FOREIGN TRADE AND FINANCE

THE MACMILLAN COMPANY
NEW YORK • CHICAGO
DALLAS • ATLANTA • SAN FRANCISCO
LONDON • MANILA

IN CANADA
BRETT-MACMILLAN LTD.
GALT, ONTARIO

Foreign Trade and Finance

Essays in International Economic Equilibrium and Adjustment

Edited by

WILLIAM R. ALLEN
University of California, Los Angeles

and

CLARK LEE ALLEN
Southern Illinois University

New York: THE MACMILLAN COMPANY

First Printing

Library of Congress Catalog Card Number: 59-7442
The Macmillan Company, New York
Brett-Macmillan Ltd., Galt, Ontario

Printed in the United States of America

FOREWORD

Presumably no one would claim that the twenty-three selections reprinted in this volume are the best things ever written in English in the area of international economics. The editors certainly make no such claim. The very notion of "best" is nebulous, for the criteria of what is best are several and varied, and an essay which may be ranked high by one standard may receive a low grade with respect to another.

In general the editors employed three criteria in determining what to include. (a) The major consideration, of course, was the quality of the *substantive content*. (b) *Manageability* by students and non-specialists was deemed important—and it hardly need be pointed out that it is not always true that an essay which meets the first condition is outstanding also with respect to the second. (c) It was desired that the *scope* of a selection be such as to place the major topic, which itself might be technical and detailed, in a significantly broad context.

We did not wish to confine the selections solely to matters of policy, to pure analytics, or to description and empiricism. There seemed little point, however, in including materials of primarily current and passing interest. We have tried to choose items which are devoted to the analytical consideration of real problems. Many of the selections are purely analytical in form, but the volume over-all has a substantial policy orientation.

There has been no attempt to treat the broad area of international economics comprehensively. This would not be feasible with a readings book—or, indeed, any kind of book—of less than encyclopedic length. Rather than including a very little of almost everything with a collection of snippets, we present a relatively small number of essays generally almost in their

v

entireties. It is inevitable in such a collection that some major topics often considered in international trade and finance courses are not represented. But the selections are directed toward the core of analysis in international economics: the bases and consequences of trade, the nature of international equilibrium and its relation to domestic equilibrium, the criteria and consequences of disequilibrium, and the means of adjustment to equilibrium.

While the articles have been arranged in five groups, in many instances the content of a selection overlaps two or more of these divisions. This is neither surprising nor undesirable. It should be beneficial for the reader to find that a given topic logically presents itself for analysis in various contexts and that a given technique often is applicable to different sorts of problems.

The editorial introductions and commentaries are intended to clarify the readings by restatement and sometimes elaboration of key points. They also attempt to place the readings in a fuller setting by discussing some matters which either are not included in the essays or are given only cursory attention. (The editors do not guarantee that the authors whose works inspired these interpretations and excursions will be gratified by their influence.) The editorial contributions are not presented, however, as a comprehensive and elaborate review of the literature. For excellent broad surveys, one should consult: Lloyd A. Metzler, "The Theory of International Trade," in Howard S. Ellis, editor, *A Survey of Contemporary Economics* (Philadelphia: The Blakiston Co., 1948), vol. I, pp. 210–254; Norman S. Buchanan, "International Investment," in Bernard F. Haley, *A Survey of Contemporary Economics* (Homewood: Richard D. Irwin, Inc., 1952), vol. II, pp. 307–350; Gottfried Haberler, *A Survey of International Trade Theory*, Special Papers in International Economics (International Finance Section, Department of Economics and Sociology, Princeton University, September 1955). The first two of these references give extensive footnote references; the latter contains a lengthy bibliography. An outstanding bibliography is in Howard S. Ellis and Lloyd A. Metzler, editors, *Readings in the Theory of International Trade* (Philadelphia: The Blakiston Co., 1949), pp. 555–625.

Obviously, the compilation of a book of readings requires the co-operation of many people. We are grateful to the various authors and publishers for permissions to reprint the selections. Problems of space compelled us to request permission in most instances to reprint only excerpts or shortened versions, and everyone who was asked kindly gave consent to such mutilation. In various significant ways, the following scholars gave special assistance: Robert E. Baldwin, Paul T. Ellsworth, Wytze Gorter, Gottfried Haberler, George Kleiner, Fritz Machlup, Charles L. Merwin, Lloyd A. Metzler, J. Carter Murphy, Ragnar Nurkse, Henry H. Schloss, and Jacob Viner. Finally, a number of journals and organizations generously gave permissions to include in the editorial sections lengthy quotations from their publications: Constable and Co., Ltd., E.P. Dutton and Co., Inc., Harvard University Press, International Monetary Fund, *Kyklos, Three Banks Review,* and the Twentieth Century Fund.

W. R. A.
C. L. A.

CONTENTS

I. International Trade Theory and Policy Issues

I. International Trade Theory and Policy Issues

INTRODUCTION

The basic questions of international trade theory relate to the *bases* of mutually beneficial exchange, the requisite *pattern* of production specialization, the *terms* on which the trade is conducted, and the *gains* from trade. The classical approach to these problems centers on the doctrine of comparative costs (advantage).[1] In 1817, David Ricardo gave a lucid exposition of this doctrine in terms of a labor theory of domestic values and a simple two-country, two-commodity model.[2] Later John Stuart Mill endorsed the Ricardian doctrine and extended it with respect to the terms of trade.[3] The Ricardo–Mill theory, somewhat elaborated by later writers,[4] remained largely un-

[1] "The classical theory of international trade was formulated primarily with a view to its providing guidance on questions of national policy. . . . This was true even of the classical discussions of the mechanism of international trade, but it was more conspicuously true in the field which is sometimes called 'the theory of international value,' where the problems were expressly treated with reference to their bearing on 'gain' or 'loss' to England, or on the distribution of gain as between England and the rest of the world. Recognition of its 'welfare analysis' orientation is essential to the understanding and the appraisal of the classical doctrine." Jacob Viner, *Studies in the Theory of International Trade* (New York: Harper and Brothers, 1937), p. 437. On doctrinal history in international economics, in addition to Viner, see James W. Angell, *The Theory of International Prices* (Cambridge: Harvard University Press, 1926), and Chi-yuen Wu, *An Outline of International Price Theories* (London: G. Routledge and Sons, Ltd., 1939).

[2] David Ricardo, *On the Principles of Political Economy and Taxation,* edited by Piero Sraffa (Cambridge: Cambridge University Press, 1951), chapter 7.

[3] John Stuart Mill, *Essays on Some Unsettled Questions of Political Economy* (1844) (London: London School of Economics and Political Science, 1948), essay I, and *Principles of Political Economy* (1848), edited by W.J. Ashley (London: Longmans, Green and Co., 1929), Book III, chapters 17–18.

[4] Notably, F.W. Taussig, *International Trade* (New York: The Macmillan Co., 1927).

3

challenged in England and in the United States for a century.[5]
After World War I, the Swedish economist, Eli Heckscher, and
his pupil, Bertil Ohlin,[6] formulated a different approach to the
bases of trade. The "modern" theory of Heckscher and Ohlin
scarcely supersedes the traditional analysis, but it powerfully
supplements it.[7]

THE DOCTRINE OF COMPARATIVE COSTS

Ricardo's arithmetical illustration of the comparative cost
principle is familiar to all students of international economics.
Suppose, he says, that in England it requires the labor of 100
men for a year to produce a unit of cloth and the labor of 120
men for a year to produce a unit of wine. In Portugal it takes
the labor of only 90 men for a year to produce a unit of cloth
and 80 men to produce a unit of wine. If there are no barriers
to trade, it will pay Portugal to specialize in the production of
wine and England in the production of cloth. By such an arrangement, England can trade a unit of cloth, which costs her

[5] A notable dissenter was Frank D. Graham, whose work culminated in *The Theory of International Values* (Princeton: Princeton University Press, 1948); see Lloyd A. Metzler, "Graham's Theory of International Values," *American Economic Review*, XL (June 1950), pp. 301–322.

[6] Eli Heckscher, "The Effect of Foreign Trade on the Distribution of Income," *Ekonomisk Tidskrift*, XXI (1919), pp. 497–512, reprinted in Howard S. Ellis and Lloyd A. Metzler, editors, *Readings in the Theory of International Trade* (Philadelphia: The Blakiston Co., 1949), pp. 272–300; Bertil Ohlin, *Interregional and International Trade* (Cambridge: Harvard University Press, 1935).

[7] Paul T. Ellsworth has strongly championed the Heckscher-Ohlin approach, but he agrees that the lineal descendant of the classical theory has its uses: "Since international price differences are the principal immediate cause and regulator of trade, a satisfactorily complete explanation must unavoidably analyze in some detail the chief reason for their existence: the widely varying degree to which different lands are endowed with the productive factors [Heckscher-Ohlin]. For dealing with the welfare problems of the gain from trade, however, this detailed discussion of why prices differ and why, therefore, geographical specialization and trade follow the lines they do, is superfluous. The theoretical explanation of the source and course of trade may be taken for granted, and attention directed to the alternative costs, in terms of income foregone, of using productive resources to produce goods at home or to acquire them by producing exports." "A Comparison of International Trade Theories," *American Economic Review*, XXX (June 1940), p. 288.

100 man-years of labor to produce, for a unit of wine, which would have cost her 120 man-years; Portugal can trade a unit of wine, which costs her 80 man-years of labor to produce, for a unit of cloth, which would have cost her 90. Both countries have benefited from the trade. Although Portugal has an *absolute* advantage over England in the production of both cloth and wine, she has a *comparative* advantage in wine production; and England, although absolutely inferior in producing both commodities, has a comparative advantage in cloth production.

With reference to Ricardo's illustration, we may note two points, the second of which stems from the first. First, he assumes that the terms of trade between England and Portugal are one unit of cloth for one unit of wine. Second, with reference to each country, the commodity in which it has the comparative advantage is also the one which it can produce at the lower cost, i.e., England can produce a unit of cloth with fewer man-years of labor than it can produce a unit of wine, and Portugal can produce a unit of wine with fewer man-years of labor than it can produce a unit of cloth. In Mill's analysis both restrictions are dropped.

Suppose, says Mill, that 10 yards of broadcloth cost in England as much labor as 15 yards of linen, and in Germany as much as 20 yards of linen. Broadcloth is more costly to produce in both countries than is linen, but since the same amount of labor that will produce 10 yards of broadcloth will produce 20 yards of linen in Germany but only 15 yards of linen in England, Germany has a comparative advantage in the production of linen, and England has a comparative advantage in broadcloth. If we assume, as Ricardo did, that one unit of broadcloth exchanges for one unit of linen, there would be no trade between England and Germany, since England would suffer by trading. If, for example, England traded 10 units of broadcloth to Germany for 10 units of linen, she would be getting 10 units of linen for the same labor expenditure that would provide her with 15 units if she produced her own linen domestically. But there is, of course, no reason why trade must be conducted on a 1 : 1 basis. If the terms of trade were 10 of broadcloth for 15 of linen, England would neither gain nor lose, and the entire benefit would accrue to Germany. If the terms were 10 of broadcloth for 20 of linen, the whole gain would go to England. At any rate between 10 of broadcloth for 15 of linen (which is the English domestic production and exchange ratio in the absence of foreign trade) and 10 of broadcloth for 20 of linen (the German domestic ratio), both countries would gain by trading. Some rate, e.g., 10 of broadcloth for 17 of linen, will be established by what Adam Smith called the higgling of the market. The equilibrium rate will be reached when the amount each country wants to import at that rate is just paid for by the amount it can export at that rate.

Mill summarizes his argument in these words:

> The law which we have now illustrated may be appropriately named, the Equation of International Demand. It may be concisely stated as follows. The produce of a country exchanges for the produce of other countries, at such values as are required in order that the whole of her exports may exactly pay for the whole of her imports. This law of International Values is but an extension of the more general law of Value, which we called the Equation of Supply and Demand. . . . But all trade, either between nations or individuals, is an interchange of commodities, in which the things that they respectively have to sell, constitute also their means of purchase: the supply brought by the one constitutes his demand for what is brought by the other. So that supply and demand are but another expression for reciprocal demand: and to say that value will adjust itself so as to equalize demand with supply, is in fact to say that it will adjust itself so as to equalize the demand on one side with the demand on the other.[8]

RECIPROCAL DEMAND SCHEDULES

Mill's analysis of reciprocal demand was set forth in graphical terms by Marshall and Edgeworth.[9] The basic notion of

[8] Mill, *Principles*, pp. 592–593.

[9] Alfred Marshall, *Money, Credit and Commerce* (London: The Macmillan Co., 1923), pp. 330–360; *idem, The Pure Theory of Foreign Trade* (1879)

comparative costs is represented in Figure I. Curve A is the production-possibility, or transformation, curve for Country A. If all of Country A's resources are devoted to the production of Commodity Y, it can produce 500 units of Y in a given time period; if all of A's resources are devoted to the production of Commodity X, 600 units of X can be produced. Assuming constant production costs, Country A can produce any combination of X and Y which is represented by a point on the linear curve A. Curve B is similarly the production-possibility curve for Country B.

Country B can produce more of both commodities than can Country A. But A has a comparative advantage in the production of Commodity Y. A can produce 5/6 as much Y as can B, but only 6/11 as much X. To look at it another

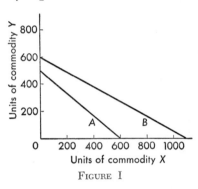

FIGURE I

way, it costs A as much to produce 500 units of Y as it does to produce 600 units of X, and, in the absence of foreign trade, X will exchange for Y in A at the rate of $6X$ for $5Y$. Similarly, X will exchange for Y in Country B at the rate of $11X$ for $6Y$. The slopes of the curves measure the respective domestic exchange ratios. Since the slopes of A and B are different (i.e., the prices of X in terms of Y, or of Y in terms of X, are different) in Countries A and B, trade between these countries would be mutually beneficial. If Country A could trade Y to Country B at some rate which would give her more than 6 units of X for each 5 units of Y and if Country B could trade X to Country A at a rate which would give her more than 6 units of Y for each 11 units of X, both countries would be better off. That is to say that the terms-of-trade line which represents the ratio at which

(London: London School of Economics and Political Science, 1930); Francis Y. Edgeworth, "Theory of International Values," *Economic Journal*, IV (March, September, December, 1894), pp. 35–50, 423–424, 606–638; *idem*, *Papers Relating to Political Economy* (New York: The Macmillan Co., 1925), vol. II, pp. 25–29.

Countries *A* and *B* exchange *X* and *Y* must be less steep than curve *A* and more steep than curve *B*.

This is demonstrated in Figure II. A broken terms-of-trade line is drawn indicating that by trading with Country *B*, Country *A* can get 3 units of *X* for each 2 of *Y*, which is more than 6 of *X* for each 5 of *Y;* another terms-of-trade line with the same slope is drawn to show that Country *B* can by trading get more than 6 units of *Y* for each 11 units of *X*. Suppose at the price of *X* indicated by the terms-of-trade line Country *A* wants to consume 300 units of *X*. This can be done by exporting 200 units of *Y* in exchange for 300 of *X*. Since *A* has completely specialized in the production of *Y* and produces a total of 500 units, she will have 300 of *Y* for her own consumption plus 300 units of *X* imported from *B*. Country *B* produces 1100 units of *X*, and, since she has exported 300 of *X* to *A*, she will have 800 units of *X* for her own consumption in addition to the imported 200 of *Y*.

Both countries have gained from trade. By trading, the "consumption boundary" of each country has been pushed beyond its "production boundary": the terms-of-trade lines lie outside the production–possibility lines. Trade is thus a means of efficient indirect production, for each country has "produced" its imported commodities at smaller alternative cost through trading than would have been required through direct production with its own resources.[10]

But how is the price of *X* in terms of *Y* established so that at those terms of trade (a) the value that Country *A* wishes to import is just equal to what she is willing to export, (b) the value of what Country *B* wants to import is just equal to what she will export, and (c) the value of desired imports of *A* equals the value of desired imports of *B*? In Figure II, the rate of 2*X* for 3*Y* is the equilibrium price. But how is the equilibrium

[10] On the welfare aspects of international trade theory, see, e.g., Gottfried Haberler, "Some Problems in the Pure Theory of International Trade," *Economic Journal,* LX (June 1950), pp. 223–240, and Robert E. Baldwin, "The New Welfare Economics and Gains in International Trade," *Quarterly Journal of Economics,* LXVI (February 1952), pp. 91–101.

price determined? To answer this question reciprocal demand
curves are helpful.

Suppose with Mill that England has a comparative advantage
in cloth production, and Germany has a comparative advantage
in linen. On the *x*–axis in Figure III we measure units of cloth
(*E*–bales), and on the *y*–axis units of linen (*G*–bales). If England devotes all of her resources to cloth production, she can

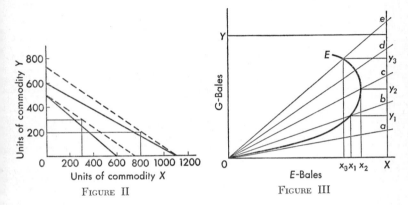

FIGURE II   FIGURE III

produce an amount equal to *OX*; the amount of cloth England
will export is measured left-to-right from *O*, and the amount
England herself will consume is measured from right-to-left
from *X*. Similarly, the total amount of linen Germany will
produce is *OY*; Germany's own consumption is measured from
Y toward *O*, and the amount she will export is measured from
O toward *Y*.

The slope of the vectors *Oa* to *Oe* may be taken to represent
alternative prices of cloth (*E*–bales) in terms of linen (*G*–
bales). If the price is represented by *Oa*, *Xa* units of linen would
exchange for *OX* of cloth, which is a relatively low price of
cloth in terms of linen. If price is represented by *Ob*, *Xb* of
linen would exchange for *OX* of cloth. As we move in a
counter-clockwise direction, we assume a higher and higher
price of cloth in terms of linen (or, what is the same thing, a
lower and lower price of linen in terms of cloth).

If the price of cloth in terms of linen is represented by *Ob*,

we may assume that England will want to import Xy_1 of linen,
which necessitates exporting Ox_1 of cloth and leaves x_1X of
cloth for domestic consumption; if the price is represented by
Oc, England will import Xy_2 of linen, export Ox_2 of cloth, and
retain x_2X of cloth; and so on. The curve OE is the locus of such
alternative equilibrium points; OE may be viewed as England's
demand-for-linen curve and also as England's supply-of-cloth
curve. As the price of linen falls from Ob to Oc, England's
total expenditure on linen increases from Ox_1 to Ox_2; since price
and total expenditure are moving in opposite directions, the
elasticity of England's demand for linen is greater than one in
this price range. As the price of linen falls from Oc to Oe,
England's total expenditure falls from Ox_2 to Ox_3; since price

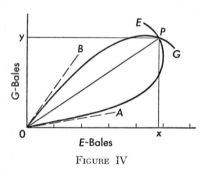

FIGURE IV

and total expenditure are moving in the same direction, England's demand for linen has an
elasticity of less than one in
this price range. If England's
demand-for-linen curve were
a vertical line, the elasticity of
demand would be equal to one,
since her total expenditure on
linen would remain constant
as the price of linen changed.

In Figure IV England's demand-for-linen curve has been
reproduced, and Germany's demand-for-cloth curve, derived
in similar fashion, has been drawn. The cost of cloth in terms
of linen in England on the assumption that there is no trade is
represented by the flatter broken line, OA; the cost of cloth in
terms of linen in Germany on the assumption that there is no
trade is represented by the steeper broken line, OB. England
will not trade with Germany unless she can get linen at a
lower cost than if she produced both commodities domestically,
and Germany will not trade with England unless she can
thereby get cloth at a lower cost. The price at which England
and Germany trade cloth and linen must, accordingly, lie
between the limits set by the domestic production costs in the

two countries. The equilibrium terms of trade will be determined by the point of intersection of the reciprocal demand curves; the equilibrium price is represented by the slope of *OP;* England will export *Ox E*–bales, and Germany will export *Oy G*–bales.[11]

Allen (selection 1) and Stevens (selection 2) further review the theory of international trade and consider its application to questions of public policy.

HECKSCHER-OHLIN APPROACH

With two commodities and two countries, the Ricardo-Mill doctrine of comparative cost demonstrates that there is a basis for mutually beneficial international trade if the respective domestic production ratios (and thus the exchange ratios in the absence of foreign trade) differ. But why do these ratios differ? Heckscher asked, what are "the *reasons for differences in comparative costs among nations?*"[12] The first major contribution of the Heckscher-Ohlin approach is to inquire more fundamentally into the ultimate bases of trade, i.e., differences in the internal cost (price) ratios, than did Ricardo and Mill, who assumed at the outset the proximate prerequisites of trade.

Differences in *relative* commodity costs (and costs, in long-run competitive equilibrium, equal prices) in two countries are traced by Heckscher and Ohlin to two considerations. There are, that is to say, two necessary conditions for trade: *relative* differences in factor (input) prices and *relative* differences in factor requirements in the production of different commodities. And relative differences in factor prices, in turn, are traced essentially to relative differences in factor scarcities in the two countries. In Heckscher's summary:

A difference in the relative scarcity of the factors of production between one country and another is thus a necessary condition for a

---

[11] William R. Allen, "The Effects on Trade of Shifting Reciprocal Demand Schedules," *American Economic Review,* XLII (March 1952), pp. 135–140.

[12] Heckscher, *op cit.,* p. 277.

difference in comparative costs and consequently for international trade. A further indispensable condition is that the proportions in which the factors of production are combined shall not be the same for one commodity as for another. In the absence of this second condition, the price of one commodity, compared with the price of another would remain the same in all countries regardless of differences in relative factor prices.

The prerequisites for initiating international trade may thus be summarized as *different relative scarcity, i.e., different relative prices of the factors of production in the exchanging countries,* as well as *different proportions between the factors of production in different commodities.*[13]

A nation will tend to specialize its production in, and export, those commodities which require for their production relatively large amounts of those factors which it has in relative abundance and which thus are relatively cheap.

The Heckscher-Ohlin approach adds a helpful instrument to the economist's tool-kit. Hansson (selection 3) uses it for analyzing historically shifting trade patterns. Metzler (selection 4) uses it for analyzing the effects of tariffs on income distribution—a problem which is not amenable to a theory couched in terms of a single input.

[13] *Ibid.,* p. 278.

1. INTERNATIONAL TRADE THEORY, COMMERCIAL POLICY AND THE ECONOMIST

William R. Allen

University of California, Los Angeles

Reprinted from *Political Science Quarterly,* LXXIII (March 1958), pp. 47–56, by permission of the publisher.

This is an elaboration of a section of my "Cordell Hull and the Defense of the Trade Agreements Program, 1933–1940," in Alexander DeConde, editor, *Isolation and Security: Ideas and Interests in Twentieth Century American Foreign Policy* (Durham, 1957). The material is used here by permission of the editor and the publisher. The paper has benefited from comments of C.L. Allen, N.V. Breckner, Wytze Gorter, and Ragnar Nurkse.

Theory is not the photograph of reality, but the criterion of the interpretation of reality.—Benedetto Croce, *History as the Story of Liberty,* p. 175.[1] . . . experience has underlined the truth and wisdom of Edgeworth's judgment: "As I read it, protection might procure economic advantage in certain cases, if there was a Government wise enough to discriminate those cases, and strong enough to confine itself to them; but this condition is very unlikely to be fulfilled."—Gottfried Haberler, *The Theory of International Trade,* p. ix.[2]

Analysis requires theory, and evaluation requires criteria. Economic elements and considerations have long been conspicuous in the structure and the determination of international relations. But foreign policy has been formulated largely by persons little versed in, and much inclined to shun, the techniques of economic analysis.

Whether the historian of foreign policy and the academician specializing in "international relations" have greater facility and interest in such analysis than has the public official is, perhaps, too delicate an inquiry to be pushed by an economist. But it may be useful to them to review very briefly the nature of international trade theory, some of its applications to questions of commercial

[1] New York, 1941.
[2] London, 1936.

policy, and the perspective of the economist in making these applications.[3]

I

The prospect of *mutual gains* to the parties in an exchange of goods, services and claims is the major motivation of market-oriented economic activity, and the conclusion that such mutual gains are possible under certain typical circumstances is the crux of economic theory. When two bargaining units place different relative valuations on things they possess, there is a range of exchange ratios, or prices, within which trade will benefit each unit. Each party is made better off by giving up some of what it values relatively little in exchange for things which it values relatively highly. Similarly, when two communities have adjusted their respective patterns of consumption and production in such a fashion as to result in different sets of relative prices, they can trade to the profit of each.

With the emergent possibility of trade between these parties, it is a short step to the principle that specialization in production, partial or complete, can *increase the total of goods and services* available for trade and consumption. The so-called law of "comparative advantage" holds that a producing unit should specialize in those commodities in which it is *relatively* most efficient. The requirement is not that each trader be absolutely more efficient in the production of its export commodities and absolutely less efficient in the production of its import commodities. It is necessary only that the *degree* of its superiority or inferiority in production differ from commodity

---

[3] When considering the use of economic analysis for purposes of, say, political-military power, the economist is in generally unfamiliar and uncongenial territory. This article is concerned with the "economics" of trade policy. A discussion so severely delimited in scope presumably will not by itself yield many positive policy proposals, but it can provide the basis of an understanding which will permit the avoidance of certain sorts of major policy errors.

For a discussion of United States foreign economic policy in a world of cold war, see Jacob Viner, "The Role of the United States in the World Economy," in R. Lekachman, editor, *National Policy for Economic Welfare at Home and Abroad* (Garden City, 1955), pp. 175–210. For excellent surveys of international trade and finance theory, see L.A. Metzler, "The Theory of International Trade," in H.S. Ellis, editor, *A Survey of Contemporary Economics*, vol. I (Philadelphia, 1948), pp. 210–254; N.S. Buchanan, "International Investment," in B.F. Haley, editor, *ibid.*, vol. II (Homewood, 1952), pp. 307–350; Gottfried Haberler, "A Survey of International Trade Theory," *Special Papers in International Economics* (Princeton, 1955).

to commodity and that it specialize in those goods where its degree
of superiority is greatest or its degree of inferiority is least.[4]

With each community specializing according to the principle of
comparative advantage and exchanging on the basis of such production specialization, each tends, first to maximize desired output
within the constraints of given resources and production techniques,
and, second and simultaneously, to achieve the highest level of
"well-being" commensurate with a given aggregate quantity and
initial international distribution of goods and services.

In sum, for the simplified case of one-person economies—in which
there are no issues associated with domestic income redistribution—
it can be demonstrated that: (a) assuming full employment of

---

[4] Much of the preceding two paragraphs can be illustrated simply with a
two-country, two-commodity model. Let the United States and the United
Kingdom prices of commodities X and Y be as follows:

U.S.	U.K.
$X = \$15$	$X = £6$
$Y = \$12$	$Y = £3$

One cannot, and need not, tell from the data given which country is productively superior, i.e., more efficient in physical input-output terms, in either of
the commodities. For purposes of illustrating the *bases* of, and the gains from,
trade, it is sufficient that the *ratios* differ: $15/12 \neq 6/3$ or, alternatively,
$15/6 \neq 12/3$. Given these respective domestic prices, mutually beneficial, two-
way trade can obtain if the rate of exchange between the dollar and the pound
lies within the limits, $\$2.50 = £1$ (derived from the ratio, $15/6$) and $\$4 = £1$
(derived from the ratio, $12/3$).

At a rate of, say, $\$3 = £1$, X in the United Kingdom is priced at an equivalent
of \$18, and Y is \$9. The United States would, therefore, specialize its production on, and export, X; it would import Y. With the price of X being \$15 and
Y the equivalent of \$9, the *international* terms of trade would be $1X$ exchanging
for $1\frac{2}{3}Y$. By contrast, in the absence of trade, in the United States the *domestic*
terms of trade would be $1X$ exchanging for only $1\frac{1}{4}Y$. Similarly, by foreign trade
the United Kingdom must export only $1\frac{2}{3}Y$ to obtain $1X$, whereas domestically
the exchange ratio requires that $2Y$ trade for a unit of X.

This analysis is based on the classical line of thought, stemming primarily
from David Ricardo and John Stuart Mill in the first half of the nineteenth
century. In the present century, theory associated with Eli Heckscher and Bertil
Ohlin has attempted to "go behind" the classical comparative-advantage doctrine and explain *why* the price ratios differ. Roughly, it is held that, from region
to region, (1) relative factor prices differ, primarily because of differences in
relative factor supplies, and (2) different commodities require for their production different factor combinations; therefore, a region tends to export those
commodities which use relatively large amounts of factors which it possesses
in relative abundance and thus which are relatively cheap. Despite the claims
and criticisms of Ohlin (*Interregional and International Trade* [Cambridge,
1935], esp. Appendix III), the Heckscher-Ohlin approach is more a complement
to, rather than a substitute for, the classical approach.

resources and given production relations and factor (input) supplies, rational operations in perfectly competitive markets will achieve a "maximum" output in the sense that it is impossible to increase the output of one commodity without sacrificing some of the output of other commodities; (b) at the same time, with production and consumption patterns which reflect different relative valuations of commodities between the two countries in the absence of trade, free and competitive trade will achieve an "optimum" distribution of some given total of commodities (which is larger than the pre-trade total) in the sense that it is impossible to increase the "well-being" of one country without decreasing the "well-being" of another country. Trade changes the allocation of productive resources, increases world production, and frees nations from the restriction of consuming only their own particular outputs. Thus we have "optimum" global distributions of alternative "maximum" national outputs.[5]

The essence of the argument for international specialization and trade, then, is that in this manner a nation may acquire more goods and services with its given resource possibilities than would be possible by itself producing directly with domestic resources all that it consumes.

[5] Economic "well-being" or "welfare" should be measured ideally in terms of psychic "satisfaction" or "utility." Unfortunately, the psychologists have not yet invented a "util-meter" by which we can measure absolutely the level of utility engendered by an incident. Since we cannot make an absolute or quantitative measure of one person's utility, we cannot compare the absolute level of well-being of one person with that of another. If, then, "interpersonal comparisons of utility" are impossible, how can we evaluate the desirability of a public policy? One answer commonly given is, if no one in the community is hurt by the policy and at least one person is helped, the welfare of the community is increased. But almost any policy will hurt some people. In this case, community welfare is still conceived to be increased if those who are helped can compensate those who are hurt by the full amount of their injury and still be themselves better off than they were initially.

All of this may seem a bit esoteric on the policy-making level. (*Cf.* Clair Wilcox, "Relief for Victims of Tariff Cuts," *American Economic Review,* vol. XL [December 1950], pp. 884–889.) But we may conjecture that a policy is "good" if it results either in more goods and services available to the community with the use of given inputs or in acquiring the same quantity of goods and services for less real cost. For a technical demonstration that, on this criterion, some trade—not necessarily free trade—is desirable, see P.A. Samuelson, "The Gains from International Trade," *Canadian Journal of Economics and Political Science,* vol. V (May 1939), pp. 195–205, reprinted in H.S. Ellis and L.A. Metzler, editors, *Readings in the Theory of International Trade* (Philadelphia, 1949), pp. 239–252. For a review of the concept of economic welfare, see K.E. Boulding, "Welfare Economics," in Haley, *op. cit.,* pp. 3–11.

There are, however, two difficulties in concluding that free trade is the only appropriate policy for a nation—one problem inherent in all exchange and one unique to multi-person economies. First, while free exchange will result in some distribution of given products that is preferred by *both* traders to the initial distribution in the absence of trade, there is an "optimum" *range* of these alternative preferred distributions within which *further redistribution will help one party only at the expense of the other*. Free trade will benefit each of the trading partners by bringing the pattern of distribution to some point in this "optimum" range, but, once there, each trader has an incentive to garner a larger share of the gains from trade to the detriment of the other. This is unacceptable to the party being hurt; also, it is ambiguous that the world economy as such is benefited, for the gain in welfare to the one party cannot be accurately weighed against the loss to the other.[6]

Second, almost any policy affecting an economy will result in changes in the distribution of internal income, which likely will be of greater importance in the short run than over the long pull. The introduction of trade can increase the total of goods and services available to a community, but if the trade injures some members of the community, it may be impossible to judge with assurance whether the total welfare of the group has been increased.

In short, a combination of two considerations—the virtual certainty that changes in trade policy will redistribute domestic income and reapportion internationally the gains from trade, and the impossibility of interpersonal and intercommunity comparisons of utility—suggests that the introduction of free trade on the part of every country will not necessarily maximize the total welfare either of the global economy or of any given national economy. Nor does the welfare optimum necessarily represent a rational objective to all parties. If, in attaining the welfare optimum, a trader—whether an economy generally or a component of it—loses and is not fully com-

---

[6] The reference here is to the so-called "Paretian social optimum." "The real significance of the Paretian welfare economics, then, is that it sets forth explicitly the distinction between those changes in social variables which can take place through 'trading'—i.e., through a mutual benefit of all parties—and those changes which involve 'conflict,' or the benefit of one party at the expense of another. In a civilization which is threatened by extinction because of an inability to solve the problem of conflict this distinction may be of considerable importance." Boulding, *op. cit.*, pp. 18–19.

pensated for its loss, what can be the basis of enthusiasm on its part for a market structure which promotes this so-called optimum?

II

Economists, who are strongly inclined to suspect monopolistic influence as nefarious, have typically been champions of substantially free trade. But modern theory does not assert unequivocally that free trade is the only economically rational commercial policy. Free trade can, indeed, contribute to efficiency in the allocation of the world's resources. But a particular nation in the world economy, like an individual producer in the national economy, *may,* under certain circumstances and especially in the short run, gain by appropriate interferences with trade. A protectionist policy, which is suspect from the perspective of the global economy, *may* be quite rational from the viewpoint and the typical criteria of an individual country. While under necessary and common conditions *some* trade is preferable to *no* trade for a country, *restricted* trade may be better than *free* trade for that country.[7]

Many specific "economic" arguments, of varying degrees of intellectual respectability, have been offered in the defense of trade barriers.

(A) One ancient and still interesting case of deviating from free trade is the support of "infant" industries. By receiving temporary protection, a "young" industry may be enabled to realize its potential, develop into a position where it can survive the rigors of unfettered world competition, and perhaps further diversify the economy. In public tariff debates in the United States during much of the period prior to World War I, this was probably the most prominent line of thought of the protectionists.

(B) Another hoary but intellectually quite uninteresting defense of protective policies stems from alleged fear of "pauper labor" abroad. In its crudest and most popular form, the argument holds that domestic producers cannot compete with foreign industries if wage rates abroad are lower than American rates. But neither the wage rate nor the total wage bill is a reliable indicator of total costs

---

[7] "The very fact that any trade takes place is an indication that both individuals are better off, since each can at the very worst refuse to trade. Economists have proved this . . . under the mistaken impression that they were at the same time proving the desirability of free trade." P.A. Samuelson, "Welfare Economics and International Trade," *American Economic Review,* vol. XXVIII (June 1938), p. 265.

per unit of output, which are determined by productivity as well as by wages. Indeed, relative productivity is the major determinant of relative wages. High real wages are founded on high productivity, not on preventing the purchase of commodities which could contribute to the importing nation's standard of living. By trading on the basis of specialization in lines in which its productivity is greatest, that is, in which it has a comparative advantage, an economy maintains its highest-wage industries and properly sacrifices its relatively inefficient industries. Economic rationality scarcely consists in subsidizing inefficiency. Nevertheless, the "pauper labor" argument has remained conspicuous in tariff debates, and it became relatively more important as the "infant industry" argument received declining stress after World War I.

(C) Under certain circumstances trade restrictions by a nation may improve its barter terms of trade, that is, the exchange ratio between its imports and its exports, and perhaps also increase its volume of imports—both results tending to enhance its gains from trade. But the terms of trade are not a very satisfactory welfare indicator, especially when improvement in the terms is accompanied by reduced imports and worsening in the terms by an increase in imports.

(D) In recent years, the development of national income theory —the "Keynesian revolution"—has clarified the nature of the relationship between changes in trade and capital flows and changes in the level of economic activity. Money national income is determined by expenditure on current national output, and, other things remaining the same, the development of an export balance will raise the level of equilibrium national income. This conclusion is so obvious intuitively that the possible effects of increased exports on money national income furnished the basis of much of the tariff debate of the 1930's.

(E) A final example stems from balance-of-payments difficulties. Many a nation during the past quarter of a century and more has found itself with a disequilibrium in its international accounts and yet been confined institutionally and politically to a limited number of adjustment mechanisms. In such cases, direct interferences have seemed to some the most convenient alternative.[8]

[8] On modern public tariff debates in the United States, see F.W. Fetter, "Congressional Trade Theory," *American Economic Review*, vol. XXIII (September 1933), pp. 413–427, and my "The International Trade Philosophy of

III

Economists are probably less inclined now than they were a generation ago to espouse a doctrinaire position in advocacy of free trade. Developments in economic theory and the degeneration of international relations appear to have been the major contributors to an intellectual environment more cordial to exceptions to the free-trade rule. Still, economists typically are reluctant even now to advocate policies of trade restriction. Such concessions from their conventional position as they are willing to make are expressed much more readily to each other than to congressional committees and to chambers of commerce.

There are good reasons for hesitancy in advocating barriers to trade even if theory suggests that they might sometimes be appropriate according to certain criteria. First, there are complex problems in noting when the prerequisite conditions for imposing restrictions actually exist, in choosing the most appropriate mode of restriction, in determining and administering the optimum degree of restriction, and in maintaining sufficient flexibility to modify the program as conditions change. It is well to keep in mind that the world is a complicated place.

Furthermore, there is the general fear that the restricted conclusions of abstract and sophisticated analysis will be expropriated and abused by persons who are poorly equipped and little inclined to appreciate the limitations of the analysis. Also, without denying certain possible beneficial effects of trade barriers, it may be that those desired results can be obtained by preferable alternative methods. An outstanding case in point with respect to public tariff debates is the possible expansionary income effects of increased exports or curtailed imports, for there are better ways to stimulate national income than by encouraging an export balance. Finally, policies of trade curtailment which might give a nation certain advantages if it were the only country following such policies may be partially or wholly offset by retaliation. Commercial warfare, an unhappy characteristic of much modern history, tends to nullify relative gains

Cordell Hull, 1907–1033," *ibid.*, vol. XLIII (March 1953), pp. 101–116, "Issues in Congressional Tariff Debates, 1890–1930," *Southern Economic Journal,* vol. XX (April 1954), pp. 340–355, and "Cordell Hull and the Defense of the Trade Agreements Program," *loc. cit.*

among countries and to make every nation absolutely worse off.[9]

But the probability that a trade-restricting nation will keep its gains, if any, only in the absence of retaliation by no means implies, as some seem to suppose,[10] that the policy-making protectionist will surely eschew the potential gains of an illiberal commercial policy. Possible gains from trade restrictions are easily visualized, and there appears to be a strong tendency for a system of free trade to disintegrate.

. . . the success of a policy of universal free trade is seriously prejudiced by the belief that countries which indulge in protection are acting contrary to their own economic interests. It is because the *laissez-faire* economist has so often believed that free trade is the *natural* state of affairs which, in the absence of stupidity and wickedness, would prevail that his attempts to establish it have not been more successful.[11]

In judging foreign economic policy, as in judging domestic policy, the presumption of most economists is that their support should go to the side of freedom, mutual advantage and competitive efficiency. The burden of proof now, almost two centuries after Adam Smith, is clearly on those who advocate restrictive, exploitative and monopolistic deviations from the economists' traditional rule of thumb. While theory does not yield an unqualified case for free trade, the bias of economists against trade interferences is both powerful and well justified.

[9] Even J.M. Keynes, who is erroneously considered by some to have been a neomercantilist, agreed that "there are strong presumptions of a general character against trade restrictions unless they can be justified on special grounds." *The General Theory of Employment, Interest and Money* (New York, 1936), pp. 338–339. For supporting liberal views of two leading innovators in the application of Keynesian analysis to international trade theory, see Fritz Machlup, *International Trade Theory and the National Income Multiplier* (Philadelphia, 1943), pp. 211–218, and Metzler, *op. cit.*, pp. 249–252.

[10] "Mr. Lerner provides an ingenious formula for the optimum rate of tax on foreign trade which a country should impose 'if it is desired to exploit the foreigner.' The technical economist will be fascinated. The commonsensical reader will be . . . altogether discouraged when he learns that if the foreigner retaliates, the formula falls to the ground and all parties suffer an economic loss." J.E. Meade, "Mr. Lerner on 'The Economics of Control,'" *Economic Journal*, vol. LV (April 1945), p. 69.

[11] R.F. Kahn, "Tariffs and the Terms of Trade," *Review of Economic Studies*, vol. XV (1), 1947–1948, p. 19.

2. New Ideas in the Theory of International Trade

Robert W. Stevens

Standard Oil Company

Reprinted from *The American Economic Review*, XLI (June 1951), pp. 369–388, by permission of the author and the American Economic Association. At the time of original publication, the author was with the Economic Cooperation Administration Special Mission to the United Kingdom; the views stated are personal views only.

I. INTRODUCTION

Postwar experience with the General Agreement for Tariffs and Trade and various other international economic organizations continues to validate a remark made by Lloyd Metzler that "The practical conduct of international trade is . . . much more a problem of negotiation and compromise than the classical economists believed." [1] It is the purpose of this paper to investigate some recent contributions to the theory of international trade which are closely related to Metzler's widely shared opinion. These contributions are based upon the central idea that the economic judgments of those in control of a country's international trade can be given formal theoretical expression, and the advocates of the new approach purport to provide us with a clear-cut graphical representation of the economizing activities of ruthless and short-sighted national states. Their methodology relies upon curves of reciprocal demand and community indifference which were first developed by Marshall and Edgeworth. After a summary of the methodology and a discussion of some of its novel implications, reasons are advanced in a final section for finding it unacceptable.

II. FOUNDATIONS IN MARSHALL AND EDGEWORTH

In *Money, Credit and Commerce*, Marshall introduced his sections on reciprocal international demand by relating them to Mill's

[1] Lloyd A. Metzler, "The Theory of International Trade," in *A Survey of Contemporary Economics,* Howard S. Ellis, editor (Philadelphia, Blakiston, 1948), p. 252.

pioneer analysis of the subject. In order to conduct his analysis in real terms, Marshall wrote, "Mill took a yard of cloth as representative of the products of one country and a yard of linen as representative of the products of the other. But it seems better to suppose either country to make up her exports into representative 'bales'; that is, bales, each of which represents uniform aggregate investments of her labor (of various qualities) and her capital." [2] By adopting this expedient, Marshall was able to express the international commodity supplies and demands of two countries in "bale units" whose embodiments of resources remain constant even though the actual commodity composition of trade is constantly changing.

Diagram I is adapted from the schedules and diagrams which Marshall used to illustrate two countries' reciprocal demand curves (or offer curves) on a single plane.[3] *OE* represents England's offer curve and *OG* represents Germany's. *OE* shows that if only a few *G* bales are available in England, they would command a high price in terms of *E* bales, and that their value in England would fall as more of them are supplied. Marshall points out that it is a *supply*-and-demand (or *reciprocal*) demand curve because it also reflects the fact that England can supply (offer) more and more *E* bales only at progressively higher prices in terms of *G* bales. The same conditions of course apply to *OG*, and a moment's inspection will show that under free trade conditions a stable equilibrium will be established at *P*, with the slope of *OP* reflecting the price (terms of trade).[4]

Edgeworth, who was familiar with Marshall's method long before it appeared in *Money, Credit and Commerce*, indicated in a preliminary way how community indifference curves could be used on the Marshallian plane.[5] To Marshall's curves he added *OT* and *OS* (Diagram II), portraying the domestic constant cost ratios of producing in Germany and in England, respectively, the goods that enter into their international trade. Then, assuming constant costs,

[2] Alfred Marshall, *Money, Credit and Commerce* (London, Macmillan, 1923), p. 157.

[3] *Ibid.*, p. 162 and p. 331.

[4] Besides Marshall's own exposition, lucid accounts of his curves of reciprocal demand may be found in G. Haberler, *The Theory of International Trade*, translated by Alfred Stonier and Frederick Benham (London, George Allen and Unwin, 1937), pp. 150–59; and in J. Viner, *Studies in the Theory of International Trade* (London, George Allen and Unwin, 1937), pp. 541–47.

[5] Francis Y. Edgeworth, "Theory of International Values," *Econ. Jour.*, Vol. 4 (1894), pp. 35–50; 423–43; 606–38.

OT and *OS* provide limits within which the terms of trade between
the two countries must fall, since trade would not take place outside
the limits thus established. He noted that, abandoning the constant
costs assumption, one might substitute "a curve of constant advantage, or 'indifference curve' . . . representing states for which the
advantage . . . is no greater than if there had been no trade."
Assuming increasing costs in both countries, such curves would "curl
inward" from *OT* and *OS*. He did not draw them, nor did he specify

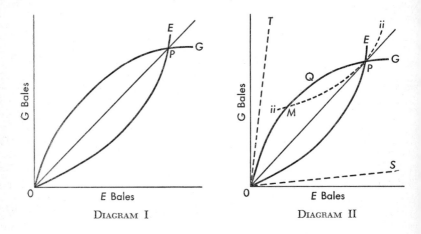

DIAGRAM I   DIAGRAM II

the existence of "families" of such indifference curves representing
for each country successively greater total satisfaction from trade.
Instead, he drew *one* such curve to illustrate the result of an English
tariff which would move the equilibrium point to the left along *OG*.
(A tariff would distort a country's offer curve in this way because it
would reduce the country's demand for imports.)

Edgeworth's community indifference curve is the broken line *ii* in
Diagram II. It must be tangent to the *OP* vector at *P* because under
free trade, trade would be carried to the point where *E*'s exporters-
and-importers are on the highest possible indifference curve, given
the terms of trade (*OP*). That is to say, a reciprocal demand curve
is the locus of points of tangency between the indifference curves
of the trading unit and the terms of trade (or price lines) it might
face. Thus *OG* is for Germany a locus of optimum positions for
steadily improving terms of trade and *OE* is a similar locus for England. It follows that a reciprocal demand curve *implies* a family of

indifference curves.[6] We shall return later to the use which Edgeworth made of his diagram.

III. THE COUNTRY AS A MONOPOLIST

First, it will be useful to outline the recent further elaboration of these early contributions by Marshall and Edgeworth. The contemporary writers examined below are assuming a "classical world" in which a tariff does not alter the level of domestic employment, but does secure an improved "swap ratio" of exports for imports. Thus we have an approach which is related to the terms of trade argument for tariffs, but not to the level of employment argument.[7]

We may begin with Samuelson's demonstration [8] that under free trade the intersection of two countries' reciprocal demand curves would necessarily lie on what is conventionally called the contract curve in the theory of bilateral monopoly, and that no movement is possible along this curve that would benefit both parties.[9] Moreover,

[6] For another application of this methodology see J.T. Dunlop and Benjamin Higgins, "Bargaining Power and Market Structures," *Jour. Pol. Econ.*, Vol. 50 (Feb., 1942), pp. 1–26.

[7] Besides the articles cited in the text, the reader may wish to consult certain other sources. An important and relatively early contribution was made by W.W. Leontief in "The Use of Indifference Curves in the Analysis of Foreign Trade," *Quart. Jour. Econ.*, Vol. 47 (May, 1933), pp. 493–503. However, his approach is not, strictly speaking, in the Marshall-Edgeworth tradition of reciprocal demand. Kaldor's *Economica* article cited in note 10 below contains a useful diagram showing the essential nature of community indifference curves and W.M. Baumol, "The Community Indifference Map: A Construction," *Rev. Econ. Stud.*, Vol. XVII (3) No. 44 (1949–50), pp. 189–97, elaborates with considerable refinement the technique of their construction. I.M.D. Little, in "Welfare and Tariffs," *Rev. Econ. Stud.*, Vol. XVI (2) No. 40 (1949–50), comments on community indifference curves from the standpoint of welfare economics.

[8] Paul Samuelson, "Welfare Economics and International Trade," *Am. Econ. Rev.*, Vol. 28, No. 2 (June, 1938), pp. 261–66.

[9] In the theory of bilateral monopoly as developed by Edgeworth and others, the indifference maps of two trading units are superimposed as in the accompanying diagram. The contract curve *CC* is the locus of tangencies of the two families of indifference curves. Of two bilateral monopolists, each would posit an indifference curve for the other and then move to the point of tangency between it and one of its own indifference curves. The final position on the contract curve would depend upon the relative bargaining strengths of the partners.

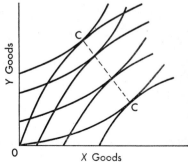

any such movement would necessarily injure the interest of one of them. Furthermore, as Samuelson points out, "There is absolutely no presumption whatsoever that (the free trade) equilibrium point is superior in any sense to any other point on the contract curve" for no welfare judgments are possible about movements on the contract curve. This is so because welfare positions in the two countries cannot be compared meaningfully. He proceeds to point out that the free trade equilibrium point would not be the "best" position on the contract curve for either single country, because each would prefer to be at the intersection of the contract curve with a higher one of its own indifference curves. Samuelson concludes, therefore, that "one country behaving like a competitor, it can be shown that it is always to the advantage of the other not to so behave, but rather to take account monopolistically of its own effect on price . . . and move the other along its offer curve up to a point of tangency of that locus with the monopolist's indifference curve."

Kaldor [10] showed this behavior diagrammatically, somewhat as in Diagram III which I have designed in order to show how the contemporary methodology has grown out of Marshall's work. He has G (France in his illustration) impose a general tariff, shifting OG to OG' and the point of trade equilibrium from P to P'. P' is a preferred position on OE for G because it is to the right of P'', where the G indifference curve through P intersects OE. He also shows that the optimum duty for G would distort OG so that it would intersect OE at Pi, where OE is tangent to the highest possible G indifference curve. A higher tariff, distorting OG to intersect OE below Pi would result in less gain, and in actual loss if the new intersection is to the left of P''. Hence Kaldor calls Pi the "optimum monopoly position" [11] and the price of wine (France's representative export in his illustration—a G bale in Diagram III) is the one which would rule if a single monopolist exported it. He observes that the introduction of import duties can produce "exactly the same effects as the introduction of monopoly," and goes on to remark that "retaliation will improve the position of the exploited country, but it might leave both countries worse off than they were originally."

[10] N. Kaldor, "A Note on Tariffs and the Terms of Trade," *Economica*, Vol. 7 (Nov., 1940), pp. 377–80.

[11] Note that G increases its *gain* from trade even though its *volume* of trade is less.

Scitovsky's contribution [12] logically follows upon Kaldor's two conclusions, for he portrays the behavior of a monopolistic entrepreneur on a diagram similar to Diagram III and also shows diagrammatically the effects of retaliation and counter-retaliation. He points out that the opportunity to move P to its "optimum" position (E' or G' in Diagram V) is not open to both countries simultaneously and, therefore, that there is a premium to be had for acting promptly. If one country does act and if each of them then proceeds to retaliate against the other, the volume of trade will steadily diminish as the two curves shift nearer to each other, but at each step

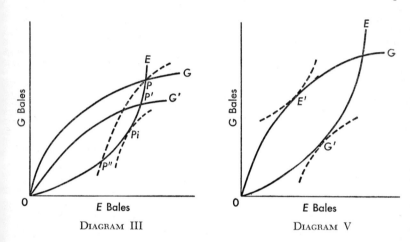

DIAGRAM III   DIAGRAM V

the tariff-enacting country moves to a better position than it would have been in if it had not fought back. As Scitovsky observes, a position of equilibrium will be reached where "the two tariff-ridden offer curves are both tangential, each to one of the other country' community indifference curves." Whether or not this position is reached before all trade stops depends upon the shapes and relative positions of the indifference curves. Scitovsky also brings out clearly how the technique of *bilateral* monopoly can be used to analyze foreign trade policies by countries which typically do not trade with only one partner. If it is supposed that any one country will not consider the danger of retaliation by *all other countries* to its own tariffs, one reciprocal demand curve (and its implied community indifference

[12] Tibor Scitovsky, "A Reconsideration of the Theory of Tariffs," *Rev. Econ. Stud.*, Vol. 9 (Summer, 1942), pp. 89–110.

curves) may be taken to represent "the rest of the world" as seen
from one country. Generalizing this procedure means that "the rest
of the world" will in fact act monopolistically, so that on the diagrams it is as if only two countries were being considered.

That this new equilibrium position, even if some trade continues,
is very likely to be one of less satisfaction for "each country" taken
singly than it enjoyed at P (before they started) is shown by
Hirschman.[13]

Despite this fairly recent accumulation of a significant body of
theory, there has been no systematic attempt to relate it to its ante-
cedents in Marshall and Edgeworth, to examine its methodological
limitations, and to contrast it with the traditional analysis of international trade by English-speaking economists.[14]

IV. THE TERMS OF TRADE AND
THE VOLUME OF TRADE

We are now in a position to appraise Edgeworth's use of his
pioneer diagram (Diagram II above). He sought to decide whether
England would be benefited by distorting its offer curve to the left
along OG by means of a tariff. He decided that if Q, the assumed
new position of equilibrium after the tariff, is above M and inside
the trade indifference curve, the inhabitants of England would be
benefited by the tariff because their terms of trade would be better.
In the light of contemporary use of this methodology, his analytical
conclusion appears curious because, in the first place, it is apparent
that England's terms of trade are better than at P at all points on OG
between O and P, and the fact that the indifference curve cuts

[13] Albert O. Hirschman, *National Power and the Structure of Foreign Trade*
(Berkeley and Los Angeles, University of California Press, 1945), pp. 44–45.

[14] Moreover, there is not unanimity among the profession that the methodology described above is the most satisfactory way to approach the problem
of how one country might reap monopoly gains from its international trade.
Lerner ignores this body of thought in addressing himself to the question, and
his treatment suffers as a result. (*Vid. The Economics of Control* [New York,
Macmillan, 1944], Chaps. 27 and 29.) He proposes that a country should follow
monopolistic principles in the various markets for its exports and monopsonistic
principles in the various markets for its imports. By neglecting the principle
of reciprocal demand he seems to suppose that, for example, the elasticity of
the foreign supply of every good is quite independent of the amount of a given
country's own exports which are offered in exchange. For a similar approach see
Stephen Enke, "The Monopsony Case for Tariffs," *Quart. Jour. Econ.*, Vol.
LVIII (Feb., 1944), pp. 229–45.

OMQP at *M* has nothing to do with this. In the second place, it is apparent that *OG* would intersect higher *E* indifference curves at *all* points between *M* and *P*, but that *MQP* is tangent to *only one E* indifference curve. In other words, as the indifference curve is drawn, it shows that improved *terms of trade* more than compensate *E* for the shrinking volume of trade along *OG* from *P* to *M*, but fail to do so between *M* and *O*.[15]

Marshall also sought to decide whether a country could gain by enacting a tariff to distort its offer curve. He concluded that a country would clearly gain if it faced a reciprocal demand of less than unit elasticity but would probably *not* gain if it faced a reciprocal demand of greater than unit elasticity.[16] The reason for this position was, of course, that if the foreign reciprocal demand is inelastic, a tariff-distorted offer curve will increase both imports and the home supply of exportable goods, while if its elasticity is greater than unity, the home supply of exportable goods will increase but imports will decrease. In this latter case, the *volume* of trade declines, although the *terms* of trade improve; and without a single index of the effect of *both* on welfare, Marshall and his contemporaries believed that the advantage did not lie with restrictive practices.

V. RESTRICTION OF THE "OUTPUT" OF EXPORTS

Until the appearance of the body of ideas summarized above, the Marshallian curves of reciprocal demand were not used for the

[15] Viner, in commenting on Edgeworth's exercise, fell into the same pitfall that Edgeworth did—i.e., failed to recognize that the indifference curves must take account of both the terms and volume of trade in so far as each affects welfare (Viner, *op. cit.*, p. 582). Benham also fails to take into account this characteristic of the methodology (F. Benham, "The Terms of Trade," *Economica*, Vol. VII [Nov., 1940], p. 360–76).

Apparently it was Edgeworth's personal opinion that his graphical exercise should not be taken too seriously, for he promptly sought to minimize the implications of his conclusion for policy. In commenting upon his own analysis, he quoted with approval a remark by J.S. Nicholson that some analytical demonstrations are "part of the casuistry of economics, like the discussions of moral philosophers concerning the occasional justification of mendacity. Free trade, like honesty, still remains the best policy."

[16] Marshall did not think this terms of trade argument for tariffs was of much importance as a practical matter. His position rested in part upon his opinion that "no country is likely to be able to throw any considerable part of the burden of her import duties on others: unless, either all her exports consist of things of which she has at least a partial monopoly; or she is the only important consumer of most of the commodities which she imports from those countries" (*op. cit.*, p. 198).

analysis of problems in the field of international trade. Rather, they were regarded as providing an interesting graphical method of representing equilibrium in trade across national boundaries and were seldom used at all except, perhaps, for intellectual exercise by economists. Those who have revived the method now reject Marshall's view that a country could probably not gain from a tariff if it faced a reciprocal demand with greater than unit elasticity. Instead, they claim that a tariff will confer a nationalistic advantage if the country faces a reciprocal demand of anything less than *infinite* elasticity. A tariff decreases the (tariff-enacting) country's demand for imports in the schedule sense, and when this is portrayed on Marshall's curves, it also amounts to a reduction in the supply schedule of exports.

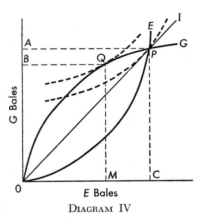

DIAGRAM IV

The content and significance of the body of thought under review can perhaps be clarified if it is provisionally accepted for a graphical demonstration of this case.

The proposition that a zero tariff is the optimum monopolistic policy if a country faces a reciprocal demand for its exports of infinite elasticity could be demonstrated as in Diagram IV. Here OI is a "foreign" reciprocal demand curve of infinite elasticity, and OE is the home country's reciprocal demand curve. If the home country follows a free trade policy (i.e., does not distort its offer curve), equilibrium would be at P. As explained above, it follows from the derivation of OE that one of E's community indifference curves must be tangent to OI at P. Therefore, P is the optimum position on OI for E and free trade is indeed the rational policy for E. It would continue to be so even if G should levy a tariff shifting the position of OI, as long as OI remains a straight line, or in other words, as long as the country faces constant terms of trade.

To assume that a single country will not consider the collective retaliation of other countries to its own tariff policies (a necessary assumption for this methodology, as pointed out above) implies that the country supplies exports to a world market in which it believes the demand (in the schedule sense) for its exports will not change as a result of its own policies. It is conventional, among those who use international reciprocal demand curves, to suppose that countries face a "curvilinear" reciprocal demand, which is to say that they realize different terms of trade for different "outputs" of exports. (Otherwise, they would face a demand of infinite elasticity and the optimum tariff would always be zero.) For a given country, this possession of a certain amount of control over its market may, of course, arise either from some degree of monopoly in its export markets or some degree of monopsony in its import markets, or both. The presence of some degree of market control in this sense is usually alluded to by stating that the given country's "strategic position" (economically) is taken as a datum. Therefore, in a single diagram, one may show the difference in the rational behavior of a country if, on the one hand, it believes that it faces an infinitely elastic reciprocal demand, and, on the other hand, it believes that the world's reciprocal demand for its exports is of less than infinite elasticity. Such a contrast is analytically similar to the Chamberlinian case of a single monopolistic firm contrasted with a competitive firm.

If the reciprocal demand for E's exports is of infinite elasticity, OI in Diagram IV, E will be in free trade equilibrium at P supplying OC of E bales in exchange for OA of G bales. Free trade is, of course, the optimum policy for E. If, however, we suppose that E does have some control over the price of its exports and faces a curvilinear reciprocal demand curve, it will restrict trade. OG, the curve of less than infinite elasticity, must begin at O and pass through P. E's equilibrium position now shifts to Q, where it supplies (fewer) OM exports in exchange for (fewer) OB imports. Because OG is curvilinear and convex to the G bale axis, and must pass through both O and P, it follows that it must be tangent to an indifference curve at a volume of E bales less than OC, and it would be rational for E to distort the reciprocal demand curve (OE) by a tariff so that it would intersect OG at Q. Thus we find that if a country were in a situation in which it believed that different terms of trade would be associated with different volumes of exports, it would rationally supply fewer exports and receive fewer imports than it would if it faced given and constant terms of trade (an infinitely elastic foreign reciprocal demand).

VI. RADICAL IMPLICATIONS OF THE METHODOLOGY

Thus far a sketch has been provided of the interesting manipulations which appear to have been made possible by theoretical refinement of basic tools worked out by Marshall and Edgeworth. In section VII below, reasons are advanced for finding the use of community indifference curves unsatisfactory, but very eminent members of the profession have subscribed—either explicitly or implicitly —to their use and, as will be pointed out in this section, without apparently recognizing all of the implications of doing so.[17] Broadly speaking, the methodology under discussion comes very close to providing us with a consistent formal theory of an important aspect of economic nationalism, and in a world which has been tormented by various forms of this virus since, say 1920, it would be a highly significant achievement if economists could provide an acceptable formal theory of the phenomenon. Therefore, this section has been added to indicate the great importance that would attach to the ideas under review—if one did not feel compelled to add a final section rejecting the methodology.[18]

A. The selection of premises

At the hands of English-speaking economists, the development of the formal theory of international trade has been largely "atomistic" and cosmopolitan in character because the premises used have been applicable to economic relations among private buyers and sellers who happen to live in different countries but conduct trade across national boundaries. More specifically, if still in terms of broad generality, it has usually been supposed that: (1) The relevant decisions in international trade are made by many, private, profit-maximizing business units and many, unorganized, income-maximizing consumers; (2) The relevant decisions tend to be made in terms

[17] H. Denis, in "A Note on the Theory of Tariffs," Rev. Econ. Stud., Vol. XII (2), No. 32 (1944–45), cites the body of doctrine under review here as constituting "important progress in the pure theory of international trade" without remarking upon the sharp break with precedent in the English-speaking world which these doctrines involve.

[18] It is clear from what has gone before that all economists do not find it necessary to reject community indifference curves. For a rather typical attitude toward this problem which does not quite finally reject them, see G. Haberler, "Some Problems in the Pure Theory of International Trade," Econ. Jour., Vol. LX, No. 238 (June, 1950), pp. 223–40.

of price and cost relationships; (3) The balance of payments of a country is a registering device rather than a guide to active policies that may themselves be systematically expounded; (4) The rôle of government is typically restricted to management of the currency.[19] Thus atomistic forces have been stressed, and have tended to lead an existence independent of any considerations of a national economic interest which might inhere in the fact of national sovereignty. Ricardo's famous remark that "Every transaction in [international] commerce is an independent transaction," [20] illustrates this characteristic of our subject.

It is against this background that the essential novelty of the ideas here under discussion appears, for they *sectionalize* the world economy into independent national economies by assuming the existence of two separate community preference systems. Such a sharp separation of distinctly national economic interests, and the *formulation of a formal theory of active national tariff behavior* would have appeared quite novel to the British classical economists. It might not have appeared theoretically "revolutionary," however, for while the British classical (and neo-classical) writers developed a cosmopolitan and "atomistic" *formal theory* of international trade, they were quite conscious of a national economic interest when they turned to the subject of economic policy.[21]

The relatively cosmopolitan character of the British classical theory of international trade is immediately apparent when List, for example, is considered. Historians of economic ideas find List difficult to "classify," and I think one reason is that his perception of the State as an economic unit capable of *economizing* in the national interest was very clear-cut. The premises for his historico-theoretical analysis

[19] It is true that writers on international economic *policy* have customarily gone farther than these assumptions would permit, but they usually proceed to appraise governmental policies in terms of a competitive international equilibrium, the very existence of which depends upon the empirical assumptions listed in the text. *Vid.* A.P. Lerner, *op. cit.*, Chaps. 27–29 for a conspicuous exception to assumptions (1), (3) and (4).

[20] David Ricardo, *The Principles of Political Economy and Taxation* (London, J.M. Dent and Sons, Ltd.; New York, E.P. Dutton and Co., 1911, Everyman Ed.), p. 85.

[21] Students of the history of economic thought will think of many citations, from Smith onwards, in support of this statement. The distinction between theory and policy is perhaps not so sharp as might first appear, however. For example, Mill's discussion of both the "infant industry" and the "terms of trade" arguments for tariffs suggests a certain ambiguity about his theoretical concept of a national economic interest.

were more inclusive than, say Ricardo's. He was very much aware that the environment of his day had *two* interesting characteristics: (1) National states existed which were the ultimate sources of power and authority; (2) International trade and investment were briskly growing, rendering various parts of the world more inter-dependent economically, and incidentally building up criss-crossing commercial ties that seemed not to be seriously thwarted by national frontiers.[22]

This is not the place to develop possible explanations of why the theory of international trade took a cosmopolitan, "atomistic" turn at the hands of the British classical economists.[23] It must suffice to point out that it *did,* and that the ideas being considered here represent a sharp break with this tradition. How sharp a break is indicated by Diagram IV. This diagram and the analysis it represents make no sense unless we postulate the existence of some kind of national economic policy agent trying to *decide* whether or not "it" faces a reciprocal demand that is less than infinitely elastic. If "it" decides that it does, its conduct is adjusted accordingly and we have a limitation to output (exports) arising on the *demand* side of the market which has the same economic effect as a negatively inclined demand curve facing a firm in ordinary partial equilibrium analysis.

A careful study of the relationship between the idea of a (collective) national economic interest and the formal theory of international trade developed by the British classical economists would be highly rewarding.[24] Pending such an investigation, it appears that

[22] It is significant in this connection that he strongly dissented from the British classical view—found in Smith, Ricardo and Mill—that free international trade would promote international amicability. On the contrary, he thought that self-respecting sovereign states other than Britain would not tolerate the "aim-less" intrusion of atomistic business forces into their domains if they did not promote economic development. International peace and free trade, he claimed, must follow, and not precede, the development of Germany to a position of economic equality with Britain.

[23] The two principal reasons are, I think: (1) Economic theory appeals to rational minds and free trade appeared to be the most rational national economic policy. Therefore, if rational public policies were to be pursued—and most of our forebears in economic theory thought they would be—free trade hypotheses were the most useful ones; (2) Being Englishmen in an Anglo-centric world, the national economic interest of their country did not appear to them as something that needed promotion by theories and policies of economic nationalism.

[24] As eminently practical citizens, of course, they thought and wrote about the national economic interest, but it almost eludes detection in their strictly theoretical work.

their thinking was somewhat ambiguous at this point but that, in the environment of nineteenth century England, such ambiguity did not have serious consequences. The essential nature of the ambiguity is indicated in a remark of Hume's which symbolizes quite well the transition from mercantilism to economic liberalism. Observing that one country need not fear the prosperity of others because they could be good customers only if they were prosperous, he said: "I shall therefore venture to acknowledge that, not only as a man, but as a British subject, I pray for the flourishing commerce of Germany, Spain, Italy, and even France itself." [25] The cosmopolitan tradition of the British classical school, I think, rested essentially upon the intellectual feat which enabled Hume to achieve this harmony between his prayers "as a man" and "as a British subject." Such a harmony would become quite cloudy if one should suppose that British subjects had some unique collective economic interest in common, and it would disappear if they were to set about pursuing such an interest at the expense of people in other countries. By selecting "atomistic" premises for their formal analysis of international trade, the great majority of British writers after Hume built up an essentially cosmopolitan theory of the subject.[26]

B. Analytical conclusions

If one recalls that the classical and neo-classical economists ordinarily drew the conclusion from their analyses that free trade was the most *rational* economic policy for a single country (regardless of what policies other countries might follow), it is immediately apparent that the economists here under discussion have in this respect, too, made a very sharp break with the precedent set by the majority of English-speaking writers on the subject.[27] Not only do they identify a range of points on the offer curve facing a country which are superior to the point of free trade equilibrium, but, in a world in which economic nationalism is fashionable (however deplored) it would clearly be to a country's interest to enact tariffs

[25] From *Of the Jealousy of Trade,* quoted by Alexander Gray in *The Development of Economic Doctrine* (New York, Longmans, Green, 1931), p. 121.

[26] An illustration of theoretical harmony is provided by the fact that the classical and neo-classical models postulated buyer-seller relationships "between countries" whose nationals *exchanged* goods. There was no theoretical model, for example, of countries in a seller-seller relationship vis-à-vis each other in third markets.

[27] An exception to free trade was thought defensible in theory, however dubious in practice, in favor of the "infant industry" argument.

promptly, if possible before its neighbors do. Scitovsky's conclusion
on this point is unequivocal: "To call the raising of tariffs on these
assumptions irrational, would be similar to calling competitive
behavior irrational."

Moreover, a little further reflection upon the probable shapes of
reciprocal demand curves applicable to "important" and "unimportant" countries would lead to the disquieting analytical conclusion
that the economic opportunity to exploit foreigners would be more
attractive to a large and important country than to a small and unimportant one.[28] Also, retaliation by others against the tariff policy
of an "important" country is more likely than retaliation against an
"unimportant" country, so that a strong economic incentive to
exploit other countries and a strong likelihood of retaliation probably occur together in practice.

The conclusion to which this analysis points is clear and unmistakable (still not attacking the concept of community indifference
curves) and has been frankly stated by Scitovsky and others. It is
that national economic sovereignty is incompatible with a stable
world system of free trade. More than this even, the analysis would
lead inexorably to the conclusion that a world-trading system of
economically sovereign countries would be very likely to degenerate
quickly into a conflict of special (national) interests and that consumers' welfare in all countries would deteriorate as the self-defeating struggle progressed.[29]

[28] In practice, much might depend upon the commodity composition of
trade. That is, a "small" country might have a monopoly in supplying one or
a few "vital" commodities. Aside from this special case, however, a large and
important country would probably be less dependent on international trade
than a small country and would therefore *have* a relatively elastic demand for
imports and a relatively elastic supply of exports. It is also probable that "the
rest of the world" would be more dependent upon trade with a large and
important country than upon trade with any particular small country, so that
a large country would *face* a less elastic reciprocal demand.

[29] One obvious criticism of the methodology under review is that it is "too
neat" to apply to so unsystematic a process as the formulation of tariff policy.
If one could accept the concept of reliable curves of reciprocal demand and
community indifference, certainly the former could not be expected to remain
symmetrical and smooth in a world of economic bellicosity. As Diagram V
brings out, such curves would make a country admirably vulnerable to exploitation by other countries, since E' and G' respectively show the alternative
optimum monopoly positions available to E and G, depending upon which
moves more promptly. It seems improbable that an economic control agency
of a country would leave itself so exposed. If G should enact (or propose to
enact) a tariff and move its offer curve toward G', E might threaten an embargo
on trade with G or, at least refuse G access to E goods for which G's demand

It should be clear that, like certain other socially unsettling conclusions that have been drawn by economists, this one would have definite roots in Ricardo. At the end of his classic illustration of the law of comparative costs, he concluded that, "It would undoubtedly be advantageous . . . to the consumers in both countries" if there were no obstructions to the movement of capital and labor across national boundaries.[30] The doctrines we are discussing would go one step further in effect and show that by breathing life into the national state, as it were, and portraying it as a rationally calculating economic unit, not only would consumers not have as large a social product as they would have if there were no (passive) national boundaries, but they would suffer a contraction in their total welfare. The probability that this would occur, *given one's acceptance of the community indifference curve methodology* and the reality of an ungoverned world, is very high since no national government which could see such a clear opportunity of immediate gain would be likely to refrain from taking advantage of it.

C. Policy implications

In one important respect the "new methodology" would lead to a conclusion that has long been familiar to English-speaking students of international trade. It is that world-wide policies of free trade are probably "best" for all of the world's consumers taken together. Placed in the context of this judgment, the analytical finding that a world-wide system of free trade would probably be economically unstable leads Scitovsky to the conclusion for public policy that "some form of compulsion is necessary to ensure free trade." According to the usual understanding of a free trade world, the bulk of international trade and investment would be carried on by private enterprises which should be able to make plans on the assumption that the international economic policies of governments will aim at relative *stability*. The incompatibility between such a world of private international transactions and the world of embattled national states suggested by the model certainly implies that without some form of compulsion administered in the interest of *all* the world's

---

is most inelastic. If governments should thus seize monopoly power over the export (or import) of certain economically strategic goods, such discontinuities would appear in the reciprocal demand curves that they would become quite unmanageable.

[30] *Op. cit.*, p. 83.

consumers, international trade and investment would appear chronically unattractive to private enterprises.

This is the policy implication of the "new methodology" which I think is most interesting. Certainly in a world struggling toward new and more inclusive political forms, the type of analytical demonstration which those who use community indifference curves purport to make would be of considerable practical significance. Therefore, if I found the methodology acceptable, I could not agree that the characterization of it which appears in the Introduction to *Readings in the Theory of International Trade* brings out its most significant aspect. There it is said that, "It is surprising . . . to find that the improvements in international price theory, when they were finally made . . . affected the basic conclusions derived from the classical theory only to a moderate extent. On questions of commercial policy, for example, Mill and Scitovsky are in substantial agreement, even though their methods of analysis and their underlying price theories are considerably different." [31] Surely it cannot be forgotten that Mill made only vague and obscure references to the existence of a national economic interest and to the policies of "collective churlishness" which might be followed (mistakenly, he thought) to promote it. On the other hand, so far from supposing that countries will rationally adhere to free trade (Mill's—and Edgeworth's—recommendation for commercial policy), Scitovsky claims to show an incentive which exists for each country to be the *first* to exploit other countries. His conclusion is unmistakable that, given economic sovereignty, we should not expect world-wide free trade to flourish and (as Mill expected) to usher in an era of international good feeling. Surely Scitovsky's most interesting finding for commercial policy is that "some form of compulsion is necessary to ensure free trade."

[31] Howard S. Ellis and Lloyd A. Metzler, in the Introduction to *Readings in the Theory of International Trade* (Philadelphia, Blakiston, 1949). It is curious to find in this "Introduction" the quoted reference to the use of community indifference curves as "finally" bringing "improvements in international price theory," and three pages later an expression of doubt as to whether or not the methodology is valid at all. On page xi we read that "the concept of a collective indifference schedule for the community as a whole . . . has frequently been called into question. But whether this affects the validity of their final conclusions [Leontief's and Scitovsky's] is a question which need not detain us here."

VII. COLLAPSING A METHODOLOGICAL HOUSE OF CARDS

The close relationship between the contemporary ideas discussed above and the terms of trade argument for tariffs which was familiar to classical and neo-classical economists has been brought out. Taken together, Marshall's reciprocal demand curves and Edgeworth's addition of a single community indifference curve may be regarded as a midway house in the progress of thought from Mill to Scitovsky. The point has also been made that reciprocal demand curves were scarcely used in the theory of international trade until their recent revival by Samuelson, Kaldor, Scitovsky and others. One reason for this hiatus in their use is that economists had little or no confidence in the practicability of the terms of trade argument for tariffs with which the curves were associated. Marshall's opinion was cited in note 16 above.[32] Haberler expressed his dissatisfaction with the argument in strong terms by writing that, "It is out of the question to deduce an argument for tariffs [on this basis]. . . . Whoever does so proves only that he has not realized the full complexity of the problem." [33] A second reason why Marshall's curves were allowed to lie fallow for so long is that the very completeness and the finality of the picture of equilibrium which they provide (and its representation in terms of real resource units) was generally thought to make them unsatisfactory tools of analysis. Edgeworth once made this point by comparing them to the hands of a clock, which move as the result of a complicated but hidden mechanism. Haberler made the same point by observing:

One can make a rough estimate of the money demand for some particular good, but it is almost impossible to estimate the elasticity of the Marshallian demand curve of a country. Guessing the shape of these curves and then reading off the result means simply jumping to the final outcome of a complicated process without analyzing it. By assuming Marshall's curves as given we really assume the result.[34]

We now know that the major reason for dissatisfaction with the terms of trade argument for tariffs (and, by implication, with the

[32] The terms of trade *argument* for tariffs has long been recognized, however, as being one of the few arguments for tariffs which might have theoretical respectability. *Cf.* Viner, *op. cit.*, pp. 298–99, 320, 322, 447.

[33] *Op. cit.*, note 4 above, pp. 294–95.

[34] *Ibid.*, p. 159.

practicability of Marshall's curves) was the non-comparability between gains which might accrue from improved *terms* of trade and
losses which would follow upon a reduction in the *volume* of trade.
We now know, too, that contemporary writers believe that, by showing community indifference curves (in terms of "bale units") to be
implicit in Marshall's reciprocal demand curves, they have succeeded
in making this community gain and this community loss comparable. To adopt Edgeworth's metaphor, the writers under review confidently set and reset the hands of the clock in order to move them
toward *points of partial equilibria* for particular countries.[35] These
countries are assumed to be actively economizing agents under
unified management, and bent upon ruthless (if short-sighted) economic aggrandizement. After carefully weighing the probable elasticity of the relevant reciprocal demands, they are presumed to enact
tariffs because (in the short run) it can be demonstrated that they
will increase the community's welfare.[36]

The preceding paragraph brings out sharply the crucial rôle of the
concept of reliable community indifference curves in the "new
methodology." In short, they must make it possible to arrive at policy
decisions in the field of international trade, and this they cannot do.
The reasons why they cannot may be analyzed under two general
headings.

A. Tariffs change the distribution of income [37]

A community indifference curve, in the first place, is a locus of
points representing a constant real income for the community as a
whole. Each curve represents a unique income distribution within
the community, and the various points on the curve show different
combinations of the goods measured on the two axes. Therefore,
through any point on a community indifference map there pass an

[35] It should be noted that such points of partial equilibria are not conceivable
under the methodology of the British classical school. Marshall and Edgeworth
only hinted at them.

[36] It is indicative of the confidence which they feel in their achievement of
making comparable two economic concepts previously thought incomparable
that the contemporary writers under review state their conclusions in the
indicative mode, whereas the classical and neo-classical economists usually use
the conditional when reaching conclusions in this field.

[37] For a good statement of some of the problems involved in inter-personal
comparisons of utility (a process implicit in the use of community indifference
curves) see W.J. Baumol, "Community Indifference," *Rev. Econ. Stud.*, Vol.
XIV (1), No. 35 (1946–47), pp. 44–48.

almost infinite number of indifference curves, corresponding to every possible *distribution* of the combination of goods represented at that point. This means that if a country should (in effect) distort its offer curve by means of a tariff, which implies some redistribution of incomes within the country, the new system of indifference curves would have a shape different from those applicable before the tariff. Therefore, the two pertinent indifference curves would have a shape different from the ("same") two applicable before the tariff. Moreover, in Diagram IV the "pre-tariff" curve tangent to P and the "post-tariff" curve tangent to Q might intersect.

Scitovsky makes the most forthright attempt to deal with this problem, and he seeks to render it manageable by explicitly confining his attention to only two of many possible hypothetical income distributions—the ones prevailing before and after the contemplated tariff.[38] He then proceeds to argue that if these two income distributions are "similar," it is unlikely that the relevant community indifference curves will intersect, and therefore the community's total welfare in the two situations will probably be comparable.[39] This courageous attempt to rescue the methodology is unsatisfactory for at least two reasons. First, a decision is called for—whether or not to enact a tariff—and the basis upon which it must be made cannot be established until *after* the tariff has been passed and *allowed to have its effect upon income distribution so that a new family of indifference curves can be drawn* appropriate to the new distribution pattern. Secondly, a comparison "before and after" is possible only if the two income distributions are "similar," and they would become "dissimilar" long before the spectacle of retaliation and counter-retaliation envisaged by Scitovsky could go very far. As soon as enough dissimilarity occurs (and this crucial criterion of "similarity" is probably not possible to define), the "before and after" families of indifference curves will intersect, suggesting not one optimum tariff but a whole range of optima.

B. Too many variables are in the premises

It is now quite apparent that there is a striking contrast between the quite vague and tenuous nature of the concept of reliable com-

[38] Note 12 above.

[39] Scitovsky appears to have certain reservations about this "solution" for at the end of the sections in which it is presented he writes, "Readers who feel uneasy about what has been said so far are *well advised* at this stage to forget about [it] altogether" (*ibid.*, italics supplied).

munity indifference curves, on the one hand, and the definite and forcefully stated conclusions which those who use them claim to reach. We have not far to seek for an explanation of the contrast: it is that the greater apparent certainty of the "findings" made with the use of community indifference curves is paid for by using assumptions which must be both very numerous and extremely restrictive. In other words, use of the new tools described above does not, in actual fact, enable one to side-step any of the old problems that have worried economists since Ricardo who have labored in this field of inquiry. A country's relative degree of monopoly in particular (potential, as well as actual) export markets, of monopsony in particular (potential and actual) import markets, the equivocal nature of various measures of changes in the terms of trade, the vexing problem of deciding whether "a country" is or is not "better off" if it secures fewer imports on better terms,[40] the baffling problem of the effect of changes in income distribution upon community welfare— all of these problems still exist in the real world, but are covered by theoretical premises in the "new methodology."

Thus—and now we have arrived at the heart of the matter—the difficulty of drawing the community indifference curves and the Marshallian curves (both in terms of "bales of resource embodiments") according to the current fashion merely replaces the difficulty which classical and neo-classical economists faced when they tried to make hard practical judgments *one at a time*. It seems, indeed, as if Haberler in 1936 were smiling in the background, remarking that "guessing the shape of these curves and then reading off the result means simply jumping to the final outcome of a complicated process without analyzing it." [41] It would be fatuous of course to

---

[40] Neo-classical writers, while they did not make much use of community indifference curves, did point to an aspect of this part of the problem which is not brought out by the contemporary writers. In Diagram III the vertical distances between OG and OG' represent the tariff revenue of G's government in terms of G bales. Clearly the underlying indifference curves which would validate OG would not be changed (in the short run, at least) by the imposition of a tariff. That is to say, in the short run, cost conditions in G's export industries and the utility functions in G for G's imports do not change. Hence it follows that G's producers and consumers—as such—are injured by the tariff: the price of imports (in their own currency) immediately rises and the market for exports contracts. As a unit, however, G country is supposedly better off, as shown by the diagram. This is so because the government's tariff revenue is reckoned along with the effects on private producers and consumers. Therefore, we must know how G's government responds to the increase in its revenue in order to assert unequivocally that "G" would be better off at P' than at P.

[41] *Cf.* note 34 above.

suppose that the neatly *symmetrical* preference systems of the diagrams were applicable in the real world. In short, it seems that those who use community indifference curves and Marshall's reciprocal demand curves have been led to formulate sweeping and positive conclusions which their underlying methodology cannot support.[42]

Perhaps one could have reached such a judgment intuitively in the first place, for it hardly seems plausible that the economic activities of national states bent upon exploiting one another could have been represented realistically by means of the almost mechanical manipulation of curves. Governments are political organizations, and their objectives cannot be satisfactorily delimited as we conventionally limit those of a business enterprise to the pursuit of maximum profit. The authorities have more to think about than the possibilities of economic gain at the expense of other countries. Moreover, even if this were not so, because tariff policy certainly affects internal income distribution, it follows that tariffs are enacted which do not represent the maximum exploitation of foreigners but maximum concessions to domestic pressure groups.

Finally, as economists should know better than some other people, conditions change rapidly nowadays and there are some grounds for hoping that the institutional structure subsumed by the ideas reviewed above may be passing away. Perhaps the concepts of consultation and mutual economic aid may in future apply more appropriately to that part of the world which still allows market forces to operate across national boundaries than the concept of ruthless and short-sighted national states bent upon exploiting one another.

[42] Were Marshall still among us, he might not be surprised at the revival of his ingenious curves of reciprocal demand and their portrayal against a background of super-imposed community indifference curves. He certainly would be surprised, however, at the easy transition from this exercise to the statement, on the basis of it, of firm conclusions about the world of affairs. He, too, enjoyed the logical intricacies of pure theory, but wrote in justification of an extensive treatment of reciprocal demand curves with "exceptional elasticities" that such explorations "derive their origin from the sport of the imagination rather than from the observation of facts." *Op. cit.,* p. 353.

3. A GENERAL THEORY OF THE SYSTEM OF MULTILATERAL TRADE

Karl-Erik Hansson

United Nations

Reprinted from *The American Economic Review*, XLII (March 1952), pp. 58–68, by permission of the author and the American Economic Association. While the writer is on the staff of the United Nations Secretariat, the views expressed are his personal views. The paper was presented at a joint meeting of the American Economic Association and the Econometric Society in Chicago, Illinois, on December 28, 1950.

In the field of international trade many theoretical discussions have been held in general terms without too much concern about what the world actually looked like. On the other hand, numerous statistical studies, with an outstanding exception to be noted here, have usually been limited to the problems of one or a few countries or particular commodities. In the present paper I shall try to strike a middle road between these two extremes. The approach may be said to build further on the empirical results found by Folke Hilgerdt with regard to the network of world trade [1] and theoretical discussions, as expounded chiefly by Bertil Ohlin,[2] based on the distribution of factors of production and the principle of comparative costs.

To refresh our memories I should like to draw attention to the now rather well-known chart of the network of world trade. In this diagram the year considered is 1928 since this is one of the last "normal" years before the system was disturbed.

The arrows in the chart indicate the direction of balances of merchandise trade, in millions of dollars, between the groups in the system by pointing from net exporting to net importing groups. The balances have been calculated on the basis of f.o.b. values, because

---

[1] *The Network of World Trade* (League of Nations, 1942); and "The Case for Multilateral Trade," *Am. Econ. Rev.*, Vol. XXXIII, No. 1, Pt. 2, Suppl. (March, 1943), pp. 393–407.

[2] *Interregional and International Trade* (Cambridge, Mass., 1933), and in more simplified direct form in *Utrikeshandel och Handelspolitik*, 4th ed. (Stockholm, 1949).

freight and other charges included in recorded c.i.f. or frontier values of imports frequently are paid to other than the exporting countries. The Tropics include central Africa, the tropical agricultural and the mineral producing countries of Latin America, and tropical Asia. The Great Plains, or countries of recent settlement in the temperate belt, briefly comprise Canada, Argentina, Paraguay, Uruguay, South Africa, Australia and New Zealand. Non-continental

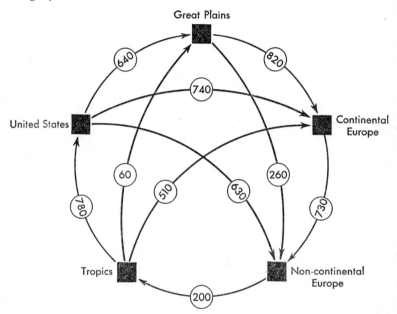

CHART 1. The system of multilateral trade, as reflected by the orientation of balances of merchandise trade in 1928. (*Source: The Network of World Trade*, Table 44, p. 77.)

Europe consists mainly of the United Kingdom. Germany, which is here included in continental Europe, may be shown separately and would then enter between the Great Plains and the rest of Europe. Thus in 1928 the countries included in the multilateral trade system accounted for nine-tenths of the world's trade. The remaining share fell on the other areas, notably China, Japan, USSR, North Africa and the Middle East, which did not fit well into the simple trade pattern.

The trade pattern was found empirically. It was discovered that the countries in the system could be arranged in the order of the direction of their balances of trade, so that each country had an import balance from practically all countries that preceded it in the list and an export balance to practically all countries that succeeded it. The countries have been grouped into a limited number of categories to give a synoptical view of the network.

This system was not a haphazard, unstable pattern shifting in form from year to year. The great significance lies in the stability of the system. This structure of world trade was built on a solid foundation, some major principles of which will now be dealt with in a theoretical approach.

A GENERAL THEORY

International trade takes place in response to the unequal distribution of the factors of production.

The simple case of three countries, A, B and C, which have an unequal relative supply of the three main factors of production, labour, land and capital, demonstrates the fundamental basis of a trade system. To begin with, we will consider only merchandise trade. We disregard here further refinement in the definition of factors of production and we also leave for the moment modifications due to variations or movements of the production factors themselves and the effects thereof, as well as the friction caused by transport costs and artificial barriers. These various elements will gradually be taken into consideration in a realistic interpretation of the multilateral system found empirically. The simple theoretical case, however, contains principles which are not materially altered by these modifications.

CASE 1.

Relative Supply	A	B	C
ample	labour	land	capital
moderate	land	capital	labour
scarce	capital	labour	land

Each country will produce and export commodities embodying chiefly the factor of production in ample supply there. The three countries choose their imports simultaneously. The greatest return or consumption satisfaction will be obtained from an imported commodity containing mainly the factor of production in the most scarce supply in the importing country. Therefore *A* will tend to import capital-intensive goods from *C* (such as textiles), *B* labour-intensive commodities from *A* (such as coffee, sugar, rubber) and *C* land-intensive merchandise from *B* (such as grains and wool). Basically the simultaneous free choice makes it possible for *A* to have an import surplus from *C*, *B* from *A* and *C* from *B* and for *A* to have an export surplus to *B*, *B* to *C* and *C* to *A*. Thus the fundamental multi-lateral trade triangle is closed and the placing of one country in relation to the others in the system is given.

Later on, in connection with a schematical illustration of the development and disruption of the actual system, the case will be considered where each group does not possess an ample relative supply of a different factor of production *and* also at the same time a scarce relative supply of a different factor of production, for instance, when capital is the most scarce factor in both *A* and *B* and when capital is the most ample factor in both *B* and *C*.

THE COUNTRY GROUPS IN THE ACTUAL SYSTEM

The countries participating in the actual multilateral system described before can be identified with the three types just mentioned, especially for the period before World War I. Thus the countries of the Tropics, with their ample labour and scarce capital supply, belong to type *A*; the Great Plains, including the United States, with ample land and scarce labour supply, belong to type *B*; and Europe, especially the United Kingdom, with ample capital and scarce land supply, belong to type *C*.

The three corner groups may be broken into six. In terms of the simple theory, continental Europe appears to come before the United Kingdom in the system, and thus closer to the Great Plains, because of the greater relative supply of land. In fact, the total net imports of the United Kingdom from continental Europe, excluding Germany, and her net imports of foodstuffs from that area in 1928 were almost identical in magnitude. These foodstuffs from continental Europe, consisting of dairy products and other processed articles, were more labour-intensive, however, than those from the Great Plains, where labour is more scarce than in continental Europe. Germany could produce substantially the same goods as the rest of continental Europe, but, in addition, she had the advantage of a wide home market and large-scale industrial production geared to the needs of Europe. Germany therefore appeared before the rest of continental Europe in the trade system due to a large export surplus of manufactured articles going to that area. For similar reasons the United States took the place in front of the rest of the Great Plains, at least from the 1890's.

The supply of production factors may be measured in terms of the total population and area in each country, and the use of machinery, as done by Wagemann,[3] or some other measurement of capital. We need not go into a discussion of such figures here or desirable refinements in quantitative presentation. Even such crude figures, when analysed simultaneously, confirm the grouping of countries by revealing quite distinct differences between the countries or groups of countries shown in the system. To take an example, the supply of capital, as measured by Wagemann, was roughly the same per capita in the Great Plains (weighted average) and Germany, but in the Great Plains that capital had to be spread over much larger land. From such considerations, it may be tempting to lead into speculation about the natural type of production, exchange of goods, standard of living, etc.

The theory based on the relative supply of factors of production leads to an explanation of the natural *grouping* of countries, into three and six corners, and of the *pulling* force in the system. A country with a certain factor supply combination may be placed in relation not only to one other country but to practically the whole world in a system. In fact, it is surprising that no attempt was made, on the basis of Ohlin's factor supply theory, to postulate the pattern of world trade before it was discovered empirically. The theory also leads to the conclusion that the major merchandise balances tend to follow the "rim" of the circular system. The natural markets and sources of supply are located along this rim. Direct cross-trade going counter to the natural direction of balances tends to be dependent on the force of the production factor in *moderate* supply. On the demand side this factor competes with the most scarce factor and on the export side it competes with the ample relative supply of that factor elsewhere. It follows that commodities embodying chiefly the factor in moderate supply in the country tend to be marginal on both the supply side and the demand side; that is to say, the imports

[3] E. Wagemann, *Struktur und Rhytmus der Weltwirtschaft* (Berlin, 1931), pp. 406–409, gives figures for machinery per capita and per square kilometre in various countries.

of such articles can be dispensed with rather easily or be replaced by domestic production, and the exports of such merchandise can be increased only at relatively high cost. The greatest possibility of adjustment to reach equilibrium thus appears to lie within this range of commodities for each country. If three countries have a *moderate* supply of a *different* factor of production, such adjustment may be quite easy in multilateral trade.

The simple case comes closer to reality when we also consider the influence of the climate and the supply of mineral resources and other factors on the *size* of balances between the three basic types of countries. The existence of a tropical climate in *A* (the Tropics) and *A* alone and the need in *B* (the United States and the Great Plains) and *C* (Europe) for foodstuffs and raw materials requiring tropical climate for their production, tend to increase *A*'s export balance to *B* and to reduce its otherwise natural import balance with *C*. Similarly, the demand for and the world distribution of mineral resources affect the net balances between the three groups in such a way that they tend to increase the export balance from *A* to *B*, and particularly from *B* to *C*, and to reduce the "natural" import balance of *A* from *C* (except for coal). "Invisible" items in the balance of payments and transport costs and other factors also affect the *size* of balances and the possibility of matching an export balance in one direction with an import balance in another. I will deal with them briefly after a schematical illustration of the development of the multilateral trade system in terms of the general theory.

DEVELOPMENT THEORY

The basic pulling force of the system is modified slowly by the fact that the production factors themselves can be moved or changed, to a certain extent. Service payments and the friction caused by transport costs and artificial barriers also play their part. The rise, working and disintegration of the system may thus be sketched in terms of shifts in the relative supply of the factors of production and these other elements. The same groups of countries as before are considered. It is realized that different rates of change may apply to different countries in the same group.

Capital and labour supply may be altered through international migration and domestic savings and population changes. Land cannot be moved, but the economic reach of land may be affected. These facts have had an important bearing on the development of the system and the present situation.

Capital was early invested by the United Kingdom in the Tropics and on the European continent. The land factor had not yet been brought into play in the Great Plains. At this time, before the 1870's, the structure of the relative supply of the three major factors of production appears to have been similar in continental Europe to that shown for A in the simple case:

CASE 2.

Relative Supply	Tropics	Continental Europe	United Kingdom
ample	labour	labour	capital
moderate	land	land	labour
scarce	capital	capital	land

Then after the Civil War and the invention of steel and steamships, the Great Plains, including the United States, came within the economic reach of Europe. In the meantime continental Europe, particularly Germany and France, had succeeded in improving the relative supply of capital through domestic savings, while the Tropics instead increased their population. Thus the relative factor supply structure appears to have taken the following form from the early 1870's:

CASE 3.

Relative Supply	Tropics	United States	Great Plains	Continental Europe	United Kingdom
ample	labour	land	land	labour	capital
moderate	land	labour	labour	capital	labour
scarce	capital	capital	capital	land	land

With the opening up of new land, such as the American Middle West, capital was shifted over especially to the United States. United Kingdom investment in Europe even started to decline. The United States-Great Plains area and the United Kingdom became complementary in factor supply. Here was an easy two-way line of exchange of capital and capital-intensive goods against land-intensive products without immediate need for triangular trade in the beginning.

During this period, from the 1870's to the 1890's, continental Europe continued its increase in industrialization and domestic savings. France and Germany supplied capital also for smaller countries on the continent. Capital became relatively more ample at least in the industrialized western countries while the population growth fell off. Primary production overseas depressed European agriculture, but food production turned to more intensive commodities, such as dairy products, for which an expanding market could be found in the United Kingdom. An increasing amount of labour also went into industries or emigrated. The close touch with the labour standard in the United States kept labour from growing into ample supply. Toward the end of the period the United States had gained wide development; largely due to increased domestic savings, capital appears to have grown into a relatively less scarce factor. More land also had become available in the Great Plains, particularly in the southern hemisphere, through inventions, such as refrigeration, and better transportation. By the 1890's, the relative factor supply structure therefore appears to have taken a new form:

CASE 4.

Relative Supply	Tropics	United States	Great Plains	Continental Europe	United Kingdom
ample	labour	land	land	capital	capital
moderate	land	capital	labour	labour	labour
scarce	capital	labour	capital	land	land

The true system of world-wide multilateral trade now came into being, and thus took the shape analysed earlier in this paper. With its growing industrialization and scarcity of labour, United States imports tended to shift from capital-intensive articles from Europe to labour-intensive goods from the Tropics. At the same time the United States, as well as the Great Plains, encouraged immigration from Europe. The ample labour supply in the Tropics was ready to meet this active demand in the United States, and in addition it had the advantage of the climatic and mineral factors. The importance of these factors is seen by the fact that China and Japan, although otherwise having on the whole the same supply structure as the Tropics, were not able to enter the system successfully on the basis of their abundant labour supply alone. With capital now in more ample supply in the United States, the United Kingdom and other creditor countries in Europe gradually lost the incentive for investing in the United States. Instead investments were shifted to the capital-scarce Tropics in response to the active demand in the United States for labour-intensive goods such as rubber. A clear export surplus, which was now developed from the United Kingdom to the Tropics, partly reflected this capital movement. The net imports of the United States and the Great Plains from the Tropics expanded; they served to cover part of the import surplus of the Tropics from the United Kingdom as well as the transfer of interest and dividend payments. The United States in turn developed a large export surplus in trade with the Great Plains on the basis of its larger capital accumulation and industrial production fitting the needs of the Great Plains. This development also facilitated the transfer of European capital via the United States, particularly to Canada. Capital continued to be scarce in the Great Plains, which were complementary to Europe in supply structure. The Great Plains as well as the United States enjoyed a growing export surplus to Europe, particularly continental Europe, which in turn found an expanding market in the United Kingdom. Germany appeared as a separate link between the Great Plains and the rest of Europe. Triangular and more complicated multilateral trade thus became intensive from the 1890's in an almost explosive fashion, after the foundation of the trade system had ripened during the preceding decades.

Before we consider the disintegration of the system and the present situation, let us now have a look at the place of transport costs and other elements.

Transport costs always cause friction by adding to the costs of goods moved. Inventions and improvements in transportation added to the mobility of goods and brought the land factor more fully into play. The development of the basic net trade triangle may have been encouraged by especially large reductions in the transport friction, in the form of low return freight rates between certain points. This appears to be the case in the net exports from the Tropics to the Great Plains and from the latter to Europe. The otherwise natural import surplus of the Tropics from Europe probably was held down somewhat by the favourable ballast rates for Europe on returning coal boats. European freight earnings helped to cover the European import balance particularly from the Great Plains. Artificial trade barriers have, of course, limited the free interplay of the relative scarcity of factors of production in a way similar to transport costs. The removal of British tariffs on foodstuffs and the protection of United States industries appear to have been especially important moves in establishing a large export surplus from the United States-Great Plains to Europe.

At least in its quantitative aspects, the development of the system was closely tied up with the transfer of payments for "services." Growing interest and dividend payments from the Tropics and the Great Plains, including the United States, served to cover a substantial part of the increasing import surplus of Europe from the Great Plains. Although for accounting purposes such payments were settled directly, the real transfer covering those payments took a "roundabout" way. Debtor countries found the natural market for their products in third countries situated between the debtor country and the creditor country in the system. Interest payments from Malaya, for example, may thus be said to have gone through the series of export balances along the rim of the diagram leading to the United Kingdom. Malaya itself had an import balance with the United Kingdom. Some capital movements also tended to take such "roundabout" routes. These financial transactions thus were served by and tended to foster multilateral trade in the system. Emigrants' remittances, tourist receipts and commission and insurance earnings similarly made it possible for Europe, and particularly for the United Kingdom, to develop large net imports of merchandise. Gold balances, finally, served an important purpose in covering net obligations at certain times and thus made the natural triangle work more smoothly.

DISINTEGRATION AND THE PRESENT SITUATION

Major changes took place slowly during the functioning of the circular trade system which finally led to its disintegration. The Tropics continued to pour the advantages of trade into an increase in population. Capital remained scarce, and the low income made it difficult to accumulate domestic savings. There were only limited opportunities for migration. The United States enjoyed high productivity which facilitated a rapid increase in domestic savings. After the closing of the "frontier" in the 1890's, land became less ample while capital grew more abundant. The United States emerged as the major capital market after World War I. The Great Plains, through capital imports and accelerated domestic savings, experienced the same development as the United States had done before. Europe lost the advantage of a relatively ample capital supply and also lost capital invested overseas. Europe was at a disadvantage because land, the scarce factor, could not be moved. Migration to the United States was also curtailed during the 1920's. The relative factor supply structure thus seems to have changed into the following pattern by the end of the 1920's:

CASE 5.

Relative Supply	Tropics	United States	Great Plains	Continental Europe	United Kingdom
ample	labour	capital	land	capital	capital
moderate	land	land	capital	labour	labour
scarce	capital	labour	labour	land	land

The United States and the Tropics became complementary in supply structure. There developed a two-way line between the United States and the Tropics with capital and capital-intensive commodities moving one way and labour-intensive goods the other. Triangular trade became less necessary. Europe was left out. Europe thus lost an important basis for covering the large import surplus from the United States and the Great Plains. The system, having been sustained by American and French capital during the 1920's, came to a spectacular end, leading to the Great Depression, with severe consequences for merchandise trade, financial transactions and currency convertibility. The traditional export surplus of the United Kingdom to the Tropics turned into an import surplus. There developed a tendency toward bilateral balancing in an effort to minimize currency pressure and to establish two-way lines of trade in response to the new situation. The basic net triangle of groups A, B and C was upset and the system of multilateral settlement disintegrated. The situation has remained the same in principle ever since but has become even more acute after World War II.

At present Europe therefore has to face a formidable problem if she is going to keep or raise the considerable imports from the United States and the Great Plains on which her standard of living largely depends. Despite trade barriers and the fact that the United States has the advantages of large-scale production in most fields, just as Germany used to have over the rest of Europe, direct exports to the United States may be raised. United States imports from Europe and particularly from the Tropics are in fact gaining momentum now during the armament boom. It may be possible for

Europe to create an export balance with the Tropics. Europe would need that export surplus, coupled with net exports from the Tropics to the United States, to cover imports from the United States. Not much of the European export balance could be left for capital investments, which are badly needed in the Tropics. Roundabout transfers of interest payments to Europe have largely fallen out. Net tourist and freight receipts may become a source of greater dollar earnings. If these measures fail and the European imports are to be kept or increased, the remaining sources are loans and grants from the United States. The prospects for capital movements to Europe are dimmed, however, by the difficulty of transferring interest payments and amortizations. The Tropics are in a more favorable situation in that respect. A new multilateral system, resembling the old one, may therefore be based on United States capital movements going through Europe to the Tropics and other underdeveloped countries, provided Europe can supply the corresponding exports to these countries in competition with American exporters. But with such a basis, the system may be fraught with the same elements of instability as during the 1920's unless international cooperation is achieved.

4. Tariffs, the Terms of Trade, and the Distribution of National Income

Lloyd A. Metzler

University of Chicago

Excerpt reprinted from "Tariffs, the Terms of Trade, and the Distribution of National Income," *Journal of Political Economy*, LVII (February 1949) by Lloyd A. Metzler by permission of the author and The University of Chicago Press; pp. 1–11, 19–20, 28–29 excerpted.

I

The classical concept of the gains from international trade was essentially a concept of increased productivity. The gains from trade, in the classical view, consisted of an increased output of all goods and services, made possible through specialization and exchange. In other words, the classical "law of comparative advantage" demonstrated that, with a given amount of productive resources in every country, it was possible, by an interchange of goods, for all countries to consume more of all commodities. In addition to its description of the potential gains from trade, the classical theory, from the time of John Stuart Mill, also gave an excellent account of how these gains are actually divided among different countries. Stated more broadly, the theory of reciprocal demand, which was added to the classical doctrine by Mill, indicated how international exchange affects the distribution of world income among countries.[1] With its strong emphasis upon productivity and upon the division of the gains from trade between different countries, however, the classical doctrine, as well as the subsequent theoretical work of neoclassical economists, seriously neglected the closely related problem of how international trade affects the division of income within each country among the various factors of production.[2] The

[1] J.S. Mill, *Essays on Some Unsettled Questions of Political Economy* (1844), Essay I.

[2] In view of the fact that the marginal-productivity theory of distribution did not appear until late in the nineteenth century and in view, further, of the generally recognized opinion that even the present theory of distribution has

classical theory and its neoclassical refinements could show well enough how a country, considered as a unit, tends to benefit from specialization and trade; but these doctrines had very little to say about how the gains of real income within each country are divided among labor, capital, and land.[3]

The division of the gains from trade among the different factors of production or, what amounts to substantially the same thing, the influence of international trade upon the distribution of national income is a subject which has received an adequate theoretical treatment only in comparatively recent times. The pioneer works in this branch of international economics were, of course, the studies which E.F. Heckscher [4] and B. Ohlin [5] made during the years between the two world wars. It is a curious fact that, just as the classical discussion of the terms of trade had neglected or left unsolved the related problem of the distribution of income, so the more recent contributions to the study of income distribution have neglected the complications arising out of changes in the terms of trade. Indeed, at the very beginning of his article Heckscher asserted that a discussion of the gains from trade has no relevance to the problem of income distribution. "No attention is paid," he said, "to the advantages one particular country may achieve, by means of protection, in altering the relation between supply and demand of a certain commodity and thereby wholly or partly letting the 'foreigner pay the duty'; since this problem has been discussed so widely, and since it is not relevant in the present connection, it

---

many deficiencies, it is perhaps not surprising that the influence of international trade upon the distribution of income was inadequately discussed by the classical economists. But, even with due allowances for the backward state of distribution theory, the lag in the development of this aspect of international trade was surprisingly long.

[3] Although the question of income distribution arose early in the nineteenth century in the English controversy over the Corn Laws, the results of the controversy in this respect were inconclusive and had no permanent influence on the theory of international trade. Cf., however, C.F. Bastable, *The Theory of International Trade* (London: Macmillan & Co., Ltd., 1903), chap. vi.

[4] "Utrikhandelns verkan på inkomstfördelningen" ["The Influence of Foreign Trade on the Distribution of Income"], *Ekonomisk Tidskrift*, (1919), Part II, 1–32. Subsequent references to this paper have been taken from a translation into English prepared by Professor and Mrs. Svend Laursen and to be published shortly in the American Economic Association's "Readings in International Trade and Finance."

[5] *Interregional and International Trade* (Cambridge, Mass., 1933), chap. ii and *passim*.

seems unnecessary to discuss it here." [6] In the historical development of the theory of international trade, questions of income distribution have thus been rather sharply separated from questions of productivity and of gains or losses to a country as a whole.

In view of this distinct cleavage in the purely theoretical aspects of international trade, it is not surprising that the practical application of economic theory to the particular problem of tariffs has suffered from a similar lack of integration. On the one hand, the concept of reciprocal demand has been employed to demonstrate how tariffs may improve a country's terms of trade—i.e., reduce the prices it pays for its imports relative to the prices it receives for its exports—but little attempt has been made to employ this same concept in showing how the resulting increase of real income is divided among the different factors of production. Indeed, there has at times been a tendency in the classical theory to deny that tariffs exert any influence at all upon the distribution of national income. [7] On the other hand, when a theory of the influence of international trade upon the distribution of income was finally developed, this theory was based in part, as the preceding quotation from Heckscher demonstrates, upon the assumption that the influence of tariffs upon the terms of trade can be neglected. But, despite this historical separation of two important aspects of tariff theory, it is easily shown that changes in a country's terms of trade are closely related in a number of ways to changes in the distribution of its national income. It is the purpose of the present paper to show some of the relations between these two distinct and heretofore largely independent branches of tariff theory. Since Heckscher's work is basic to the later studies of tariffs and income distribution, it seems advisable to present a brief summary of his principal conclusions.

Heckscher began his discussion, as did the classical economists, with the assertion that trade between countries depends upon the

[6] Heckscher, *op. cit.*, p. 2.

[7] The following statement by Taussig illustrates the point: "The general proposition that a high rate of wages is a result of high productiveness of industry is simple and undeniable. . . . Beyond doubt there remain questions which are more difficult. Just how and through what channel or mechanism does high productivity lead to the high wages? And what determines the share of the total product, be that great or small, which shall go to the laborer, the employer, the owner of capital, the owner of land? But these questions, the most important and perhaps the most complex in the field of economics, *lie quite outside the tariff controversy* . . . " (quoted from *Free Trade, the Tariff, and Reciprocity* [New York, 1920], p. 54). Italics added.

law of comparative advantage, i.e., upon the fact that the ratio of the cost of production of two commodities is different in one country from the corresponding cost ratio in another. Unlike the classical economists, however, Heckscher placed great emphasis upon the way in which the supplies of various factors of production affect comparative costs. He argued, in particular, that comparative costs in one country differ from those in another primarily because the relative degree of scarcity of some factors of production differs between countries and because different commodities require varying proportions of the factors of production.[8] Suppose, for example, that one country, Alpha, has a large amount of land per worker as compared with another country, Beta. The ratio of rent to wage rates will then be lower in Alpha than in Beta, since land in the former country will be used to the point where its marginal product is relatively small. Consider, now, the comparative costs in the two countries of producing two products, wheat and textiles. Since wheat requires a larger amount of land per worker than textiles do, the money cost of producing a unit of wheat, relative to the cost of producing a unit of textiles, will be lower in Alpha than in Beta. In other words, Alpha will have a comparative advantage in wheat, the product requiring relatively large amounts of its abundant factor, while Beta will have a comparative advantage in textiles.

It is a simple step from these basic propositions concerning comparative advantage to the final conclusions of Heckscher with respect to the distribution of income. Suppose that Alpha and Beta are initially isolated and self-sufficient but that trade is finally opened up between the two countries. Alpha, the low-rent country, will then export wheat and Beta, where rents are comparatively high and wages low, will export textiles. This exchange of goods has a definite and predictable influence upon the demand for land and labor in the two countries. In each country the demand for factors of production is increased in the export industry and reduced in the industry competing with imports; but, as Heckscher pointed out, the proportions in which the factors of production are required in the export industry are not exactly the same as the proportions in which they are released by the industry competing with imports. In the present illustration the expansion of the wheat industry in Alpha requires, at prevailing wages and rents, a small number of workers per acre of land, while the contraction of the textile industry, under

[8] Heckscher, *op. cit.*, p. 6.

the pressure of competition from abroad, releases a relatively large number of workers and only a small amount of land. The shift of resources from textiles to wheat thus increases the relative scarcity of land in Alpha, the country which initially had a comparatively large supply of that factor. Wages per unit of labor accordingly fall in Alpha, relative to rent per unit of land. In other words, the shift in production which was brought about by international trade has given land, the relatively abundant factor in Alpha, a larger share of the total product. An analogous argument could easily be presented —and, indeed, has been presented both by Heckscher and, later, by Ohlin—to show that in Beta, where land is relatively scarce and labor abundant, international trade increases wage rates relative to rents. The central feature of the Heckscher-Ohlin analysis is thus the proposition that international trade, by increasing the demand for each country's abundant factors, tends to equalize the relative returns to the factors of production in different countries.[9]

With this brief introduction, we may now examine the relation of

[9] Whether international trade achieves a *complete* or only a *partial* equalization of relative and absolute factor returns in different countries has been a controversial issue. Heckscher, working with a simple model in which the coefficients of production were fixed, argued that the equalization would be complete in both an absolute and a relative sense. Thus, on p. 15 of the article previously cited, he said: "With fixed supplies of the factors of production and the same technique of production in all countries, we have seen that the final effect of international trade, with unimportant reservations, is the equalization of the *relative* prices of the factors of production. We must next inquire whether the equalization will be *absolute* as well as *relative*, i.e., whether rent, wages and interest for the same qualities of the factors of production will amount to the same real return in all countries. This proposition has not thus far been demonstrated, but it is an inescapable consequence of trade." If the coefficients of production were variable, on the other hand, Heckscher believed that substitutions of one factor for another would lead to different techniques of production and hence to differences in relative and absolute factor returns between countries (*ibid.*, p. 16). It was this latter conclusion, rather than the former one, which was subsequently adopted and elaborated by Ohlin and which became more or less the generally accepted view (*op. cit.*, pp. 37–39). Samuelson, however, in a recent study prepared independently of Heckscher's work, has shown that the equalization of relative and absolute returns may be complete even when account is taken of factor substitutions. In other words, Heckscher's first conclusion—i.e., the conclusion that equalization is *complete*— is applicable even to the case of variable coefficients of production (P.A. Samuelson, "International Trade and the Equalization of Factor Prices," *Economic Journal*, LVIII [June, 1948] 163–84). This suggests that the theory of international trade might have been advanced considerably, in the English-speaking world at any rate, by an earlier translation of Heckscher's pioneer article.

the Heckscher-Ohlin theory to the tariff problem. In view of the tendency of international trade to equalize relative factor returns among different countries, it might seem that the owners of a factor of production which is relatively scarce in a given country would have a strong interest in restricting international trade; for by so doing they could preserve the relative scarcity which might otherwise be threatened by competition from abroad. In a country with an abundant supply of land and a limited supply of labor, for example, the working class might well benefit by tariffs on manufactured goods. Superficially at least, the Heckscher-Ohlin analysis lends support to the pauper-labor argument for tariffs.

Against this view, it may be objected that the conclusions with regard to the influence of trade upon the distribution of national income take account only of the *relative* position of a particular factor of production and make no allowance for the fact that the *absolute* return of the scarce factor may deteriorate even when its relative position improves. Tariffs interfere with the allocation of resources, and, if the real income of an entire nation is thus reduced by protective duties, it may be small compensation to the scarce factor that it now obtains a larger share of the reduced total. Fifty per cent of a national income of 75 is clearly worse than 40 per cent of a national income of 100.[10] But this possibility of a divergence in the movements of *real* and *relative* returns need not detain us further; for Stolper and Samuelson, in a study which forms a sequel to the works of Heckscher and Ohlin, have shown that the real return and the relative return of a particular factor of production are likely to move in the same direction.[11] In other words, if a tariff increases the share of the national income accruing to the working class, it will also improve the workers' standard of living, and conversely. According to the Stolper-Samuelson argument, a country with a comparatively small labor supply could thus increase its real wage rate by means of protection, even though national income as a whole were thereby diminished. To use a common expression, the workers would get not merely a larger share of a smaller pie but a share which was larger, in absolute magnitude, than their previous

[10] Unless conspicuous consumption and social standing are more important than the absolute standard of living.

[11] W.F. Stolper and P.A. Samuelson, "Protection and Real Wages," *Review of Economic Studies,* IX (1941), 58–73.

smaller share of a larger pie. The detrimental effects of the tariff would be shifted entirely upon the country's "abundant" factors of production.

These results follow directly from two assumptions. The first is that a tariff causes factors of production to be shifted from export industries to industries competing with imports. If labor, as before, is taken to be the country's relatively scarce and high-cost factor of production, it follows from the Heckscher-Ohlin conclusions that the export industries will be those requiring a comparatively small amount of labor in relation to other factors, while the industries competing with imports will require a large proportion of labor to other factors. In the absence of changes in factor prices, the shift of resources brought about by a tariff accordingly leads to a scarcity of labor and an excess supply of land and other factors. Wage rates rise relative to rents, and in all industries a substitution of land for labor occurs. This brings us to the second fundamental assumption, namely, that the marginal physical productivity of a given factor in any industry depends exclusively upon the proportion of that factor to the other factors of production. More explicitly, it is assumed that the marginal product of a factor declines as the ratio of that factor to others in a particular industry is increased. Stolper and Samuelson show that, when wages rise relative to rents, the resulting substitution of land for labor causes the ratio of labor to land to decline in all industries. To put the matter another way, the surplus of land and scarcity of labor arising from the shift of resources from exports to industries competing with imports can be eliminated only if there is a reduction, in all industries, in the ratio of labor to land. But if this occurs, then, according to our second assumption, the marginal product of labor must have increased in all industries, compared with the former position of equilibrium. If competitive conditions prevail or if the degree of monopoly is about the same in one industry as in another, it follows that the real wage rate must have increased, regardless of whether this real return is measured in export goods or in the commodities of the industries competing with imports.

Although this conclusion concerning the influence of tariffs upon real wages represented a definite improvement in the theory of tariffs, a number of questions still remained unanswered. Like the earlier works on the subject, the later study by Stolper and Samuelson made no allowance for changes in the terms of trade. The rigid separation between the classical theory of the gains from trade and the modern theory of the distribution of income has thus continued to exist even in the most recent contribution to the subject. This naturally raises the question of whether modifications in the existing theory of tariffs are required if changes in the terms of trade and in the distribution of income are considered simultaneously. The classical theory of the gains from trade demonstrated that, under certain conditions of international demand, a country could increase the external purchasing power of its exports by means of tariffs on imports and that, if this favorable movement in its terms of trade were sufficiently large, the real income of the country imposing the tariff might be increased despite the unfavorable effects of the tariff upon the allocation of resources. Now, since Stolper and Samuelson assumed that a country's external terms of trade were unaffected by a tariff, they were actually considering the least favorable case possible with respect to the real income of the country imposing the duty; the tariff, in the Stolper-Samuelson argument, interfered with the allocation of resources without bringing about any offsetting favorable movement in the terms of trade. Real income of the country as a whole was therefore unambiguously reduced by the import duty.

Let us consider, for a moment, a more favorable case. Suppose that a particular country's exports and imports are important influences on world markets and that a tariff reduces the external prices of imports, relative to the prices of exports, to such an extent that real income for the country as a whole is clearly increased. How does this alter the conclusions summarized above concerning real and relative wage rates? Assuming, as before, that the country has a scarcity of labor and therefore imports commodities requiring a large amount of labor, it might appear at first glance that the tariff would increase real wages, perhaps to a considerable extent; for, if the real as well as the relative returns of labor are increased by a tariff even when the duty reduces real income of the country as a whole (the Stolper-Samuelson case), it might seem that the rise in real wages would be even greater if real income as a whole were increased. To return to our previous analogy, it would surely seem better for labor to receive a larger share of an increasing pie than to receive a larger share of a diminishing pie. Although this argument seems plausible, it is actually misleading, for the improvement in terms of trade affects not only real income as a whole but also the degree of scarcity of the so-called "scarce" factors. Paradoxical as it may seem, when changes in the terms of trade are taken into consideration, tariffs or other impediments to imports do not always preserve or increase the scarcity of the scarce factors of production. Under some conditions of international demand the industries competing with imports and the scarce factors of production, which are usually required in large amounts in such industries, may benefit from free trade and suffer from protection.

The precise conditions of international demand required to bring about such an unexpected result are described in Section II. The argument is presented by means of the familiar Mill-Marshall schedules of reciprocal demand.[12]

II

Whether a tariff injures or benefits a country's scarce factors of production depends largely upon how it affects the output of exports and of commodities competing with imports. If output expands in the industries competing with imports and contracts in the export industries, the increased demand for scarce factors of production in the expanding industries will normally exceed the supplies made available in the contracting export industries; and, as Stolper and Samuelson have shown, the real returns as well as the relative shares of the scarce factors in the national income will thus be increased. In a large part of the nontechnical literature dealing with tariffs, and even in some of the technical literature, a shift of this sort is normally taken for granted; indeed, it is frequently regarded almost as a truism that tariffs injure export industries and benefit industries competing with imports. Nevertheless, when both primary and secondary price changes are taken into consideration, this is by no means a self-evident proposition. To be sure, the tariff itself is the cause of a direct increase in the domestic prices of imports over and above world prices, and this constitutes an immediate benefit to the industries competing with imports. But, on the other hand, the tariff is also the cause of a series of events which tend to reduce the

---

[12] The reader will recognize that in adopting this method I have not added anything essentially new to the well-known classical technique. My purpose, rather, is to apply this technique to a problem which was seldom discussed and never strongly emphasized in the classical literature. In doing this, I have made particular use of the classical theory in the form in which it was expounded by A.P. Lerner ("The Symmetry between Import and Export Taxes," *Economica*, III [new ser., 1936], 308–13).

world prices of the country's imports relative to the prices of its exports—i.e., to improve the terms of trade—and this secondary reduction of world prices of imports relative to exports may more than offset the initial primary increase.

Now it is reasonable to suppose that resources will not be permanently shifted from the export industries to the industries competing with imports unless the net effect of all primary and secondary price changes is an increase in the domestic prices of imports (including tariffs) relative to the domestic prices of exports. Whether a tariff increases or reduces the real and relative returns of the scarce factors, therefore, depends upon the magnitude of the favorable movement in the terms of trade, compared with the size of the tariff. If the former is greater than the latter, the final effect of the tariff will be a reduction of the domestic prices of imports relative to the prices of exports, and resources will accordingly be shifted from industries competing with imports to the export industries. In other words, the industries producing commodities for export will expand, after tariffs are imposed, while industries competing with imports will contract, an outcome diametrically opposite to the usual expectation. Suppose, for example, that the ratio of the world prices of a country's imports to the world prices of its exports is initially taken to be 1:1. Suppose, now, that a tariff of 50 per cent ad valorem is placed upon all imports and that, as a result of the ensuing reduced demand for imports, the ratio, in world prices exclusive of tariffs, of import prices to export prices falls to 1:2. The domestic price ratio, which differs from the world price ratio by the amount of the tariff, will then be 1.5:2, compared with 1:1 before the tariff was imposed. The tariff has thus reduced the domestic prices of imports relative to the prices of exports, and a transfer of resources from the "protected" industries to the export industries may accordingly be anticipated. Under these circumstances the effects of the tariff upon the distribution of income are exactly opposite to the conclusions reached by Stolper and Samuelson; the scarce factor of production, i.e., the factor relatively most important in the industries competing with imports, suffers both a relative decline in its share of the national income and an absolute decline in its real return. The most important factor of production in the export industries, on the other hand, enjoys both a relative and an absolute increase of income.

The magnitude of the favorable movement of the terms of trade which occurs when tariffs are imposed obviously depends upon conditions of international demand in a way that has been familiar to all economists at least since the time of Mill. It is therefore appropriate to state the argument in terms of the Mill-Marshall equations of reciprocal demand. As before, I shall assume that there are two countries—Alpha and Beta—producing two commodities—wheat and textiles—and that, for the reasons discussed above, Alpha has a comparative advantage in the production of wheat, while Beta has an advantage in textiles. In Figure 1, the curves A and B represent the reciprocal demand schedules of the two countries, Alpha and Beta, for imported textiles and wheat, respectively, under conditions of free trade.[13] Equilibrium is established at the point P, which implies that Alpha imports an amount OT of textiles in exchange for OW of wheat. Suppose, now, that Alpha imposes an ad valorem duty of 50 per cent upon imported textiles. If we neglect

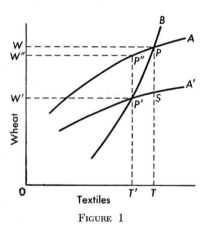

FIGURE 1

for a moment the effects of the spending of the proceeds of the tariff by the government of Alpha, it is clear that the initial effect of the tariff is to reduce the demand schedule facing the exporters of textiles in Beta from A to A'. In other words, textile importers in Alpha will now be willing to give to the exporters in Beta only TS units of wheat for OT of textiles; a money value equal to the additional amount, SP, which citizens of Alpha formerly gave to Beta, now goes to the Alpha government as a duty. This means that SP is 50 per cent of TS or that TS is two-thirds of TP, and similarly for any other point, such as P', on the new demand schedule.

After the tariff has been imposed, the new equilibrium in terms

[13] In all the figures the reciprocal demand schedules are assumed to depend not only upon conditions of demand but also upon conditions of production. The elasticity of a given reciprocal demand schedule is thus a combined result of substitutions on the part of consumers and shifts of resources on the part of producers (see W.W. Leontief, "The Use of Indifference Curves in the Analysis of Foreign Trade," *Quarterly Journal of Economics*, XLVII [1933], 493–503).

of quantities actually traded is at P', at which point OW' units of wheat are exported by Alpha and OT' units of textiles are imported. Unless B is a straight line from the origin, which implies that the demand in Beta for the exports of Alpha is infinitely elastic, it is obvious from Figure 1 that the tariff will improve the terms of trade of Alpha. The fraction OT'/OW' is clearly larger than OT/OW, which means that Alpha obtains more units of textiles for a given amount of wheat than was true under free trade. Or, to put the matter another way, the world price of textiles, exclusive of the tariff, has fallen, relative to the world price of wheat. The bargaining position of Alpha, the country imposing the tariff, is thus improved. Such an improvement in Alpha's terms of trade is, of course, completely explained by the classical theory of international trade and would not need to be considered further except for its influence upon the distribution of income. In order to see how the tariff has affected the distribution of income in Alpha, we must look at domestic prices rather than at world prices. This means that the tariff must be added to the world price of textiles. Measured in terms of their export commodity, the total outlay of the residents of Alpha for imported textiles, including their outlay for the tariff, is not OW', in Figure 1, but OW'', an amount 50 per cent greater than OW'. In other words, in terms of value actually expended, the residents of Alpha are giving up the equivalent of OW'' units of wheat for OT' units of textiles; the domestic ratio of exchange is therefore given by the fraction OT'/OW''. Now, since OT'/OW'' is less than OT/OW in Figure 1, it is obvious that, with the schedules of reciprocal demand there assumed, the tariff has caused the domestic price of textiles in Alpha to rise, relative to the price of wheat; land and labor are therefore shifted from wheat to textile production; and the relative share of labor in the national income, as well as the real wage rate, is increased.

It is easily shown that this conclusion is valid for reciprocal demand schedules other than those depicted in Figure 1, as long as the demand of Beta for the products of Alpha is elastic. The foregoing argument may therefore be generalized as follows: If the world demand for a country's exports is elastic and if we neglect the effects of government expenditures on the demand for imports, (1) a tariff always increases the domestic prices of imports relative to the prices of exports; (2) the improvement in the terms of trade is not sufficient, in this case, to offset the tariff itself; (3) the protected

industries become more profitable, relative to the export industries;
(4) resources are shifted from the latter to the former; and (5) the
real returns to the country's scarce factors of production, as well as
these factors' share in the national income, are increased. The
Stolper-Samuelson conclusion is thus valid, even when changes in
the terms of trade are taken into account, as long as the demand for
exports is elastic.

When the demand for exports is inelastic, the conclusions of the
last paragraph must be reversed. This situation is depicted in Figure
2, where the demand of Beta for the product of Alpha is assumed to
be inelastic at the equilibrium point, P. In other words, in the neighborhood of P the residents of Beta are willing to give up decreasing
amounts of textiles in exchange for an increasing amount of wheat.

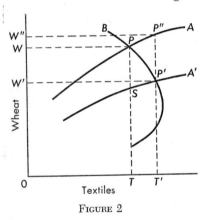

FIGURE 2

The notation is the same as in
Figure 1. The original equilibrium is at P; but, after the tariff
is imposed, the point of balanced
trade moves to P', at which point
Alpha gives up OW' units of
wheat in exchange for OT' units
of textiles. As before, the terms
of trade move in favor of Alpha.
Indeed, in the present example a
greater amount of textiles is obtained for a smaller amount of
wheat, and the favorable movement in the terms of trade of

Alpha is now so great that the domestic price of textiles, including
the tariff, is lower, relative to the price of wheat, than it was before
the tariff was imposed. This is shown in Figure 2 by the fact that
OT'/OW'' is greater than OT/OW.

When the demand for a country's exports is inelastic, the foregoing argument shows that a tariff, far from protecting the industries competing with imports, may actually make these industries
worse off than under free trade. In Figure 2, for example, the tariff
on textile imports into Alpha reduces the domestic price of textiles,
relative to the price of wheat, and leads to a shift of resources in
Alpha from the textile industry to the wheat industry. This result is,
of course, well known from the classical and neoclassical theories of
international trade; but, so far as I am aware, its implications for

the distribution of income have never been fully discussed. Figure 2 implies that, when the demand for a country's exports is inelastic, the scarce factors of production—those required in comparatively large amounts in the import industries—actually suffer both a relative and an absolute decline in income when tariffs are increased. Although it seems paradoxical, the scarce factors of production and the industries competing with imports, under the conditions of Figure 2, actually achieve economic gains from free trade and suffer losses from protection. In other words, if labor is the scarce factor of production and the standard of living is therefore high, a country is not likely to be able, by means of tariffs, to protect its workers from the competition of "cheap foreign labor" unless the demand for its exports is elastic.

Nothing has been said, as yet, about how the government which imposes import duties disposes of the resultant revenue. In this respect the preceding discussion of Figures 1 and 2 is deficient, for the manner in which the government revenues are spent will obviously influence the reciprocal demand schedule of the country introducing the tariffs. If the customs revenues are used in part to purchase imported goods, for example, the reciprocal demand schedule of Alpha will not fall from A to A' but will lie somewhere between these two curves. In the classical discussion of this question two limiting examples were usually considered: the customs revenues were assumed to be spent either entirely upon the export goods of the taxing country or entirely upon imports.[14] The reader will no doubt have recognized that Figures 1 and 2 belong to the first of these alternatives. No part of the tariff proceeds, in these two illustrations, is spent on imported goods; for, if it were, the reciprocal demand schedule would not fall, as assumed in the figures, by the full amount of the tariff. Moreover, it is easy to see that both diagrams implicitly assume the full proceeds of the tariffs to be spent on goods formerly exported from Alpha. Thus at the new equilibrium point, P', Alpha exports OW' of wheat to T. The equilibrium point, P', however, is stated in world prices, and this equilibrium corresponds to a domestic ratio of exchange in Alpha, including tariffs, of OT' units of textiles for OW'' units of wheat. In other words, at the new domestic price ratio, exporters in Alpha offer OW'' units of wheat, an amount which exceeds the purchases

---

[14] See, e.g., A. Marshall, *Money, Credit, and Commerce* (London, Macmillan & Co., Ltd., 1929), pp. 344–48.

of wheat in Beta by $W'W'''$. The supply of wheat is thus not equal to the demand unless this excess supply is purchased by the government of Alpha. But the excess supply of wheat, $W'W'''$, is simply the amount of duties collected by the government of Alpha, measured in the export product of that country. Figures 1 and 2 are thus implicitly based upon the assumption that the tariff-imposing country uses the entire proceeds of the tariff to purchase goods from its own exporters.

III

The aspect of tariff theory which the preceding discussion outlines most sharply is the potential or actual conflict of interests that may arise between a country's relatively scarce factors of production and the remainder of the economy. The classical dictum that real wages and the returns to other factors of production depend upon productivity remains true in a general way, of course; but the preceding argument shows that this dictum cannot be applied to the particular problem of tariffs without numerous reservations and exceptions. It cannot be asserted, for instance, that tariffs necessarily reduce productivity and thereby lower the real incomes of all factors of production. In the first place—and this is an argument of which the classical economists were fully aware—tariffs, under favorable circumstances, may improve a country's terms of trade so much that real income for the country as a whole is thereby increased. But this is a familiar argument to which the present paper has made no particular contribution. The point to be emphasized is a second reservation, namely, that the returns to each of the factors of production do not necessarily move in the same direction as general productivity or real income of the economy as a whole. In other words, regardless of whether a high-tariff policy increases or diminishes real income for a country as a whole, such a policy is likely to affect some factors of production favorably and others adversely. This point of view, in fact, might be stated even more strongly: the real income of a country's scarce factors of production is not likely to be increased by a tariff unless world demand is such that the tariff clearly diminishes the country's total income; and, conversely, the scarce factors are not likely to be injured by a tariff unless the tariff benefits the rest of the economy.

To clarify these propositions, consider a country having a comparative scarcity of labor and importing commodities with a high labor content. Stolper and Samuelson have shown that, *if the terms of trade are not affected,* a tariff in such a country will probably increase both the real wage rate and the proportion of the national income accruing to the working class. Now, if the terms of trade remain unchanged, this means that the tariff, while disrupting the allocation of resources and thereby tending to reduce real income for the country as a whole, has not succeeded in bringing to the economy the benefits of a more favorable bargaining position in world markets. In other words, when the terms of trade remain unaltered, a tariff causes an unambiguous reduction in a country's real income as a whole. But this is precisely the condition, according to the Stolper-Samuelson argument, when a tariff increases the absolute and relative return to labor, the country's scarce factor of production. If I may return to an earlier metaphor, the scarce factor of production receives a larger piece of a smaller pie. But what if the size of the pie is increased by the tariff? How does labor fare under these circumstances? An increase in real income for the economy as a whole is, of course, possible, provided that the tariff causes a sufficient improvement in the terms of trade to offset its interference with the allocation of resources. A substantial improvement in the terms of trade could take place, however, only if the foreign demand for the country's exports was inelastic; and in this event, as we have seen, there is a strong probability that the tariff, far from protecting the industries competing with imports, would actually injure these industries and lead to a transfer of resources from them to the export industries. This shift in resources would reduce the degree of scarcity of labor and thereby lead to a reduction in both its relative and its absolute return.

The conflict of interests which the preceding summary emphasizes is in sharp contrast to the doctrine of a harmony of interests which occupied such a prominent place in the work of many nineteenth-century liberal economists. The preceding argument has shown that, with respect to problems of commercial policy, the economic interests of such broad groups as manual workers, landlords, and capitalists are not likely to coincide. A policy of reducing tariffs may therefore be the source of widespread political cleavages, quite apart from the pressure which is inevitably exerted by the industries immediately affected. This, of course, is no argument against reducing trade barriers. Rather, it is simply an indication that the political conflicts inherent in tariff reduction may have a much broader base than would be supposed from concentrating one's attention upon the protected industries alone.

IV

In concluding this paper, a word should be said about the relation of the arguments presented here to the earlier work of Heckscher and Ohlin. As noted in Section I, the well-known view of both Heckscher and Ohlin is that international trade tends to equalize the relative returns to different factors of production among the trading countries. In other words, it is their view that trade increases the relative demand, and therefore the relative return, of the factor of production which is comparatively most abundant and comparatively cheapest in a particular country. In this manner wages tend to be raised relative to the returns to other factors of production, in countries which have a large population in relation to their other resources. Superficially it might seem that any measure, such as a tariff reduction, which reduces the impediments to international trade, would have these same effects. In a country with a large supply of land, for example, it might be expected, following the Heckscher-Ohlin argument, that a tariff reduction would increase rents and lower wages. But we have found in Section II that, if the demand for a country's exports is inelastic, this result does not necessarily follow. Under some conditions with respect to international demand a reduction of tariffs may *increase* the demand for a country's scarce factors and *reduce* the demand for its abundant factors. How can this conclusion be reconciled with the view of Heckscher and Ohlin that international trade always increases the demand for a country's abundant factors?

Despite superficial differences, the conclusions reached in this paper are essentially consistent with those of Heckscher and Ohlin. The contradictory appearance of the conclusions is attributable entirely to a difference in the point of comparison. When Heckscher and Ohlin say that international trade increases the demand for a country's scarce factors, they mean that the demand is increased *compared with the demand in a state of complete isolation.* In other words, they are comparing free trade or restricted trade with a state of affairs in which there is no trade at all; and this is by no means the same as comparing trade under one tariff system with trade under smaller tariffs. The argument presented in Section II, that an increase in customs duties may reduce the demand for a country's scarce factors of production, was limited in its application to tariff changes within a range for which the foreign demand for the country's exports had a certain degree of inelasticity. In other words, the argument was valid only for movements along a limited part of the foreign reciprocal demand schedule. Now, in order to make the present analysis comparable to that of Heckscher and Ohlin, we should have to consider an increase in tariffs so large that all imports were eliminated. In short, all tariffs on all commodities would have to be completely prohibitive. From the nature of the reciprocal demand schedules, however, it is apparent that if tariffs were gradually increased to a level where they threatened to cut off all trade, the point of equilibrium would sooner or later move to a position where the foreign demand for the tariff-imposing country's exports was elastic. Thereafter, any further increases in tariffs would increase the demand for the country's scarce factors and reduce the demand for its abundant factors, in the manner envisaged by Heckscher and Ohlin. When the present technique is applied to changes in foreign trade as great as those envisaged by Heckscher and Ohlin, my conclusions are thus in agreement with theirs. An appearance of conflict arises only when one attempts to apply to the entire reciprocal demand schedule an argument which is applicable only to a segment of that schedule.

I. *International Trade Theory and Policy Issues*

COMMENTARY

The essays of Part I raise a variety of important issues, some of which—balance of payments disequilibrium, international adjustment processes, the gains from and conditions of multilateral exchange—will be considered in more detail later. This Commentary will center on Metzler's analysis of tariffs (selection 4).

The Stolper-Samuelson tariff analysis, reviewed by Metzler, showed that "there is a grain of truth in the pauper labour type of argument for protection." [1] Thus, as Metzler has observed elsewhere:

In the United States during the early nineteenth century, for example, our comparative advantage in agriculture was clearly governed by the large amount of land per worker. Under these circumstances, the tariffs which were imposed upon manufactured imports may well have improved the standard of living of the working class as a whole, since labor is a more important factor in manufactures than in agriculture. . . . We would no doubt agree today with Taussig that "no economist of standing would maintain that a protective tariff is the one decisive factor in making a country's rate of wages high," but it is doubtful whether we would also agree that "no economist . . . would sanction the pauper-labor argument for tariffs." [2]

However, the Stolper-Samuelson model did not allow for changes in the terms of trade. Metzler's contribution is to make

[1] Wolfgang F. Stolper and Paul A. Samuelson, "Protection and Real Wages," *Review of Economic Studies*, IX (November 1941), reprinted in Howard S. Ellis and Lloyd A. Metzler, editors, *Readings in the Theory of International Trade* (Philadelphia: The Blakiston Co., 1949), p. 356.

[2] Lloyd A. Metzler, "The Theory of International Trade," in Howard S. Ellis, editor, *A Survey of Contemporary Economics* (Philadelphia: The Blakiston Co., 1948), p. 248.

allowances for such changes—allowances which sometimes change the nature of the results of imposing the tariff.[3]

METZLER ON TARIFFS

In the Introduction to this Part, it was explained how a reciprocal demand curve can be derived from a production possibility curve and alternative terms-of-trade lines. For purposes of reviewing Metzler's article, it is convenient to derive reciprocal demand curves from ordinary curves of demand for imports and of supply of exports.

It should be recalled that any point on a reciprocal demand curve indicates an amount of exports which a country is willing to give up for the indicated amount of imports. In money terms, at any point on the curve the value of exports equals the value of imports. In Figure Ia, we have the demand schedule of Alpha for textiles, its import commodity. Alpha has a comparative advantage in wheat, and her supply of wheat is indicated in Figure Ib. If the price of textiles is $10 per unit, Alpha will buy none; the value of her imports is zero, and therefore the value of her wheat exports (and thus the quantity of her exports) is zero. In short, if we are at point *I* on the demand curve in Figure Ia, we are also at point *I* on the supply curve in Figure Ib.

At a textile price of $8, the quantity demanded is 2, and the value of textile imports is thus $8 \times 2 = 16. The value of wheat exports must accordingly be $16; at a price of $2, this implies a quantity of $16/2 = 8$. Thus point *II* in one figure corresponds to point *II* in the other.

And so it goes. Any given point on the demand schedule has a corresponding point on the supply schedule. While we are in the elastic portion of the demand curve, a fall in the price leads not only to an increase in quantity, but to an increase in money value; a higher money value, in turn, implies an increase in the quantity of wheat supplied. That is, in the range of *elastic* demand, both quantities move in the *same* direction when the price of wheat changes. And when price changes in the **inelastic** range of demand, the quantities move in **opposite** directions.

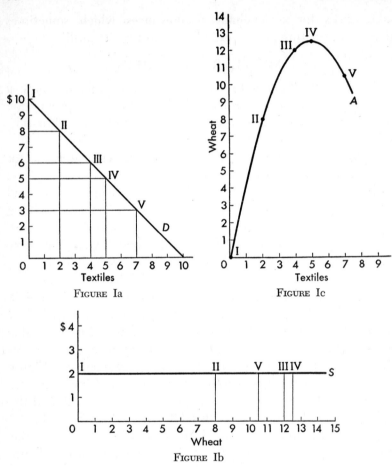

FIGURE Ia

FIGURE Ic

FIGURE Ib

³ For a further modification of the Stolper-Samuelson analysis, see Kelvin Lancaster, "Protection and Real Wages: A Restatement," *Economic Journal* LXVII (June 1957), pp. 199–210.

This is seen in Figure Ic, where the pairs of points in the demand and supply diagrams are plotted with respect to the quantities involved. Alpha's reciprocal demand curve, which measures alternative quantities of wheat supplied and corresponding quantities of textiles demanded, rises from the origin at a decreasing rate, hits a maximum (at point *IV*), and then falls. The curve has an elasticity greater than one where it rises, equal to one at point *IV*, and less than one where it falls. Thus, the elasticity of demand (Figure Ia) "controls" the elasticity of reciprocal demand (Figure Ic): where demand is elastic, the corresponding point or segment of reciprocal demand is elastic (e.g., points *I, II, III*); where demand is inelastic, so is reciprocal demand (e.g., point *V*); where elasticity of demand equals one, the same is true of reciprocal demand (point *IV*). The reader can verify with experimentation that demand elasticity "controls" reciprocal demand elasticity so long as the demand curve is sloping downward from left to right (or is vertical) and the supply curve slopes upward (or is horizontal).

Now assume that Alpha levies a tariff of 50 per cent (i.e., 50 per cent of the "world" price exclusive of the tariff) on textile imports. How is this represented in the figures?

We may assume that the imposition of the tariff does not shift the supply curve. Nor is the demand schedule *in the eyes of domestic consumers* affected: e.g., consumers in Alpha were willing before the tariff to pay $6 per unit for 4 units of textiles, and after the tariff is levied they are still willing to do so. However, now that the government of Alpha is collecting one-third of the total price as an import tax, the price *to Beta's exporters* (i.e., the "world" price) is only $4. We may call *D'* the "net" demand curve, i.e., the "world" (or "international") curve exclusive of the tariff.

Translating these results into reciprocal demand curves in Figure IIc, the effect of the tariff is to lower Alpha's reciprocal demand curve; the amount of wheat offered internationally for any given quantity of textiles is now two-thirds the quantity offered previously.

The Metzler analysis centers on *shifting domestic resources* and the consequent effects on the *marginal productivities* of those resources. The determinant of resource-shifting is *changing relative domestic prices*.

Suppose that there are two factors, land and labor, and that textiles are relatively "labor intensive" and wheat is relatively "land intensive." Alpha had a comparative advantage in wheat

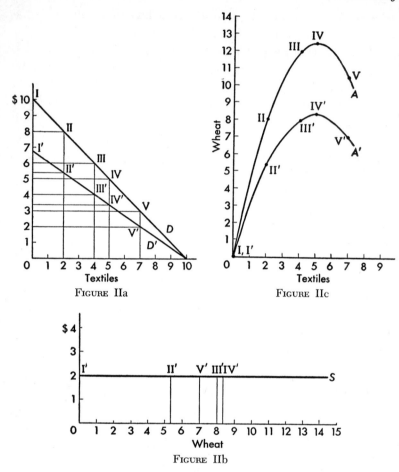

Figure IIa

Figure IIc

Figure IIb

when trade opened, and she exports wheat and imports textiles, but both Alpha and Beta produce some of both products. If the effect of Alpha's tariff is to raise Alpha's domestic price of textiles relative to the domestic price of wheat, resources will tend to shift out of the wheat industry into textile production. This is illustrated in Figure III. Before the tariff, Alpha is producing at point *P*, the relative prices of wheat and of textiles being indicated by the slope of the line tangent at *P* to the production possibility curve (*AB*). If the price of textiles rises relative to the price of wheat, i.e., if it now takes more units of wheat to equal in the market one unit of textiles, the tangent line becomes steeper, and the point of tangency slides down the production possibility curve to, say, point *P'*. In moving to *P'*, obviously the output of wheat has contracted, and textile output has expanded.

The decline in wheat output releases "much" land and "little" labor, but the expansion of the textile industry calls for "much" labor and "little" land at the initial ratio of factor prices. The price of labor is thus bid up relative to the price of land. Producers tend to substitute the relatively cheap input for the expensive factor; the ratio of land/labor rises in *both* the wheat and the textile industries. This increase in the land/ labor ratio decreases the marginal productivity of land and raises that of labor. Since, in the competitive model assumed here, the price per

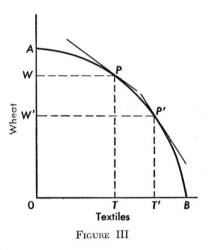

FIGURE III

unit of input equals the marginal product of that input, the real *absolute,* as well as relative, return to land falls, and the return to labor rises. This is Metzler's first case, in which the reciprocal demand of Beta is elastic.

If Beta's curve is inelastic, as in Metzler's second case, we have opposite changes in Alpha's relative prices and shifts in resources, leading to an increase in the returns to land and a fall in labor's returns.

It may be useful to comment further on two key points: (a) the effect of the tariff on relative output prices and (b) how the land/labor ratio can increase or decrease in *both* industries when the total quantities of land and of labor for the economy remain constant.

(a) We can illustrate arithmetically Metzler's analysis of changing relative product prices in Alpha. The table below represents his Figure I.

	WHEAT			TEXTILES		
	Quantity	*Price*	*Value*	*Quantity*	*Price*	*Value*
Initial situation	1000	$1	$1000	1000	$1	$1000
Post-tariff world situation	640	$ .75	$ 480	800	$ .60	$ 480
Post-tariff domestic situation	960	$ .75	$ 720	800	$ .90	$ 720

It is assumed that the values of imports and of exports are equal, both before the tariff and (at a different level) after the tariff is imposed. The tariff rate is 50 per cent of the price of imports exclusive of the tariff (or 33⅓ per cent of the price inclusive of the tariff). As a result of the tariff, the volumes of both wheat and textiles fall, but proportionately wheat falls more. Trade is still balanced, so the price of wheat has risen *relative to* the price of textiles. This refers to *world* prices. The *domestic* price of textiles is 50 per cent higher than the world price—and is higher than the price of wheat: the domestic price of textiles has risen *relative to* the price of wheat.

In Metzler's Figure I, "a money value equal to . . . *SP*" is the government's customs receipts. Indeed, Metzler assumes that all the receipts are spent on wheat—an assumption which is modified in a section of his essay not reprinted. Customs receipts equal 800 × $.30 = $240, and at a price of wheat equal to $.75, $240 purchases 320 wheat; wheat exports of 640 plus government purchases of 320 total 960. In other words, the *world* equilibrium trade ratio (corresponding to point *P'*) is 640/800; the *domestic* ratio (corresponding to *P''*) is 960/800. The former is smaller, and the latter is larger, than the initial ratio (corresponding to *P*) of 1000/1000.

Not all the figures are completely arbitrary: we know in what *direction* some must move, and, in other cases, given certain data we know certain *conditions* which must be satisfied by others or *limits* within which others must fall. For example, we

know that the quantities of both wheat and textiles must fall
after imposition of the tariff and that wheat must fall proportionately (in this illustration, absolutely) more. Again, assuming that we have the initial data and also the post-tariff
data for textiles, we know that the post-tariff quantity of wheat
must lie within certain limits. Not only must wheat be less
than textiles (640 < 800), but wheat must be greater than
533⅓; if wheat is 533⅓, then the price of wheat is $.90, but the
price of wheat must be less than $.90 (which is the price of
textiles inclusive of the tariff). In other terms, the following
limiting ratio of post-tariff world volumes of wheat and textiles
must obtain: $W'/T' = P_m'/[P_m'(1 + t)]$, where t is the tariff
rate, and P_m' is the post-tariff world price of imports.

We may similarly review Metzler's case in Figure II.

	WHEAT			TEXTILES		
	Quantity	Price	Value	Quantity	Price	Value
Initial situation	1000	$1	$1000	1000	$1	$1000
Post-tariff world situation	700	$ .80	$ 560	1120	$ .50	$ 560
Post-tariff domestic situation	1050	$ .80	$ 840	1120	$ .75	$ 840

The assumptions are the same as before: trade is always
balanced, and the tariff rate is 50 per cent. But this time, the
volume of textiles increases. Again the *world* price of wheat
rises relative to the *world* price of textiles. This time, however,
even in terms of *domestic* prices the price of wheat rises relative
to the price of textiles. Given the initial situation and the post-
tariff situation for textiles, wheat must be less than 746⅔, for at
746⅔ the price of wheat is $.75, and it is required in this case
that the price of wheat be greater than $.75.

(b) It is not difficult to show that the land/labor ratio can
change in the same direction in both industries. Assume that in
Alpha there are 300 units of labor and 250 of land. When, in our
Figure III, Alpha is producing at point *P*, the textile industry
employs 200 labor and 150 land; the wheat industry uses 100
labor and 100 land. Now suppose that, as in Metzler's first case,

the relative price of textiles rises, and production moves to P'. It is assumed that all land and labor continue to be employed, but in different ratios in the two industries, corresponding to new relative factor prices.

If the wheat industry tries to reduce factor inputs in the old 1 : 1 ratio and the textile industry wishes to absorb them in a ratio of 1⅓ : 1, there will be some unemployed land—or a deficit supply of labor relative to the quantity of land available. Rent falls and the wage rate rises. Therefore, entrepreneurs in *both* industries wish to use less labor per unit of land.

Wheat producers do not wish to contract by releasing, say, 40 labor and 40 land, but they might well release 40 labor and 35 land. And textile producers will expand by hiring 40 labor and 35 land. Thus, if 40 labor and 35 land shift from wheat to textiles, we are left with 60 labor and 65 land in wheat and 185 land and 240 labor in textiles. $60/65 < 100/100$ and $240/185 < 200/150$: although there is a fixed ratio of labor to land for the entire economy, the ratio can fall in both industries (when the industry ratios are initially different). And—to complete the line of thought—the marginal product of labor rises and the marginal product of land falls in both industries, for in both labor has more land with which to work, and therefore real wages rise and real rents fall in both, i.e., throughout the economy.

II. The Balance of Payments and Equilibrium

II. The Balance of Payments and Equilibrium

INTRODUCTION

The essays of Part II deal with interpretation of the balance of payments. They are concerned with the *meaning* and the *measurement* of equilibrium and disequilibrium in the balance of payments and with some of the possible *causes* of disequilibrium; in addition, they pose the problem of alternative methods of *adjustment* in cases of disequilibrium, but this broad area of analysis is considered more fully later.

THE NATURE OF THE BALANCE OF PAYMENTS

The balance of payments of an economic unit is an accounting record of the transfer of goods, services, claims, and gifts between the unit and generally the rest of the world over a period of time. Any economic unit, including a person, has its balance of payments. Here the unit of interest is the nation, and we shall deal, therefore, with the balance of *international* payments, typically over a year.[1]

On the one hand, the balance of payments lists *credits, receipts,* or *plus* items; this is the *export* side, listing exports of goods, services, securities, and gold (and also receipt of gifts). On the other hand, there are *debit, payment,* or *minus* entries— the *import* side.

Except for gifts (commonly designated "*unilateral* trans-

---

[1] On accounting details, consult United States Department of Commerce, *The Balance of Payments of the United States, 1949–1951* (Washington: Government Printing Office, 1952) and International Monetary Fund, *Balance of Payments Manual* (2nd ed., January 1950). See also Donald G. Badger, "The Balance of Payments: A Tool of Economic Analysis," *International Monetary Fund Staff Papers,* II (September 1951), pp. 86–197, and John M. Letiche, "Balance of Payments," *Encyclopaedia Britannica* (1958), vol. II, pp. 956A–958.

fers"), each transaction is a two-way exchange: there is a trading of assets, with something received for every export and with payment made for every import. On the credit side, there is listed the assets which the nation transfers to the rest of the world. These things obviously are not in themselves actual receipts—quite the contrary—but their export establishes claims on the rest of the world. Entries on the credit side *give rise* to receipts; the *forms* in which these claims are exercised or receipts are manifested are listed on the debit side. Alternatively, we may say that the debit side shows what has been acquired from abroad and which necessitates payment, and the credit side shows the ways in which payment was made for these imports.[2] Even gifts are recorded in "double-entry" fashion: the merchandise or security movement is listed in usual fashion, and the books are balanced by entering an equal value on the other side of the balance of payments as unilateral transfers, or donations.

Capital movements may appear to be exceptions to the rule that exports are listed on the credit side and imports make up the debits, for so-called "capital exports" are debits, and "capital imports" are credits. However, this seeming inconsistency stems from referring to the *"thing"* being imported or exported when speaking of goods, services, and gold and emphasizing the *payment* for the "thing" being imported or exported when speaking of capital. If American investors buy British bonds or real estate or bank books (i.e., build up balances in English banks), the value of the thing being bought is listed as a debit. But such purchases are called capital exports: U.S. investors are sending capital abroad—to pay for the purchase of an asset.

[2] "The same rules of debit and credit that are applied in corporation accounting are applied in the balance of payment, namely to debit increases in assets and decreases in liabilities and to credit decreases in assets and increases in liabilities. . . . Thus an export of merchandise is a credit because it reduces the exporting country's assets, and the same is true with respect to the rendering of services to foreign countries, although in the latter case the 'asset' is intangible, and is actually transferred at the moment of its creation. Again, to draw a parallel with commercial accounting, all sales are credits. . . ." Department of Commerce, *op. cit.*, p. 17.

Consider two transactions. (1) Englishmen buy tractors from a U.S. firm. The firm ships the tractors and draws a draft, i.e., an order to pay, on the English importer. The exporter probably will sell the draft for dollars to an American bank (foreign exchange dealer), and the bank will collect pounds from the importer and thus build up an account in a London bank. In the U.S. balance of payments, we would list the value of the tractors under merchandise exports (credit) and the accumulated bank balance as a short-term capital outflow (debit): the American economy as such has given up (exported) tractors and acquired (imported) claims on England in the form of a bank deposit. The exchange dealer loses dollars and gains pounds, thus moving "capital" from the U.S. to the U.K. (2) American investors buy British bonds. They make payment by buying pounds owned by U.S. exchange dealers in London banks and then transferring the pounds to the British seller of the securities. The exchange dealers gain dollars and give up pounds. The American economy has thereby acquired long-term claims on England in the form of bonds and financed the purchase by reducing its short-term claims in the form of demand deposits: in the U.S. balance of payments, a long-term capital outflow (debit) is matched by a short-term capital inflow (credit).

Capital movements thus involve changes in international claims. A U.S. capital export, or outflow, consists of either (a) an increase in U.S. claims on foreigners or (b) a decrease in foreign claims on the U.S. A U.S. capital import, or inflow, consists of either (a) an increase in foreign claims on the U.S. or (b) a decrease in U.S. claims on foreigners.

Since *each* transaction, including gifts, is recorded by double-entry, i.e., since each transaction is "financed" or balanced somehow, it follows that the *total* of transactions over a period will balance. Total credits equal total debits. This inevitable, purely bookkeeping balance is not informative. The question is not *whether* the balance of payments balances, for it always will, but *how*—at what *level* of transactions, with what *composi-*

tion of transactions, and within what *framework* (or subject to what *constraints*) of economic conditions and public policy.

Since the fact of overall balance is not interesting, balance of payments analysis must center on the relationships of various sub-categories, or components, of the total statement. As a first approximation, we may distinguish the current account from the capital account. If a given transaction in itself affects the international debtor-creditor status of a nation, i.e., if it is manifested in a change in international claims, it is a capital transaction; otherwise it is a current item. Merchandise and services trade obviously are current; also in the current account are dividends and interest from international investments, for the payment or receipt of investment income does not constitute a change in the principal of the investment. Gold movements may be considered separately, but in general they have a closer analytical relationship to capital movements than to current transactions: an acquisition of gold, like an accumulation of bank balances abroad, increases generalized command over foreign assets. Unilateral transfers are neither current nor capital—they are simply mechanical, bookkeeping "plug" entries— and are usually listed separately, especially when they have bulked so large during and after World War II.

HISTORICAL DATA AND GROWTH STAGES

Very generally, the nature of the American international accounts since World War II can be thus summarized (with items listed in the order of quantitative importance):

CREDITS	DEBITS
Net current account export balance	Net unilateral transfer outflow
	Net capital outflow
	Net gold import

During the 1920's, the picture was similar but with smaller absolute magnitudes:

CREDITS	DEBITS
Net current account export balance	Net capital outflow
	Net gold import
	Net unilateral transfer outflow

In both periods large export balances on current account were "financed," and thus made feasible, by American investment abroad, imports of gold, and gifts. Since the balance of payments must balance overall, if the net debits had been smaller, the current account surplus would have been smaller. Conversely, the current account surplus made possible the outflows of capital and gifts and the inflow of gold. If foreigners had not spent on goods and services so many of the dollars made available to them, foreign dollar bank balances and other dollar assets could have increased, making the *net* U.S. capital outflow and/or gold imports that much smaller.

As a final illustration of balance of payments interrelationships, consider the somewhat different situation of the 1930's:

CREDITS	DEBITS
Net current account export balance	Net gold import
Net capital inflow	Net unilateral transfer outflow

Here net capital movements did not help to finance the current account surplus, but rather added to the credit balance to be financed in small part by American gifts and mainly by a "gold avalanche" into the U.S.

Historical U.S. balance of payments date are summarized in Table I.

Arranging the data by groups of years may suggest an "inherent logic" in the evolution of a nation's balance of payments. Some writers have attempted to identify a system of "stages" through which a country will tend to move in its international accounts. One six-stage system runs:

I. Young debtor	IV. Young creditor
II. Adult debtor	V. Adult creditor
III. Mature debtor	VI. Mature creditor

Table I

UNITED STATES BALANCE OF PAYMENTS BY PERIODS

Millions of Dollars

(Annual averages in parentheses)

	1850–1873*	1874–1895*	1896–1914*	1914–1918†	1919–1929	1930–1933	1934–1939	1940–1945	1946–1949	1950–1957
Current Account	−2758	−707	1781	10,771	19,129	2267	3403	40,073	32,560	40,880
	(−115)	(−32)	(94)	(2154)	(1739)	(567)	(567)	(6679)	(8140)	(5110)
Goods and services	−1854	1163	4821	10,411	11,977	262	1458	37,882	29,021	27,131
	(−77)	(53)	(254)	(2082)	(1089)	(66)	(243)	(6314)	(7255)	(3391)
Investment income	−904	−1870	−3040	360	7152	2005	1945	2191	3539	13,749
	(−38)	(−85)	(−160)	(72)	(650)	(501)	(324)	(365)	(885)	(1719)
Unilateral Transfers	330	−440	−2850	−711	−5111	−1061	−1062	−41,844	−16,293	−41,079
	(14)	(−20)	(−150)	(−142)	(−465)	(−265)	(−177)	(−6974)	(−4073)	(−5135)
Long-term Capital	1000	1000	1000	−11,078§	−8959	321	2035	−2851	−14,598	−10,162
	(42)	(46)	(53)	(−2216)	(−814)	(80)	(339)	(−475)	(−3650)	(−1270)
Short-term Capital	—	—	—	5	632	−1974	3918	5156	−221	5213
				(1)	(57)	(−494)	(653)	(859)	(−55)	(652)
Gold	1098	112	−174	−1044	−1126	−99	−10,697	−2284	−4479	1707
	(46)	(5)	(−9)	(−209)	(−102)	(−25)	(−1783)	(−381)	(−1120)	(213)
Errors and Omissions	330	35	243	2057	−4565	546	2403	1750	3031	3441
	(14)	(2)	(13)	(411)	(−415)	(137)	(401)	(292)	(758)	(430)

* Fiscal years.
† July 1, 1914–December 31, 1918.
§ Includes net government short-term capital.
Source: United States Department of Commerce, *Survey of Current Business*, July 1954, pp. 14-15, June 1956, p. 24, March 1957, p. 16, June 1958, p. 12.

The major categories of the balance of payments (omitting unilateral transfers) for the various stages might be as follows: [3]

	I	II	III	IV	V	VI
Net Current account	−	0	+	+	0	−
Net goods and services	−	+	+	+	−	−
Net Investment income	−	−	−	+	+	+
Net Capital and gold account	+	0	−	−	0	+

How neatly may we superimpose this scheme on the U.S. balance of payments data? It appears that the period, 1850–1873, clearly belongs in stage I. It is open to question how to classify 1874–1895: one could argue that it is a continuation of stage I, but the current account balance is so small that the period approximates stage II. 1896–1914 may be designated stage III if we include unilateral transfers in the capital and gold account. 1914–1918 would seem to be in stage IV. But does the U.S. ever move beyond stage IV? Apparently not: beginning in World War I, the U.S. has persistently had a current account surplus (with both components of the current account being positive) and generally a negative capital and gold account.

Whether the failure of the U.S. to move into stage V is to be deemed desirable or undesirable turns on the criteria employed. Unfortunately, it is not uncommon for Americans to advocate two foreign economic policies of dubious consistency, *viz.*, maintenance of a surplus on current account and, at the same time, repayment by foreigners of previous U.S. loans.[4] Assum-

---

[3] Cf. Charles P. Kindleberger, *The Dollar Shortage* (Cambridge: The Technology Press and New York: John Wiley and Sons, Inc., 1950). After mature creditors (stage VI) consume "all their foreign capital, or even some time before, [they] . . . may be regarded as eligible to start the growth cycle over again as young debtors" [p. 76].

We are assuming that a debtor nation is, on balance, remitting interest and dividend payments (stages I–III) and that a creditor is receiving net income payments (stages IV–VI). While reasonable, this need not be the case.

[4] For example, in the Congressional debates of 1934 on the original Reciprocal Trade Agreements bill, there was frequent bitter condemnation of foreign debtors who had dishonorably defaulted on their solemn agreements and expression of fear that the Administration would cancel all or part of the debts; yet the same men were violently opposed to a program which might lead to increased imports, even noting specifically that imports for the very purpose of enabling foreigners to make debt payments were undesirable!

ing that "repayment of previous loans" means a net capital flow to the U.S., these dual objectives require a positive current account and a positive capital account—which is manifestly impossible if these accounts exhaust the balance of payments.

We can salvage something of this general viewpoint only by elaborating the alternatives:

	A	B	C
Current account	−	+	+
Goods and services	+	+	+
Investment income	−	+	+
Unilateral transfers			− ⎫
Capital account ⎫	+	+ ⎫	⎬ −
Gold account ⎭		− ⎭ } − +	⎭

Under alternative *A*, we keep the capital and gold account positive by making income transactions negative and larger than exports of goods and services. But in historical fact, the income account has been positive by a sizable amount since World War I. Under alternative *B*, both the capital and the current accounts are positive because the gold account is segregated and made negative and arithmetically larger than capital by the amount of the current account surplus. Under alternative *C*, we again group capital and gold into a single, positive account and also have a positive current account through the device of introducing debit unilateral transfers arithmetically equal to the sum of the current and capital-gold accounts. It is apparent from alternatives *B* and *C* that it is possible to receive debt repayments and also to have an export balance on current account—if the U.S. is willing to take great quantities of gold for reburial in Fort Knox or to give away large amounts of goods, services, and claims.

American efforts to resist entry into stage V are scarcely rational—assuming that the criterion of rationality is maximization of American living standards. As an adult creditor, a nation is, on balance, neither exporting nor importing capital and gold, and it finances net imports of goods and services with its net income from foreign investments. And net imports of goods and services means that the rest of the world is contributing more to the consumption of the creditor nation than the creditor is contributing to the rest of the world. The penalty of entering stage V is simply the necessity of accepting higher standards of living.[5]

It is sometimes suggested that there is a virtual inevitability in the movement of the balance of payments from one stage to another. And a common reason offered for the inevitability rests on the relationship between flows of foreign investment income and amortization of old loans, on the one hand, and new capital movements, on the other. Thus a young creditor (stage IV) will eventually find that the return amortization flow plus the receipt of investment income is greater than the new capital outflow. If amortization alone is still less than new lending, then investment income is greater than imports of goods and services, and we would have the following situation, which lies between stages IV and V and may be labelled IVa:

	IVa
Current account	+
Goods and services	−
Investment income	+
Capital and gold account	−

If this trend of variables continues, amortization will first equal new lending, making both the capital and the current accounts zero and giving stage V, and then exceed new lending, moving the balance of payments to stage VI.

Domar has demonstrated that it is not inevitable, on these grounds, that the balance of payments move even to stage IVa, much less stages V and VI.[6] Let I be foreign investment income, A be amortization of past foreign loans, G be new (cur-

[5] See Clark Lee Allen, "El Problema de la Balanza de Pagos de Estados Unidos: Necesidad de Aceptar Niveles de Vida Mas Altos," *Revista Economia Salvadorena*, IV (1955), pp. 66–71.

[6] Evsey D. Domar, "The Effect of Foreign Investment on the Balance of Payments," *American Economic Review*, XL (December 1950), pp. 805–826, reprinted in *idem, Essays in the Theory of Economic Growth* (New York: Oxford University Press, 1957), pp. 129–153.

rent) gross lending, X be exports of goods and services, and D be total outstanding foreign loans. If $G > I + A$, the balance of goods and services (the remainder of the balance of payments) is positive; if $G < I + A$, there is an import balance of goods and services.

Table II gives a period analysis, with the period being a year. I and A received in *one* year are (constant) fractions—i and a, respectively, of D at the end of the *preceding* year; D at the end of *one* year equals $G - A$ in *that* year plus D at the end of the preceding year. G rises at a constant rate, r. X in *one* year equals G minus I and A in *that* year. It is assumed that $i = .02$, $a = .1$, and $r = .04$.

The ratio of "inflow" to "outflow," $(I + A)/G$, rises at a decreasing rate and would eventually level out at a constant value.[7] If this ratio levels out at a value of less than unity, i.e., if $I + A < G$, we are left with a persistent export balance; if the ultimate ratio is greater than unity, i.e., if $I + A > G$, the balance of payments will then show an import balance. Domar deduced that $(I + A)/G = (a + i)/(a + r)$. That is, whether the ratio is greater or less than unity, and thus whether there is finally an import or export balance, depends on whether i is greater or less than r. In Table II, the limiting value of $(I + A)/G = .857$, and an export balance remains. Indeed, after reaching a minimum before $(I + A)/G$ reaches its equilibrium value, the export balance slowly rises as the *absolute*

---

[7] $(I + A)/G$ rises and reaches a constant ("equilibrium") value when the rate of increase in the inflow equals the rate of growth in the outflow, i.e., when

$$\frac{\Delta I + \Delta A}{I + A} = \frac{\Delta G}{G}$$

or, since $\Delta G/G = r$, when

$$\frac{\Delta I + \Delta A}{I + A} = r.$$

Note further that

$$\frac{\Delta I + \Delta A}{I + A} = \frac{\Delta D}{D}.$$

Thus we reach the equilibrium value of the inflow-outflow ratio when $\Delta D/D$ has fallen to the level where $\Delta D/D = r$.

Table II

Year	Investment income (I)	Amortization (A)	Gross lending (G)	$\dfrac{I+A}{G}$	Exports (X)	Accumulated debt (D)
1	2		100		100	100
2	3.88	10	104	.115	92	194
3	5.655	19.4	108.16	.215	84.88	282.76
4	7.339	28.276	112.486	.302	78.555	366.970
5		36.697	116.985	.376	72.949	447.258
11	16.165	80.825	148.023	.655	51.033	875.451
12	17.509	87.545	153.944	.682	48.690	941.850
13	18.837	94.185	160.102	.706	47.080	1007.767
19	26.796	133.979	202.581	.793	41.806	1408.393
20	28.168	140.839	210.684	.802	41.677	1478.238
21	29.565	147.824	219.111	.809	41.722	1549.525
22	30.991	154.953	227.875	.816	41.931	1622.447
23	32.449	162.245	236.990	.821	42.296	1697.192

increases in $I + A$ become smaller than the increases in G. A low enough interest rate (relative to the rate of growth in capital outflow) or, alternatively, a high enough rate of growth of lending (relative to the interest rate), will prevent the movement of the balance of payments beyond stage IV.

5. Three Concepts of the Balance of Payments and the So-called Dollar Shortage

Fritz Machlup

The Johns Hopkins University

Reprinted from *The Economic Journal,* LX (March 1950), pp. 46–48, by permission of the author and The Royal Economic Society.

The confusion concerning the meaning of a deficit or a disequilibrium in the balance of payments is almost as old as the study of political economy. But never before has it been so widespread; and rarely so systematically exploited. To be sure, most of the people who speak and write of the so-called "dollar shortage" are honestly confused. But there are probably some who know better and try to take advantage of the general confusion for political purposes if only out of patriotic motives. In any case, we have no right to abet confusion through continued equivocation. Three fundamentally different ideas are continually called by the same name. For the sake of clearer thinking they should be distinguished.

What is indiscriminately called the balance of payments may be: I. *A Market Balance,* i.e., a balance of supply and demand; or II. *A Programme Balance,* i.e., a balance of hopes and desires; or III. *An Accounting Balance,* i.e., a balance of credits and debits.

The market balance of payments is a model of a given situation in the foreign-exchange market, characterised by the effective demand and supply of foreign exchange at the given exchange rate and at alternative, hypothetical rates. This is an *ex ante* concept for use in the analysis of the foreign-exchange market, with major emphasis on the effects which changes of the exchange rate might have upon the amounts of exchange effectively demanded and supplied.

The programme balance of payments is a statement of sources and uses of foreign funds, expected or planned, over a future period of one or more years, based upon the nation's capital and consumption requirements, and on a programme of meeting an excess of requirements over resources by recourse to foreign finance expected or sought. This also is an *ex ante* concept, not for analysis but for use in planning, forecasting or negotiating, with major emphasis not on what is effectively demanded, but on what is felt to be desirable with reference to some accepted standards.

The accounting balance of payments is a record of all transactions, real and financial, which have taken place over a past period of one or more years between the country's residents and residents of other countries, the record being kept in the form of double-entry book-keeping, with each credit entry balanced by an offsetting debit entry, and vice versa. This is an *ex post* concept based on statistical information and estimates for use chiefly in the description of past developments and perhaps also in the appraisal of the present position of one nation in relation to others.

The meaning of a deficit in the balance of payments is, of course, categorically different for each of the three basic concepts. But also within each concept the meaning of a deficit is by no means clear. There may be several different deficits depending on a number of arbitrary definitions, assumptions, hypotheses, judgments or objectives, even after one has decided whether one speaks of a market, a programme or an accounting balance.

I. THE MARKET BALANCE OF PAYMENTS

In an attempt to define a dollar shortage or a deficit in the dollar balance of payments in the market sense (or supply and demand sense), one should be deliberately vague on certain points in order to allow for differences in assumptions and hypotheses which can be legitimately made.

A dollar deficit in a country's market balance of payments may be tentatively defined as an excess of dollar amounts effectively demanded at the given exchange rate by would-be purchasers (who are not restricted by specially adopted or discretionary government control measures) over the dollar amounts supplied at that exchange rate by would-be sellers (who are not motivated by a desire to support the exchange rate).

1. The phrase *"effectively demanded"* is to mean that the would-be buyers possess and are willing to part with the domestic money to pay for the foreign exchange. Effective demand for dollars means supply of domestic money in exchange for dollars; and excess

demand for dollars means excess supply of domestic money in the exchange market. Of course, total cash balances, bank credit outstanding and incomes are assumed to be given.

The concept of a "given" demand for dollars has several implications: (*a*) The case of a continuing credit expansion, of a continuous "feeding" of demand by the creation of additional bank credits or other forms of money is ruled out.[1] (*b*) When an excess demand for dollars is met by sales from monetary reserves (for the sake of maintaining exchange-rate stability) these sales tend to reduce domestic circulation and, thus, the would-be buyers' ability to sustain the given demand for dollars.[2] We must understand the effective demand as that which would-be buyers of dollars can exercise before their buying power may be impaired through dollar sales out of monetary reserves. (*c*) When an excess demand for dollars is reduced through an increase in the price of the dollar, *i.e.*, a depreciation of the currency, the reduction of dollar sales out of official reserves and the improvement in the foreign balance on current account may result in an increase in the domestic money supply and income level, and thus, in an increase of the demand for dollars.[3] Again, the "given" demand for dollars cannot show these repercussions of the change in the exchange rate.

In order to show the repercussions of changes in income, our working model should include, in lieu of a "given" demand for dollars, a family of demand curves with different income parameters. As long as we try to deal with a "given" demand, we have to assume that the buying power which makes this demand effective is unchanged. This assumption, I am afraid, limits the use of a

[1] The process of a continuing expansion would be represented by a continuing shift of the demand curve for foreign exchange upward and to the right (and of the supply curve upward and to the left). At a fixed exchange rate the excess demand for foreign exchange would continually rise, and with freely flexible rates the successive "deficits" in the market balance of payments would regularly be eliminated by continual increases in the price of the dollar.

[2] The "deflationary" effects of dollar sales out of monetary reserves would come to an end when the income flow is reduced to such a level that current savings out of received incomes are low enough to be adjusted to the reduced rate of "investment" (domestic investment minus the import balance).

[3] The existence of a continuing dollar deficit on current account at a stabilised dollar rate may be consistent (as was indicated in the preceding footnote) with stationary income equilibrium if the rate of saving has adjusted itself to the import balance. If, then, the depreciation reduces the dollar deficit, the domestic income flow must increase and, depending on the marginal propensity to import, the effective demand for dollars must also increase.

market model which includes only a "given" demand curve to short-period analysis.

2. The phrase *"at the given exchange rate"* may mean any exchange rate whatever, but the excess demand for dollars would then be purely hypothetical. More often the "given" exchange rate will refer to the one actually prevailing, at least at the outset of the imagined process. Most often it will refer to the rate fixed and maintained by the monetary authorities.[4]

3. The phrase *"not restricted by specially adopted or discretionary government control measures"* is the most delicate part of the definition; it is designed to prevent the definition from becoming unnecessarily narrow and to make it applicable to a variety of assumptions. A given demand curve for dollars assumes a large number of "underlying" conditions including the levels of income and buying power, the supply and demand conditions for all domestic and foreign products, and also the existence of governmental obstacles, incentives or prohibitions. Import tariffs, import quotas, import prohibitions, subsidies for home-made substitutes of foreign products, excise taxes on goods containing imported materials, limitations on foreign travel and hundreds of similar governmental measures are among the factors determining a country's effective demand for dollars. To assume "absence of all government intervention" would be silly if the model is to aid in the analysis of reality. On the other hand, to assume the existence of comprehensive foreign-exchange controls (allocation controls) and to include in the effective demand for dollars only those amounts which the control authorities will actually authorise would be worse, because it would define away the very problem we are out to solve, the excess demand for dollars. On what grounds, then, should we distinguish governmental control measures that can be assumed as given among the factors determining the effective demand for dollars from other measures that cannot be so included?

The answer to this question will usually be suggested by the

[4] Underlying the whole market analysis is usually the notion that the size of the excess demand is a function of the exchange rate and that in all probability an exchange rate could be found at which the excess demand is zero. Nevertheless, there are theories denying the existence of an equilibrium exchange rate under certain conditions and, under other conditions, asserting that the equilibrium may be unstable. In any event, the model of the foreign-exchange market with given supply and demand functions serves equally those who believe and those who do not believe it probable that there is always an exchange rate which can equate the dollar amounts demanded and supplied.

setting of the problem to be solved. For example, if with a given set of non-discretionary control measures the problem is to analyse the possible effects of depreciation without a change in the controls, the "given" demand will surely be on the basis of the existence of the controls. An absolutely effective prohibition of capital exports—if such a thing can exist—may exclude the demand for dollars by would-be capital exporters and reduce the relevant demand to that by importers of foreign goods and services. If the problem includes a comparative evaluation of specific (non-discretionary) control measures, the best procedure might be to work with two demand curves, one including, the other excluding, the effects of the controls in question. If the problem is to find out whether existing restrictions which were adopted merely for the duration of an emergency can be abandoned, these restrictions will be assumed to be absent so that one may see the picture of a possible market balance or imbalance without the use of the restrictions. If controls are of a kind that can be administered only with a discretion which in turn is affected by the size of the excess demand, then the "given" demand should certainly not reflect the exercise of these controls.[5]

4. The phrase *"not motivated by a desire to support the exchange rate"* is designed to separate the sales of foreign exchange out of monetary reserves and out of foreign stabilisation loans from the sales properly regarded as the "supply" of exchange in the market in which the balance between supply and demand is being analysed.

The "market supply" is by no means confined to transactions on income account, that is, to the proceeds from sales of exported goods and services (and certain donations). It includes also all those transactions on capital account (and all those donations) which are not the result of deliberate efforts to satisfy an effective demand for foreign exchange that could not otherwise be satisfied at the given

---

[5] Ardent believers in a free economic order may have a bias towards thinking of the effective demand always as if it were as "pure" as possible, *i.e.*, unaffected by restrictive government controls. Ardent believers in centralised planning, on the other hand, may refuse even for theoretical analysis to abstract from foreign-exchange restrictions, except in order to prove that a free market is inherently unstable and injurious to the national interest. The technique of analysis implied in the concept of the market balance dictates neither of these prejudices, although, as was said before, the logic of the conception of a demand function of determinate elasticity forbids us to include in the function the probable effects of discretionary restrictions (where the exercise of the restrictions is not restricted by any stated rules but only by the *ad hoc* rulings of the administrators).

exchange rate. Long-term capital imports, that is, direct investment by foreigners and the proceeds from the sale of securities to foreigners, are unquestionable components of the market supply of foreign exchange. And there is no reason why the market supply should not also include the foreign exchange derived from official (governmental or institutional) loans for relief, rehabilitation, reconstruction and development. Of short-term capital imports, the autonomous ones, such as funds of foreign capitalists placed in the country (whose balance of payments is being analysed) either for safekeeping or in order to profit from interest differentials are also clearly eligible for inclusion in the market supply of foreign exchange.[6] The "market supply" of dollars includes all those dollars that come to the exchange market as effective demand for domestic money. In other words, these dollars are offered because the would-be sellers want domestic money.[7]

Excluded from the "market supply" are the dollars sold out of the gold and foreign-exchange reserves of the monetary authorities, and

[6] Doubtful is the inclusion of short-term capital imports of private exchange speculators. These might be either foreigners willing temporarily to increase their balances (claims) in the country, or nationals willing temporarily to reduce their foreign balances or to increase their foreign debts. They are motivated by expectations of profiting from a merely temporary weakness of the domestic currency in the exchange market. In an analysis of the position of the monetary authorities, the foreign funds made available by exchange speculators might possibly be regarded as part of the market supply of foreign exchange, because this supply will relieve the pressure upon the monetary authorities and reduce the drain of official monetary reserves. From other points of view it seems preferable not to include the speculators' funds in the market supply of foreign exchange, especially since some of the consequences of these speculative transactions are very similar to those of reductions of the gold or exchange reserves of the monetary authorities. On these questions see my article on "The Theory of Foreign Exchanges," *Economica*, 1939 and 1940, especially pp. 42 ff. Reprinted in *Readings in the Theory of International Trade*, Philadelphia, Blakiston, 1949, pp. 149 ff.

[7] Many of the comments made above regarding effective demand have analogous relevancy for the market supply. The offer of foreign exchange, for example, may be the consequence of governmental measures stimulating the exports of merchandise or prohibiting the holding of foreign balances (claims); and it may depend upon the problems at hand whether the effects of the "interventions" should be included in or excluded from the market supply. There is also again the question of changes in the domestic income level affecting the exportability of home products and the flow from other sources of supply of foreign exchange. This either calls for a family of supply curves with different income parameters or it limits the use of a "given" supply curve to problems for which changes in income can be legitimately disregarded.

out of foreign stabilisation loans, and the rate-pegging purchases of domestic currency by foreign monetary authorities and international institutions such as the International Monetary Fund. These are the funds which are made available for the purpose of meeting all or part of the deficit in the market balance; they are supplied in order to support the exchange rate, not in order to get domestic currency.

5. Every supply-and-demand analysis has several *time* aspects: it pictures a situation prevailing at a particular moment of time and expected to last for a definite or indefinite period of time; it deals with quantities offered or demanded per unit of time; and it expresses the changeability of these quantities in response to changes in price with a certain time interval allowed for the adjustment. We are concerned at this point with how long the situation depicted by the market curves is expected to last. This is a time aspect of great significance in policy decisions. If an excess demand for foreign exchange is expected soon to give way to an excess supply, the problem of the "dollar shortage" is surely quite different from what it would be if no change was expected in the foreseeable future.

Disregarding day-to-day and even seasonal fluctuations, and speaking only of deficit periods long enough to constitute serious problems for monetary authorities intent upon maintaining exchange-rate stability, we may distinguish three kinds of cases: (*a*) The excess demand is judged to be cyclical in character, that is, associated with a particular phase of a national or international trade cycle, and hence likely to disappear in due time even without any special measures on the part of the governments concerned. (*b*) The excess demand is judged to be associated with structural or monetary factors expected to change before long in consequence of certain measures taken by the government or of certain developments afoot in the economy. (*c*) The excess demand is judged to be associated with conditions not expected to change significantly in the foreseeable future. Cases (*a*) and (*b*) are those in which the International Monetary Fund would consider sales of dollars against the currency temporarily in excess supply. In case (*c*) the I.M.F. would favourably consider a depreciation of the currency in excess supply.

6. There are several different *policies* for dealing with a deficit in

the market balance of payments. *A*. The excess demand for dollars at the given exchange rate can be reduced or removed by altering the rate. The proper adjustment of the exchange rate is typically a depreciation of the domestic money, i.e., a higher price for the dollar. *B*. The excess demand for dollars can be satisfied at the given exchange rate through sales of gold or dollars by the national or international monetary authorities. *C*. The excess demand for dollars can be left unsatisfied, the short amount supplied being distributed among would-be buyers by rationing, administrative allocation or similar discretionary restrictions of foreign-exchange transactions. *D*. The excess demand for dollars can be reduced or removed by monetary and fiscal measures reducing the money circulation and income flow of the country. *E*. The excess demand for dollars can be reduced (though rarely removed) by restrictive commercial policy, thus reducing, through higher import barriers, the demand for dollars (a shift which ordinarily will imply increased domestic demand for other things including exportable goods, and thus tend to reduce the supply of dollars [8]). *F*. The excess demand for dollars can be reduced (though rarely removed) by persuading other countries to a more liberal commercial policy, thus increasing, through reducing their import barriers, the supply of dollars (a shift which ordinarily will imply increased domestic demand for imports and dollars [9]).

Policies *E* and *F*—import barriers and removal of export barriers—have in common with policy *D*—deflation—that they are attempts to remove the gap between the supply and demand curves by shifting them until they intersect at the existing exchange rate. Policy *A*—exchange depreciation—attempts to close the gap by movements along the existing curves towards the point where they intersect. Policy *B*—exchange stabilisation—attempts (by rate-pegging sales out of reserves) to fill the gap between the existing curves at the existing exchange rate. Policy *C*—exchange restrictions—leaves the

---

[8] This reservation need not be relevant where policy *E* is adopted after policy *C* has been in use for a considerable time and the particular import demand that is now eliminated by new import barriers had been in any case unsatisfied under existing exchange controls. Policy *E* then merely reduces the demand for imports and dollars without reducing actual imports and purchases of dollars.

[9] Where policy *F* is adopted on top of policy *C*, the new supply of dollars may merely allow some previously existing but unsatisfied import demand to be satisfied. The qualification concerning an increase in demand is then not relevant.

existing curves, the existing rate and the existing gap as they are, but suspends the free market.[10]

Depreciation as well as deflation are apt to reduce real wages, the former by raising prices of imports and possibly increasing exports at the expense of home consumption, the latter by lowering money incomes in the economy. Policies A and D are unpopular for these reasons, and B and C are the monetary policies preferred by most politicians and many political economists. Since B, however, drains the foreign reserves of the country, C—restrictions—are relied upon in increasing degrees. Foreign loans strengthen the reserves for continuing policy B, but as soon as foreign loans give out, policy C becomes more stringent and the "dollar shortage" is perpetuated. This policy is rationalised by the contentions that deflation would lead to Communism, and that depreciation would under trade-union pressure become inflationary and, thus, could not eliminate the excess demand for dollars. It is true that trade-union pressure for excessive wages will lead either to unemployment or to inflation (open or repressed), and that inflation (even if repressed) results in permanent dollar shortages unless the price of the dollar is allowed to rise continually along with or ahead of wage-rates. If it is politically disastrous to permit large-scale unemployment and politically impossible to outlaw disequilibrating wage increases, a policy of continual exchange depreciation might be the only alternative to a policy of permanent restrictions or abolition of the market system.[11]

[10] The system of "freely fluctuating exchange rates" adopts policy A as an automatic regulation of the market balance of payments. Under such a system a dollar shortage in the market sense could not last even for a quarter of an hour. Any gap between supply and demand that threatened to develop at one exchange rate would immediately be closed by the market finding a rate that would squeeze out the excess demand. Whether the rate fluctuations under such a system would be enormous or moderate would depend on various elasticities, about the size of which we know little. In all systems used in actual practice, several of the policies dealing with an excess demand for exchange are used in combination. Of the two commercial policies, F is usually a pious hope, E—import barriers—an impious fact. Of the four monetary policies, the gold standard combined policies B and D—stabilisation and deflation. Most of the systems now in use (e.g., United Kingdom) combine policies B and C—stabilisation and restrictions. Some systems (e.g., France) combine policies A, B and C—depreciation, temporary stabilisation and restrictions. In at least one case (Italy) we have recently observed a combination of all four types of monetary policy.

[11] A "temporary suspension" of the market mechanism pending certain anticipated improvements of domestic productivity and possible foreign tariff reductions would in fact turn out to be permanent. The alternative policy of

Needless to say, assertions about what is politically "disastrous" or "impossible" are matters of political opinion, the validity of which is difficult to judge.

7. In contrast to the programme balance of payments, to be discussed presently, it makes no sense to *forecast* the market balance of payments for a future period into which the present market conditions can hardly continue—unless we believe that we know the future market conditions. The market balance of payments refers to a given exchange rate under given conditions of supply and demand. Changes in wage-rates, interest-rates, production costs, consumers' tastes, tariffs, fiscal policy, credit policy, capital movements, etc., will alter the market conditions for foreign exchange so significantly that it is nonsense to predict the size of the excess demand for a time a year or two away. Sometimes, perhaps, one may predict that the underlying conditions are likely to change in the near future so as to reduce the gap between supply and demand of dollars that exists at the present exchange rate. Or one may deny that they are likely to change sufficiently to eliminate the gap soon. Or one may try to estimate, nay, guess, the size of depreciation that might suffice to close the gap under given conditions. But a pretence of quantitative precision in forecasts of the market balance of payments cannot be taken seriously.[12]

---

countering any excessive wage increases by continual depreciation was apparently what Lord Keynes regarded as most feasible. (See "The Objective of International Price Stability," *Economic Journal*, 1943, p. 186.) There is a good chance that the threat of continual depreciation will make trade unions ready to agree on schemes for wage stabilisation (or wage increases in measured steps).

[12] Some of the differences between market balances and programme balances, particularly the difference in predictability, can be clarified by an illustration from another field. The housing shortage in the market sense is sure to continue for a long time if rentals are held at the controlled levels. One may try to guess the increase in rentals sufficient to eliminate the excess demand under given supply and demand conditions. But it is impossible to forecast the amount of excess demand for next year; although we may be certain that supply conditions will not have changed considerably, demand may be completely different. For example, another round of wage increases under full employment or a reduction in the income tax might easily double the excess demand; or an increase in food prices might cut it in half. The housing shortage in the programme sense, on the other hand, can well be predicted, because the amount of dwelling space which we regard as desirable depends chiefly on the (perhaps) predictable number of families—not on their disposable incomes and on the rentals they must pay.

II. THE PROGRAMME BALANCE OF PAYMENTS

The second concept of a balance of payments does not offer as many difficulties of definition as did the first concept. The definition of the deficit in the dollar balance of payments in the programme sense (or hopes and desires sense) calls merely for enough flexibility to take account of differences in judgment and in objectives.

A dollar deficit in a country's programme balance of payments may be defined as an excess of dollar amounts needed or desired for some specified purposes (assumed to be important with reference to some accepted standards) over the dollar amounts expected to become available from regular sources.

1. The phrase *"needed or desired"* is to emphasise the contrast to the phrase "effectively demanded" that was used in the definition of the market balance of payments. The relevant magnitude in the programme balance is not the effective demand—based on the people's ability to pay—but the "requirements" computed by experts and based on what they regard as the nation's needs or desires. These needs or desires refer to the imports from abroad required to sustain certain levels of domestic consumption and capital formation.

2. The phrase *"for some specified purposes"* need not mean exact import specifications according to detailed blueprints in a comprehensively planned economy, but may refer to global figures put down as targets or forecasts in an aggregative national budget, or even to mere projections of import totals required to supplement domestic output in the achievement of certain levels of consumption and rates of development. Given these levels of consumption and rates of development, given the productive resources available in the country, and given a certain export target, the total import requirement can be deduced by addition and subtraction.

3. The phrase *"with reference to some accepted standards"* indicates that the levels of domestic consumption and the rates of domestic capital formation are, in this context, matters of political judgment. Since the programme is usually submitted in justification of governmental measures or requests, the objectives must conform to some standards widely accepted as fair and reasonable. With regard to consumption goals, the maintenance of the existing

plane of living, or the return to one attained prior to an emergency, will usually be considered as a fair objective; lifting the plane of living will most easily be accepted as a reasonable objective if it can be couched in terms of public health and social security. With regard to capital accumulation, proper goals may include the reconstruction of plant worn or torn by war or other catastrophies, improvement of plant capable of securing quickly an increase in productivity such as to make the nation self-sustaining at a satisfactory living standard or any kind of development work promising to raise consumption from notoriously sub-standard levels. But it will be shown later that the "requirements," in all actual situations, are at least as much a matter of how much foreign finance appears to be obtainable as they are of how much appears to conform to "accepted standards."

4. The phrase *"expected to become available from regular sources"* is to exclude the emergency sources. The foreign finance designed to fill the dollar gap is thus separated from the dollar amounts from more regular sources upon which the programme makers are counting when they estimate the gap that remains to be filled. These, in other words, are the dollar amounts to be received as proceeds from exports of goods and services, and from loans and investments by foreign capitalists if such are safely expected. Whether dollar loans or grants firmly promised by foreign governments are included among the available dollar amounts before calculation of the deficit or, instead, are regarded as parts of the financing provided to meet the "existing" deficit is a matter of taste. There seems to be an inclination to consider foreign loans or grants for "special projects" among the ordinary "transactions supplying foreign exchange," but to put "general-purpose" loans or grants down as "compensatory official financing" sought and obtained in response to an existing deficit in the programme balance of payments.[13]

5. The programme balance of payments is always set up for a definite *period of time*, usually one year, sometimes two, three or four years. In a programme for two or more years it is customary to show declining deficits in successive years in order to emphasise the beneficial effects of the aid to be received in the first year. (This

[13] Cf. International Monetary Fund, *Balance of Payments Yearbook, 1938, 1946, 1947*. Washington, 1949, p. 10. On the inconsistencies involved in such procedures see Section III below.

definiteness contrasts strongly with the indefinite and probably brief time period to which a given market balance of payments could refer. Every slight change in market conditions, every act of fiscal or monetary policy, might drastically change a deficit in the market balance.) Since the programme is presumably independent of the whims of the markets it is possible to plan a deficit of definite size for one or more years ahead.

6. The existing *foreign-exchange rate* is not as essential for the programme balance as it is for the market balance of payments. The amounts of dollars effectively demanded and supplied will vary if the price of dollars changes; but the amounts of dollars needed or desired for certain national purposes may be entirely independent of the price of the dollar. If the dollar becomes more expensive in terms of domestic currency, people will not be able to buy, on their given incomes, so many things for which dollars are required. But they may still need or desire these things and this is what counts for the dollar deficit in the programme balance of payments. With regard to the programme balance, the foreign-exchange rate may possibly be a factor in the effective steering of productive resources for the attainment of the production and export targets set in the programme. But the more comprehensive the price and allocation controls in the economy, the less relevant will be the foreign-exchange rates.

7. It is in the assumptions about the *level of incomes* that the difference between market balance and programme balance of payments becomes most strikingly apparent. An increase in money and real income will most likely increase a dollar deficit in the market balance, but decrease a dollar deficit in the programme balance. In the market, the dollar gap will be widened at a given exchange rate, because people can buy more and, thus, more goods will be imported and fewer goods made available for export. In the programme, the dollar gap will be narrowed, because people produce more and, thus, fewer goods need be imported and more goods may be made available for export.

8. Six *policies* for dealing with a deficit in the market balance of payments were previously mentioned. Two of them, exchange depreciation and deflation, are of little relevance for the programme balance, because relative prices are not of the essence in judging what the nation needs, desires or can do without. The other policies remain relevant. Import barriers and exchange restrictions are among

the main instruments of implementing the programme: only for needed or desirable imports are dollars made available. Exchange stabilisation (in the sense of sales of dollars out of reserves of the monetary authorities) is often a part of the programme of covering the deficit: the programme may seek foreign loans and grants for the larger portion of the deficit, but draw on the dollar reserves of the nation to finance the rest. In a sense, however, one should really not speak of policies of "dealing" with a deficit in a programme balance of payments. For this is not a deficit which first "exists," and then is "dealt with." Instead, it is a deficit which is programmed when there is a chance to finance it. There is no sense in drawing up a programme balance with a dollar deficit when there is no hope of finding the funds required to carry out the programme. The entire programme is built around the potentialities of finding the foreign finance for the deficit.[14]

9. That the dollar deficit in the programme balance of payments is conditioned by the *financing potentialities* explains our previous remark that the so-called "standards" underlying the nation's requirements are not only flexible but, perhaps, even secondary to the appraisal of the financing potentialities. No matter how fair and reasonable are the standards on the basis of which a country would "need" large amounts of dollars, any programme balance showing a deficit too large to be financed would quickly be revised. Thus, a realistic appraisal of how much foreign finance might possibly be obtainable (from other than "regular" sources) will be the chief determinant of the deficit. This would make the dollar shortage (in the programme sense) merely a function of the financing potentialities. In actual fact, of course, the strength of the case, resting on the validity of the standards, might influence the willingness of other nations to finance a larger deficit and, besides, matters are even more complicated than that because the authorities in most countries constantly confuse in their thinking the programme balance of payments with the market balance. It is chiefly the programme bal-

---

[14] The staff of the International Monetary Fund recognises the planned character of most of the dollar deficits and considers it erroneous to assume "that in some way a deficit develops and financing must then be found for it. . . . Unless it is financed, the deficit cannot come into being." Again, "the monetary authorities engage in compensatory financing of a deficit upon which they have deliberately decided." International Monetary Fund, *Balance of Payments Yearbook, 1938, 1946, 1947.* Washington, 1949, p. 23.

ance by which the economic benefits of a foreign loan can be judged. A loan to finance a persistent deficit in the market balance would be beneficial only if something could be gained by postponing the correction of a fundamental maladjustment of the exchange rate.

10. Apart from its use in foreign diplomacy and domestic politics the programme balance of payments is a *forecast* of future developments. The forecasting involved in the programme balance makes sense even for periods for which forecasting of a market balance would make no sense. This does not mean that the forecasting will usually be proved correct by the actual developments. Where a nation allows some degree of economic freedom and permits free enterprise to perform some of the international transactions, it may find that some things do not go according to plan, that not all targets are reached, and that the programme must be revised in several respects. Yet, even if the forecasts eventually turn out to be wrong, they often make sense at the time they are made.

As in all forecasting and programming, past experience plays a dominant role in the computation of a programme balance of payments. The figures of past imports and exports are the chief material used by the programme makers, and projections of these figures into the future, with certain revisions up or down, are their most common method. There seems to be a tendency on the part of forecasters to underestimate the pliability of the trade balance in free market economies.[15] This is probably so because many economists

[15] In the forty-eight years from 1867 to 1914 France had import surpluses in forty-four years, and export surpluses only in the four years (1872-75) during which she paid war tributes to Germany. Despite this example of the pliability of the trade balance, John Maynard Keynes in the discussion of the German transfer problem regarded the trade figures as "sticky." When he wrote his famous article on "The German Transfer Problem" (*Economic Journal*, 1929) he had only the 1927 trade statistics available. It showed a German import surplus of RM 2,847 million. In 1928 the import surplus was only RM 1,229 million, by 1929 the balance had changed into an export surplus of RM 36 million, and in 1930 and 1931 the export surplus reached RM 1,642 million and RM 2,872 million, respectively. In the years before 1930 the changes were chiefly increases of exports with merely small decreases of imports; during the later years, after the onset of the world depression, the imports fell most drastically. The 1927 imports had been RM 13,801 million, the 1932 imports were RM 4,666 million. It may be said that these drastic changes in the trade balances had undesirable consequences. True enough. But this means merely that quick change may hurt, not that it is difficult to achieve; and that a forecast of a deficit based on past trade figures is in the nature of a programme, not a market balance, with the purpose of avoiding "undesirable" consequences.

underestimate the price elasticities and income elasticities which determine the flows of goods and services in free economies. Another reason may be that they take import figures as an expression not of effective demand but rather of the needs of the nations, and are loathe to programme a significant reduction in imports that would hurt. In any case, while past trade balances are of little relevance in sizing up the market balance of payments, they are important in shaping the programme balance of payments.

The *ex ante* character of the programme balance of payments is self-evident, but to the extent to which hopes are fulfilled and targets attained, the *ex post* record of international transactions may tally with the programme.

III. THE ACCOUNTING BALANCE OF PAYMENTS

The third concept of the balance of payments, the statistical record of a country's international transactions in the form of a fully balancing accounting statement, offers difficulties of definition only when it comes to define a deficit or surplus. If for all one-sided international transactions the accountants make offsetting entries on "donations" account, the only possible difference between the totals of credits and debits can be "errors and omissions," reflecting statistical deficiencies, not economic phenomena. Although everybody agrees that the accounting balance of payments "necessarily balances," many choose to present it as showing a surplus or deficit in some meaningful sense.[16]

Thus, *a dollar deficit in a country's accounting balance of payments may be defined as an excess of dollar amounts entered on the debit side of certain accounts in the annual record of its international transactions over the dollar amounts entered on the credit side of the same accounts, the accounts being selected from the full, necessarily balancing statement in order to throw light upon problems connected with market or programme balances of payments.*

[16] Cf. International Monetary Fund, *Balance of Payments Yearbook 1938, 1946, 1947*: "The balance of payments of a country necessarily balances. It is a system of double-entry bookkeeping under which total credits equal total debits. There can be no surplus or deficit in the balance of payments as a whole" (p. 4). Nevertheless, "the Fund's staff has endeavored to develop a concept of balance of payments surplus or deficit that would facilitate consideration of the problems of the Fund" (p. 5).

1. The phrase *"certain accounts"* serves as recognition of the fact that a complete statement of all accounts cannot possibly show a credit or debit balance, while "certain accounts" can. If these accounts, taken together, show a credit balance, the remaining accounts, taken together, must show a debit balance, and vice versa.

2. The phrase *"debit side"* stands here also for various other captions alternatively used in statements of international transactions, such as "payments," "imports," "passive" and "increase in gold or foreign assets" or "decrease in foreign debts," the latter two captions referring to gold and capital movements (provided such items are among the selected ones).

3. The phrase *"international transactions"* does not mean that every single transaction with foreigners is separately entered in the record; net changes in gold holdings and in foreign assets and debts can adequately reflect the net results of all individual transactions on gold and capital accounts.

4. The phrase *"credit side"* stands here also for various other captions alternatively used, such as "receipts," "exports," "active" and "decrease in gold or foreign assets" or "increase in foreign debt."

5. The phrase *"accounts selected"* is intended to reflect the fact that the ideas as to what is a significant selection have varied most widely. For a long time writers stressed only merchandise accounts, and up to this day many concentrate their attention on current accounts (income accounts).[17] Official donations are sometimes excluded, so that transactions on current account consist of goods, services and private donations. Others have felt that long-term capital movements (or at least private long-term capital movements) should be included among the accounts showing the significant balance.[18] This would leave movements of monetary gold and short-term capital (and perhaps official long-term capital movements) as the items offsetting or financing the surplus or deficit. There are

---

[17] Cf. *Report of the ECA Mission to the United Kingdom,* London, 1948, p. 3, where the proposition that "the period from 1930 to 1938 showed a deficit in the balance of payments running at the rate of £27 million per year" refers to the "trade" balance plus "net invisibles."

[18] Cf. International Monetary Fund, *Balance of Payments Yearbook 1938, 1946, 1947,* p. 5 illustrating "the necessity of including private capital movements if the impact of the balance of payments on the exchange problem is to be assessed."

several more possible combinations of accounts, separating private and official short-term capital movements, or using other sorts of breakdowns. A "new approach," [19] recently developed by the International Monetary Fund in its search for a "working concept of surplus or deficit in the balance of payments," [20] will be discussed presently.

6. The phrase *"in order to throw light"* indicates the purpose, but not necessarily the result of selecting certain items of the accounting balance of payments to show a credit or debit balance. The light thrown by the balance of chosen items is more often deceptive than helpful, particularly in the analysis of the market balance of payments. Even the most careful selection of items in an accounting statement cannot indicate whether the particular transactions were "autonomous" or "induced," which is the significant thing in market analysis.[21]

7. On first thought it may appear that no difficult *time problems* are involved in the concept of a deficit in the accounting balance of payments, with all accounts recording *ex post* the transactions that have actually occurred during the year. Unfortunately, this is not so if the accounting balance is supposed to explain the situation in the foreign-exchange market. There may be, within a year, several changes, back and forth, from excess demand to excess supply of foreign exchange, that is, a succession of deficits and surpluses in the market balance of payments. But apart from this, the trade statistics of one year may contain imports or exports prepaid in the previous year or payable in the next year, in amounts not cancelling each other, so that the offsetting short-term capital movements would not reflect any "balance of payments pressures" in the foreign-exchange markets. Many other kinds of peculiar timing constellations may make the accounting balance absolutely irrelevant for any market balance over the year.

8. The accounting balance of payments tells nothing about the

[19] *Yearbook,* p. 24.
[20] *Yearbook,* p. 5.
[21] In an analysis of the foreign-exchange market it is essential to distinguish, for example, between imports which give rise to additional demand for foreign exchange, and imports which are induced by additional supply of foreign exchange. The accounting balance of payments, regardless of the way the accounts are selected, cannot say anything about such problems. All imports are considered as representing a demand for foreign exchange.

relationship between *foreign-exchange rates* and the market balance of payments.[22] Aggregative elasticity studies are absolutely unreliable.

9. The impossibility of using an accounting balance of payments as an *indication of the market balance of payments* can perhaps be better understood by imagining cases of perfect balance in the accounting balance, no matter how the accounts are selected. (*E.g.*, assume a perfect balance of trade, a perfect balance of invisibles and no net movements of monetary gold or capital.) We still could not see from the accounting balance whether the equality of annual exports and imports was achieved: (*a*) by a stable market balance with supply and demand unchanged during the year, (*b*) by a flexible adjustment of exchange rates to changing supply and demand conditions, (*c*) by a flexible adjustment of domestic-income levels by means of fiscal and monetary policies compensating any autonomous influences upon supply and demand for foreign exchange maintained at a stable rate (or by an orthodox gold-standard policy, which, conceivably, might do the same thing), (*d*) by a flexible adjustment of tariffs, subsidies and prohibitions compensating any other influences upon supply and demand for foreign exchange maintained at a stable rate, or (*e*) by suspending the free market, requisitioning all foreign exchange from exporters and rationing it among favoured importers. These are surely very different situations in the foreign-exchange market. Only the first of the five cases of perfect accounting balances may be described as one of a perfect market balance.

10. The thought of using an accounting balance of payments as indication or explanation of difficulties with the market balance of payments is too tempting to be given up lightly. The staff of the

---

[22] Where the exchange rates were kept stable over the years, it is, of course, not possible to learn from actual import figures anything about the exchange-rate elasticities of demand for imports. Where exchange rates changed during a year, the accounting balance of payments for the whole year cannot possibly show the effects of the rate changes. But even if we ever had a clean comparison between two periods (without overlapping anticipations or commitments), with two different exchange rates, we still could not derive the relevant elasticities, because autonomous capital movements and domestic income levels in the two periods may have been very different. For example, while one naturally supposes that a higher price of the dollar would reduce imports into a country, a foreign loan granted to it at the time of the depreciation might enable it to import more rather than less.

International Monetary Fund worked hard to solve this problem. In 1948, they reported progress [23] and, in 1949, success.[24] They admitted that the new concept that they had developed was "still in the experimental stage," and "will undoubtedly be modified" in the process of application. But they considered it "to have reached a sufficiently well-defined stage to assist in analysing problems of international exchange." [25]

The new concept, called *Compensatory Official Financing*, is provisionally defined as "the financing undertaken by the monetary authorities to provide exchange to cover a surplus or deficit in the rest of the balance of payments." [26] It can be said of every single item, or group of items, that it covers a surplus or deficit in the rest of the balance of payments; this is in the nature of any accounting statement. Hence, what this definition apparently tries to single out is those operations which have the sole or primary purpose of providing foreign exchange in response to a situation that has arisen in the foreign-exchange market. The main criteria, therefore, are the *purpose or motive* of the operations and the *stimuli* to which they are supposed to respond. In the analysis of any particular financing operation, the analyst's decision on its purpose should depend on whether the operation would have been undertaken also "for its own sake," that is, even if there had been no excess demand for foreign exchange.[27] And the decision on the stimulus should depend on

[23] "It is of great importance for the Fund *to know the financial pressures on the monetary authorities* resulting from international transactions and how they are met. In the preparation of the Manual serious consideration was given to the possibility of setting up a final item . . . that would have been entitled 'Official operations to finance a deficit or surplus in the balance of payments.' The deficit or surplus would, by definition, have represented the balance of all transactions other than these official operations, and the official operations themselves would have represented *the response of the monetary authorities to the pressures arising from the balance of payments*. It was decided, however, not to set up an item of this character, because of the difficulty of determining without analysis in each particular case how certain transactions should be classified." International Monetary Fund, *Balance of Payments Manual*, Washington, 1949, p. 8. (Italics are mine.)

[24] "The staff has developed a concept of compensatory official financing . . . ," a "concept that would facilitate consideration of the problems of the Fund." International Monetary Fund, *Balance of Payments Yearbook 1938, 1946, 1947*, Washington, 1949, pp. 4–5.

[25] *Yearbook*, p. 5.

[26] *Yearbook*, p. 5.

[27] "There is a wide range of financing . . . in which it is a matter of interpretation whether or not the operations have been compensatory; the decision in these instances rests upon whether the financing was in response to general

whether without the financing operation the "balance-of-payments pressures" would have resulted in some serious events in the foreign-exchange market, such as depreciation, additional restriction measures, default on governmental obligations or the like.

In applying the new concept to their statements on the "Financing of International Transactions," the staff of the Fund met with perplexing paradoxes. That they included foreign-exchange transactions of *private* commercial banks of all countries except the United States under the heading of compensatory *official* financing was probably good judgment, inasmuch as most of these banks are merely the lengthened arms of the respective monetary authorities. But the judgment concerning many intergovernmental loans and grants was so poor, I am afraid, as to deprive the new concept of most of its meaning.

U.N.R.R.A. aid, for example, was entered as compensatory financing for the recipient countries, because "it was directed to needy countries that could not make international payment for it out of their own resources." [28] That the recipient countries could not have paid for the U.N.R.R.A. supplies is certainly correct, but irrelevant for the question, because the supplies would not have been bought and, hence, would not have had to be paid for. The goods were supplied without charge, not because the countries had an excess demand for foreign exchange, but because they had an unsatisfied need for food and other necessary materials; not because there was an excess supply of local currency in the dollar market, but because people were hungry and the production lines were disrupted. If in any of the recipient countries the price of the dollar had been so high, or the holdings of domestic money had been so low, that people could not afford to demand dollars, that is, if there had not been any "pressures" on the market balance of payments, this surely would not have disqualified such a country from receiving U.N.R.R.A. aid. The grants, therefore, cannot be called compensatory of any pressures in the exchange markets.

The same inconsistent application of the new concept was made in the case of E.R.P. loans and grants. Although it was recognised by the staff analysts that "project loans" are not "*compensatory* offi-

---

balance-of-payments pressures or whether it was for a particular project or other special purpose that would have been financed anyway for its own sake." *Yearbook*, p. 10.

[28] *Yearbook*, p. 11.

cial financing" but *"special* official financing," [29] E.R.P. aid, loans as
well as grants, were put down as "compensatory." The failure to
observe the criteria adopted for the new concept can be appreciated
by asking what were the principles of allocating the E.R.P. funds
among the recipient countries. The comparative pressures in the
foreign-exchange markets? the comparative excess demands for
dollars? the comparative need of exchange-rate adjustments? the
comparative rigour of exchange controls? None of all these. Not the
pressures in the foreign-exchange markets, but the potentials for
improvement in the productive use of domestic resources were
fundamental guides in the allocation of loans and grants under the
E.R.P. programme.[30]

11. We can now diagnose a part of the confusion in the application of the new concept. The balance-of-payments pressures which
Compensatory Official Financing is supposed to relieve are, in one
place, taken to refer to the market balance and, in another place, to
the programme balance of payments. E.R.P. loans or grants are
surely compensatory of deficits in the programme balances of the
recipient countries, even if they are not compensatory of deficits in
their market balances of payments. But there can be no doubt that
problems of the market balance were originally what the designers
of the new concept had in mind; they specifically mentioned the
"use of the Fund's resources, exchange-rate adjustments and exchange controls" as the problems the consideration of which was to
be facilitated by the new concept.[31]

Some of the inconsistencies in the application of the streamlined
accounting balance of payments obviously bothered the staff writers
of the Fund. This is apparent from the discussion of the differences
between balance-of-payments deficits in free exchange markets and
in controlled exchange markets. The argument runs as follows:
Where the "exchange markets are free and the authorities undertake
to maintain a stable rate of exchange," this undertaking *"forces"* the
authorities to finance any deficit that should arise. But where the

[29] "The development of the project, rather than the development of balance-
of-payments deficits, governs disbursements under the [project] loan. A project
loan may in fact be extended to a country that is enjoying a balance-of-payments surplus." *Yearbook,* p. 12.
[30] A critic of this statement has said that the E.R.P. dollars will always relieve
the pressures in the foreign-exchange market and cover part of an existing
dollar deficit in the market balance. Even this need not be true. The E.R.P.
funds may be used for purposes for which there was no effective demand before
the E.R.P. aid was granted.
[31] *Yearbook,* p. 5.

exchange markets are controlled, so that the authorities supply only as much exchange as they wish or are able to afford, they "engage in compensatory financing of a deficit upon which they have *deliberately* decided." Hence, this "planned deficit is different from the unplanned deficit of the free exchange market." But—although the staff writers had stated before that a deficit in the balance of payments can *exist* only if and in so far as it is *financed*—they nevertheless conclude that "in either case," that is, with unplanned or planned deficits, "the amount of compensatory financing is the measure of the extent to which the *existing* balance of payments has *forced* the authorities to take financial action." [32]

At the bottom of these manifest contradictions lies a neat piece of circular reasoning. Originally the idea of the staff was to call compensatory that amount of financing that was designed to provide exchange to cover a balance-of-payments deficit. Now they have ended up with measuring the balance-of-payments deficit by the amount of financing that they choose to call compensatory. This noble accounting balance is not even a distant relation of the market balance of payments. As a matter of fact, the deficit in the market sense, the excess demand for dollars, was defined away when the staff of the Fund assumed that "a country exercising an effective exchange control," by cutting down "its outpayments to whatever it finds to be the level of its international receipts," can *eliminate the deficit.* [33] A "dollar deficit," in the sense of this peculiar way of reasoning, is then the amount of dollars made available by monetary authorities—even if the excess demand is much greater—and the amount of dollars made available by foreign governments for general purposes—even if the effective excess demand for dollars in the exchange market is larger, smaller, nil or negative.[34] This arbitrary accounting balance measures nothing but itself.

[32] *Yearbook*, p. 23. (All italics are mine.)

[33] *Yearbook*, p. 23. (Italics are mine.)

[34] The actual state of the foreign-exchange market can be judged by mental experiment: by postulating the removal of all allocation and rationing controls and asking what amounts of dollars would have to be sold or bought by the monetary authorities in order to stabilise the exchange rate, and what would happen to the exchange rate in a free market if no dollars were added to or sold out of official reserves. In some European countries the price of the dollar would surely have declined in a free exchange market if the dollars available from ERP aid had been offered for sale. This certainly does not mean that these countries do not need the aid. On the basis of the potential benefits to their economies, their need for this dollar aid—*i.e.*, the deficit in their programme balance of payments—may be more urgent that in the case of countries with large excess demand for dollars.

IV. CONCLUSIONS

Deficits in the market balance, programme balance and accounting balance of payments mean very different things. A persistent deficit in the *market* balance of payments—an excessive amount of domestic money wanting to be exchanged into foreign money—indicates that the nation's monetary, fiscal and wage policies (and the resulting money incomes and product prices) are incompatible with the foreign-exchange rates. A persistent deficit in the *programme* balance of payments—repeated plans to liquidate foreign assets, to attract foreign investors, to contract foreign debts and to negotiate foreign grants—indicates that programme makers believe foreign funds could be obtained and would materially contribute to the recipient nation's development, improvement of plant, productivity of resources and plane of living. A persistent deficit in the *accounting* balance of payments, with one of the customary selections of accounts, indicates that the nation in the past has been able to live partly on its foreign assets and/or to secure foreign loans or grants.

There is no necessary relationship between these deficits; indeed, a deficit in one of the three sense may be compatible with a simultaneous surplus in one of the other senses.[35] For example, a country with a deficit in its program balance of payments may have a surplus in its market balance of payments. The government of that country may be anxious to obtain foreign funds for a development program and may have succeeded in impressing a foreign mission with the urgent needs for a development loan. These needs (not satisfied out of other sources) constitute the program deficit. But the government may have been pursuing a conservative fiscal and monetary policy, avoiding deficit spending and credit expansion. Thus, the market demand for foreign exchange would not be inflated, and the market supply at the given exchange rate may be such that the monetary authorities can make current net additions to their exchange reserves. This surplus in the market balance of payments may prevail despite the recognized deficit in the program balance, certainly as long as the latter remains only on paper; but it may persist even after the foreign loan to cover the program deficit has been granted

---

[35] *Editors' note:* The following four paragraphs were written by Professor Machlup in the spring of 1958 and replace a paragraph in the original publication.

if the government—though perhaps ill-advised—continues its anti-expansionary policies and keeps national spending to a minimum. In this case the foreign funds required for the program may be supplied in the open market before an effective market demand for them has developed.

The opposite constellation is also conceivable: a deficit in the market balance and a surplus in the program balance of payments. Such a surplus is of course nothing but an opinion of some planners or experts, who hold that the country, much wealthier than others, is able to save much more than others, but lacks sufficient investment opportunities at home. In its own interest, they conclude, the country "ought" to have steady capital exports.[36] At the same time, however, the country may have been indulging in deficit spending and credit expansion, and/or several foreign countries may just have devalued their currencies, with the result that there exists an excess demand for foreign exchange—a deficit in the market balance of payments—in the rich country with its program surplus.

The possibility of a deficit in the program balance and a surplus in the accounting balance of payments is easily conceived. A country may have been paying reparations, or repaying foreign loans, or investing abroad because of political insecurity at home, and thus its balance on current account may show a surplus. Yet the experts may agree that the country is in urgent need of capital imports to bolster its development. (As, if, and when foreign capital is actually obtained and used for buying foreign goods, the accounting surplus may disappear and give place to an accounting deficit.)

A deficit in the accounting balance and a surplus in the market balance of payments may co-exist in a country receiving loans and investments from abroad while abstaining from expansionary domestic monetary policies. The supply of foreign exchange, increased by the foreign funds becoming available on capital account, may be partly sold in the open market, thus depressing the price of foreign money to the lower limit tolerated by a policy of exchange stability, and partly purchased by the monetary authorities. To the extent that the foreign exchange finds sellers in the market it goes to pay for

[36] Distinguish the "ought" of capital exports to help other nations and the "ought" of capital exports to provide outlets for potential over-saving and to avoid underemployment at home. Only in the latter case could one speak of a "surplus" in the program balance of payments; in the former case the capital exports would only be designed to cover deficits in the program balances of other nations.

the import surplus, that is, to finance a deficit in the balance of payments on current account; to the extent that it is purchased by the monetary authorities it will be regarded as a surplus in the market balance of payments.[37]

Under these circumstances, much of the current talk about dollar shortage makes little sense. A country may have a large effective demand for dollars—if the supply of domestic money is relatively large and the price of the dollar relatively low. This does not indicate the urgency of the need for any dollar aid sought to increase the productivity of the nation's resources and to improve its plane of living. And neither the urgent need nor the effective demand for dollars is indicated by accounting records reflecting past financing operations.

In the evaluation of the benefits of a loan to a nation "suffering

[37] A diagrammatical illustration of the situation described above may be helpful.

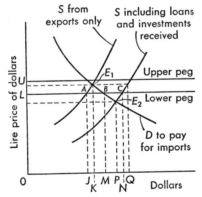

OU = upper peg (selling price of dollars maintained by monetary authorities);

OL = lower peg (buying price of dollars maintained by monetary authorities);

KE_1 = hypothetical equilibrium rate, if no foreign capital were received;

PE_2 = hypothetical equilibrium rate, if none of the foreign capital received were re-exported by adding it to the foreign exchange reserve.

With the dollar price at the lower peg, there will be a *surplus* in the market balance of payments in the amount of MN dollars or $MNCB$ lire, and a *deficit* in the balance of payments on current account (which is the most widely used variant of the accounting balance) in the amount of JM dollars or $JMBA$ lire.

This description of a "situation" should be distinguished from a description of an "adjustment to a change," namely, from the situation in which no foreign capital had been received (and the equilibrium rate KE_1 had been "actual," not merely hypothetical) to the situation prevailing when the supply of dollars received from foreign capitalists becomes effective (with domestic income and expenditures still unchanged). In this case one would say that at the former equilibrium rate the market surplus would be KQ dollars, and that this would result in (a) a fall of the dollar rate to the lower peg, (b) a reduction in the market surplus from KQ to MN dollars, (c) a reduction in commodity exports by JK dollars, (d) an increase in commodity imports by KM dollars, and (e) an increase in exchange reserves by MN dollars.

from a dollar shortage," its programme balance of payments will be of major significance. For it will indicate what the nation intends to achieve with the aid requested, the consumption levels and the plant improvements that it visualises. The current market balance of payments of such a nation is not so significant in this respect. For if the market deficits are persistent, loans will only postpone the necessary adjustments of relative prices and exchange rates. It is for the evaluation of the usefulness of such adjustments that the deficit in the market balance of payments is most relevant. The connection between the two kinds of dollar shortages is chiefly political. It may be that the improvements in the nation's economy which are to result from the financing of the programme deficit may give its government the political security it needs for carrying out the price and rate adjustments necessarily involved in the elimination of the deficit in the market balance of payments.

In discussions of the equivocal "dollar shortage" we should insist on full identification of the concept employed. We may then discover that many of the existing differences of opinion—in the diagnosis of as well as in the therapy for concrete cases—can be easily resolved, and the rest can be reduced to questions of unknown facts or of irreconcilable political philosophy.

6. The Cause and Cure of "Dollar Shortage"

Frank D. Graham

Excerpt from "The Cause and Cure of 'Dollar Shortage,'" *Essays in International Finance* (International Finance Section, Department of Economics and Sociology, Princeton University), January 1949; pp. 1–9 excerpted. Reprinted by permission of the publisher. At the time of original publication, the author was with Princeton University.

I. INTRODUCTION

Lack of balance in the international accounts, and the consequent "shortage" of dollars and certain other currencies, are phenomena for which there are almost no precedents before World War I. On the contrary, in the pre-1920 literature on empirical international trade, we find frequent expressions of surprise at the speed, facility, and automaticity with which equilibrium was restored after any major disturbance. It would be naïve to suppose that the difference between past and present is wholly accidental. Yet most of such "explanations" as have so far been offered are worse than Taussig's famous remark with respect to some of the early situations that "it all just happened," since the thesis of chance, however unsatisfying, is certainly to be preferred to highly irrational fantasy garbed in pseudo-scientific habiliments. The true explanation, however, is very simple and is not far to seek. Before World War I, we had effective pecuniary machinery for securing equilibrium in the international accounts while, since 1920, our pecuniary institutions have been all but perfectly designed to prevent it.

II. FORMER AND PRESENT INTERNATIONAL MONETARY MECHANISMS

The typical national monetary system in the period prior to 1914 was either an "essentially unmanaged" gold standard or an independent currency with free exchange markets.[1] Either system would readily restore equilibrium in disturbed international accounts, not, as is ordinarily supposed, by changing the prices of a currently debtor (or creditor) country's exports relative to those of its imports but by changing the relationship of the price-level of all internationally traded goods to that of purely domestic commodities in the several national entities. As soon as such a change occurred (in consequence of an international transfer of gold or an alteration in exchange rates) a shift in both consumption and production, in all affected countries, was inaugurated, with attainment of equilibrium a ready and inevitable result.

A gold-standard, currently-debtor country, losing gold without resort to any "offsetting" technique, would suffer a decline in its money supply, in its money-income, and in the price-level of *domestic* commodities. The prices of internationally traded commodities, however (whether exports or imports of the country in question), would tend to remain unchanged since they would be demanded, and supplied, not only by the country *losing* gold but by many other countries (including those *receiving* gold).[2] The upshot of the segmented movement in domestic-international price relationships following an international transfer of gold was, therefore, that consumers in the currently debtor country would find that internationally traded commodities were now relatively dear. Even with a *given*, and, *a fortiori*, with a *lowered* domestic money income, they would thereupon almost certainly reduce their takings both of imports and of exportables (leaving more of the latter to be exported). Such a country's *producers*, however, would tend to concentrate on the new relatively high-priced internationally traded commodities (both import-competing and exportable commodities) and would, under the stimulus of a persisting loss of gold, continue to do so until not only the discrepancy between imports and exports was eliminated but the composition of industry in the country in question had become adjusted to the requirements of the new equilibrium

---

[1] By an "essentially unmanaged gold standard" is meant a standard under which the monetary authorities essayed no longe-range control of the national money supply in substantial disregard of international movements of the money material, but confined their attention to short-term smoothing operations.

[2] There is no reason to suppose that the influence on the prices of internationally traded goods of the country losing gold, or, indeed, receiving it, would be dominant over that of all the rest, and the respective influences of the countries losing and receiving gold would tend to cancel one another.

in the international accounts.[3] The restoration of equilibrium would, of course, be facilitated, and completed, by the occurrence of converse phenomena in countries originally receiving gold.

The same consequences would ensue in the case of a currently debtor country of independent currency and freely mobile exchange rates. The fall in the exchange value of the currency of any such country would raise the *domestic-currency* price of internationally traded commodities but would leave the prices of domestic commodities unchanged. The new price relationships in the affected country would operate in the same way as those just described for currently debtor countries under gold-standard conditions. Converse movements in currently creditor countries of independent currency would parallel the situation in gold-standard countries *receiving* gold.

From 1920, or thereabouts, to the present time, however, the vogue of "managed" currencies, whether gold or paper, has consigned this mechanism to oblivion. Monetary and credit management has consistently sought to "offset" the effects above depicted and has endeavored to relieve the "pressures" without which the said effects will not be achieved. For, if successful efforts are made to keep domestic prices from falling when an ostensibly gold-standard country is losing gold (and from rising when it is receiving gold), or to keep the exchange rates between a given inconvertible and other currencies fixed despite a state of unbalance in the international accounts, there will be nothing to prevent the indefinite continuation of the current price relationships and we shall then get a perpetuated disequilibrium with a consequent chronic "shortage" of what will now become very "hard" currencies.

The inherent contradiction between a nostalgic yearning for the fixed exchange rates appropriate to unmanaged gold standards (with national price-levels moving in substantial uniformity) and the modern desire for national monetary independence as a prerequisite to monetary management in the interest of high-level employment (with national price-levels moving in aberrant relationship to one another) is the real explanation not only of the present unbalance

---

[3] The presumptive decline in the output of domestic commodities would, of course, steadily operate to raise their prices once more to the level of the internationally traded goods and, in a process of oscillation of sales, might lead to oscillatory international movements of gold. But this would not prevent the eventual attainment of equilibrium in the international accounts with all price relationships then substantially as they had originally been.

in international trade but of the inter-war tendency for the world's gold to move to our shores, of the strong demand abroad for stabilization loans from this country, and of the "shortage" of dollars in the outside world when the gold supplies of foreign countries had been more or less exhausted and the United States was no longer inclined toward foreign investment.

III. EXCHANGE RATES AS PRICES, AND THE EFFECTS OF "CONTROLS"

Exchange rates are prices. In a free market there is never a shortage of any commodity in the sense that the amounts of that commodity demanded and supplied, at the free market price, are out of equilibrium. It is, in fact, the function of a free market price to bring them to equality. There will, on the other hand, *always* be a "shortage" of any commodity if its price is somehow held below what marginal buyers in a free market would be prepared to give for it. The "shortage" of dollars in the foreign world is therefore solely and simply explicable in the fact that the dollar is made available to residents of foreign countries, in necessarily rationed amounts, at lower prices in their respective currencies than, in a free market, they would be prepared to pay for the given supply.

Under the unmanaged gold standard it was possible to have substantially fixed exchange rates, *and also a free exchange market,* only because the purchasing powers of the exchange currencies over domestic goods were automatically altered in opposite directions in countries respectively losing and receiving gold. That is to say, that any tendency toward a shift beyond the gold points, in the relative values of the currencies in direct exchange the one for the other, was automatically nullified by a flow of gold attended by corresponding, but opposite, shifts in their relative value vis-à-vis *domestic* goods within their respective spheres of circulation. The external and the internal values of each of the several currencies were thus automatically kept in the relationship that would at once procure fixed exchange rates together with the composition of national outputs, and the price structure, that would promote equilibrium in the international accounts.

In the case of independent currencies and a free exchange market a similar shift in the relationship between the internal and external values of any one of them was achieved through a more sustained

movement of exchange rates with results more or less the same as
those attained under the "unmanaged" gold standard with its very
slight exchange-rate movements followed by the shift to an alternative mechanism.

With a few notable exceptions (*viz.* the hard currencies other
than the dollar) the degree of internal inflation of the dollar has, at
most times, been less (or, as the case might be, the degree of deflation has been greater), ever since World War I, than that of any
synchronous movement in the internal value of other currencies.
Combined with a widespread predilection for the attainment, and
maintenance, of fixed exchange rates, this has meant that there has
been a persistent tendency toward the sale of dollars on the exchange market at prices, in other currencies, below the figure which
the respective purchasing powers of the dollar and other currencies
would warrant. We can say either that the price level in the United
States has persistently been relatively low, on the basis of the established exchange rates, or that the exchange value of the dollar has
persistently been low on the basis of existing price-levels. However
the matter is put the upshot has been a chronic excess of American
commodity exports over imports, and that "shortage" of dollars
which, in otherwise not unrespectable quarters, has been "explained"
in terms of intractable inelasticities of international demand, of an
overweening American productivity, or of some mysterious forces
operating, it would seem, in complete disregard of well-established
economic laws. The notion, stemming from a firm grasp of the doctrine of comparative advantage, that neither national productivity
nor poverty has anything to do with *balance* in international trade
(except, perhaps, that poverty will operate to *ensure* it) has been
treated with a contempt that it is very far from deserving. The fact
is that we need never look to anything more recondite than an inappropriate relationship between the internal and external value of
the currency of any country, rich or poor, to have a *complete* explanation of a lack of balance in its international accounts.

It will, perhaps, be worth while specifically to note a few of the
many attempts in the inter-war period, to preserve fixed exchange
relationships in the face of national price-level kinetics which did not
warrant maintenance of the established rate. The so-called, and
widely lauded, international cooperation involved in these attempts
was actually the primary factor in frustrating equilibrium and the
free movement of commodities in international trade (both of which

it professed to foster), since it removed the incentives toward these ends without which they will never be attained.

In the latter half of the twenties the Federal Reserve Board pursued a policy allegedly designed to promote the preservation of the gold standard in Britain after convertibility of the £ sterling had been restored at a rate against gold, and the dollar, which is now universally conceded to have been too high. The effect, and perhaps the immediate aim of the Board's policies was to relieve the pressure on the British to deflate, and thus to prevent adoption of the only British policy which, in the absence of inflation in the United States, could produce equilibrium in the international accounts at the $4.86 rate for the £. Like all such attempts this policy merely cumulated maladjustments until the British lost all their gold and the £ fell with a crash in 1931.

Take now the case of German reparations. The Dawes Plan—hailed as a restorer of the gold standard in Germany and as a rational solution of the problem of German reparations payments—provided that, whenever pressure should develop on mark exchange, the transfer of reparations was to be stopped though the money involved in the payments within Germany of the untransferred sums was not necessarily to be abstracted, *pro tanto*, from the internal circulation. The Plan thus deliberately abandoned the only mechanism by which it could have been made to work, and it in fact worked only so long as lavish loans to the Germans, advanced by American investors, relieved the Germans of the necessity of increasing the ratio of their exports to their imports. Collapse was immediate when these loans were no longer forthcoming. It is worthy of note, however, that Germany automatically attained a balance in its international accounts on several occasions, before and after this period, when the Germans were in desperate straits for international means of payment but could get no foreign aid. This should surely occasion no surprise. It is, indeed, a truism, but it is a truism we seem peculiarly prone to forget.

Let us look now at the Tri-partite Agreement of 1936 which once more sought to establish, and maintain, fixity of exchange rates between the currencies of the participants but without a trace of any mechanism for coordinating the purchasing powers of the currencies concerned. Of this effort it need only be said that the outbreak of war merely confirmed the collapse that was already under way.

IV. THE INTERNATIONAL MONETARY
ORGANIZATION

It would seem that, after all this, we might have learned that we cannot both have our cake and eat it. We should know that we must either forgo fixed exchange rates *or* national monetary sovereignty if we are to avoid the disruption of equilibrium in freely conducted international trade or the system of controls and inhibitions which is the only alternative when the internal values of independent currencies deviate—as they always tend to do—from what was, perhaps, a correct relationship when the fixed rates of exchange were set up. Yet the old error was, to all intents and purposes, again repeated in the International Monetary Organization which did not much curtail national monetary sovereignty. It is true that some concessions were made to the consequent demand for flexibility in exchange relationships. But there is, nevertheless, a strong bias in the statute toward the ideal of rates maintained unchanged for an indefinitely lengthy period, and not even the slightest provision for the adoption, by the various participating countries, of the congruent monetary policies without which a system of fixed exchange rates simply does not make sense.

It can be confidently asserted that it is only in the most extreme cases, or otherwise under the rarest of circumstances, that, in a still strongly Mercantilistic world, a group of nations will concede the case for a reduction in the relative exchange value of the currency of any one of them since this will have the effect of increasing, on third markets, the competition of the devaluing country with the exporters of the others, and of increasing its sales to, and reducing its purchase from, those other countries. Yet, in view of the more or less justifiable horror with which sharp deflations are regarded, such a devaluation may be a practically indispensable condition of the restoration of a free market equilibrium. When, then, countries insist upon national monetary sovereignty—as they will—the goal of free enterprise requires, at the very minimum, that, if exchange rates are to be bound *at all*, a covenant run with the contract to establish a presumption that a country may, at its own discretion, with impunity, and without the consent of any other country, lower (or raise) the exchange value of its currency at any time and in any degree. (If it does not have this power it does not, of course, possess *full* sovereignty.) The presumption might be rebuttable, that is to say, there might be provision for the imposition of concerted sanctions whenever there was clear evidence that the devaluating action was taken with predatory intent. But the burden of proof should always lie on those who oppose a devaluation. The adoption of the suggested rule would be to universalize the practice under the British Exchange Equalization Account, especially in the years from 1934–1936. It is my conviction that the Equalization Account then provided Great Britain, and the world as a whole, with the best exchange situation we have had since World War I. With a flexible exchange rate the British international accounts automatically came into a balance that they have not known, before or since, during the period of monetary management in the modern sense, and the Equalization Fund might well have become the exemplar for all later "improvements" in international monetary organization.

There is, of course, good reason for so much exchange control as is necessary to prevent wide, non-functional, hour-to-hour, or day-to-day, fluctuations in rates, and also to stop fear-inspired flights from currencies. So much, the Equalization Account provided. Anything beyond this limited "control," however, should be anathema. The attempt to keep rates fixed over substantial periods of time, during which the relationship between independently determined national price levels is changing, is certain to cripple trade, evoke disequilibrium in the international accounts, and distort the composition of production in the several trading countries. A world of independent national currencies requires exchange rates that are readily mobile, in a free market, as the means of maintenance of a free international economy and, if exchange rates are not allowed to move in response to a practically inevitable shift in the relationship between uncorrelated national price levels, the ensuing exchange overpricing of the currency of a country of relatively rising price level not only, as already shown, puts a damper on its exports, and a premium on imports, but sets its production in a mould that will surely bedevil even the *eventual* balancing of its international trade structure. Export industries, and industries competing with imports, are rendered unprofitable, while domestic industries, including those ministering to investment beyond the saved income of the community and, therefore, furthering the inflation, are given a shot-in-the-arm. Industries in the former of these categories will thereupon wither while those in the latter wax. Balance in the international accounts can then be attained, if at all, only by drastic controls of imports, and a forced draft on exports, so that any prospect of a free economy goes out of the window.

Once the composition of the national industry is distorted under a currency overpriced on the exchange market, moreover, the power of vested interest, and the fear of unemployment in the overdeveloped domestic trades if the process is reversed, operates to keep the distortion in being. The notion then grows up, and is supported with a plethora of pseudo-erudition, that it is *impossible* for the country in question to balance its international trading position. This may, in very truth, be the case so long as the existing composition of its industry is maintained.

The Western World is yearning for free markets in face of the fact that it has, quite unwarrantably, lost faith in the free-market price as an (all but perfect) peace-time allocator of resources. It has for years, and even decades, been interfering in markets, and adopting *ad hoc* therapies and prophylactics in compensation of one economic ill after another, without any regard for ultimate consequences. It has thus been steadily undermining the general health of the patient. We are in urgent need of a fundamental diagnosis which, in my opinion, would compel the conclusion that, along with certain other agencies, the International Monetary Organization should, if not discarded, be radically transformed. The Organization asserts that it has no fixed ideas, that its administration is flexible, and that it can meet requirements as they arise. But there is little, if any, overt evidence of this, and persistence along the present lines will frustrate the very purpose for which the Fund was set up in that it will cumulate disequilibria, multiply and perpetuate controls, and shore up shaky structures until they finally collapse in all-round devastation. As things now are, the Fund even if it eventually sanctions a currency devaluation, must, if it is to restore equilibrium, permit a greater change in the exchange rate than would otherwise have been necessary. This follows from the fact that the devaluation should not merely be sufficient to rectify the current-account position of the country concerned but also clear up the floating debt accumulated under the prior overpricing of the country's currency as well as provide a strong incentive toward a reconstitution of its industry. The depreciation would, sooner or later, provoke a counter disequilibrium and require a revaluation in the opposite direction. All this is fundamentally much more disruptive of international business

than a free exchange rate is ever likely to be. The practice of changing rates by intermittent steps has the further disadvantage of violat-
ing the rule against giving a speculator a "sure thing." In doing so it
greatly enhances noxious speculation to the extreme discomfort of
the monetary authorities.

We are in urgent need of a substantially automatic international
monetary mechanism, persistently working toward equilibrium in
the international accounts, so that we do not cumulate the disequilibria that now continue to plague us. If we will not accept coordinated monetary systems we must frankly face the fact that fixed
exchange rates, even with a gesture toward flexibility, are a vicious
anachronism.[4] The only real solution is the operation of the price
mechanism in a free exchange market to equate national supply and
demand in international trade.

[4] When a country has used its autonomous right, under the International
Monetary Fund constitution, to effect a 10% change in the value of its currency,
is it precluded, *forever,* from any further similar action? Or does some Statute
of Limitation finally apply?

7. A LECTURE ON THE DOLLAR PROBLEM

Sir Donald MacDougall

Oxford University

Reprinted from *Economica, XXI* (new series) (August 1954), pp. 185–200, by permission of the author and the publisher.

Delivered at the London School of Economics and Political Science on 2nd March, 1954. This version was written later from notes used during the lecture. Apart from minor changes, it is intended to be as faithful a record as possible of what was said. The statistical results are provisional. Fuller explanations and more detailed development of the arguments used are reserved for a book which it is hoped will be published by Messrs. Macmillan & Co. Ltd. in 1955. [This book, *The World Dollar Problem: A Study in International Economics,* was published in 1957 (by St. Martin's Press in the United States). Some of the arguments in this article have been modified and some of the statistical results revised.]

The title of this lecture is obviously too wide. It is impossible to deal with the whole dollar problem in fifty minutes. It is necessary to select a few aspects, and even some of these can be dealt with only superficially. I am not clear in my own mind about the answers to some of the questions I shall raise; so perhaps you will regard this as a preliminary report—a throwing out of ideas, some of which may, I hope, be at least provocative.

SOME DEFINITIONS

One of the things there is no time to discuss is the definition of the dollar problem, but I must say briefly what I shall mean by it. I shall be talking about the *world* dollar problem, and not the dollar problem of Britain, the Sterling Area, or Europe; and about the *United States* dollar problem, not the problem of balancing trade between the whole of North America and the rest of the world.

I shall define a solution of the dollar problem as a situation in which there is an easy balance of payments between the United States and the rest of the world on current account, but allowing for normal long-term loans and grants. This balance must be achieved, or expected to be achieved, over a longish period, without discriminatory restrictions against American goods, and while preserving a reasonably high and free level of trade in the rest of the world, a reasonably high level of employment and rate of expansion (an important point), and reasonable terms of trade between the United States and the rest of the world.

This is, of course, an imprecise and question-begging definition. But I think this is probably inevitable because the dollar problem is partly a political one. And, if I may be allowed to say so in this School of Economics and Political Science, politics is not a very precise subject. The dollar problem is political in the sense that, for example, though it might be soluble if the rest of the world made sufficient sacrifices, yet, if it is thought politically undesirable or impracticable for these sacrifices to be made, the dollar problem remains.

I might mention in passing that, according to this definition, there can be a dollar problem even if currencies are convertible. Others have taken a different view. For example, Professor Mikesell, the American economist, has claimed that "during the 1930's there was no general dollar shortage since the key currencies were all convertible into dollars." This is true in the sense that no special shortage of dollars was apparent to the monetary authorities of the various countries, since other currencies could be freely converted into dollars. But there may still be a real dollar problem in such circumstances, according to my definition, if convertibility is maintained only at the expense of, for example, heavy unemployment in the rest of the world, as in the 1930's, or severe import restrictions against American goods.

So much for definitions. The main question I wish to consider is whether the dollar problem is chronic, whether it will be with us for the rest of our lives. But, to clear the ground, I should like to give brief answers to two preliminary questions—

First, has the dollar problem ever existed?

Secondly, does it still exist?

HAS THE DOLLAR PROBLEM EVER EXISTED?

The first question may seem a strange one to a British audience that has lived through the past eight years. But it has been argued, mainly perhaps in America, but also over here, that there never can be a real dollar shortage, because it is always curable by sufficient devaluation of non-dollar currencies and sufficient deflation in the non-dollar world. I have unfortunately no time to discuss this question. I can only say, briefly and brutally, that, in my view and according to my definition, the dollar problem could not have been solved in this way, at least in the early post-war years.

IS THERE STILL A DOLLAR PROBLEM?

It is not so easy to answer my second preliminary question—is there still a dollar problem?—because there has been a great improvement since the early post-war years.

In the free world outside the United States, industrial production has nearly doubled since 1946, and is now about half as great again as it was before the war. Food production in the free world outside North America has risen by perhaps one-quarter, although it has, unfortunately, not caught up with the rise in population since before the war, especially in the Far East.

Mainly as a result of this great recovery of production in the rest of the world the United States balance of payments has become much less one-sided. In the first two post-war years—1946–47—the rest of the world paid for only one-half of its purchases from the United States by earnings in that country. In the next two years—I am taking pairs of years because of the two-year cycle that has been apparent in the American balance of payments during most of the post-war period—the fraction was two-thirds; in the following two years, six-sevenths; and in the last two years—1952–53—the rest of the world has paid for about 95 per cent of its purchases from the United States, leaving out of account throughout military goods and services supplied free by the American Government.

This improvement has, moreover, been accompanied by, I should say, a relaxation of discriminatory restrictions against American goods, and, on the whole, of restrictions on non-dollar trade. The terms of trade have become better for the rest of the world, not worse; and there has not been much serious unemployment. There has therefore, according to my definition, been a great easing of the dollar problem.

There is also the much publicized fact that, during the fifteen months from the summer of 1952 to the autumn of 1953, the United

States was actually losing gold and dollars to the rest of the world at a rate of $2½ billion per annum.

In the light of all these encouraging facts, it is tempting to think that the dollar problem has been virtually solved. I think this would be a false deduction. A gain of $2½ billion per annum is by no means excessive for rebuilding the still exiguous reserves of the non-dollar world, especially as the United States was very prosperous during the period in question. It is right and proper that a surplus of at least this size should be earned in such periods to offset deficits when the United States is less prosperous.

A margin of $2½ billion is only about 5 per cent of the rest of the world's annual transactions with the United States, and we know from experience how quickly the position can be reversed. For example, in the year following the outbreak of war in Korea, the rest of the world was gaining gold and dollars from America at a considerably greater rate; and within a few months we were in the middle of another dollar crisis.

I therefore suggest that the margin during these fifteen months should, in prudence, be wholly discounted; and we are left with, at best, a balance. But this was not an easy balance. It was a precarious one, since it depended on, first, $2 billion a year of U.S. government loans and grants, other than military supplies. This is broadly "economic aid," which the Randall Commission has recommended should be brought to an end as soon as possible, at least on a grant basis.

The balance depended, secondly, on nearly $2½ billion a year of American military expenditure abroad. A considerable part of this expenditure is temporary, or at best precarious (though I am not suggesting that there is any danger of a large reduction in the near future), since it consists of off-shore purchases and of expenditure on military works abroad which will, presumably, sooner or later be completed.

The balance depended in the third place on $4 billion worth of military supplies given free by the American Government. If this form of aid ceased or was reduced, it might have to be replaced, in part at least, by the recipient countries.

Lastly, the balance depended on the suppression of demand for American goods through discriminatory restrictions imposed by other countries. I do not propose to put a figure to this nor to the total of the four points I have mentioned, but I am prepared to say that, in my view, there is still a real underlying gap of, shall we say, "a good many billions of dollars."

The gap is certainly much smaller than it was seven or eight years ago. But it is still uncomfortably large and it would be a grave mistake to think that it could be at all easily closed by devaluation or deflation or in any other way, without risking other serious difficulties.

IS THE DOLLAR PROBLEM CHRONIC?

I have answered two questions and that is enough. The dollar problem has existed and still exists. I am afraid I do not propose to answer my third and main question—is the dollar problem chronic? —for the good reason that I do not know the answer.

You may say that this is not a very interesting or useful question to ask. For, if I am right in thinking that there is still a dollar problem, surely we shall have to carry on for the time being with the same sort of policy as has been followed in recent years, irrespective of whether the problem is ultimately soluble or not.

I do not agree with this argument. I believe that a view on the longer-run dollar problem is of great importance in framing policy. If we think the dollar problem is permanently insoluble, there may be a case for starting here and now to build some kind of permanent non-dollar bloc in isolation from America. If, on the other hand, we think the problem is not necessarily insoluble, there is a strong argument for patience and for avoiding a course that would inevitably be fraught with grave economic and political dangers.

In our policy during the next few years, it is not just what we do that matters, but the way we do it. There is all the difference in the world between (i) working with the United States for one multilateral world, or even one-and-a-half worlds (perhaps the sort of world outlined by Mr. Day in his recent stimulating book on *The Future of Sterling*), while explaining that it would be foolish to rush into it too quickly; and (ii) telling the Americans that they are impossible people to live with, that they are bad creditors and have a stagnating, fluctuating economy, and that we therefore propose to make our own independent arrangements.

Such a line would, incidentally, be rather tactless at a time when the Americans are pouring $20–$25 billion a year into the rest of the world, when their level of activity has been much higher and more stable since the war than anyone dared to hope, and when their barriers to imports are no higher than those of many other countries.

I therefore conclude that it is interesting and useful to ask the question: "Is the dollar problem chronic?" I do not know the answer. I am not too optimistic. But, in view of the great improvement during the past eight years, one cannot be unduly pessimistic.

I should like to deal with the question by considering four main lines of argument that have been used in the attempt to show that the dollar problem is chronic.

First, the appeal to the experience of the last forty years.

Secondly, arguments drawn from the fact that the American productivity is so much higher than productivity elsewhere.

Thirdly, arguments derived from the belief that productivity grows faster in the United States than in the rest of the world. (This type of argument is sometimes confused with the second, but is quite different.)

Fourthly, arguments based on the whole economic and political structure of the United States in relation to the rest of the world. This type of argument examines the outlook for American exports, imports and foreign investment and, taking account of political considerations, reaches gloomy conclusions.

This is not a comprehensive list of arguments, and some of them overlap. But I hope you will accept the classification for the purposes of this lecture. I propose to remind you briefly of what the arguments are, and spend a longer time on criticism of them. This does not mean that I am necessarily optimistic. But the arguments tending to establish the chronic nature of the dollar problem have probably received more attention in this country, and I should perhaps try to do something to redress the balance.

A. The appeal to past experience

First, the appeal to past experience. It is argued that the dollar problem has been with us most of the time since 1914—for the last forty years—and there is therefore a presumption that it will continue.

The trouble with this argument is that there was no dollar problem during the prosperous period of the 1920's (say, 1923–29), at least according to my definition, and, I think, according to most authorities. And the rest of the period was abnormal. It consisted of two great wars and their aftermath and one great slump, in the 1930's.

If, then, there are no more big wars and no more big slumps, there may be no more big dollar problems. At least, it would be a bold man who would prophesy chronic dollar shortage simply on the basis of the last forty years' experience, especially in view of the great improvement since the end of the second world war.

B. Productivity higher in the United States than in the rest of the world

The second line of argument, in its crude form, argues that, since productivity is higher in America than it is elsewhere, all American goods will be cheaper than those produced in the rest of the world. This can, of course, be easily refuted by the theory of comparative costs.

There is, however, another form of the argument which is much more serious. It is what I call the "films argument." It has been well described in a recent book by Professor Nurkse, who has drawn on the so-called "demonstration effect" of Professor Duesenberry. In simplified form the argument runs as follows:

Higher productivity in America means higher standards of living there. As a result of modern means of communication these standards are becoming better and better known in other countries, and there is more and more attempt to emulate them. This is impossible because productivity is so much lower in the rest of the world. There is thus a constant tendency for countries other than the U.S. to live beyond their means, through pressure for higher consumption today and pressure on or by governments to carry our large investment programmes to raise the standard of living tomorrow. This means inflationary pressure, a tendency to balance of payments deficit with the United States, in other words, dollar shortage.

This may well be the strongest argument for chronic dollar shortage, but I feel bound to mention some difficulties I have in accepting it fully. Drawing first on my own personal experience, the only American newspaper I read at all regularly—the *New Yorker*—is full of advertisements which seem to be largely devoted to persuading Americans to buy foreign goods, not the other way around. I sometimes wonder, too, whether there may not in time be a reaction against attempts to spread the American way of life such as that exemplified by the Coca Cola stall I saw a few years ago on the roof of Milan Cathedral.

More seriously, the argument I am discussing would lead one to expect an inverse relation between a country's standard of living and the state of its balance of payments. But this is not evident in the real world. Since the end of the war, at least, many relatively rich countries, like France, Britain and Australia, have had recurrent balance of payments difficulties, while relatively poor countries like Portugal and many of the British Colonies have had reasonably favourable balances of payments.

Nor is there any clear inverse relationship between the closeness of a country's contact with the United States and its balance of payments. The Central American republics, for example, have in general had more comfortable balances of payments since the war than many other countries with comparable standards of living but in less close contact with the United States.

We must remember, too, that Americans, as well as other people, desire a higher standard of living. They are, after all, the most exposed to high pressure salesmanship and advertisement. And we are often told that one reason for the higher American productivity is the great desire of the American worker to improve his lot, while the Briton, for example, is more content as he is.

Throughout history, moreover, the masses in most countries have been exposed to the "demonstration effect" through the sight of the very high standards of living of the rich in their midst, standards most conspicuously displayed. One wonders why a few American films and American soldiers in their country should suddenly make so much difference.

It may be, of course, that the presence of G.I.'s, for example, has shown that it is possible for the *masses* to be well off, and shaken long held fatalistic beliefs in the inevitability of poverty except for the very few. But this is extremely vague. I am straying into the realms of sociology, about which I know even less than I know about politics. Despite the questions and difficulties I have raised, some of which are not wholly fair and most of which have answers, I think there may well be a great deal in this line of argument. But I doubt whether the evidence is really strong enough to conclude that, for this reason alone, the dollar problem is necessarily chronic.

The higher level of American productivity may, of course, have another consequence. Since it leads to a higher real income per head, it may make it easier for Americans to save, and this may make possible a higher rate of increase of productivity in America. But this takes me on to the third type of argument.

C. The faster rate of growth of American productivity

The arguments connected with the faster rate of growth of American productivity have been well and elegantly analysed by Professor Hicks in his Inaugural Lecture as Drummond Professor of Political Economy in Oxford.

I am in general agreement with his first main proposition. This is, very simply, that, if American productivity is rising faster than productivity elsewhere, and American money incomes do not rise correspondingly faster or nearly so, there will be recurring balance of payments crises in other countries because their prices will be continuously getting out of line. The argument stated thus is, I believe, generally true (though not necessarily so). But I think the model used by Professor Hicks tends to exaggerate the difficulty because it assumes—

First, that productivity in the rest of the world is stationary, whereas in fact it goes up quite a lot;
Secondly, that American money wages do not normally rise as fast as American productivity, whereas in fact they often do.

Professor Hicks concludes, on the basis of these assumptions, that money wages in the rest of the world will have to fall if equilibrium is to be maintained with the United States. This would, of course, raise very difficult problems. But in fact it may not be necessary.

It is quite likely that in the future American wages may rise by as much as, say, 4–5 per cent per annum in peace time. Hourly factory earnings have risen by an average of about 4 per cent per annum during this century, leaving out the years when America was at war (when the rise was accelerated) and the great depression of the 1930's (which caused wages to fall). Since the end of the last war American wages have been rising by, on average, as much as 7 per cent per annum.

The problem for the United Kingdom, for example, may therefore be, not to reduce money wages, but to limit the rise to, say, 3–4 per cent per annum, while American wages are rising by, say, 4–5 per cent per annum. This may be very difficult indeed, but it is not necessarily an impossible task for wages policy, especially when we remember that, since the end of the war, British hourly earnings in manufacturing *in terms of sterling* have gone up no faster than American hourly earnings *in terms of dollars* despite the devaluation of 30 per cent.

Professor Hicks also analyses the consequences of different rates of growth of productivity in different industries; improvements in productivity may be what he calls "import-biased" or "export-biased." That part of his argument relevant to our problem seems to be as follows. Productivity in American agriculture is increasing relatively slowly. The United States is an exporter of agricultural products. This is bad for the rest of the world and will turn the terms of trade against them.

I find it hard to apply this argument to the present situation. Since before the war, American productivity per man-hour seems to have gone up faster in agriculture than in industry, not slower. Secondly, the United States is a net importer of agricultural products, not a net exporter; only about one-fifth of her exports consists of agricultural products. Thirdly, the terms of trade—Professor Hicks' measure of the dollar problem—have moved against the United States and not in her favour.

I find certain other difficulties in Professor Hicks' analysis. For example, I am sorry that he ignores differing income elasticities of demand for his different types of goods; I think these can be very important. And he seems at times to confuse the *dollar* problem with what I call the *British* problem of paying for our imports from all parts. But I have no time to discuss these questions. I may well have misunderstood him but, though I find his analysis most stimulating, I doubt whether, in its present form, it can be applied to the problem now before us.

I now wish to be rather unorthodox and cast some doubt on the general belief that American productivity does increase so much faster than productivity in the rest of the world—at least in peace time. I think we sometimes suffer from an optical illusion here. We can easily be misled by comparing a recent pre-war year (such as 1937 or the average of 1934–38), when the United States was depressed, with a post-war year like 1949 or 1950 when the rest of the world had not fully recovered from the war. In making comparisons of Britain and America we can also be misled if we ignore the very fast growth in the American population. This is increasing by nearly one million every four months—there are one million more Americans today than there were at the beginning of last term. The American population has risen by 25 per cent since 1937, a year often used for comparisons with the present. During the same period the United Kingdom population has risen by only about 7 per cent.

I have been making some calculations about long-term trends in production—not productivity—in the United States and in the rest of the world (excluding Russia and China for which there are no good figures). Here are some preliminary and provisional results.

Raw Materials. Since 1913 production of raw materials as a whole has increased more quickly in the rest of the world than in the United States. This is true even if allowance is made for the growth of synthetic production and even if we include Canada with the United States and not with the rest of the world.

Food. United States production of food has, it is true, more than doubled since 1900. But the American population has risen very nearly as much, and there has been only a very small growth in food production per head of the population. The figures are less reliable for the rest of the world, but it seems likely that food production has gone up in roughly the same proportion as population.

Manufactures. During the last fifty years production of manufactures has increased faster in the United States—by about $3\frac{1}{2}$ per cent per annum against $2\frac{1}{2}$ per cent per annum in the rest of the world. But this has happened only during the two great wars, not in peace time. During the decade before the first world war it seems that manufacturing production was growing at roughly the same rate in America and in the rest of the world. During the inter-war years it was growing faster in the rest of the world—not only in the slump of the 1930's when the U.S. was more depressed than most other countries, but also during the prosperous years of the 1920's. Since the end of the second world war production has, of course, increased much more in the rest of the world—very much faster in the early post-war period and at about the same average rate as in the U.S. in more recent years.

It is true that the United States' fast rate of growth during the wars has more than offset her slower growth in peace time. But if we try to allow for the much greater dislocation and damage caused by the wars in the rest of the world, by ruling out the years of war and only two extra years for the aftermath in each case—if we assume that these years never happened in the rest of the world—we find that the rate of growth outside America is raised from $2\frac{1}{2}$ to $3\frac{1}{2}$ per cent per annum, the same as in the United States.

If we take these three main forms of physical production together (raw materials, food and manufactures) it seems that physical output in the rest of the world has increased roughly as fast as in the United States, making a modest allowance for the two wars and allowing for the faster growth of the American population.

It is, of course, possible that total output of goods *and services* per *man-hour* has increased faster in the United States, even in peace time, if (i) leisure has been increasing faster in the United States, though it is by no means certain that this has been an important factor, or (ii) the output of services has been increasing faster in America—probably more significant. In general, total output per man-hour probably does increase faster in the United States than in the rest of the world, even in peace time. But the difference may not be nearly so great as is sometimes supposed.

D. The economic and political structure of the United States in relation to the rest of the world

The fourth line of argument is in terms of economic and political structure. Here again I shall begin by outlining briefly some arguments—mostly rather familiar—that tend to establish the chronic nature of dollar shortage. I shall consider in turn United States exports, imports and foreign investment.

1. U.S. exports. It can be argued that there will always be a large and insistent demand for American manufactures, because the Americans always have the latest things; and for American primary products, because the United States, with her vast natural resources and large supplies of capital and technology, is the one place where primary production can be rapidly expanded whenever the rest of the world goes short. And the rest of the world may well go short, at least from time to time, especially of food.

Professor Dudley Stamp, in his stimulating book, *Our Underdeveloped World,* has suggested that the main scope for increasing world food production in the forseeable future lies in North America and Russia. (There are also possibilities of large increases, percentagewise, in such countries as Australia, New Zealand, and the Argentine, but these are of much less importance in absolute terms.) Leaving out Russia—at the expense of ignoring some interesting possibilities—we are left with a picture of food production growing mainly in North America while the main increase in the population to be fed, in absolute numbers, is in the rest of the world. This suggests a tendency for the rest of the world to demand American food.

2. *U.S. imports.* It is argued that the United States can produce almost anything in replacement of imports, again because of her vast natural resources, her large number of technologists who are constantly discovering substitutes for imports, and her plentiful capital which makes it possible to exploit these discoveries quickly and cheaply.

There tends, moreover, to be political pressure to replace imports, not only because of the American political system, but also because there is comparatively little opposition from consumers. The extra cost to them is often hardly noticeable because imports form so small a fraction of the national income and the additional cost of home production is often not very great.

3. *Foreign investment.* It is argued that there is no great incentive for Americans to invest abroad. This is largely, I think, because the United States is the major under-developed country in the world, and yields are therefore very high on investments within her borders. In this respect the United States today is very different from the United Kingdom in the nineteenth century.

It is also argued that the Americans have little experience of foreign investment; and since they had their fingers burnt in the inter-war years, they demand a high extra risk premium.

Lastly, if the balance on annual foreign investment and income on this investment taken together is to become more favourable for the rest of the world, American investment abroad has to increase year by year at a rate greater than the yield on foreign investments. It is argued that the latter is high, perhaps as much as 15 per cent, and that American annual investment abroad is unlikely to increase so fast. (This argument, of course, ignores the favourable effects on the rest of the world's balance of payments of American foreign investment that encourages the production of commodities which will earn or save dollars.)

Counter-arguments

So much for all these rather familiar, but none the less powerful, arguments. Now may I give you some arguments on the other side —some reasons why the dollar problem may not be so difficult to solve? I wish to suggest that United States exports may be potentially vulnerable and United States imports what I call "potentially explosive."

First, then, the potential vulnerability of American exports, taking primary products and manufactures in turn.

The United States is an important net exporter of only four major *primary products:* grain, coal, cotton and tobacco. It may be that the very large exports of grain and coal since the war—far higher than pre-war exports—have been merely a flash in the pan, the result of temporary shortage in the rest of the world resulting from the dislocation caused by the war. U.S. exports of raw cotton are threatened by synthetic production abroad. Her tobacco exports are relatively small in dollar value and production in the rest of the world could fairly easily increase faster than consumption.

American exports of *manufactures* are vulnerable because American wages are so high. They are over three-and-a-half times the British per hour, compared with only two-and-a-half times before the war. The margin is still greater if the comparison is made with many other industrial countries. But U.S. productivity is not three-and-a-half times as high in many lines; it must always be remembered that American techniques are generally available to other countries. It may be, too, that the industrialisation of new countries will hit the United States as it has hit Britain in the past. Cars and refrigerators may prove to be the cotton textiles of tomorrow.

Now for the potentially explosive nature of American imports. This arises from the fact that many American imports are supplementary to home production and form only a marginal part of total consumption. For example, the United States draws about 5 per cent of her iron ore supplies from abroad, 5–10 per cent of her lumber and oil and perhaps 20 per cent of her copper.

This means that, if the United States pursued a protectionist policy, she could easily whittle away her imports. This is one of the frightening possibilities. If, on the other hand, she pursued a reasonably liberal policy, her imports could expand greatly if consumption ran even a little ahead of production.

This is what has been happening with raw materials throughout the present century. The United States has been changing from a net exporter to a net importer of one commodity after another, and especially of oil, most of the metals and forest products. In perhaps over-simplified terms, the frontier has been reached. America has exploited her easiest mines and wells and cut down her virgin forests. The annual drain on American timber suitable for the saw-mills is now 50 per cent in excess of the annual growth.

Taking raw materials as a whole we find that during the first half of this century American production has been increasing by roughly 1½ per cent per annum, while her consumption has been growing by 2 per cent per annum. Such a small difference may seem relatively unimportant but over a period of decades it can have quite striking results.

In 1900 the United States was producing about 15 per cent more raw materials than she was consuming, the balance being "net exported." By 1925 consumption had nearly caught up with production. By 1950 it was 10 per cent greater. If these trends continue, American consumption of raw materials in 1975 will be nearly 25 per cent in excess of production. (Physically, this is not unlikely, since the United States seems to be using up her reserves of nearly all important minerals, except coal, faster than the rest of the world.)

If this does happen during the third quarter of the century, a rise in total American consumption of raw materials of two-thirds (roughly the possible increase forecast by the Paley Commission) would increase her net imports of raw materials between three and four times. This is what I mean by the "explosive potentialities" of American imports. There is a kind of "scissors" effect. The curve of consumption is rising more steeply than the curve of production and the difference between the two curves—net imports—rises very much faster, proportionately, than either of the two curves.

In food the same sort of thing has been happening, but to a rather less striking extent. American food imports have trebled in quantity during this century and are now about as big as our own. The United States has changed from a net exporter to a net importer of food. Fifty years ago her exports were twice the value of her imports. Now her imports are nearly twice the value of her exports. This has been a fairly steady trend interrupted only by the two world wars and their aftermath.

I would be the first to admit that American production of food can easily go up as fast as American consumption. There is great scope for increasing yields per acre, which are far lower than in N.W. Europe. But if this were done by the method recommended by Professor Stamp—the copying of N.W. European methods, which means small-scale, mixed farming—and if this required a good deal of labour, I sometimes wonder whether American food might not become rather expensive.

But I am no agricultural expert. In practice, American food production probably will rise at least nearly as fast as consumption. I should like to emphasize, however, that even a small, temporary failure of production to keep pace with consumption could put an enormous extra demand on to world food supplies moving in international trade.

Possible effects on the United Kingdom

This could be a serious matter for the United Kingdom. It is a sobering thought that, roughly every seven years, Americans eat an extra amount of food equal to the whole of our food imports. This is, of course, because there are so many of them, because they multiply so rapidly, and because they eat so much.

It may be objected that the United States does not import the same kind of food as we do—that they import things like coffee. My reply would be, first, that all food, including coffee, uses agricultural resources which could usually be devoted to other purposes, at least in the long run. In the second place, the United States *is* a big importer of a good many foods which Britain also buys from abroad, such as sugar, cocoa, fish, certain vegetable oil, oilseeds and oilcake. She is even a substantial importer of beef. I was rather shocked to discover recently that, in the years 1951 and 1952, American imports of beef and veal were half as great as our own. (Admittedly, these were bad years for us because of trouble with the Argentine.) But these American imports, though large in relation to ours, were only about 4 per cent of American consumption. If, therefore, the United States were to take 8 per cent of her beef and veal supplies from abroad instead of 4 per cent this would deprive us of half our own imports, at least on the 1951–52 level.

When people tell me that the United States could get meat and dairy produce from abroad at only perhaps half the price paid to her own farmers, I sometimes thank providence for American agricultural protectionism.

All this reminds us that, if the Dollar Problem were solved by a large increase in American imports of primary products, this might simply reveal in all its nakedness the British (or European) Problem of paying for imports of food and raw materials in a world where demand for these is growing rapidly. We might be out of the frying pan into the fire, and have a terms of trade problem substituted for a dollar problem.

Such an outcome is, fortunately, not inevitable. We might get the best of both worlds—and solve both our problems—if primary production abroad expanded sufficiently rapidly to meet both the growing demands of America and those of Britain and other industrial countries at a reasonable price.

There is also, however, a third and alarming possibility. We might be both in the frying pan and in the fire. This could happen if the output of primary products abroad expanded so slowly, and their prices rose so much, that they priced themselves out of the American market; the Americans might find it cheaper to produce for themselves. If this happened, we could have both a dollar problem and a terms of trade problem.

It seems then that the expansion of primary production overseas may be one of the keys to both of our problems. What are the prospects? It is impossible to say, but it is not necessary to be too gloomy, at least judging by past experience.

We have seen that since 1913 the production of raw materials has increased faster in the rest of the world than it has in the United States. At the same time, consumption of raw materials has been increasing faster in the United States than in the rest of the world. The United States has obtained about one-third of her extra needs from abroad (by importing more and exporting less). The rest of the world has used over one-quarter of its extra production to "feed" the growing demands of American industry.

Food production has, it is true, increased rather more slowly in the rest of the world than it has increased in the United States. But it has at least roughly kept pace with population. The rest of the world has not become more dependent on United States supplies, as an analysis based on Professor Stamp's argument might have led one to expect.

The price elasticity of demand for U.S. imports

One final point before summing up. Thinking about these problems has suggested to me that, contrary to popular belief, the price elasticity of demand for U.S. imports may be quite high, at least in the longer run, and *when American import prices rise*. For there are then great possibilities in the United States of (i) producing synthetic substitutes for imports, (ii) economising in the use of imported materials (switching from timber to steel, from sisal to wire; more intensive use of scrap; making tin cans without tin; and so on), (iii) using America's own natural resources. For example, if the price of imported oil rose 20–25 per cent I understand that the vast American reserves of oil shale would become economic to exploit. Similarly, if the price of foreign iron ore rose sufficiently, it would pay to use the huge low-grade reserves in the United States.

All this may, unfortunately, have a tendency to pull the American demand curve for imports over to the left. For whenever foreign prices rise—even temporarily—this may encourage a large and rapid development of substitutes and the like. But if, later, foreign prices fall, this will not restore the old demand for imports; because the new technical knowledge acquired will not be lost and the new synthetic factories take a long time to wear out. The whole comparative cost structure has in fact been altered to the disadvantage of the rest of the world.

If there is a "kinked" demand curve for American imports, this may also mean a tendency to dollar shortage for another reason. If the rest of the world were to run into *surplus* with the United States, equilibrium could be easily and quickly restored by a fairly small rise in prices in the rest of the world. But when the rest of the world has a dollar *shortage*, it may be much more difficult to restore equilibrium because a fall in the rest of the world's prices may have only a slow and painful expansionary effect on American purchases from abroad. If, therefore, there are random fluctuations in the factors affecting trade between the United States and the rest of the world, there may be longer periods of dollar shortage than the reverse—in other words, a tendency to dollar shortage.

CONCLUSION

On the main question of whether the dollar problem is chronic I am, as I have said, an agnostic. This is because there seem to me to be strong forces working in each direction, and it is hard to say which will come out on top.

It may be that the most important factor will be a tendency of the rest of the world to live beyond its means, in the vain attempt to emulate American standards. But the factors connected with economic and political structure may be equally important. If, as many would argue, these also work against solving the dollar problem, the outlook may be bleak. But if they work favourably—and I have given some reasons for thinking that this may not be impossible— they may overcome any tendency of the rest of the world to live beyond its means.

Prophecy about the dollar problem is as difficult and dangerous as prophecy about the balance between savings and investment. Those who, before the war, claimed that a tendency to unemployment was inevitable in an advanced economy have had to eat their words. It may be that those who now foresee chronic inflation will prove to be equally wide of the mark. Likewise, in my opinion, it would require a very courageous man to forecast either chronic dollar shortage or its absence during the coming decades. I for one lack the necessary courage.

8. AMERICAN PRODUCTIVITY AND THE DOLLAR PAYMENTS PROBLEM

E.M. Bernstein

Reprinted by permission of the author and of the Harvard University Press, Cambridge, Mass., from *The Review of Economics and Statistics*, XXXVII (May 1955), pp. 101–109. Copyright, 1955, by the President and Fellows of Harvard College. At the time of original publication, the author was Director of the Research Department of the International Monetary Fund; the views stated are personal views.

The recent postwar payments difficulties were probably more widespread and of greater magnitude than those that emerged after World War I. There is no evidence, however, that the postwar payments difficulties were fundamentally different in origin or that they have been more persistent than those after World War I. It has been fashionable, nevertheless, to speak of the postwar payments problem this time as one of dollar scarcity, and this concept seems to be the basis for far-reaching and wholly unjustified conclusions regarding the causes of recent payments difficulties and the proper direction of future payments policy.

PAYMENTS DIFFICULTIES AND SCARCE CURRENCIES

If there is to be a real understanding of the postwar payments problem, it is essential to distinguish between a true dollar scarcity and widespread payments difficulties. The causes of a true dollar scarcity must lie in economic conditions and economic policies in the United States. Otherwise, the so-called dollar scarcity would merely be the focal point for the payments difficulties of a number of countries, which difficulties could originate in economic conditions and economic policies outside the United States.

The so-called dollar scarcity of the postwar period was actually a scarcity of real resources. A large number of countries decided to maintain a level of consumption and investment that was in excess of their output and that could not be covered by normal borrowing. In some instances, the destruction of production facilities made it difficult to limit consumption and investment to the low level of output of the early postwar years. In other instances, expectations of consumption and investment exceeded what the economy could produce. Whatever the cause, for political, social, and economic reasons, consumption and investment were allowed to exceed output, and the excess manifested itself as a balance of payments deficit. Because the goods demanded could be procured quickly, easily, and relatively cheaply in the United States, the payments deficits were very largely (although not exclusively) with this country.

There can be no great objection to using the term "dollar scarcity" or "dollar shortage" to describe the postwar payments problem, provided the terminology does not lead us to ignore its true nature and to prescribe false remedies. If the actual basis for the postwar payments problem was a widespread but temporary shortage of real resources, then deficits were necessary and desirable, and the proper policy was to provide the deficit countries with additional resources. This was, in fact, done through the Marshall Plan and in other ways. On the other hand, if the actual basis for the postwar payments problem was an inability to sell available export goods to the United States, then deficits were unnecessary and undesirable, and the proper policy would have been to find means to increase the demand for imports in the United States.

Although the postwar payments problem was fundamentally caused by a shortage of real resources, undesirable financial and exchange policies may have contributed to the inability of countries to sell as much of their exports to the United States as they would have wished. Definitely, however, it was not inadequacy of aggregate demand in the United States that made it difficult for countries to sell as much of their exports on tolerably good terms as would have been necessary for a fully employed but balanced internal economy. Because of such implications as to causes and remedies, it seems preferable to reserve the concept of a dollar scarcity to the case intended at Bretton Woods—a marked inadequacy of dollar receipts arising from a sharp decline in United States imports.[1]

---

[1] This is the view expressed in my paper, "Scarce Currencies and the International Monetary Fund," *Journal of Political Economy*, LIII (March 1945), 1–14. That paper presented the views of the American technicians at Bretton

In any event, the concept of dollar scarcity provides no real explanation of the postwar payments difficulties unless the term can be linked to real economic forces working in the United States and in the world economy. One reason frequently put forward as the alleged cause of the postwar payments difficulties is the more rapid growth in productivity in the United States than in other countries. It has even been suggested that the problem is a very old one, that there has long been a chronic dollar scarcity, but that it was clearly recognized only in the postwar period because it became much more acute. As Professor Williams puts it, the "wars hastened processes of change already under way, and . . . the successive short run crises have been primarily the symptoms of longer-run and deeper-seated maladjustments in international relationships that go back for at least three-quarters of a century." [2]

More recently, as the payments of the rest of the world with the

---

Woods. My impression is that the concept of dollar scarcity was used by the British economists to describe the same problem. See, for example, what Keynes wrote in an analysis of the future of dollar payments: "All that can be said on the other side [against Keynes's view that the dollar payments problem can be solved] is that these figures do not show what would happen in a period of slump in the United States and of full employment in the rest of the world." *Economic Journal*, LVI (June 1946), 173.

Professor Lionel Robbins explicitly distinguishes the dollar shortage we have had from the dollar scarcity that was feared. In his essay on the dollar shortage, he says: ". . . the dollar shortage which has actually emerged is entirely different in respect of origin from the shortage predicted by those to whom Keynes alluded." (*The Economist in the Twentieth Century*, London, 1954, p. 42.)

[2] John H. Williams in the Stamp Memorial Lecture, *Economic Stability in the Modern World* (London, 1952), p. 9.

Professor D.H. Robertson, in *Britain and the World Economy* (London, 1954), pp. 56–57, also subscribes to the view that the "dollar shortage is not a purely wartime or postwar phenomenon, but traces of it, to put it mildly, can be found over the preceding quarter-century."

Professor J.R. Hicks, in "An Inaugural Lecture," *Oxford Economic Papers*, N.S. V (June 1953), 131, is quite explicit. "It is true that the forms in which the dollar problem has actually appeared have constantly tempted us to regard it as something much less deep-rooted . . . A special explanation of the difficulties which were being experienced by European countries in settling their dollar debts could always be found. But the continuance of the same consequence, the same dollar shortage, as the result of these various 'causes' has by now become very striking. That there is some general influence underlying these particular manifestations can now no longer be doubted. It is hard to see that there is another general force which would account for what has been happening than the disparity in growth of productivity which we have been discussing."

For a full discussion of other views along similar lines, see Charles P. Kindleberger, *The Dollar Shortage* (Cambridge, Mass., 1950), esp. ch. 8.

United States, before receipt of economic aid, have approached balance, there has been less emphasis on the so-called intractability of the dollar problem. Nevertheless, the fear persists that the improvement in dollar payments is temporary and that the postwar dollar scarcity may recur, although on a more moderate scale. Above all, there is still a tendency to regard the United States as too formidable a competitor in international markets. The supposed adverse effects of American productivity on international payments are put forward as reasons for maintaining discrimination against dollar trade and for avoiding the heightened international competition that is implicit in establishing convertibility of the currencies of the large trading countries.

The assertion that productivity in the United States is increasing at a greater rate than in other countries requires considerable qualification. More likely, the differences in per capita output between the United States and some other technically advanced countries are proportionately about the same now as they were half a century ago, and for a few countries absolute differences between per capita output and that of the United States have actually declined during recent decades.[3] It will be assumed, nevertheless, that productivity in the United States is increasing more rapidly than in other countries, and the question will be considered whether disparate rates of growth in productivity can or must cause a dollar scarcity and a world-wide payments problem.

Relative differences in productivity are the very basis for international trade, and differences in the rate of increase in productivity in various countries merely intensify or moderate this basis for international trade. There is nothing in traditional economic analysis that would indicate that a world-wide payments problem could emerge from different rates of increase in productivity in various countries.[4] There may, however, be cases in which failure to make adjustments promptly to changing productivity relationships may cause widespread and persistent payments difficulties.[5] Individual

---

[3] Sir Donald MacDougall in "A Lecture on the Dollar Problem" at the London School of Economics, March 7, 1954, published in *Economica*, N.S. XXI (August 1954), 192, states: "I now wish to be rather unorthodox and cast some doubt on the general belief that American productivity does increase so much faster than productivity in the rest of the world—at least in peacetime."

[4] This is the point emphasized by F.D. Graham in "The Cause and Cure of Dollar Shortage," *Essays in International Finance* (Princeton, 1949).

[5] Professor D.H. Robertson observes "that when one of the partners to its operation is a country of multifarious resources and towering strength, the law

countries, of course, may be confronted with severe payments difficulties, temporary or persistent, because of the consequences of a
rapid increase in productivity in other countries, particularly in so
large an economy as the United States.

PRODUCTIVITY AND COMPETITIVE COSTS

To simplify the first approach to the problem, assume that productivity in the United States increases uniformly in the three
sectors of the American economy—export goods, import-competing
domestic goods, all other domestic goods. Assume also that productivity is unchanged in other countries. Assume further that the
general level of incomes (for convenience, wages) rises in the
United States promptly in proportion to the increase in productivity.
In that case, money costs of production would remain unchanged
for all types of goods. The competitive position of foreign producers
in terms of costs would be precisely what it was before the increase
in American productivity. They could compete in the United States
and in third markets with their export goods, and in their home
markets against American export goods, on the same relative price
basis as before the increase in American productivity.

In fact, such a general increase in American productivity ought to
bring about a strengthening of the payments position of other countries. With the increase in incomes in the United States, the general
level of demand would rise—for import goods as well as for domestic
goods. As incomes in other countries would not have risen, their
demand for United States exports would be unchanged. In the first
instance, there would be a larger increase in United States imports
than in United States exports, and a deficit would emerge in the
balance of payments. In order to assure a sufficient increase in
United States exports to balance the increase in imports, it would be
necessary for wage rates in the United States to rise somewhat less
than the increase in American productivity.[6]

---

of comparative advantage, for all its inexorable truth, needs a string of footnotes." (*Britain in the World Economy*, p. 62). The essence of Professor
Robertson's point is that large and rapid changes in productivity in the United
States impose frequent and costly adjustments in the trade patterns of other
countries which they may be unable to undertake.

[6] This is the conclusion reached by H.G. Johnson, "Increasing Productivity,
Income-Price Trends and the Trade Balance," *Economic Journal*, LXIV (September 1954), 462–85. Increases in productivity in a one-product economy have
effects similar to a uniform increase in productivity in all industries.

The case is not essentially different if there is also a uniform increase in productivity in the rest of the world, but at a lesser rate than in the United States. One new factor would have to be taken into account. Assume that in other countries, as in the United States, wages are increased in proportion to the increase in productivity. The relative price-cost position is, therefore, unchanged. But if other countries have a higher income elasticity of demand for imports than the United States, difficulties could emerge. For the increase in incomes in the rest of the world, even if smaller than in the United States, could result in a larger increase in the demand for United States exports than in the United States demand for imports. The cause, however, would not be that American productivity had risen too much, but that it had risen too little relative to that of the rest of the world.

The assumption that the increase in productivity is uniform in all sectors of the American economy is favorable for avoiding a dollar payments problem. Let this now be modified to assume that in the United States productivity in the export industries increases uniformly and more rapidly than in other sectors of the economy. Assume that in other countries, however, productivity in the export industries increases uniformly but less rapidly than in other sectors of the economy. Finally, assume that in all countries wages rise in proportion to the average increase in productivity and that the average increase in productivity is considerably greater in the United States than in other countries.

As the increase in productivity in the United States export industries will be greater than the average of American industry, United States export production costs and prices will tend to fall. In other countries, because the increase in productivity in their export industries will be less than the average for all industry, export production costs and prices will tend to rise. On a price-cost basis the competitive position of their exporters will have been impaired in third markets where they compete with American exports. It may or may not have been impaired in their home markets where their home goods compete with American exports and in United States markets where their exports compete with American home goods.

The strengthening of the price-competitive position of United States exporters does not itself indicate that the payments position of the rest of the world will be impaired. For it is also assumed that incomes have risen substantially more in the United States than in the rest of the world. If the income elasticity of demand for imports is not very much lower in this country than abroad, the effects of the larger increase in United States incomes may offset the effects of the relative fall in United States export prices, and United States imports may increase as much as United States exports. If the income elasticity of demand for imports in other countries is substantially higher than in the United States, however, the effects of the larger increase in incomes on United States imports may not be enough to offset the effects of the stronger price-competitive position on exports.

In brief, if increases in productivity in American export industries run ahead of those in other industries, and if increases in productivity in foreign export industries lag behind those in other foreign industries, then the price-competitive position of American exporters will become stronger if wages in all countries are increased in proportion to the average increase in productivity. The payments problem that would then emerge could be attributed to the exceptionally rapid increase in productivity in American export industries. Alternatively, it could be attributed to a mistaken wage policy (in the United States or abroad) which relates the increase in wages to the increase in *average* productivity.

PRODUCTIVITY CHANGES AND ECONOMIC ADJUSTMENTS

Changes in productivity are very likely to require adjustments of some kind, either to avoid or to correct imbalance in international payments. Where the changes in productivity are of a uniform character—that is, where they are spread over the entire economy or over one entire sector, such as the export industries—the adjustments that must be made are essentially of a monetary character. They should not, in general, require far-reaching structural changes in the economy.

The classical theory assumes that balance of payments equilibrium in gold-standard countries is established through price, wage, and exchange rate mechanisms. In such a world the general level of money incomes is in the long run related to the production of gold, modified by institutional changes that limit the dependence of monetary policy on reserves of gold. If the growth in the money supply is at approximately the same rate as the increase in aggregate production, money incomes can rise about in proportion to the increase in productivity. In any one country in which productivity is increasing more rapidly than in the world as a whole, money incomes will, of course, rise differentially to about the same extent as the differential increase in productiivty. This is the general relationship between incomes and productivity that is inherent in the classical theory of trade and payments.

Nassau W. Senior, in an attempt to relate money wages more specifically to productivity, held that a proper balance of payments will be maintained when wage rates in each country reflect the productivity of labor in the export industries.[7] This statement, while emphasizing a very essential point, is incomplete. It implicitly assumes a highly elastic supply schedule for a country's exports and a highly elastic demand schedule for the rest of the world's imports. More refined adjustments in the wage-productivity relationship may be necessary to maintain international balance. In particular, the wage-productivity relationship must take account of the effect on imports of an increase in incomes associated with greater productivity. In short, if the income elasticity of demand for imports in a country is high, it will not be able to raise incomes as much for the same increase in productivity as another country with a lower income elasticity of demand for imports.

The adjustments necessary to offset differential increases in productivity present no special difficulty—apart from the usual difficulty of implementing monetary policy.[8] Increases in productivity ordinarily proceed over large segments of the economy at a more or less constant pace, differing for each country. Where a rapid increase in productivity in a great trading country strengthens its export industries generally, the adjustment necessary to restore a competitive price situation can be made by simply slowing down the rate at which wage increases are made in other countries particularly affected by this export competition. Where such an adjustment of

---

[7] Nassau W. Senior, "The Cost of Obtaining Money," reproduced in No. 5 of the *Series of Reprints of Scarce Tracts in Economics and Political Science* by the London School of Economics. The reference is to p. 13 of this reprint.

[8] Compare Professor Hicks' statement in his Inaugural Lecture: "For monetary difficulties are in principle capable of being eased, if not wholly dissipated, by appropriate institutions. Thus if the difficulty which we find is purely monetary, it ought to be possible to find a means of doing something about it; but if the monetary problem hides a real problem, no monetary wizardry can conjure it away." *Op. cit.*, p. 123.

wage policy cannot be made, the only alternative is to restore the price-competitive position through exchange rate adjustment.

The discussion has hitherto been concerned with uniform changes in productivity at a more rapid rate in the United States than in other countries, either in the economy as a whole or in the export sector of the United States economy. These rather artificial assumptions were made to isolate the pure productivity impact and to generalize the impact on the world as a whole. The fact, of course, is that increases in productivity are by no means uniform throughout the United States economy and their impact cannot be the same on all countries. Increases in productivity in the United States takes place in particular industries, and it is the impact of such particular increases in productivity on other countries that must be considered.

Although it may very well be true that a rapid increase in productivity in the United States does not adversely affect the dollar payments position of *all* other countries, it does not follow that particular countries or groups of countries would not feel an adverse effect from an increase in American productivity in some industries. These countries or groups of countries may occupy so important a position in the world economy that adverse effects upon their payments position may seem, mistakenly, to indicate a world-wide payments problem. Any meaningful analysis of the effects of a rapid increase of American productivity on the payments position of other countries must differentiate among countries and among the industries in which the increase in productivity takes place.

PRODUCTIVITY AND U.S. EXPORTS

It has already been shown that a rapid increase in productivity in United States export industries can strengthen the competitive position of American exporters if wage policy in the United States and abroad is such as to lead to a relative fall in United States export prices. In practice, the problem arising from a rapid increase in productivity does not emerge as one covering all export industries and affecting all other countries in the same way. The increase in productivity cannot be uniform for all American exports. Instead, there are certain industries which from time to time, and even over long periods, show a more rapid increase in productivity than output generally, so that no conceivable wage policy could prevent those goods from falling in price, even if the average level of all prices or of all export prices in the United States were constant. Some countries are producers of the same or competitive goods; other countries are consumers of the same or competitive import goods. The balance of payments effects cannot be the same for all countries and these differences require special emphasis.

If the United Kingdom, for example, competes with the United States in exporting certain products to third countries, then a relative fall in American prices for such exports can lead to payments difficulties for the United Kingdom. Its exports of these products will decline, exports of other products will not necessarily rise, and aggregate export receipts of the United Kingdom will tend to fall. Of course, wage policy or exchange policy could be adjusted to act on the United Kingdom's competitive position in such a way that the decline in its exports of those goods for which American productivity has increased most would be offset by the increase in its exports of other goods. But the need for such an adjustment in policy indicates the existence of a payments problem.

If the impairment of the United Kingdom's competitive position should cover an important segment of its total export trade, her problem could very well be much more difficult than putting into effect a suitable monetary policy. "Under no system of monetary policy," said Professor Robertson in 1931, "can things be very pleasant for a country which finds the productivity of other countries in competitive goods increasing faster than its own." [9] And as Professor Williams emphasized, in such cases "the traditional explanation of how adjustment comes about, through money flow and its effect on comparative price levels or through income changes, misses the point that these adjustments would be at the expense of real income." [10]

There is nothing in these views that differs essentially from the accepted analysis. A century and a quarter ago, Senior noted precisely this point. In the lecture previously cited, he said:

Many economists have maintained that no country can be injured by the improvement of her neighbours. If the continent, they say, should be able to manufacture cottons with half the labour which they now cost in England, the consequence would be, that we should be able to import our supply of cottons from Germany or France at a less expense than it

[9] *The International Gold Problem* (Oxford University Press, 1932), p. 46.
[10] *Op. cit.,* p. 14.

costs us to manufacture them, and might employ a portion of our industry now devoted to the manufacture of cottons, in procuring an additional supply of some other commodities. These opinions have such an appearance of liberality, that I am sorry to dissent from them. But it must be remembered that England and the continent are competitors in the general market of the world. Such an alteration would diminish the cost of obtaining the precious metals on the continent, and increase it in England. The value of continental labour would rise, and the value of English labour would sink. They would ask more money for all those commodities, in the production of which no improvement had taken place, and we should have less to offer for them. We might find it easier to obtain cottons, but we should find it more difficult to import everything else.[11]

To recognize that the United Kingdom will have a payments problem under these circumstances is not to say that there will be a world-wide payments problem. The countries that import the goods for which United States export prices are lower *may* find their payments position strengthened as a consequence of the better terms of trade. In the 1870's, for example, when Western Hemisphere wheat production was greatly increased and the price of wheat was greatly reduced, the Western European exporters of wheat ran into difficulties. On the other hand, the Western European importers of wheat benefited from the new and cheaper supplies. The problem was met by Western European exporters shifting to the production of dairy and meat products.

Where the sole effect of an increase in United States productivity is to shift the American supply schedule for exports, the payments effects are mixed, adverse to some countries and beneficial to others. The problem is different where the increase in productivity is accompanied not only by a shift in the supply schedule for exports, but by a shift in the demand schedule for imports in other countries. This is what is likely to occur when the change in United States productivity takes the form of supplying new goods. Under such circumstances, the importing countries have a better all round collection of American export goods which they want to buy. Their

---

[11] *Op. cit.*, pp. 25–26. Jacob Viner, *Studies in the Theory of International Trade* (New York, 1937), pp. 462–64, cites this quotation from Senior on third-country competition. It is worth noting, as pointed out by Viner, that few of Senior's contemporaries gave adequate consideration to the adverse effect on England (an old supplier) of competition from a new supplier.

larger imports of the new goods is only partially offset by smaller purchases of other United States exports and smaller purchases of the export goods of other countries. Countries importing from the United States, as well as countries competing with United States exports, may then have a payments problem unless the United States demand for imports is increased to an equivalent extent.

A good deal has been made of this point in recent discussions. It is inevitable that the emergence of new goods will result in changing trade patterns. For a time, the country which is the source of the innovation may have great competitive advantages in the export of such goods; but it need not follow that this advantage will continue. Although the automobile is regarded as typifying American mass production, European countries are now supplying the major part of the world's exports of automobiles. This may be partly due to restrictions on imports of American cars in some countries. In large part, however, exports of European cars are indicative of the fact that in many markets they are competitive on a price, quality, and style basis.

PRODUCTIVITY AND U.S. IMPORTS

An increase in United States productivity matched by a rise in wage rates will increase money incomes in the United States and the demand for imports as well as home goods. It is conceivable, however, that the increase in productivity will be especially great in certain domestic import-competing industries. Under such circumstances, the effect of increased incomes on the demand for imports generally may be offset by the decreased demand for those import goods which competing output at home has displaced.

Increases in productivity do result in such behavior from time to time, although the decrease in demand for specific imports is unlikely to be on such a scale as to offset the increase in demand for imports generally that accompanies an increase in the real incomes. Nevertheless, the decrease in the demand for specific imports may be important for some countries. The rapid growth of American manufactures in the nineteenth and twentieth centuries resulted in a steady decline in the ratio of United States imports coming from the industrial countries of Western Europe. There may have been no absolute reduction in our total imports, even from such countries, but whole classes of goods formerly imported in considerable volume have dwindled to insignificance on the import list.

In recent years, some of the most important United States imports of the 1920's and 1930's have lost relative and even absolute ground in the American market. Silk is a prime example for it was a leading import in the 1920's and early 1930's and has now been largely displaced by such artificial fibers as rayon and nylon. There have been a number of other quite important import commodities affected by technical developments in the United States and abroad. The payments position of the countries that depend on such exports is obviously weakened by improvements in productivity that diminish the demand for their products. That is quite different, however, from saying that world-wide payments difficulties can be attributed to the rapid increase in productivity in the United States.

It may be worth noting that apart from the income effect of an increase in productivity on the general demand for imports in the United States, technical developments may be of a character that increases the demand for specific imports. For example, the development of the automobile brought an enormous increase in the demand for imported rubber. The development of the electrical industry and of electrical appliances increased the demand for imported copper. The range of imported commodities for which this is true is very wide. Improvements in productivity may be specifically import-requiring developments as well as import-economizing ones.

TERMS OF TRADE

There is one indirect effect of changes in American productivity which is of special importance—helpful to some countries, harmful to others—but favorable to the dollar payments position of the world as a whole. An increase in American productivity means an increase in output and income in the United States. Under such circumstances, the prices of raw materials may rise relative to the prices of manufactured goods. Such a rise in prices of primary products may be due to the fact that the increase in technical efficiency in the raw materials producing industries may not be as great as the increase in productivity in the manufacturing industries. This is apparently what Professor Hicks had in mind when he said that "things have become more difficult for the United Kingdom, mainly because the rate of growth in productivity in agriculture has slowed up." [12] In fact, there is no evidence that productivity in agriculture has failed to keep pace with productivity in the economy as a whole.[13]

The rise in the prices of raw materials relative to the prices of manufactured goods seems to be due to the shift in the supply schedule for the factors of production rather than to any noticeable lag in productive efficiency in the basic industries. For the United States, such a rise in prices cannot have great consequences. A 10 per cent rise in prices for raw materials, constituting a small fraction of total consumption and investment, is no burden to a people whose incomes are 20 or 30 per cent higher, particularly if the rise in prices is necessary to call forth the larger supplies required to meet their demand. From a balance of payments point of view, the effect may also be of much less importance to the United States than to the industrial countries of Europe. The United States is a large exporter as well as importer of such commodities although, of course, a net importer.

The effect of a rapid increase in United States productivity on

[12] *Op. cit.*, p. 132. Essentially the argument of Hicks on productivity and the dollar payments problem comes down to the point that productivity has not increased as rapidly in the industries supplying U.K. imports as in the industries competing with U.K. exports.

[13] On the basis of data prepared for the Joint Committee on the Economic Report, relative changes in man-hour productivity in agricultural and non-agricultural employment in recent years have been as follows:

INDEX OF PRODUCTIVITY IN AGRICULTURAL AND
NONAGRICULTURAL EMPLOYMENT IN THE UNITED STATES

	(1910–14 = 100)		(1935–39 = 100)	
	Agricultural	Private Non-agricultural	Agricultural	Private Non-agricultural
1946	165.9	187.4	130.8	118.7
1947	164.8	183.9	129.9	116.6
1948	190.8	190.6	150.4	120.8
1949	190.2	197.9	150.0	125.4
1950	216.6	209.8	170.8	133.0
1951	200.5	211.8	158.1	134.2
1952	205.7	217.3	162.2	137.7
1953	217.1	224.0	171.2	141.9

It is worth noting that the study projects an increase of 42 per cent in productivity in nonagricultural employment in the same period. This table is adapted from "Potential Economic Growth of the United States During the Next Decade," p. 34.

the terms of trade is not of small importance, however, to other industrial countries. Because the United States accounts for a very large part of the world consumption of raw materials, the prices of these products are sensitive to increases in demand occasioned by a rapid rise in output and incomes in the United States. The rise in import prices in a country like the United Kingdom may even be greater than the increase in its own productivity, so that there is not only an adverse movement in the commodity terms of trade, but also in single factoral terms of trade. Between 1937 and 1953, for example, weekly wage rates in the United Kingdom rose less than import prices, so that the amount of labor a British worker must perform to acquire a unit of imports may have risen in the past 17 years.[14]

In recent years, great importance has been attached to the effect of the change in the terms of trade on the payments position of Western Europe. One important cause of the change in the terms of trade since the prewar years has been the great increase in United States industrial production, although it has also been affected by the large increase in industrial production in Europe and elsewhere. Undoubtedly, the change in the terms of trade has adversely affected the payments position of some industrial countries. By the same token it has strengthened the payments position of countries exporting raw materials. This has resulted in great changes in the pattern of international payments. It cannot be the cause of a world-wide dollar payments problem.

CONCLUDING OBSERVATIONS

The rapid increase in productivity in the United States has been a striking phenomenon, and it is not surprising that some people have sought in it the cause of the postwar dollar problem. The effects of a rapid increase in United States productivity are too complex and too diverse to explain the payments problems of so many different countries. The effects of an increase in American productivity must be analyzed in specific terms and in general terms. The increase in productivity in each specific industry must be considered in rela-

[14] While the commodity terms of trade deteriorated by about 21 per cent between 1935 and 1953, the single factoral terms of trade deteriorated by about 5 per cent. Ely Devons, "Statistics of United Kingdom Terms of Trade," *Manchester School*, XXV (September 1954), 273.

tion to its effect on export competitors, import suppliers, and on the terms of trade. The specific effects may be adverse for some countries, beneficial for others. The aggregate of the specific effects on the balance of payments of all other countries with the United States may be favorable under certain conditions and at certain times, adverse under other conditions and at other times. No firm conclusion as to the aggregate impact of *specific* effects can be drawn even from historical experience.

There can be no doubt, however, as to the *general* effects of an increase in United States productivity. An increase in productivity—more particularly in total production—is merely the counterpart of an increase in real incomes. An increase in income means an increase in demand for imports, as well as for home goods. Unless the specific effects of an increase in United States productivity are clearly adverse to the payments position of other countries, the general effects are certain to be such as to lead to a strengthening of the dollar payments position of the rest of the world. Indeed, the greater the increase in United States productivity, the wider the field over which the increase in productivity has taken place, and the more sustained the increase in productivity, the more likely it is that the general effects will be favorable to the payments position of the rest of the world as a group.

The analogy between the general effects of an increase in productivity and business prosperity is worth noting, although admittedly it is not perfect. Prosperity in the United States is helpful to the payments position of other countries largely because it means an expansion of incomes and production. The economic growth of the United States, brought about by an increase in productivity, is helpful to the payments position of other countries for the same reason. It is true that a cyclical expansion is not ordinarily accompanied by technical changes which can adversely affect the competitive position of exports of other countries either in the United States or in third markets, while increases in productivity may have such specific effects for some commodities and for some countries. The general effects of growth and cyclical expansion are, however, the same.

It should be borne in mind that payments difficulties are not those of an amorphous group, "the rest of the world," with a single country, the United States. Payments difficulties are experienced by individual countries, and their payments difficulties are the resultant of the world economic environment and of their own economic policies.

Certainly, rapid changes in productivity in the United States affect other countries, but not in the same way or to the same extent for all. The impact of the United States on the world economy is very great, and changes in the American economy, including changes in productivity, have repercussions on producers and consumers in all parts of the world. Changes in the American economy may necessitate adjustments abroad, just as they necessitate adjustments at home. There is no way by which a country can isolate itself from the dynamics of a progressive world economy, including rapid changes in United States productivity, without paying a high price in well-being and efficiency.

II. The Balance of Payments and Equilibrium

COMMENTARY

THE MARKET AND PROGRAM BALANCES

Machlup (selection 5) feels that the accounting balance of payments is of doubtful analytical value. In any case, for the interesting problems of prediction and of public policy, the accounting balance can be of use only as a supplement to, or means of interpreting, the market and program balances.

Machlup points out that the surplus-deficit status of one type of balance of payments does not imply the nature of the status of another type. He illustrates this geometrically with respect to the market and accounting statements. Following is a geometric interpretation of possible relationships between the market and program statements.

Suppose that the U.K. is the country in question, and the U.S. is the rest of the world. In Figure I, dollars (the foreign currency) are measured horizontally, and the pound price of the dollar is measured vertically. D_m is the market demand for dollars, S is the market supply, and D_p is the "program demand" for dollars.[1] D_p is drawn vertically on the assumption that the U.K. program calls for the acquisition of a certain quantity of U.S. goods and services and thus calls for a certain number of dollars irrespective of the exchange rate. As indicated in the diagram, at sufficiently low pound prices of the dollar, the

[1] It can be objected the D_p is not a "demand" curve, for a genuine schedule of demand for one item implies a schedule of supply of the thing being expended. D_m, the market demand for dollars, is a reflection of a market supply of pounds. But D_p does not in itself reflect pound supply: it is simply a statement of the number of dollars required to fulfill the government's program. Perhaps D_p should be named "program requirement," "program proposition," "program stipulation," or "programmed expenditure." Regardless of the name, it is stated in terms of dollars and can thus be plotted in the diagram.

program calls for a smaller expenditure of dollars than would be normally demanded in the foreign exchange market. In this case, D_p will be the actual demand only by somehow curtailing market demand.[2]

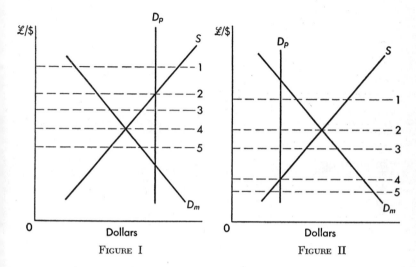

FIGURE I   FIGURE II

At a given exchange rate, if $S > D_m$, there exists a market surplus; if $S < D_m$, there is a market deficit. Similarly, there is a program surplus if $S > D_p$ and a program deficit if $S < D_p$.[3] Accordingly, we have the following market and program combinations at alternative exchange rates in Figure I:

At level 1, market surplus and program surplus
At level 2, market surplus and program balance

[2] Drawing D_p vertically suggests that the market demand as such may not be permitted to be operative at *any* exchange rate. Rather D_p is the total foreign exchange expeditures of the economy (private plus official) specified in the government's program. Alternatively but presumably less realistically, one might conceive of the government's not restricting private demand for foreign exchange and simply adding a given quantity of foreign exchange required for the government's own expenditures to D_m at every exchange rate. Thus if D_p were to pertain only to the government's own programmed requirements, the new demand curve, $D_m + D_p$, would be parallel to D_m.

[3] Although program demand itself is assumed to be independent of the exchange rate, the surplus-deficit status of the program balance of payments is affected by the exchange rate, for the quantity of dollars normally supplied is a function of the rate.

At level 3, market surplus and program deficit
At level 4, market balance and program deficit
At level 5, market deficit and program deficit

In Figure I, at rates of exchange below the relatively high level 2, there is a program deficit. One might expect that for purposes of negotiating for dollar aid, D_p will be placed sufficiently far to the right that a program deficit will obtain at the current exchange rate (and even at a substantially devalued pound)—although at the current rate the quantity of dollars normally supplied may be greater than the quantity normally demanded. But in principle it is obviously possible, even if atypical, for D_p to be smaller than the free market equilibrium quantity, as in Figure II. Again we have five market-program combinations.

At level 1, market surplus and program surplus
At level 2, market balance and program surplus
At level 3, market deficit and program surplus
At level 4, market deficit and program balance
At level 5, market deficit and program deficit

There is a certain asymmetry in the program deficit cases and the program surplus cases. A program deficit is an excess of *desired* expenditures over normal supply of foreign exchange, and unless extraordinary financing (conspicuously including aid from foreign governments) is forthcoming, *actual* expenditures will be no larger than normal supply. By contrast, it is within the power of the domestic authorities to make the program demand the effective, or actual, demand when it is smaller than normal supply. On the assumption—reasonable for at least a restricted time—that S is not appreciably affected by shifting D_p, with an exchange rate at, say, level 3 in Figure II, the U.K. government could use direct controls to curtail dollar expenditures to the amount of D_p, and the gap between D_p and S at that rate could take the form of increased official holdings of gold and dollar assets.

Mendershausen joins Machlup in denying the significance of past international accounts in measuring dollar shortage.

"There is not a single item or any residual of items in the international account of any country, including the United States itself, that could be accepted as representative of a past dollar shortage, whatever may be known about the considerations that led to specific transactions. . . . There is no international convention declaring that certain balance of payments features are expressions of a dollar shortage, and it is doubtful that one would be of much use; for the lack of dollar means felt in certain places at certain times may or may not find its reflection in the balance of payments statistics, and if it does—because the shortage was filled—it may not be a simple matter to locate its incidence in the statistics."[4]

At any rate, the significant conception of "dollar shortage" is in terms of "judgments of the future, not accounts of the past."[5] For Mendershausen, dollar shortage is a problem of political economy, centering on a particular process of foreign aid negotiation and administration, and he adopts Machlup's program balance of payments.

It may occur, in one country or in many, that the inflow of dollars expected by the community for a period of time in the future falls short of the desired or planned dollar expenditures. The expectations, the desires, and the gap between them may be presented by government authorities in a statement of international receipts and payments for the period. In this manner, an expected dollar shortage may be announced and measured, for one country or many. But such a statement will hardly ever be made if not for the purpose of producing the means to fill the expected gap. The announcement would serve chiefly as the basis for a request of United States aid, or of aid from intermediary institutions that command United States dollars. . . . A statement of dollar shortage has the nature of a proposition, made for the purpose of obtaining aid that would close the gap. . . . As long as [the propositions] are not accepted in international negotiations as at least a reasonable estimate of additional dollar finance to be provided, the propositions remain an expression of opinion and so does the magnitude of the dollar shortage to which they refer. But if the propositions are accepted, the dollar

[4] Horst Mendershausen, "Foreign Aid With and Without Dollar Shortage," *Review of Economics and Statistics*, XXXIII (February 1951), p. 39.
[5] *Ibid.*, p. 40.

shortage is determined. It is determined *ex ante* by agreement on the extent of the measures designed to overcome it.[6]

As a matter of history, the conception of negotiated dollar shortage scarcely has meaning:

To the extent that the dollar shortage presented in a proposition is covered by aid of one sort or another, it ceases to be a shortage. Requirements are covered by a dollar supply. To the extent that the proceeds of the measures fall short of the estimated gap and that no other developments make up the discrepancy, the dollar shortage likewise ceases to be of operational significance. Some dollar purchases, private or public, that were hoped and planned for have to be left unrealized, owing to a lack of dollar exchange. . . . As an *ex post* concept, the "dollar shortage" is only meaningful insofar as it indicates the experience of failures to fill previously expected dollar requirements.[7]

If dollar shortage is a phenomenon only of programming and negotiating, it follows that if—wisely or not—"the United States firmly declared itself unwilling to listen to announcements of dollar shortages abroad, there would be no more dollar shortage." And, indeed, "Soviet Russia has had no dollar shortage— at least since 1947; China lost its dollar shortage in 1949; and Yugoslavia has acquired one of late."[8]

THE ACCOUNTING BALANCE

Not everyone rejects as useless or uninteresting the analysis of the accounting balance of payments. However, "equilibrium" and "disequilibrium" in the accounting statement are difficult to define, and they are a matter of debate in principle; to distinguish and measure with tolerable accuracy the conceptual categories and variables is well nigh impossible.

Since the balance of payments balances overall, Bloomfield suggests that "the concepts of . . . equilibrium, deficit, and surplus must clearly imply the segregation from a country's aggregate international transactions of those items that are of a 'balancing' or 'induced' character. . . . In theory at least, the

[6] *Ibid.*, pp. 39–40.
[7] *Ibid.*, p. 40.
[8] *Ibid.*, pp. 41, 42.

items to be excluded should be those 'passively' induced by fluctuations in the net balance on account of all other balance-of-payments transactions and serving to 'offset' such fluctuations." [9] Similarly, Meade distinguishes between "autonomous" entries in the balance of payments and "accommodating" items. Autonomous payments and receipts have taken place for reasons other than the status of the balance of payments; they were not motivated or determined by other items in the balance of payments. Accommodating items, by contrast, were induced by other entries and served to fill the gap left in the balance of payments by the net autonomous entries.

The "balancing" items are traditionally considered to be gold and short-term capital. (For example, when U.S. exports of merchandise build up pound balances in U.K. banks, as described in the Introduction to Part II, this capital outflow is implicit in the payment process, "induced" by the originating merchandise transaction, and appears in the U.S. balance of payments as a debit entry offsetting the credit merchandise entry.) However, for gold-producing countries, gold exports may be best considered as normal autonomous merchandise rather than "balancing" movements. More serious, some short-term capital movements (perhaps accompanied by gold movements) may be autonomous and even disequilibrating, as with "capital flights" in the unsettled conditions of the 1930's. Furthermore, capital movements which may be classified as long-term by the time criterion (more than one year) may serve the function of a balancing item, as with the 50-year Anglo-American loan of 1946, which was motivated by U.K. balance of payments considerations rather than the profit and income objectives of normal long-term investment.

Meade avoids equating short-term capital with balancing transactions. In the balancing category, he includes *all* "induced," or accommodating, items. Since each entry is classified as either autonomous or accommodating, the net of all autonomous items is equal (with opposite sign) to the net of accom-

[9] Arthur I. Bloomfield, *Capital Imports and the American Balance of Payments 1934–39* (Chicago: University of Chicago Press, 1950), p. 223.

modating items. If the autonomous items are a net debit, the balance of payments is in deficit disequilibrium. This deficit—which must be matched by accommodating finance—is called a "true" balance of payments deficit by Meade.[10]

Unfortunately, this type of approach may suggest that the so-called "autonomous" balance consists of entries which literally are not determined to any extent by the remainder of the balance of payments. It may imply that the "true" deficit (or surplus) is a fact which does exist, with an independent life of its own, and which now must, and inevitably will, be financed. But actually, of course, the autonomous balance does not *first* spring full-blown from nowhere and is *then* financed. If the financing were not feasible, the autonomous balance could not appear. For some purposes or from some perspectives, accommodating financing may be conceived to be induced by autonomous transactions. However, one could at least as meaningfully argue from another viewpoint that the availability of the financing induced the gap which could be filled. When the financing is no longer available—when gold reserves and assets abroad which can be liquidated are exhausted and when aid from abroad is no longer forthcoming—the autonomous gap can no longer persist. Conversely, if the available financing were increased, perhaps because of additional foreign aid, the supposedly autonomous gap could and probably would grow larger.

The staff of the International Monetary Fund developed the concept of "compensatory official financing" to facilitate analysis of problems relating to "action undertaken or proposed by the monetary authorities of member countries to deal with their exchange problems." The concept is defined as "the financing undertaken by the monetary authorities to provide exchange to cover a surplus or deficit in the rest of the balance of payments."[11] Compensatory official financing is "the financing that the monetary authorities undertake to settle inter-

[10] J.E. Meade, *The Balance of Payments* (London: Oxford University Press, 1951), pp. 3–13.

[11] International Monetary Fund, *Balance of Payments Yearbook, 1938, 1946, 1947* (Washington, 1949), p. 5.

national transactions" and is "essentially a modernized version of the movement of international reserves." It measures "the financial burden that the balance of payments creates for the monetary authorities." [12] Such financing includes movements in international reserves (monetary gold, foreign assets "at the disposition of the monetary authorities," liabilities to foreign official and banking institutions other than the I.M.F. and the World Bank), purchases from and sales to the I.M.F., official transactions in outstanding long-term obligations, and long-term official loans and official grants "extended or received for balancing international transactions." [13] Thus to movements in international reserves are added other transactions supposedly of an "equilibrating" nature.

The Fund maintains that the concept of compensatory official financing is as appropriate in measuring balance of payments pressures at a given exchange rate when the deficit is "planned" as when the exchange market is free.

Discussion of balance of payments deficits often implies that in some way a deficit develops and financing must then be found for it. This was never the case even under the gold standard. Unless it is financed, the deficit cannot come into being. Under the gold standard, however, there was an unlimited offer on the part of the monetary authorities to finance any deficit that appeared. More generally this is the situation wherever exchange markets are free and the authorities undertake to maintain a stable rate of exchange. Because in this case the authorities can never know in advance just how much balance of payments financing they will be called upon to provide, it is easy to regard the deficit as coming first and the financing afterward even though the two are inevitably simultaneous.

In the postwar world few exchange markets are free. . . . Theoretically, a country exercising an effective exchange control can cut down its outpayments to whatever it finds to be the level of its international receipts. It can eliminate the deficit.

[12] International Monetary Fund, *Balance of Payments Manual* (Washington, January 1950), p. 108.
[13] *Yearbook, op. cit.*, pp. 5–20; *Manual*, pp. 108–109; International Monetary Fund, *Balance of Payments Yearbook 1948* (Washington, 1950), pp. 22–23.

To do so, however, may put a severe strain on the economy, and the Government may well prefer to sustain essential imports by using monetary reserves or borrowing abroad or, if possible, negotiating outright grants. In taking action along these lines, the monetary authorities engage in compensatory financing of a deficit upon which they have deliberately decided. This "planned deficit" is different from the unplanned deficit of the free exchange market. The latter can be controlled only by general measures such as fiscal or credit policy, the precise effects of which are unpredictable; the planned deficit, however, can be rigidly controlled by direct measures.

In either case, however, the amount of compensatory financing is the measure of the extent to which the existing balance of payments has forced the authorities to take financial action. Since the full range of international transactions must balance simultaneously in free markets as well as controlled, all that is significant about movements of gold or monetary reserves, or, more broadly, compensatory official financing, is that they reflect financial pressures on the monetary authorities arising out of a balance of payments within which authorities are attempting to maintain orderly exchange conditions. Compensatory official financing is the response of the authorities to these pressures.[14]

Machlup contends that this position hopelessly confuses the market and the program balances of payments and that it falls into the trap of measuring a deficit by the "compensatory" financing which made the deficit possible:

The balance-of-payments pressures which Compensatory Official Financing is supposed to relieve are, in one place, taken to refer to the market balance and, in another place, to the programme balance of payments. . . . But there can be no doubt that problems of the market balance were originally what the designers of the new concept had in mind. . . . Originally the idea of the staff was to call compensatory that amount of financing that was designed to provide exchange to cover a balance-of-payments deficit. Now they have ended up with measuring the balance-of-payments deficit by the amount of financing that they choose to call compensatory.

Donald Badger, formerly on the staff of the I.M.F., has re-

[14] *Yearbook, 1938, 1946, 1947*, p. 23.

plied that Machlup's criticism of compensatory official financing is based on an unrealistic distinction between the market
balance and the program balance.

. . . Machlup attaches a number of unnecessary limitations to his
concept of the market balance. In particular, he is prepared to
extend his definition to cover the effects of tariffs, quotas, and prohibitions of a protective nature, but he is not willing to extend it to
cover the effects of controls introduced for balance of payments
purposes. The program balance is introduced to deal with the situation where controls of this nature are employed, but it is further
differentiated from the market balance by being defined in terms of
"hopes and desires" rather than "effective demand." This ignores the
fact that once a government program is adopted and the necessary
steps to implement it have been taken, the demand becomes effective
and, consequently, part of the market.[15]

Machlup holds that in the market balance of payments "to
assume the existence of comprehensive foreign-exchange controls . . . and to include in the effective demand for dollars
only those amounts which the control authorities will actually
authorize" would "define away the very problem we are out to
solve, the excess demand for dollars." Badger argues, on the
other hand, that discretionary controls frequently are administered at constant levels of severity for prolonged periods.
Thus for all practical purposes they become simply another
of the market conditions underlying demand for dollars, and
their effects may be included in a "realized market balance," as
distinguished from a "pure market balance" which excludes
such effects.

Furthermore, Badger contends, Machlup has criticized the
notion of compensatory official financing for failure to give
results which its creators did not intend it to give.

Machlup's exclusion of exchange and trade controls from his definition of the market balance seems to be due to a desire to measure

---

[15] Donald G. Badger, "The Balance of Payments: A Tool of Economic
Analysis," *International Monetary Fund Staff Papers*, II (September 1951),
p. 150.

something more than the actual gap between effective demand and market supply which has to be filled by official financing. He seems to be trying to define the market balance in such a way that the absence of a surplus or deficit will indicate that the balance of payments is in equilibrium. No such claim has been made for the concept of compensatory official financing. All that is indicated by the absence of a surplus or deficit, in the sense in which the terms are used by the Fund's staff, is that, given the actual conditions affecting the exchange market in the period under review, there has been no need for supplementary financing by the monetary authorities on either side of the market. . . . the purpose of the concept of compensatory official financing is to cast light on the strength of a country's exchange position within the framework of certain "given" conditions (including controls and other government policies). . . .

The task of making the balance of payments present facts in the most enlightening way must be distinguished clearly from the task of determining the appropriateness of alternative corrective measures which might be taken in the light of these facts. . . . In diagnosing fundamental disequilibrium, only the size of the gap between supply and demand has to be taken into account. In considering the appropriateness of different corrective policies, however, information is needed about the elasticities of the supply and demand curves and the extent to which these curves would be shifted by particular changes in the underlying conditions. One of Machlup's criticisms of an *ex post* concept of surplus or deficits is that it does not give reliable information of this kind. This is not a valid criticism of the concept itself; it is merely a warning against attempts to use the concept for purposes for which it is not intended. All that can be claimed for the concept of surplus or deficit which has been elaborated here is that it provides a measure of the gap between supply and demand under the conditions that prevailed during the period under review. The task of balance of payments analysis is to throw as much light as possible on the factors contributing to this situation. To pass from this point to the diagnosis of fundamental disequilibrium requires detailed analysis of many other series of economic data. Even when this point has been reached, the hardest task of all remains— that of determining the most appropriate corrective measure. The balance of payments can play a part, but a rather limited part, in this task.[16]

[16] *Ibid.*, pp. 150, 162, 196–197.

MEASUREMENT OF DOLLAR SHORTAGE

The foregoing discussion indicates that there is no obvious or generally accepted manner of using historical data to measure past dollar shortage. There is disagreement on the very conception of dollar shortage as reflected in the accounting balance of payments. In addition, it may be impossible to specify with assurance what components of an actual balance of payments statement correspond with a particular analytical category, e.g., "accommodating capital movements."

The I.M.F., as we have seen, has attempted to measure dollar shortage by means of its compensatory official financing approach. Other methods of measurement can be used, with widely varying results. For example, one may specify that net changes in foreign long- and short-term investment in the U.S. plus net U.S. gold import or export measures a dollar "surplus" or "deficit" for the rest of the world. The remainder of the U.S. balance of payments can be grouped into a net credit category, called "dollar use by foreigners," and a net debit category, or "dollar supply to foreigners." This method yields, as Table I indicates, a net dollar deficit for the period, 1946–1949, and a surplus for 1950–1957.

Table I

MILLIONS OF DOLLARS
(Annual averages in parentheses)

	1946–49	1950–57*
Dollar Use by Foreigners		
U.S. exports of goods and services, including military transfers under aid programs	67,628	174,712
	(16,907)	(21,839)
Loan-repayment by foreigners	1796	4833
	(449)	(604)
Errors and omissions	3031	3326
	(758)	(416)
	72,455	182,871
	(18,114)	(22,859)

Table I—Continued

MILLIONS OF DOLLARS

(Annual averages in parentheses)

	1946–49	1950–57*
Dollar Supply to Foreigners		
U.S. imports of goods and services	−35,068	−133,901
	(−8767)	(−16,738)
U.S. private capital outflow (long- and short-term) and private remittances	−6172	−17,688
	(−1543)	(−2211)
U.S. government unilateral transfers and capital outflow	−26,445	−43,686
	(−6611)	(−5461)
	−67,685	−195,275
	(−16,921)	(−24,409)
Dollar Surplus or Deficit (−)		
Increase or decrease (−) in foreign dollar assets (long- and short-term)	−291	10,697
	(−73)	(1337)
U.S. gold exports or imports (−)	−4479	1707
	(−1120)	(213)
	−4770	12,404
	(−1193)	(1551)

* Figures for 1957 are preliminary.

Sources: United States Department of Commerce, *Survey of Current Business,* July 1954, p. 15; *ibid.,* June 1956, p. 24; *ibid.,* March 1957, p. 16; *ibid.,* March 1958, p. 16.

Table II presents another schema. Here balance of payments disequilibrium is conceived to be measured by the sum of the current account balance (plus errors and omissions) plus net private long-term capital plus net private unilateral transfers. The balance of these items will be equal to net government unilateral transfers and capital plus net private short-term capital plus gold. According to this method, there was a large dollar deficit for the rest of the world in both post-war periods, although on an annual average basis the deficit was smaller in the latter period.

The Department of Commerce has used variants of both

Table II

MILLIONS OF DOLLARS

(Annual averages in parentheses)

	1946–49	1950–57*
Dollar Use by Foreigners		
U.S. current account surplus	32,560	40,811
	(8140)	(5101)
Errors and omissions	3031	3326
	(758)	(419)
	35,591	44,137
	(8898)	(5519)
Dollar Supply to Foreigners		
U.S. private long-term capital outflow	−2929	−7879
	(−732)	(−985)
U.S. private remittances	−2545	−3780
	(−636)	(−473)
	−5474	−11,659
	(−1369)	(−1457)
Dollar Deficit		
U.S. government unilateral transfers and capital outflow	−25,417	−40,114
	(−6354)	(−5014)
U.S. private short-term capital inflow or outflow (−)	−221	5929
	(−55)	(741)
U.S. gold exports or imports (−)	−4479	1707
	(−1120)	(213)
	−30,117	−32,478
	(−7529)	(−4060)

* Figures for 1957 are preliminary.

Sources: Same as for Table I.

methods.[17] Both can be defended (and criticized), and they do not exhaust the possible ways of rearranging the balance of pay-

[17] On the method of Table I, *cf.* United States Department of Commerce, *Survey of Current Business,* July 1954, pp. 10, 13, and on the second, *idem, The United States in the World Economy* (Washington, 1943). On the latter, see the critical comments of Gottfried Haberler, "Dollar Shortage?" in Seymour E. Harris, editor, *Foreign Economic Policy for the United States* (Cambridge: Harvard University Press, 1948), pp. 427–432. The approach of Table II is similar also to that used in [Randall] Commission on Foreign Economic Policy, *Staff Papers* (Washington, February 1954), chap. I.

ments data. Obviously calculations of "dollar shortage" must
be handled with care.

VIEWS OF THE "DOLLAR SHORTAGE"

The essays and the Commentary of Part II illustrate the differences of opinion concerning the conception and cure of
"dollar shortage." There are differences, first, as to the meaning
of the term, dollar shortage, and, indeed, as to whether in any
significant sense there is or can be such a thing as dollar shortage. Among those who profess to recognize the existence of
dollar shortage, there are differences as to whether it is temporary (or could be made temporary because it is readily amenable to correction) or chronic. And among those who consider
dollar shortage to be a persistent phenomenon, there are differences as to its causes and the appropriate modes of dealing
with it.

The views on dollar shortage range from Harrod's charge
that "this allegation of a 'world dollar shortage' is surely one
of the most brazen pieces of collective effrontery that has ever
been uttered. . . . In fact it is no more than the young man
going forward and living beyond his resources without leave" [18]
to Balogh's contention that "the dollar problem is not of a
transitory nature; nor can it be solved by 'orthodox methods,'
without aggravating the malaise not only of the world but even
of the United States." [19]

Graham (selection 6) forcefully presents the "orthodox"
view that the so-called dollar shortage is the consequence of
pegging exchange rates within an unacceptable monetary and
fiscal setting. Since the rates are pegged at levels below free
market equilibrium, the quantity of dollars demanded by the
rest of the world is naturally greater than the quantity supplied.
Robertson agrees that dollar shortage is the manifestation of
nations living beyond their means:

[18] Roy F. Harrod, *Are These Hardships Necessary?* (London: Rupert Hart-
Davis, 1947), p. 43.
[19] Thomas Balogh, *The Dollar Crisis, Causes and Cure* (London: Blackwell,
1949), p. xiv.

. . . the more fully developed countries of the Eastern Hemisphere have clung tenaciously to ways of life and standards of consumption which they could no longer afford; the less developed ones have aimed at a pace of advance which they had no possible means of implementing. Balance could have been attained by now if the former had shaken off their crippling rigidities and the latter had toned down the exuberance of their visions. . . . balance always *can* be attained between any two trading areas, however great the gap between them in productive power, provided that the less richly endowed area accepts the standard of life to which its relative efficiency entitles it, and does not keep kicking against the pricks by adhering obstinately to occupational immobility and utopian social policy, buttressed by monetary inflation and an overvalued exchange.[20]

Others, as MacDougall and Bernstein (selections 7 and 8) point out, hold that recurring balance of payments strains may be inherent in differing national rates of growth in productivity.[21] According to the analysis of Hicks, if United States productivity rises relatively rapidly and if such improvements are centered in United States export industries, the rest of the world will gain in real income. To a lesser degree, the rest of the world will gain if the improvements are uniformly spread over United States production. But the rest of the world will be worse off if the productivity gains are concentrated in American import-competing industries. Hicks suggests that the third case has characterized the twentieth century. Furthermore, even when relative increases in United States productivity make gains possible for the rest of the world in *real* terms, unless appropriate adjustments are made in prices and incomes, the rest

[20] Sir Denis H. Robertson, *Britain in the World Economy* (London: George Allen and Unwin, Ltd., 1954), pp. 55–56.

[21] Even Robertson wonders (*ibid.*, p. 58), "What is to happen if country A is not only better endowed than country B, but if the disparity of endowment between them is continually *increasing* through the cumulative mutual interaction of capital accumulation and technological progress? It is true [on the basis of the principle of comparative advantage] that at any given moment there will still be *some* distribution of function between the two countries which, if it could be instantaneously attained, would be in the best interests of both. But the task of attaining it, and then of abandoning it almost immediately for a new one, may surpass the human capacity for adjustment in what is, *ex hypothesi,* the weaker country."

of the world may experience *monetary* payments difficulties.[22] However, MacDougall (selection 7), while pessimistic that the "orthodox" policy of exchange rate adjustment would solve the dollar problem, discounts also the Hicks thesis on the ground that it is not clear that in fact productivity has increased more rapidly in the United States than elsewhere. Letiche agrees that the United States rate of productivity growth has not been greatly different from that of Western Europe generally, and he doubts further than United States growth has been concentrated in import-competing industries.[23]

No one denies that there have been balance of payments strains of varying degrees of severity since World War I. Hicks' analysis is one attempt to formulate a *general* theory of such phenomena: in the 1920's the dollar problem

was entangled with war debts; in the nineteen-thirties with world depression and the flight of capital before Hitler; in the nineteen-forties with war damage, more war debts, and the Cold War in international trade. A special explanation of the difficulties which were being experienced by European countries in settling their dollar debts could always be found. But the continuance of the same consequence, the same dollar shortage, as the result of these various "causes," has now become very striking. That there is some general influence underlying these particular manifestations can now no longer be doubted. It is hard to see that there is any other general force which would account for what has been happening than the disparity in growth of productivity. . . .[24]

However, Ellis suggests that one can recognize the fact of recurring difficulties and still doubt that there is "some general influence underlying these particular manifestations":

If an unfortunate citizen were to fall victim to yellow jaundice, then to an automobile accident and then to a plunge into icy water while skating, next to pneumonia and finally to a fall from a step-

[22] J.R. Hicks, "An Inaugural Lecture," *Oxford Economic Papers*, V (new series) (June 1953), pp. 121–135.

[23] J.M. Letiche, "Differential Rates of Productivity Growth and International Imbalance," *Quarterly Journal of Economics*, LXIX (August 1955), pp. 371–401.

[24] Hicks, *op. cit.*, p. 131.

ladder while trimming roses, we might call him a "chronic" invalid. But I doubt it. Similarly the shortage of dollars is not something arcane, inevitable and inveterate, but the result of a series of impacts, all in the same direction.[25]

On the one hand are the "orthodox" economists who deny any inevitability of disequilibrium and contend that the prescriptions for adjustment, designed to keep an economy living within its international means, are conceptually clear-cut—although scarcely painless. On the other hand, there are some who attempt to identify certain institutional or "structural" factors or certain propensities not readily subject to control which will produce persistent or chronic dollar shortage. As Harris reminds us, the suggested causes of chronic dollar shortage are numerous and varied in nature:

According to Kindleberger, it is the tendency toward depression and stagnation in the United States (excess of savings) with relative inflation (excess of investment) in other countries; according to Williams, it is the size of the United States, its strong and improving competitive position, its relative independence of imports; according to Hicks, it is the varying rate of gains of productivity, and particularly in import-competing industries in the non-dollar-short countries; according to Balogh, it is the greater technical gains in the

[25] Howard S. Ellis, "The Dollar Shortage in Theory and Fact," *Canadian Journal of Economics and Political Science*, XIV (August 1948), p. 364.

Mendershausen (*op. cit.*, p. 58) has thus summarized two views of the dollar shortage: "According to the one, the outside world is, or tends to be, persistently short of dollars, owing to economic facts in this country and abroad. This may be called the 'persistent-fact' theory of the dollar shortage. According to the other, the outside world need not be persistently short of dollars, and was not, at least until some time in the 1940's. By its efforts it could achieve a more even balance of trade with the United States, and so could the United States from its side; but somehow the efforts are lacking, too weak, or are being frustrated. This may be called the 'recurrent-frustration' theory of the dollar shortage. According to the first viewpoint, the dollar shortage is a fact to be lived with, an economic disequilibrium that may be righted by dollar finance or other means, but that has a way of reappearing despite such measures owing to some deeply rooted economic tendencies. According to the second, the dollar shortage is a state of affairs, or mind, that need not be lived with. It is a result of human fallacy, e.g., a deviation from 'orthodox economics' or faulty planning, or of short period calamity, that might be tided over by temporary dollar aid but that would require no permanent provision in our scheme of things."

United States and the propensity to depression if savings are not invested in the United States and to great gains in productivity if they are; according to Nurkse, it is the tendency of countries with lower standards of living to emulate the consumption standards of the United States, with unfortunate effects on savings and the balance of payments; according to Samuelson, it is natural for poor countries to receive aid or borrow from rich countries and then repudiate.[26]

One may argue, and argue effectively, that there is no "inevitable" dollar shortage—no dollar shortage which is an integral part of the grand design of the universe—and still fear that in fact the world will stumble and bumble from one balance of payments crisis to another. One may thus share MacDougall's opinion that "it would require a very courageous man to forecast either chronic dollar shortage or its absence during the coming decades."

[26] Seymour E. Harris, *International and Interregional Economics* (New York: McGraw-Hill Book Co., 1957), p. 233.

III. The Adjustment Process: Changes in Prices and Incomes

III. The Adjustment Process: Changes in Prices and Incomes

INTRODUCTION

The discussions of Part II indicate that the concept of balance of payments "disequilibrium" and the causes of disequilibrium, however defined and measured, are not without ambiguity. But despite the difficulties of definition and measurement, there is no question that from time to time economies do in fact suffer balance of payments strains—strains which may degenerate into full-blown crises of great public importance, with political and even military repercussions.

"Disequilibrium" connotes a state of variables which cannot normally persist; net forces of change impinge upon the variables, driving them toward or away from equilibrium values (depending on whether the situation is "stable" or "unstable"). If a balance of payments is in disequilibrium, something must "give way." What are the pertinent variables in such a problem, i.e., what are the alternative methods of balance of payments adjustment? There are three obvious market variables: exchange rates, national incomes, and national price levels. These variables will differ in importance according to the international monetary arrangement. Under a gold standard, exchange rates are substantially constant, and thus the burden of adjustment falls on incomes and prices; if exchange rates are free to move, income and price changes are less conspicuous. If all three market variables are held constant, the disequilibrium may be perpetuated by suppressing certain of its normal consequences through imposing some sort of "exchange control" or "quantitative restrictions" on trade.

THE PRICE-SPECIE-FLOW ADJUSTMENT MECHANISM

In a famous passage which constitutes an incisive refutation of the mercantilistic concern for a "favorable" balance of payments, David Hume, in 1752, outlined the nature of the price-specie-flow mechanism which was to be central to the classical theory of international trade. He wrote:

> Suppose four-fifths of all the money in Great Britain to be annihilated in one night. . . . Must not the price of all labour and commodities sink in proportion . . . ? What nation could then dispute with us in any foreign market, or pretend to navigate or to sell manufactures at the same price, which to us would afford sufficient profit? In how little time, therefore, must this bring back the money which we had lost, and raise us to the level of all the neighbouring nations? Where, after we have arrived, we immediately lose the advantage of the cheapness of labour and commodities; and the further flowing in of money is stopped by our fulness and repletion.
>
> Again, suppose that all the money of Great Britain were multiplied fivefold in a night, must not the contrary effect follow? Must not all labour and commodities rise to such an exhorbitant height, that no neighbouring nations could afford to buy from us; while their commodities, on the other hand, became comparatively so cheap, that, in spite of all the laws which could be formed, they would be run in upon us, and our money flow out; till we fall to a level with foreigners, and lose that great superiority of riches, which had laid us under such disadvantages? [1]

Hume concludes that "a government has great reason to preserve with care its people and its manufactures. Its money, it may safely trust to the course of human affairs, without fear or jealousy." [2]

It is interesting to note the similarity of Hume's analysis to that of F.W. Taussig, written over a century and a half later:

> Suppose, now, that the total exports do not suffice to pay for the total imports. Then they must be paid for in specie. Will that specie flow out for an indefinite time? and what likelihood is there that a balance will permanently remain to be paid in this way?
>
> The accepted answer to these questions and in essentials the accurate one, is that the flow of specie sets in motion forces which

---

[1] David Hume, "Of the Balance of Trade," reprinted in Arthur Eli Monroe, editor, *Early Economic Thought* (Cambridge: Harvard University Press, 1945), p. 325.

[2] *Ibid.*, p. 338.

sooner or later stop the flow. When specie leaves a country, prices tend to fall. Hence that country becomes one in which it is advantageous to buy. Lower prices stimulate exports. Conversely, the country to which the specie flows tends to have rising prices. It becomes one in which it is advantageous to sell. Higher prices stimulate imports. Hence the flow of specie has an automatic limitation. The greater it is, the more certain is it likely to cease. Merchandise exports and imports on the whole and in the long run balance, in consequence of the effect of the quantity of money on prices.[3]

The traditional description of the adjustment mechanism usually ran in terms of the gold standard, that is, it was assumed that the price of gold in terms of the money of each country is fixed within narrow limits, and there is freedom of movement of gold among the several trading countries. The result—which is elaborated in the Introduction to Part IV—was that the rate of exchange could fluctuate only within the limits set by the specie (gold) points: if the rate of exchange rose above the "mint par of exchange" by as much as the costs of the shipment of gold, gold would be exported to make international payments; if the rate fell below the mint par by an amount equal to the cost of shipping gold, some of those holding claims on foreigners would import gold rather than accept the discount on foreign bills. Adjustments in the balance of payments had to be worked out, accordingly, through changes in prices and incomes rather than by large movements in the rate of exchange.

The process by which the balance of payments was kept in balance may be briefly outlined.[4] If the total current payments that Americans, for example, want to make to foreigners just equals the amount of the total payments which foreigners want to make to Americans, the current account is in balance, and the "inventories" of foreign exchange dealers remain constant. Assume now, however, that Americans' demand for English goods increases by $50 million per week with no change in

[3] Frank W. Taussig, *Principles of Economics* (New York: The Macmillan Co., 1911), p. 458.
[4] *Cf.* J.E. Meade, *An Introduction to Economic Analysis and Policy* (London: Oxford University Press, 1937), Part V, chapter II.

the British demand for American goods. Dealers in foreign exchange will be receiving additional dollars and will be paying out additional pounds. If $5 = £1, the deposits of American exchange dealers in United States banks will increase $50 million per week, and deposits in British banks will fall £10 million per week. The balance of payments is kept in balance through a capital transfer: dealers' assets have been converted from British money to American money, and in the U.S. balance of payments a short-term capital inflow (a credit) finances the current account import balance (a debit).

If American payments continue to exceed receipts by $50 million per week, exchange dealers will soon find their sterling balances depleted, the dollar price of the pound will rise to the U.S. gold export point, and gold will be exported to the U.K. The gold shipment (a credit) has now replaced the capital transfer, at least in part, and the balance of payments continues to balance.

It is possible also that U.S. exchange dealers will supplement the capital movement which is implicit in the payments mechanism when American claims on England fall and U.K. claims on the U.S. rise with separate, explicit borrowing in London. U.S. dealers are especially willing to borrow pounds in London in order to accommodate U.S. importers if the dollar price of the pound has already hit the ceiling (gold point) and if short-term interest rates in New York have risen relative to London rates.

Thus far the deficit on current account has persisted. It is acceptable to draw down foreign balances, export gold, and borrow abroad up to a point. But eventually *short-term financing* of the deficit must give way to a *long-run adjustment* to equilibrium.

As the U.S. continues to lose gold, American banks will find their reserves depleted. To protect their reserve position they will sell securities, thus tending to lower security prices and increase interest rates, and loans will be curtailed. The higher interest rates and the reduction of the money supply will discourage investment and other spending and cause American prices and incomes to fall. Conversely, the increasing stocks of gold in England will increase English bank reserves, interest rates will fall and the money supply will increase, and British prices and incomes will rise. As American prices fall and British prices rise, there will be a tendency for American imports to decrease (in volume and, it is hoped, also in value) and for American exports to increase, and eventually—with the balance of payments deficit corrected—the export of gold from the U.S. will stop.

The requisites for the successful operation of the gold standard have been summarized as follows:

1. The chief countries should adopt internal policies designed to prevent violent fluctuations in domestic money income and prices, except as induced by adjustment pressures.

2. Countries losing gold should allow their money incomes and prices to fall, and countries gaining gold should allow their incomes and prices to rise.

3. Costs of production, i.e., prices of factors, must fall as prices fall.

4. The total supply of gold reserves available for central banks must be sufficient to form adequate backing against that volume of monetary transactions which is necessary to prevent a world-wide slump in money prices and incomes. If, for example, an increase of 2 per cent per year in central banks' note issues and deposit liabilities is just sufficient to prevent unemployment or boom, gold reserves also should be increasing at the rate of 2 per cent per year.

5. The appropriate rate of exchange must be chosen. Suppose, for example, that the U.S. is not on the gold standard but England is, with one ounce of gold worth £5. At $5 = £1, we may assume, the balance of payments is in equilibrium. If now the U.S. should go on the gold standard at 1 ounce of gold equal to $20, i.e., $4 = £1, the U.S. would lose gold, prices and incomes would fall, and unemployment would develop in the U.S.

6. If a country receives a large amount of interest or reparations from abroad, its balance of payments would be in equi-

librium only if it lends abroad more than it borrows or imports more goods and services than it exports.[5]

Again we may turn to Taussig for a summary of the neo-classical view of the adjustment process:

In the last resort, when all expedients for adjusting and equalizing the payments between nations have been utilized and exhausted, specie will flow in payment of balances. When trade is following its ordinary peaceful course, in a world not racked by political or economic cataclysms, it is likely to flow in small volume, even in driblets. Each driblet, slight tho it be, affects a susceptible spot, and tends to be minimized by reaction in some other part of the delicate adjustment. But if there be a succession of such influences—if there be a continued lack of equilibrium between a country's debits and credits—something more happens. There is then no way of resisting the inevitable readjustment. Sustained changes in the demand for goods, or continuing remittances on other than merchandise account, will show their consequences sooner or later in the international distribution of specie. *Then* the question becomes one of changes in prices and money incomes. . . . And the question arises, too, whether in the slow process of adjustment toward the eventual outcome there may not emerge, when the final survey has been completed and the last consequences have been verified, a residuum of unexplained phenomena—puzzling occurrences that cannot be brought into accord with even the most guarded theoretical formulation.[6]

It is clear that the central equilibrating force in the price-specie-flow mechanism was price changes induced by gold flows. The quantity theory of money was basic to the analysis.

[5] *Ibid. Cf.* John H. Williams, "Monetary Stability and the Gold Standard," in *Postwar Monetary Plans and Other Essays* (New York: Alfred A. Knopf, 1947, 3rd ed.), p. 178: ". . . the gold standard works best (1) when banking systems are fully loaned up to the limit set by their reserves, so that the flow of gold must cause a proportional variation in the amount of credit; (2) when capital movements and goods movements are sensitive to each other, requiring but little flow of gold to induce equilibrium in the balance of payments; (3) when the demand for international products is elastic, so that a fall in prices will produce an increase in value of exports relative to imports, and contrariwise; (4) when unit costs of production are responsive to money price variations, so that, when prices change in response to increases or decreases of gold, production and trade will respond to the movement of prices."

[6] Frank W. Taussig, *International Trade* (New York: The Macmillan Co., 1927), pp. 220–221.

Taussig referred to "a residuum of unexplained phenomena—puzzling occurrences." Adjustment came with "surprising exactness and speed," and "it must be confessed that here we have phenomena not fully understood." [7] Still, as Metzler observes, "no substantial revisions of the accepted theory were made until Keynes published his *General Theory* [1936]. Thereafter, the missing link in the classical theory became almost self-evident: the rapid adjustment of a country's balance of payments which Taussig had observed, and which seemed to occur without the assistance of price changes or changes in central bank policy, was found to be largely the result of induced movements of income and employment." [8]

THE FOREIGN TRADE MULTIPLIER

For close to 200 years, the Humian price-specie-flow mechanism—elaborated after Hume primarily to include operations of a fractional-reserve banking system—furnished the core and the bulk of the substance of international adjustment theory. While national income effects were not completely omitted from early theory,[9] the role of income changes in the adjustment mechanism has been systematically detailed and emphasized—perhaps overemphasized—only during the past 20-odd years.[10]

[7] *Ibid.*, p. 239.

[8] Lloyd A. Metzler, "The Theory of International Trade," in Howard S. Ellis, editor, *A Survey of Contemporary Economics* (Philadelphia: The Blakiston Co., 1948), p. 215.

[9] See the survey by Jacob Viner, *Studies in the Theory of International Trade* (New York: Harper and Brothers, 1937), pp. 290–311. Viner, who argues that the income element in adjustment has been overly stressed in recent years, agrees that "while it is not true that the classical economists wholly ignored income changes, it is true that they did not give income changes a prominent and important role in their formal expositions of the theory of the international mechanism." *International Trade and Economic Development* (Glencoe: The Free Press, 1952), p. 32.

[10] The case for abstract income models has been put as follows: "Frequently it becomes important to know whether there are equilibrating forces in international trade other than price adjustments [*Footnote:* The term 'price adjustment' denotes, in the present context, any movement of monetary variables and is understood to include interest- and exchange-rate fluctuations.], and if so, how these other forces operate. Thus, for example, if two countries which

Although modern national income theory stems mainly from Keynes' *General Theory* [11] and Keynes was much interested in international economics, he himself did not carry far forward the extension of income theory to include elements of foreign commerce. This extension was soon developed by several writers.

Omitting government spending and taxing and omitting also, for the moment, foreign trade, we may use the following income model:

$Y = C + I$, with respect to income determination
$Y = C + S$, with respect to income disposal

That is, money national income (Y) is determined by, and indeed consists of, spending (consumption and investment) on current domestic output; and the income thereby created is disposed of in consumption and saving. Further, $\Delta Y = \Delta C + \Delta I$, and $\Delta Y = \Delta C + \Delta S$. Dividing the latter equation by ΔY, we obtain $1 = \Delta C/\Delta Y + \Delta S/\Delta Y$. Since $\Delta C/\Delta Y$ is, by definition, the marginal propensity to consume, and $\Delta S/\Delta Y$ is the marginal propensity to save, it is apparent that the sum of the marginal propensities to consume and to save is unity: $1 = c + s$; and $1 - c = s$.

In the words of Keynes, the "multiplier" states "a precise relationship, given the propensity to consume, between ag-

---

are trading with each other have substantial amounts of unemployment, and if, because of minimum-wage laws, union restrictions, or custom, money wages are relatively inflexible, equilibrium of the balance of payments and the balance of trade cannot be obtained readily by adjustments of prices and money costs. If it is assumed, in addition, that the two countries are on gold standards with sufficient reserves so that central-bank policies are not affected by gold movements, then changes in the rate of interest and the exchange rate may be ruled out. The consistency of domestic changes with the maintenance of external equilibrium will then depend upon the way in which variations of investment and consumption in one country react upon investment and consumption in others. The effects of such changes are isolated . . . by setting up a model of trade between two countries in which variations of prices, interest rates, and the rate of exchange are impossible." Lloyd A. Metzler, "Underemployment Equilibrium in International Trade," *Économetrica*, X (April 1942), pp. 97–98.

[11] John Maynard Keynes, *The General Theory of Employment, Interest and Money* (New York: Harcourt, Brace and Co., 1936).

gregate employment and income and the rate of investment." [12]
Symbolically, if k represents the multiplier, $k = \Delta Y/\Delta I$. More
generally, the multiplier is the relationship between *any*
"autonomous" injection (or disinjection) of expenditure, i.e.,
a change in spending not induced by a prior change in income,
and the (ultimately) resulting change in income.

Taking investment as the injection, we may rewrite $\Delta Y =
\Delta C + \Delta I$ as $\Delta I = \Delta Y - \Delta C$. Since $k = \Delta Y/\Delta I$, then

$$k = \frac{\Delta Y}{\Delta Y - \Delta C}, \quad \text{and} \quad k = \frac{1}{1 - \Delta C/\Delta Y} = \frac{1}{1 - c} = 1/s.$$

That is, the value of the multiplier is equal to the reciprocal
of the marginal propensity to save. And $\Delta Y = k\Delta I$.

The mechanics of the multiplier process can be best visualized by means of "period" analysis. Note that the income in
any given period is equal to expenditure (consumption and
investment) in that *same* period; but the income thus generated in any given period is disposed of (through consumption
and saving) in the *following* period.

Table I

$c = .8; s = .2$

Period	C	S	I	Y
1	900	100	100	1000
2	900	100	100	1000
3	900	100	200	1100
4	980	120	200	1180
5	1044	136	200	1244
6	1095.2	148.8	200	1295.2
*	1300	200	200	1500

We start, in periods 1 and 2, with an equilibrium level of
income, i.e., a level which persists or is self-sustaining. An
equilibrium level of income is characterized by the equality of
saving and investment *in a given time period:* if the rate of
"leakage" out of the current level of income exactly offsets the

[12] *Ibid.*, p. 113.

rate of "injection" into the current income stream, the income level does not change. Now, in period 3, the level of investment rises autonomously to 200, and the income equilibrium is upset. Income will not reach a new equilibrium until saving again equals investment: income must rise far enough to induce the community to save 200 each time period. Income rises at a decreasing rate and eventually levels off at 1500. The increase in the income level of 500 induces an increase of 400 in the consumption level and an increase of 100 in the saving level. It has been assumed that $c = .8$ (which, incidentally, is not equal to the *average* propensity to consume, C/Y, either before the injection or after the multiplier process has worked itself out) and $s = .2$, giving the result that $k = 5$.

Tables may be constructed in terms of *changes* in the variables, and the figures give the changes from the *initial* situation which existed prior to the injection. We may thus rewrite Table I.

Table Ia

$c = .8; s = .2$

ΔC	ΔS	ΔI	ΔY
		100	100
80	20	100	180
144	36	100	244
195.2	48.8	100	295.2
400	100	100	500

A simple way to introduce foreign trade into this scheme is (a) to replace autonomous changes in investment with autonomous changes in exports and (b) to add induced imports to the income-disposal equation. Exports represent a form of expenditure on current domestic output and thus are a determinant of income, an injection; imports involve spending, but not on *domestic* output, and they are a mode of disposing of income, a leakage. Thus, $\Delta Y = \Delta C + \Delta X$, and $\Delta Y = \Delta C + \Delta S + \Delta M$. In this case, $1 = c + s + m$, and $k_f = 1/(1-c) = 1/(s+m)$.

Introduction 201

Table II

$c = .5; s = .2; m = .3$

ΔC	ΔS	ΔM	ΔX	$\Delta(X - M)$	ΔY
			100	100	100
50	20	30	100	70	150
75	30	45	100	55	175
87.5	35	52.5	100	47.5	187.5
200	40	60	100	40	200

As before, an equilibrium level of income is upset by autonomous injection of expenditure—this time expenditure by foreigners, rather than by domestic investors—on current domestic output. And again we reach a new equilibrium level of income when the induced leakages—here imports as well as saving—rise to the level of the injection. But since ΔM is only part of the leakage, ΔM will not rise to the level of ΔX; when the new income equilibrium is attained, there remains an export balance. Since $\Delta S + \Delta M = \Delta X$, then $\Delta S = \Delta(X - M)$. The initial export balance would be entirely eliminated only if there were no change in saving, i.e., if $s = 0$.

Viner (selection 9) and Meade (selection 10) comment on aspects of the adjustment alternatives generally. Triffin (selection 11) takes up the gold standard, and Nurkse (selection 12) considers the application of income theory to the problem of internal and external equilibria.

9. WORLD EQUILIBRIUM

Jacob Viner

Princeton University

Excerpt, slightly modified, reprinted from "The Role of the United States in the World Economy," in Robert Lekachman, editor, *National Policy for Economic Welfare at Home and Abroad* (Garden City: Doubleday and Co., Inc., Copyright 1955), pp. 175–210; pp. 189–192 excerpted. Reprinted by permission of the author and the Trustees of Columbia University.

It should be the fundamental objective of our economic policy to bring about the establishment of a satisfactory economic equilibrium between our economy and the rest of the free world. The elimination of dollar scarcity, in the sense of recurrent dollar deficits in foreign balances of payments grudgingly to be financed by dollar grants, should be regarded as a major phase of the establishment of satisfactory equilibrium. However, this is not the whole story.

DEFICITS IN PAYMENTS

Balance of payments deficits, even "chronic" ones, can arise out of a variety of circumstances differing widely in character and basic significance. They can arise alike out of prosperity and out of economic distress, from overambitious or overimpatient programs of economic development and from economic deterioration. Whether countries are prosperous or in distress, whether their economies are expanding or stagnant, they will have balance-of-payments difficulties if they are undergoing inflation at a more rapid rate than prevails in the countries with which they have close trading relations, or if they are maintaining the exchange values of their currencies above their equilibrium levels and are not fully offsetting the resultant pressure on their balances of payments by quantitative controls of the volume of their imports.

Poverty is not of itself sufficient to produce continuing deficits in balances of payments. If there are no holdings of internationally liquid assets, of hard currencies and gold, to draw on, and if there is no assured access to foreign credit or justified reliance on foreign aid to finance deficits as they accrue, the deficits are bound to come to an end in one way or another. In the nineteenth century, when governments in the main did not interfere with the course of commodity prices, when interest rates were determined by free market forces, when gold holdings and holdings of foreign balances were the determinants of national stocks of money, adverse balances of payments soon were followed by rises in interest rates, declines in the volume of bank credit, contractions in the rate of domestic investment, relative declines in export prices as compared to import prices, and consequent termination of balance-of-payments deficits through decreases in imports, accompanied often by increases in exports. This manner of adjustment could be painful to the members of the community and could be costly to the economy, but in the absence of the power or the will to borrow abroad there was no escape from it. The impact of a balance-of-payments deficit then bore soon on individuals and firms, and the responses which they had to make to these impacts were necessarily such as operated to restore international equilibrium.

METHOD OF EQUILIBRATION

Today in most countries little is left of this automatic process of international equilibration. Dealings in foreign exchange are now largely monopolized by official agencies, and whether individual business can buy abroad and pay debts abroad no longer depends directly on their own, or their bankers', international liquidity, but on whether the official custodians of the national stock of foreign currencies permit them to do so. A deficit on current account in a country's balance of payments today, consequently, often registers itself only in the central bank or other official agency. This agency can respond to the deficit by allowing its holdings of foreign currency to shrink without further action. If it follows this procedure there is no reason why the balance-of-payments deficit cannot continue until the central bank's holdings are exhausted. The government may succeed in obtaining financing of the deficits for a time by foreign credits or grants. As long as this can be managed, the deficits can continue indefinitely. Or the monetary authorities may allow the national currency to depreciate on the exchange markets, and this may restore even balance. Or the authorities may not do any of these things, but may instead apply or extend quantitative import restrictions, and this may bring the deficits to an end by what is equivalent to brute force. Or the banking authorities may, by tightening rediscount privileges or raising reserve requirements of commercial banks or by increasing taxes and reducing government expenditures, reduce the national money supply and the level of internal business activity and thus induce businessmen to diminish their purchases abroad and to look more actively for export markets to offset the decline in their domestic sales. Whatever the detailed procedures, however, when adjustment of international balances occurs today, in most of the world it occurs because governments make the appropriate decisions, and it occurs in accordance with the timing and the severity of these decisions, rather than on the initiative of individuals and individual business firms, as was once the case.

POSTWAR INFLATION

The period since the end of the war has been largely a period of universal inflation, and all of it has been a period of marked inflation in at least a large part of the world. This means, of course, that governments permitted this inflation to occur, or even positively promoted it. It would be unfair, however, to fail to acknowledge that the forces leading to inflation were powerful, that many governments were weak, and that the measures required to bring inflation to an end were always difficult politically to apply, or at least were deemed so in advance. Many governments probably were convinced that to end the inflation by the measures available would involve dangers of mass unemployment and of popular discontent, and some governments may have feared that positive action to end inflation might result in their political defeat, perhaps by armed revolution. There were always at least a few economists, however, who insisted that these fears were exaggerated. Some countries finally did take the steps necessary to bring the inflation and the balance-of-payments deficits to an end, and in no case did economic or political disaster follow.

What the economists now say who earlier had regarded the balance-of-payments deficits of most countries as chronic, as due to something called "structural disequilibrium," which balancing of national budgets and tightening of credit would not suffice to cure and might intensify, I do not know. If they are not maintaining a discreet silence, I suppose that they are claiming either that the countries which have regained balance-of-payments equilibrium were able to do so as the result of fortuitous good luck which was not shared by the countries still in deficit or have succeeded only in attaining a balance which is precarious and will not last; or that the restoration of balance-of-payments equilibrium was not worth the cost it entailed. It is probably too early for definitive judgment on these issues, but so far the evidence seems clearly enough to show that when skillfully managed, restoration of balance-of-payments equilibrium is neither as difficult nor costly, as a rule, as even the most optimistic forecasters had foretold.

Satisfactory international economic equilibrium, however, does not necessarily involve elimination of balance-of-payments deficits, and balance-of-payments equilibrium does not necessarily suffice for satisfactory international economic equilibrium. Countries which have opportunities for profitable economic development requiring more capital than domestic savings can supply can with benefit to themselves and to the world economy adjust their economies to continuing balance-of-payments deficits on current account, provided they can find long-term financing abroad at acceptable rates of interest and terms of ultimate repayment.

On the other hand, countries which by austere fiscal and monetary policies or tight quantitative restrictions on imports succeed in keeping their balances of payments from running into deficits may nevertheless be failing to meet urgent needs for economic betterment, may be undergoing persistent economic stagnation and mass poverty, and may be building up underlying popular discontents and frustrations which eventually will explode in major revolution.

The state of a country's balance of payments, therefore, should be regarded as only one of the many significant factors requiring attention before it can be determined whether its economy is in a healthy or in an unhealthy state, whether it needs external help or not, and if it does need help, in what form and to what extent. Countries may be prospering despite the fact that they have not tried, or having tried have failed, to bring their balances of payments into equilibrium. It may be the countries which have not let their international finances get out of order that are in greatest need and most deserving of our help. We should not let balance-of-payments situations exert predominant weight in our appraisals of the needs of foreign countries and in our decisions as to what countries we help and in what manner and degree.

10. THE DOLLAR GAP

J.E. Meade

University of London

Excerpt from *The Atlantic Community and the Dollar Gap* (London: Friends of Atlantic Union, July 1953); pp. 13-25 excerpted. Reprinted by permission of the author and the publisher.

Between the middle of 1945 and of 1952 the United States and Canada in the post-war Anglo-American and Canadian loans, in Marshall Aid, and in economic aid under the Mutual Security Administration have provided a net sum of no less than $31,000 million to the countries of Western Europe, a sum which is equivalent to no less than 29 per cent of all American and Canadian exports during these years. In addition countries outside the dollar area have lost reserves of gold in the finance of some part of their dollar purchases. Yet in spite of this unprecedented use of special dollar resources all the countries of the sterling area and of the European Payments Union, with the exception of Belgium and Switzerland, have had continuously to impose strict limitations upon imports from and payments to the dollar area. It would be useless to attempt to assess what the actual requirement of additional dollar resources would have been in the absence of such dollar restrictions; but it would clearly have been very great indeed. The dollar gap has been the overwhelming persistent structural disequilibrium in the payments arrangements of the countries of the Atlantic Community since the end of the second world war.

(1) SOLUTION BY DISCRIMINATORY RESTRICTIONS

In circumstances such as this discrimination in restrictions on imports from and payments to the dollar area have been inevitable. Suppose that the United Kingdom and France have deficits on their balances of payments which each intends to control by means of quantitative restrictions on its imports; and suppose that these deficits are matched by a surplus on the United States' balance of payments. The United Kingdom and the French governments then restrict imports in order to put their balances of payments into equilibrium. But there is little point in their restricting imports from each other with the same severity with which they restrict imports from the United States. If the British refuse to buy French wines and the French to purchase British motorcars, it will cut off profitable trade between the two countries; but except to the limited extent to which it induces the French wine merchant and the British motorcar manufacturer to seek an alternative market for their products in the United States, it will do nothing to remove the world disequilibrium in the balance of payments. That will be removed by a restriction of the British and French imports from the United States, not by a refusal of the two deficit countries—the United Kingdom and France—to trade with each other.

Now it would be quite possible to organise a permanent solution of the dollar problem by means of a system of strict discriminatory restriction against dollar imports into the non-dollar world. In the absence of any special dollar aid the severity of the restrictions on dollar payments might have to be very great; but with a sufficient cut-back in the standards of consumption of dollar goods in the non-dollar world, it could no doubt be done. There are, however, a number of important reasons why an alternative solution should if possible be found.

In the first place, the organisation of the free western world into two distinctly separate financial blocs with a severe control over trade from the dollar to the non-dollar part of the Atlantic Community is not likely to provide the best economic background for the strong and rapid growth of political, cultural, and military union. Discrimination against their products in non-dollar markets may create resentment among United States and Canadian traders. The free flow of ideas is stopped when there are difficulties in obtaining books from or in travelling to other parts of the Atlantic Community. A gold curtain will never be as strict or as abhorrent as an iron curtain; but it is nevertheless a real impediment to unity.

In the second place, a rigid barrier against the purchase of dollar goods in the non-dollar world—particularly if it is accompanied by high tariffs on imports into the dollar world—will greatly restrict the possibilities of profitable trade. Even in the middle of the twentieth century there remains much good sense in the old free-trade view that all can gain if each country specialises on the things in the production of which it has the greatest comparative advantage or the least comparative disadvantage. We may all stand to gain if the United Kingdom can purchase timber from Canada and sell railway equipment to West Africa, who can sell cocoa to the North American continent. The countries of the Atlantic Community are not yet rich enough to accept a solution of payments problems which sacrifices important possibilities of raising productivity all round by a fruitful division of labour between them.

But, in the third place, the persistence of a dollar gap which is warded off only by the perpetuation of strict discriminatory restrictions against dollar purchases is likely to cause increasing stresses and strains within the non-dollar part of the Atlantic Community. The British Commonwealth presents a good illustration of this fact. Canada is a member of the Commonwealth but is in the dollar area, and discrimination against dollar goods by the United Kingdom and other parts of the sterling area involves discrimination against Canadian products. This has led to a growing dependence of Canada upon her trade with the United States in place of her trade with the United Kingdom. Between 1938 and 1950 Canadian imports from the United States rose from 63 to 67 per cent and from the United Kingdom fell from 18 to 13 per cent of her total imports; and in the same period her exports to the United States rose from 32 to 65 per cent and to the United Kingdom fell from 41 to 15 per cent of her total exports. To this extent the gold curtain has weakened the economic ties of the British Commonwealth.

Other parts of the Commonwealth might be tempted in the future to copy the example of Canada and join the dollar area. The West African colonies and Malaya, for example, with their exports of cocoa, rubber and tin are some of the chief earners for the sterling area of dollars, which they and the other members of the area must then by some process parcel out for use among themselves. If these colonial territories, which are growing up to political freedom, could choose for themselves, they might choose to join the dollar area and use their dollar earnings for their own purposes. They could do so more easily than Canada who normally had a large excess of imports from the United Kingdom. Economically Canada might have been tempted to preserve her export markets in the United Kingdom by joining the sterling area and discriminating in her imports in favour of United Kingdom over United States products. She chose to make a huge reorientation of her export sales to the United States. The dollar-earning colonial territories start with a large surplus of exports to the United States and could more easily relax their restrictions on dollar goods without having to face any structural reorientation of their export trade. In the long run a free British Commonwealth can hope to remain economically coherent only if United Kingdom and other sterling area products are made so competitive with dollar products that the dollar earners within the Commonwealth freely choose to use their dollars to buy the cheap and efficient products of the other parts of the sterling area.

But to find a means of coping with the dollar gap other than by discriminatory restrictions on dollar payments is not easy. It is not to be attained by some simple jugglery with financial mechanisms and institutions. It can be achieved only by extensive readjustments of economic policies of many kinds both in the dollar world and also in the non-dollar world. The action which is required is becoming familiar knowledge. The main question now is whether the governments and the peoples concerned have a sufficiently lively appreciation of the great objective for them to be willing to face the many awkward political decisions which are necessary for its achievement. Here there is room for no more than a brief enumeration of the sort of action which is required both by the deficit countries of the non-dollar world and by the surplus countries of the dollar world to make an alternative solution possible.

(2) DOMESTIC FINANCIAL POLICIES

The extent of any dollar gap is greatly influenced by the domestic monetary and budgetary policies of the countries of the Atlantic Community. If a country adopts an expansionist policy of cheap money (which makes it easy to borrow new money for new expenditures on capital development), of low taxation (which leaves much additional purchasing power in the hands of the private citizen) and of high government expenditure (which inflates the public demand for goods and services), then there will be an inflation of demand for goods and services within that country. Some part of this increase will represent an increased demand for imports or for goods which would otherwise be available for export. In this way the expansionist domestic policy will have increased the country's deficit, or reduced its surplus, on its balance of payments.

And conversely if a country adopts a domestic policy for monetary and budgetary deflation. It will import less and will release more of its own products for export.

This means that a very special duty is laid on the deficit non-dollar members of the Atlantic Community to avoid domestic inflation, and indeed to disinflate. In the modern world it is impossible and—the writer of this pamphlet would add—highly undesirable that the deficit countries in the interests of their balance of payments should indulge in a domestic deflation on a scale which would give rise to serious unemployment problems at home. But they have an unequivocal duty to disinflate domestically up to the point which is compatible with the maintenance of a high level of employment at home.

And similarly with the surplus dollar countries. It would not be desirable to demand of them that they should go into an uncontrolled domestic inflation in the interests of equilibrium in the world's balance of payments. But it is most emphatically incumbent upon them to inflate as much as is compatible with their domestic financial health and, above all, to avoid any recession of demand.

Since 1945 the problem has been one of controlling inflations in the deficit countries. The dollar gap—in so far as it has been due to domestic policies—has not been caused by an American slump. Indeed, as the following figures show, there has been a very considerable inflation on the North American continent, but unfortunately this has been accompanied by persistent inflations in the deficit countries of Western Europe.

INDICES OF MONEY INCOMES AND PRICES IN NATIONAL CURRENCIES
(1951 as a Percentage of 1946)

	National Income	Retail Prices	Wage Rates
United States	154	133	148
Canada	176	148	163
United Kingdom	137	134	143
France	350	364 (a)	–
Italy	150 (b)	190	156 (b)
Netherlands	182	138	135

(a) Food in Paris
(b) Compared with 1947

But the situation may well change. The most hideous threat which hangs over the Atlantic Community on the economic side is the devastation which would be caused by a serious slump in the United States. Even a minor recession would cause very great difficulties. In the United States the demand for imports is particularly sensitive to fluctuations in the domestic level of activity. In the Great Depression between 1929 and 1932 the dollar value of the United States national income fell by about 45 per cent, but the dollar value of her imports fell by no less than 70 per cent. In the recession between 1937 and 1938 the United States national income fell by about 5 per cent, but the value of her imports fell by 35 per cent. In the minor recession of 1949 the United States national income did not fall, it merely ceased to rise; but the value of her imports fell by about 7 per cent.

These facts make it patently clear that if anything more than a minor recession were allowed to occur in the United States the prospects for dealing with the dollar problem without severe discriminatory restrictions would become impossible. And even if only a minor recession occurred—a 10 per cent fall in United States imports represents an intensification of the dollar gap by no less than $1,100 million a year—the problem would be quite insoluble without many other simultaneous aids and alleviations, of which the most important will be mentioned in the following sections.

(3) THE STABILISATION OF PRIMARY PRODUCT MARKETS

The United States demand for industrial materials is most sensitive to fluctuations in domestic activity, since in times of contracting trade and falling prices a running down of stocks is likely to occur simultaneously with a contraction of current consumption. The overseas sterling area (i.e., the sterling area excluding the United Kingdom) exports many such materials. Thus in the Great Depression of 1929–32 when the value of the total United States imports fell by 70 per cent, the value of her imports from the overseas sterling area fell by 80 per cent; in the recession of 1937–38 when the value of her total imports fell by about 35 per cent, the value of her imports from the overseas sterling area fell by 50 per cent; and in the minor recession of 1949 when the value of her total imports fell by 7 per cent, the value of her imports from the overseas sterling area fell by 15 per cent.

Of great assistance, therefore, to the solution of the dollar prob-

lem would be the institution of international buffer stock schemes
for such materials as tin, rubber, etc., which would maintain the
demand for such materials in times of recession and falling demand
and which would increase the supply of such materials out of the
international stock in times of inflated private demand. If the finance
for such schemes came largely from dollar sources, this would even
out the dollar gap. It would put more dollars onto the world market
when the private demand for such materials was low; and it would
reabsorb dollars when private demand was high, materials were
being sold from the official stocks, and dollars were thus being
absorbed by the buffer stock authorities.

(4) INTERNATIONAL RESERVES

If trade restrictions and exchange controls over current payments
are to be removed, the members of the Atlantic Community must
have adequate reserves of gold or of other internationally acceptable
means of payment. This is especially important in view of the enormous fluctuations in payments which, as we have seen, would result
from comparatively small fluctuations in business activity in the
United States. Indeed, there is much to be said for the organisation
of some special fund of great dimensions (e.g., of special drawing
rights in some body like the International Monetary Fund) which
might be used by countries if, but only if, a serious strain on their
balance of payments developed as a result of a depression of demand
in other countries.

But apart from fluctuations due to domestic booms and slumps, in
the modern world inventions and changes in technique are constantly taking place; demand is liable to shift from butter to guns
and from guns to butter; economic development is continually
changing the pattern of demand; and so on. Such changes are bound
to cause variations in the demand for the products of different countries; and in the absence of control by quantitative regulation of the
volume of trade and payments, gold or other reserves must be available to meet the first shock upon a country's balance of payments
while the price adjustments considered in the next section are given
an opportunity to put matters right.

It is not always realised how very inadequate are the reserves of
some parts of the Atlantic Community at the present time. In the
United Kingdom the holding of gold and dollars represents the

reserves held not only against the United Kingdom's balance of payments but also against fluctuations in the payment position of the rest of the sterling area. Measured against either of these possible calls the post-war holdings are utterly inadequate in comparison with the pre-war position. At the end of 1938 the United Kingdom's reserves were sufficient to finance her import bill for nearly nine months; at the end of 1951 they were sufficient to finance her imports for only just over two and a half months. In the immediate pre-war period the United Kingdom's reserves were slightly greater than the total of her short-term sterling liabilities; in the middle of 1952 they covered only about one-sixth of her sterling liabilities.

A substantial increase in reserves is thus an essential condition for a system of really free payments within the Atlantic Community. There are many ways in which they might be brought about.

(i) The non-dollar deficit countries might by very austere disinflations at home and by very severe discriminatory restrictions against dollar goods generate a surplus on their balances of payments, and they could use the dollars so earned to build up their reserves. After a period they could then move towards a system of freer payments on the basis of the large reserves so accumulated. But it is not wise to cure a headache by cutting off the patient's head.

(ii) Special dollar stabilisation grants or loans might be sought from the United States; but this solution suffers from the severe disadvantage which any nephew must experience when he has to touch his rich uncle on yet one more final occasion.

(iii) The dollar price of gold might be raised once and for all. This would increase the dollar purchasing power of all the gold reserves already held by the non-dollar countries. It would have the advantage of not requiring the appropriation of any dollar funds by the United States Congress. Moreover, it would not only increase once and for all the value of existing reserves, but it would lead to a considerable rise in the amount of dollars paid out by the United States annually for the purchase of newly mined gold. If the dollar price of gold were doubled (so that the price of gold were restored more nearly to its pre-war relationship with other prices which have in general at least doubled), the annual receipts of the sterling area for its present gold output would increase by no less than $500 million—a very substantial contribution to the closing of the dollar

gap. This solution suffers, however, from a number of serious disadvantages. It distributes the once-for-all increase in reserves solely
on the principle of giving to those who start with the largest gold
reserves; it gives the whole of the annual dollar aid to the gold
producers—in particular to South Africa and the U.S.S.R.; and it
encourages the essentially silly use of economic resources in digging
up gold on the Rand for the sole purpose of reburying it in Fort
Knox.

(iv) The United States might set up an exchange equilisation
account endowed with a large initial fund of dollars, and the authorities in control of it, in co-operation with the exchange equalisation
accounts of the other countries of the Atlantic Community could
give support to currencies which were temporarily under heavy
pressure. This solution might leave too many important international
decisions solely in the hands of national governments and, in particular, of the United States administration.

(v) Finally, some form of international or supranational exchange
equalisation fund might be instituted for this purpose. For example
a revivified International Monetary Fund with much enlarged
quotas and a more appropriate form of administration might serve
this purpose. To those who, like the author of this pamphlet, wish
to see the functional co-operative institutions of the Atlantic Community developed, this will provide the most attractive solution.

(5) VARIATIONS IN EXCHANGE RATES

In the modern world national governments are not willing to
undertake domestic inflations or deflations as the main means for
bringing their balances of payments into equilibrium, regardless of
the domestic hardships which may be caused. Moreover, in the
interests of forming a unified market in the Atlantic Community,
we wish to rule out the use of direct controls over trade and payments. Also it is impossible to conceive of deficit countries living
permanently upon inexhaustible stocks of gold and other reserves.
We must find yet another means as the basic instrument for achieving lasting readjustment to fundamental structural changes in balances of payments. Only one such instrument remains, namely a
variation in the rate of exchange between the currencies of the
deficit and of the surplus countries.

When the currency of a deficit country is depreciated in terms of the currency of a surplus country this tends to raise the price of the surplus country's products in terms of the currency of the deficit country and to reduce the price of the products of the deficit country in terms of the currency of the surplus country. The surplus country, is, therefore, likely to purchase somewhat more of the products of the deficit country which are now cheaper to it; and the deficit country is likely to purchase somewhat less of the products of the surplus country which are now more expensive for it. If these shifts in trade are sufficiently responsive to changes in relative prices, if—that is to say—the imports of the deficit country fall sufficiently and its exports rise sufficiently when the value of the deficit country's currency is depreciated, then this will provide an effective mechanism for the final adjustment of balances of payments.

If we are to build a system of free trade and payments in the Atlantic Community, we shall have to rely largely upon variations in exchange rates. Some people, like the author of this pamphlet, would draw the conclusion that the best mechanism would be a system of freely floating exchange rates in a free foreign exchange market which was subject only to the intervention of national exchange equalisation funds or, preferably, of a supranational fund. Others would see more merit in exchange rates which were pegged at fixed levels, these levels being, however, subject to periodic or occasional revision. This is a controversial question. But whatever may be the merits of the choice between freely floating rates and the occasional revision of pegged rates, all would agree that in modern conditions, if trade and current payments are to be freed from direct control, much more frequent changes in rates will be necessary than under the old regime of the more or less automatic gold standard.

A variation of exchange rates will be one of the instruments which the deficit non-dollar countries might use to ward off the effects of a business recession in the United States, though it is doubtful whether alone it could suffice to cope with a serious American depression. A slump in the United States would cause a heavy fall in the real purchasing power of consumers on the North American continent and this would in any case reduce the export markets of producers in other countries. But this inevitable development would be unnecessarily intensified if as a result of the slump United States products fell, say, 10 per cent in dollar price while money costs of the products of other countries remained unchanged. The adverse effects of the fall in American real purchasing power would be intensified by a new and additional price advantage for American products. If dollar prices fell by 10 per cent, then an appreciation of the dollar (i.e., a depreciation of other currencies) by 10 per cent would restore the previous relationship between dollar prices and non-dollar prices. In the absence of such an exchange-rate variation an absolute domestic deflation of 10 per cent within the economies of the other countries would be needed to restore the old price relationship. In the absence of either of the price adjustments (and deliberate domestic deflations of this magnitude would be unthinkable), the need for discriminatory restrictions against the purchase of dollar products would be greatly intensified.

But apart from its usefulness as a means of meeting a temporary recession in other countries, the depreciation of a country's currency may be needed to meet a more permanent structural change. Suppose that, because of economic development in previously unindustrialised countries, the demand for United Kingdom textiles falls and that this puts some strain on the United Kingdom's balance of payments. Some depreciation of sterling might put the situation right, if the consequential cheapening of British products in foreign currencies caused a considerable expansion of the same or of alternative British export markets.

But the danger of the use of variations in exchange rates in such circumstances arises if the channels of trade are not responsive to changes in relative prices. If, in the hypothetical case just quoted, there is not a considerable expansion of British exports when their price is somewhat cheapened in foreign currencies, then a very large depreciation of sterling and a very large fall in the price of British exports relatively to the price of foreign products may be necessary to restore equilibrium to the balance of payments. In this case the United Kingdom would suffer a very serious change in the terms of international trade against her; she would obtain much less imports for each unit of exported product. She would avoid this change if she had met the deficit in the first place by a direct quantitative restriction of her imports.

From this we may draw two conclusions.

First, these considerations reinforce the arguments given above for believing that a substantial increase in the gold or other reserves of the deficit countries is a *sine qua non* for the successful adoption of a system of free payments within the Atlantic Community, for one cannot expect price adjustments to have their full effect upon the channels of trade immediately. British exports will be fully expanded by a depreciation of sterling only when sufficient time has elapsed to allow the consequential cheapening of British products to break a way for them into foreign markets. The United Kingdom must have sufficient reserves to finance her deficit while this adjustment is taking place.

Second, everything possible must be done to make international markets as responsive as possible to variations in relative prices and costs. The next section will deal with policies which will have this effect.

(6) COMMERCIAL POLICIES

If, in the interests of building up a system of free Atlantic payments, the deficit non-dollar countries were to remove their import restrictions and their exchange controls over current payments, there might be a sharp change in the terms of trade against them. The freeing of their payments would put them into deficit; to remove this deficit by an alternative means they would have to depreciate their currencies; and if the deficit were sufficiently large or the channels of trade were insufficiently responsive to price changes, this might involve a very considerable deterioration in their real terms of trade with the dollar half of the free world.

This development could be avoided if the dollar half of the free world, and in particular the United States, simultaneously took measures to remove its barriers against imports so that the exports of the non-dollar half of the free world were expanded *pari passu* with the expansion of its imports.

Too little credit is often given to the United States for the extent to which its tariffs have been reduced in recent years. The average *ad valorem* incidence of its duties on dutiable imports has fallen from about 45 per cent in 1934 to about 12½ per cent today. The United States tariff is now at a lower level than ever before in its recent history. This has occurred as a result of its Trade Agreements Programme and of the general rise in prices which has greatly reduced the *ad valorem* incidence of the specific element in many duties. Nevertheless, much remains to be done.

(i) The United States administration should obtain powers to go as far as the elimination of those duties (e.g., on British woollens) which really do still greatly impede trade. Some part of the statistical reduction in the United States tariff has undoubtedly been due to cutting out the unimportant, because unnecessary, parts of the tariff system.

(ii) Perhaps more important is the elimination from the General Agreement on Tariffs and Trade of the escape clause which enables a government to remove a concession if as a result of it imports come in in such amounts as seriously to injure the domestic industry. If the industry is in fact uneconomic, it ought to be injured and even eliminated by imports. It is a serious deterrent to potential exporters to the United States to know that the United States administration, however enlightened its own approach may be, is actually required by Congressional Legislation to remove a concession if by their selling efforts the foreign exporters do really effectively cut into an American market.

(iii) The simplification of the United States customs procedure is another way in which an important contribution might be made to increase the United States demand for imports. Legislation on this matter has been bogged down in Congress.

(iv) The "Buy American" legislation which requires governmental authorities in the United States to give a preference to United States products in their purchases should be repealed.

(v) The removal of subsidies on United States shipping and shipbuilding and of regulations which require that parts of United States trade should be carried in United States ships would free to price-and-cost competition another important market in which the United States would often find itself at a serious disadvantage.

The adoption of these policies by the United States would mean that the deficit non-dollar countries could simultaneously remove or relax their direct controls over dollar payments without thereby being subjected to an intolerable pressure upon their gold reserves or upon the exchange value of their currencies and their international terms of trade. But it would have another equally important though less spectacular advantage. The clearance of the channels of international trade from all these trade barriers would mean that purchasers the world over were much more readily influenced by changes in the relative prices of the products of different suppliers. In any future disequilibrium in the balance of payments which may occur—and such phenomena will, of course, be continually cropping up in a more or less acute form—a variation in relative prices brought about either by appropriate domestic financial policies or by an appropriate exchange rate adjustment would be much more effective as an instrument for restoring balance.

11. National Central Banking and the International Economy

Robert Triffin

Yale University

Excerpt from "National Central Banking and the International Economy," *International Monetary Policies*, Postwar Economic Studies No. 7 (Washington: Board of Governors of the Federal Reserve System, September 1947) pp. 46–81; pp. 46–63 excerpted. Reprinted by permission of the author and the Board of Governors.

The growth of nationalistic policies in a world of growingly interdependent nations is one of the apparent paradoxes of our age. Interdependence has proved to have disadvantages as well as advantages, and its disadvantages have at times resulted in a resurgence of extreme nationalism. Countries have become engulfed in wars which in the past would never have concerned them, and they have suffered from economic depressions having their origin in far distant lands. Nationalism persists in part as an effort to preserve or rebuild the crumbling natural boundaries which once protected countries from the political conflicts and economic maladjustments of other parts of the world. The many cases in which international crises have been intensified by nationalistic measures of defense by one country and retaliatory action by others have tended to overshadow the real and challenging problem responsible for these measures. Nothing can be gained by denying or ignoring its existence.

Our internationalism is often short-sighted in this respect. In the monetary field, for example, we are prone to stigmatize exchange control or exchange devaluation, but slow to suggest workable alternatives to meet or prevent the exchange shortages which bring about such measures of defense. Perhaps this is one reason why so little progress has been made in practice toward the elimination of exchange control and competitive devaluation, notwithstanding their condemnation by economists and statesmen alike.

A more constructive approach toward the problem is now in the process of effective realization. The recently created International Monetary Fund is specifically designed to promote international monetary stability through the concerted action of all member countries. The legal powers of the Fund may be grouped into two broad categories. First, the Fund has the financial machinery to help the members to maintain free and stable exchanges by supplementing their gold and foreign exchange resources in case of need. Thus at least one cause of monetary instability will be removed or considerably weakened. There is now an alternative to unilateral resort to currency depreciation or exchange restrictions during a period of severe even though temporary exchange shortages. Secondly, the Fund will wield a degree of influence over policy decisions of member countries. In some cases the Fund has only the power to make recommendations, or the right to be consulted. In others, such as parity changes or the establishment of exchange control, action by a member is subject to the Fund's authorization or approval.

In actual practice, however, the effective power and influence of the Fund may be far greater, or it may be far smaller, than its legal authority. Although the Fund has no right to impose specific domestic monetary or credit policies, it may develop a leadership and moral influence far beyond the scope of formal official recommendations. On the other hand, although in theory the Fund can forbid a country to engage in either currency devaluation or exchange control, such prohibition may prove to be unenforceable in the face of severe exchange shortages. Currency devaluation and exchange control are often the outcome of basic disequilibria in a country's international position and, in such a case, cannot be eliminated by mere legal provisions as long as the root causes remain, even with the best of will on the part of the country affected.

The ultimate success or failure of the Fund will depend in no small part on its ability to devise, in collaboration with member countries, workable and realistic standards of domestic as well as international monetary policy. This will require a bold revision of the traditional concepts and dogmas associated with the gold standard theory. The orthodox gold standard mechanism implied a more or less passive acceptance by each country of the automatic monetary adjustments necessitated by fluctuations in its balance of payments. This view was reaffirmed in the twenties by the Cunliffe Committee and played a major part in the studies and recommenda-

tions of the League of Nations in the monetary field. It is in
direct contradiction to the increasing trend, both in theory and
practice, toward independent monetary management by individual
countries.

The events of the thirties, the increasing influence of Keynesian
economics, and finally the financial impact of World War II have
destroyed the institutional and ideological framework of the automatic gold standard. Tomorrow's currencies will be managed currencies. The only question at issue—and it is a fundamental one—is
the direction toward which management will work, and the extent
to which national objectives can be reconciled with international
balance. Any attempt to enforce rigid solutions patterned after
orthodox gold standard doctrines would be even more futile in the
postwar period than it has proved to be in the interwar period.

CENTRAL BANKING AND THE GOLD STANDARD

The main problem considered in this paper is the reconciliation
of domestic monetary policies with the prerequisites of international
balance. In its purest form, the gold standard solved the problem
automatically by eliminating one of its terms: the domestic volume
of money escaped the control of national authorities and was determined automatically by international market forces. Monetary
circulation was made up of gold and subsidiary coin; it expanded or
contracted, not as a result of conscious monetary policy, but in accordance with the net movements of the international balance of
payments. A favorable balance of payments brought gold into a
country and expanded the circulating medium. An unfavorable
balance produced the opposite effect.

These movements were regarded as self-adjusting through their
influence on national price and cost levels and on interest rates.
International balance, if disturbed, would be restored because of the
effects of the ensuing domestic contraction or expansion on relative
cost and interest levels at home and abroad and the resulting shifts
in trade and capital movements. The automatic monetary contraction produced by gold exports would raise interest rates and attract
capital from abroad. It would at the same time exert a downward
pressure on domestic prices and costs, thus stimulating exports and
discouraging imports. Both of these movements—capital and trade
—would tend to correct the balance of payments deficit in which

they originated.[1] A surplus in the balance of payments would also be self-corrective. Gold imports would expand monetary circulation, lower interest rates, increase prices and costs, and stimulate capital exports and merchandise imports while discouraging exports. These processes would continue until foreign payments and receipts were again brought into balance.

This type of analysis contemplates a particularly rigid form of the gold standard in which there is no room for national sovereignty over currency or money. The only circulating medium is gold itself, i.e., an international standard largely impervious to national manipulation or managament. In actual practice, the gold standard never existed in such pure and unadulterated form. The value of the theoretical model discussed so far does not lie in its descriptive realism, but in the fact that it inspired so much of the academic thinking and legislative controversies regarding national and international monetary mechanisms during the nineteenth and even the twentieth century.

The coexistence of national means of payment, side by side with gold itself, deeply modified the practical functioning of the gold standard by freeing the domestic money supply from rigid dependence on balance of payments fluctuations. Little attention is usually paid, in this respect, to the latent antinomy between central banking and the classical gold standard. And yet the automatic monetary mechanism of the pure gold standard would obviously leave little room for what is today conceived as one of the primary functions of central banking action; namely, monetary management by the central banking authorities. An element in the confusion of thought on the subject is the lack of adaptability of our language, which reflects and tends to perpetuate outmoded habits of thought. Unchanging terminology has obscured fundamental institutional changes. Just as the gold standard of the twenties was basically different from the gold standard of earlier days, the central banks of today bear little resemblance to the central banks of the nineteenth century.

Indeed the original pattern of central banking had little or nothing to do with monetary management, which was left to the automatic

---

[1] Modern theories of international trade and capital movements would incorporate two further major elements in this analysis. One is the elasticity of supply and demand for imports and exports, the other the direct income effects associated with balance of payments disequilibria.

regulation of the pure gold standard. The functions of central banks
were purely ancillary ones, and even their power of issue was not
designed to interfere with or supplant the controlling role of gold
over the money supply. The shift from monetary automatism to
monetary management was slow and gradual. The evolution of the
Bank of England is most revealing in this respect.

The Bank Act of 1844 had as its objective the restoration of an
unmanaged gold standard, ruled exclusively by fluctuations in the
balance of payments. Variations in the total note issue of the Bank
of England would correspond exactly to the movements of gold
itself in the reserves of the Issue Department. Any inflow or outflow
of gold would produce a corresponding increase or decrease in the
volume of money, just as would have occurred if the circulation had
consisted exclusively of gold coin. The Issue Department of the
Bank of England therefore played a purely passive role and could
not exert the slightest influence on the volume of money.[2]

Whatever central banking functions this system left to the Bank
of England pertained, not to the Issue, but to the Banking Department. No such functions, however, were originally intended by the
authors of the Act. In the years immediately following the Bank
Act, the Banking Department was regarded merely as a commercial
bank "to be managed in the same way as any other private bank." [3]
It was only gradually, and at the initiative of the Government rather
than of the Bank itself, that the special position and responsibilities
of the Banking Department came to be clearly recognized and
accepted by the Bank authorities. Even then, these responsibilities
did not extend to the broad and modern concept of monetary management, but merely to the function of "lender of last resort." This
function, moreover, did not imply the issue power since, in principle
at least, fluctuations in the note issue continued to correspond
exactly to fluctuations in the gold assets of the Issue Department.

As "lender of last resort," however, the Banking Department,
through its credit and investment operations, would relieve tem-

[2] The only channel for interference with market forces lay in changes in the
amount of the "fiduciary" issue, which was not covered by gold. Outside of
one brief and minor exception, no such change occurred prior to the First
World War.

[3] "Evidence of the Governor and Deputy Governor of the Bank of England
before the Secret Committee of the House of Commons on the Commercial
Distress" (Mar. 7, 1848), in T.E. Gregory, *Select Statutes, Documents and
Reports relating to British Banking, 1832–1928* (London, 1929), Vol. II, p. 28.

porary shortages of cash in the commercial banks. In doing so it would interfere with the process of readjustment contemplated in the gold standard theory, since it would offset the deflationary internal effect of a deficit in the balance of payments and thus prevent its ultimate correction. The drain on the limited note reserves of the Department would continue until their exhaustion made it impossible for the Bank to continue its assistance to the market unless the limitation on its fiduciary issue was raised or suspended.[4] Thus the "lender of last resort" operations were conceived as a mere temporary palliative, to be accompanied by other measures tending toward a fundamental readjustment similar to the one which would have taken place automatically under the pure gold standard.

The most important instrument used toward that end was the management of the discount rate. Credit was made available in times of crisis, but at higher rates which led to a general rise of interest costs and contraction of credit. In the words of the Cunliffe Committee, this would result in "a decline in general prices in the home market which, by checking imports and stimulating exports, corrected the adverse trade balance which was the primary cause of the difficulty." [5] In this way, central banks could perform their mission of lender of last resort—could provide credit institutions, in times of need, with the liquid funds necessary to tide them over temporary panics and difficulties—while still transmitting to the economy the external pressures arising from balance of payments disequilibria under the pure gold standard system. They could expand credit in times of favorable balances and contract it, except for temporary assistance to the banks, in times of unfavorable balances. The general effect of this policy would be similar to the automatic results of gold inflows or outflows under a purely metallic monetary standard, at least as far as the direction of the movements was concerned.

The hiatus between gold and total monetary circulation introduced by deposit banking, however, could greatly increase monetary fluctuations and affect their incidence. Under a fractional

[4] In the first crisis following the Bank Act, the Bank refused full support to the market until authorized by the Government to exceed its legal fiduciary issue. Similar authorizations were granted, but not used, in 1857, 1866, and 1914. In the more recent period, further expansions have been made possible under the Currency and Bank Notes Acts of 1928 and 1939.

[5] "First Interim Report of the Committee on Currency and Foreign Exchanges after the War," in T.E. Gregory, *op. cit.*, Vol. II, p. 337.

reserve system of commercial banking, given the fairly stable ratio maintained by British banks between cash and deposits, the deposit component of monetary circulation would increase or decrease by several times the amount of the increase or decrease in the cash reserves of the banks. Banking expansion and contraction would also affect the cash balances of some individuals and firms which, under the pure gold standard, might not otherwise have been touched, at least directly, by the monetary fluctuations resulting from disequilibria in the country's balance of payments. Finally, because of the narrow gold base which it maintained, the Bank of England, in order to defend its reserve position, was led to follow credit policies which not only permitted but also reinforced the automatic contraction resulting from the retirement of its notes in exchange for gold. The net effect of the banking superstructure erected upon the gold standard basis was monetary fluctuations of far greater amplitude than they would have been under a pure gold standard.

The departure from the pure gold standard mechanism, implicit in the operations of deposit banks, was carried even further under the "rules of the game" so much publicized in the twenties by central bank and League of Nations experts. "Whenever gold flowed in, the central bank was expected to increase the national currency supply not only through the purchase of that gold but also through the acquisition of additional domestic assets; similarly, when gold flowed out, the central bank was supposed to contract its domestic assets also. In this way the influence of gold movements on the domestic credit base was to be magnified, and magnified in accordance with the central bank's reserve ratio. With a ratio of 33 per cent, for instance, any net increase or decrease in the gold reserve was supposed to create a threefold expansion or contraction in the total credit base." [6]

The "rules of the game" were presented as synonymous with the rules of the gold standard itself. Their effects, however, were vastly different from those envisaged by the theory. Under the pure gold standard, balance of payments disequilibria produced only an equivalent amount of expansion or contraction in the monetary circulation, while under the "rules of the game" they fostered in addition a secondary expansion or contraction many times the original one. This multiple expansion or contraction was defended as a way to speed up international readjustments and to conserve the country's

[6] League of Nations, *International Currency Experience*, 1944, pp. 66–67.

international reserves, but the result was achieved only at the cost of much greater domestic instability.[7] No wonder the "rules of the game" encountered increasing resistance, and that their breach became more characteristic of monetary policy than their observance. The breakdown of the gold standard in the interwar period has often been ascribed in part to the unwillingness or inability of central banks to play the gold standard game in accordance with its supposed rules.[8] It should again be emphasized, however, that these rules did not fit the pure gold standard theory and that consequently their observance would have impeded rather than advanced the objectives of the classical mechanism of international adjustments. Thus, the monetary policy of the United States in the twenties has often been interpreted as a "sterilization" or "neutralization" policy, and criticized as contrary to gold standard rules. In fact, however, the total money supply (deposits and currency outside banks) increased from June 1920 to December 1924 by 7.2 billion dollars, or about 4.5 times the increase in gold reserves during the same period. In 1925–29, the money supply rose by 7.6 billion in the face of a *decrease* in gold reserves. For the period as a whole, therefore, monetary circulation increased by 14.8 billion dollars, while the increase under a pure gold standard would have been less than 1.5 billion. Mr. Nurkse's discussion of neutralization policies in the United States and other countries demonstrates his point that, contrary to the "rules of the game," "central Banks' international and domestic assets . . . moved far more often in the *opposite* than in the same direction." [9] This does *not* mean, however, that the primary impact of the gold flows was fully offset or neutralized, or even that their influence on monetary circulation was not multiplied several times by commercial banking expansion. Thus, in spite of neutralization policies, gold flows may well have exerted at least as much influence on the money market as they would have under classical gold standard assumption.

The most significant development of the period, however, was the growing importance of domestic factors as the final determinant of

[7] This instability, moreover, had a very different incidence than that attaching to the primary contraction or expansion associated with gold flows under the pure gold standard. It bore especially heavily on bank borrowers and investment activities. See F.A. von Hayek, *Monetary Nationalism and International Stability* (London, 1937), pp. 25–32.

[8] See especially Lionel Robbins, *The Great Depression* (London, 1934).

[9] *International Currency Experience*, pp. 68–88 and 237–40.

monetary policies. While international gold flows continued to stimulate domestic monetary expansion or contraction, the total volume of money was no longer controlled by them. Factors of a purely domestic nature also tended to shape monetary developments in a manner totally alien both to the classical gold standard mechanism and to its "rules of the game" interpretation, or rather misinterpretation. Central bank powers were no longer used to transmit automatically to the domestic economy the upward or downward pressures of surpluses or deficits in the balance of payments, regardless of national policy objectives. On the contrary, central banking policies came to be defined less and less with reference to the state of the gold reserves or the prerequisites of international balance, and more and more in terms of domestic price stability, the promotion of fuller employment, etc. This tendency was greatly reinforced in the thirties through the general adoption of national recovery programs based on domestic monetary and credit expansion and supported by exchange control and currency devaluation. Thus the latent contradiction between the international and automatic monetary regulation characteristic of the pure gold standard on the one hand, and the evolution toward autonomous and discretionary monetary management by national central banks on the other, was accentuated by practical policies even though it was not readily incorporated into theoretical analysis.

The swing of the pendulum may now have reversed its direction. The experience of the thirties has demonstrated the pitfalls of monetary isolation along purely national lines and the difficulties of reconciling domestic stability and prosperity with international disequilibrium. The Bretton Woods Agreements, without returning to the full subordination of national monetary policies to the single goal of exchange stability, have sought to re-establish some mechanism designed to protect the international economy against autarchic excesses in the monetary field. Member countries agree to cede to the Fund a considerable measure of control over modifications in their exchange rates or the imposition of exchange restrictions. To make possible this partial renunciation of national monetary sovereignty, the International Monetary Fund undertakes to make available to member countries, in times of need, additional exchange reserves necessary to finance temporary deficits in their balance of payments. The Fund, however, does not attempt to restore an automatic international monetary standard. Central banks and other national monetary authorities are left free to determine domestic monetary policies as long as they do not use the resources of the Fund "in a manner contrary to the purposes of the Fund." The success of the new institution will thus depend largely on the soundness of the national monetary policies followed by its members, and on the successful solution by each member country of the basic conflict between domestic goals of action and the preservation of international balance. Fundamental disequilibria, if not corrected by domestic measures of readjustment, would perpetuate the need for new borrowings from the Fund or would force recourse to currency devaluation or exchange control. The assistance provided by the Fund is a limited right of borrowing, equivalent to a mere increase in the members' international reserves, together with some protection against arbitrary and damaging monetary action by other members.

No attempt is made, however, to lay down detailed "rules of the game" for the new international standard which would prevent or correct fundamental international disequilibria. And yet, it is well recognized that persistent deficits in a country's balance of payments would ultimately lead to the exhaustion of its limited drawing rights on the Fund, as well as of its gold and foreign exchange reserves. Once such a situation is reached, the whole Fund machinery becomes ineffective,[10] and no paper commitments can maintain free and stable exchange rates. Correction of international disequilibria is thus crucial to the successful functioning of the new international monetary standard.

THE CORRECTION OF INTERNATIONAL DISEQUILIBRIA

Notwithstanding the important divergencies between the classical gold standard theory and its modern "rules of the game" version, both types of analyses coincide in some important respects. Balance of payments disequilibria are ascribed to international cost and price disparities, and their correction is made to depend on the elimination of such disparities through automatic, or induced, domestic monetary expansion or contraction.

---

[10] The day of reckoning could, of course, be postponed as long as the Fund was willing and able to grant, under Art. V, Sec. 4, additional drawing rights to meet the deficit.

These views of the mechanism of international adjustment under gold standard assumptions are open to grave question. First, they fail to distinguish between a fundamental disequilibrium in one country's international position and world-wide disturbances in balances of payments associated with cyclical fluctuations. Secondly, the explanation of the readjustment of a country's balance of payments is vitiated by the underlying and totally unrealistic assumption of near-perfect competition between nations of roughly equal strength and importance in world trade.

Cyclical vs. fundamental maladjustments

The classical explanation of balance of payments maladjustments runs in terms of price and cost disparities between *one country* and the rest of the world. While applicable to many important instances of disequilibria, this analysis does not exhaust all possible causes of deficits in a country's international transactions. The most cursory examination of statistical data clearly shows that many of the most specticular disequilibria in balances of payments are world-wide in scope, and must be traced to cyclical fluctuations of an international character rather than to national price and cost maladjustments.

In the decade prior to the war, for instance, the dollar value of world trade fell by more than 60 per cent between 1929 and 1932, increased by 23.5 per cent from 1936 to 1937, and fell again by 12.5 per cent during 1938. If the major cause of these fluctuations had resided in international price and cost disparities, it would be expected that high-cost countries would have shown a decrease in exports and an increase in imports, whole low-cost countries would have shown movements in the opposite direction. The striking fact, however, is that, in spite of differences in amplitude, both exports and imports moved *in the same direction* for practically all trading countries. Clearly, the major force impinging upon their trade was international in character, and associated with a world cycle rather than with maladjustments in individual countries.

To take a concrete illustration, in the short space of three years (1929–31), Colombia lost 80 per cent of its central bank gold and foreign exchange reserves. Total exports fell from 122 million dollars in 1929 to 67 million in 1932, a decline of 46 per cent. Coffee, the major export item (about 60 per cent of total export values), suffered a reduction of 45 per cent. If this contraction in coffee exports had been due to disparities in production costs between Colombia and other major coffee exporting countries in competition with her, we would expect these other countries to have expanded their exports at the expense of Colombian producers. The fact is, however, that during the same period total exports and coffee exports of all other competing coffee countries were also falling in similar, or even larger proportions. This coincidence in time of export fluctuations in these countries was also characteristic of the recovery period 1933–37, the 1937–40 decline, and the record levels of exports reached during the more recent war years. It might of course be argued that, even though no price disparity was evident as between the various coffee exporting countries, all of them were suffering simultaneously from the consequences of excessive price and cost levels as compared with the rest of the world, and that the classical prescription for readjustment still remained applicable to the group as a whole. This position, however, would be hard to defend in view of the fact that the export prices for typical coffee grades had fallen to nearly one-half of their 1928 level by 1930 and to not far from one-third by 1931, without resulting in any substantial recovery of quantities exported.

Indeed, for most agricultural countries, large export receipts and favorable balances of payments usually coincide with high and not with low levels of domestic and export prices. The reason for this is that their export volume and export prices fluctuate as much with demand as with supply conditions, if not more. That is, they are largely determined by international rather than domestic factors. Major fluctuations in export values result primarily from cyclical movements in economic activity and income in the buying countries, and not from changes in the relationship of domestic price or cost levels to prices and costs in other competing or buying countries. Thus, for many agricultural and raw material countries, the international cycle is mainly an imported product. Such is also the conclusion of the League of Nations' Delegation on Economic Depressions. "General depressions would seem to result mainly from fluctuations in investment and employment in industrial countries." [11]

[11] League of Nations, *Economic Stability in the Post-War World* (1945), p. 291. The clearest case is provided by the brief depression of 1938 in which world exports to the United States fell by over 35 per cent in a single year, while United States exports decreased by only 7 per cent. It is not denied, of course, that other factors—including price disparities—may be simultaneously operating in bringing about or accentuating a major depression.

Whenever this is true, the classical prescription for remedial policy becomes as misleading as the diagnosis on which it is based. Deflationary efforts at readjustment by individual countries are largely self-defeating because they aggravate the depression rather than cure the disequilibrium. Any initial success that they may have in curbing imports or expanding exports aggravates the difficulties in their supply and export markets as well as in competing countries, and leads to similar and mutually offsetting measures of defense or retaliation. It should be noted that the argument applies equally to remedial action through currency devaluation and through internal price changes. Under the conditions described, both price deflation and currency devaluation spread from country to country and accentuate the international deflation. While some categories of exports may expand under the stimulus of price reductions, the expansion will often be insufficient to compensate for the decline in unit prices, especially in the case of agricultural or raw material exports faced with an inelastic world demand. The burden of readjustment then falls upon imports, the reduction of which further aggravates income contraction abroad and the effective demand for each country's exports.

The situation described presents a strong analogy with that of oligopoly, where efforts by one seller to cut into his competitors' markets are thwarted by the competitors' retaliation and the ensuing price war. The expansionary effect of a decline in one country's prices upon its exports is largely offset by simultaneous, or retaliatory, price decreases by competing countries. Thus the effective elasticity of demand for one country's exports becomes merged with the much lower elasticity of world demand for products of the types the country exports.[12] Sales can be expanded on a stable basis only in so far as lower prices stimulate world consumption, a result that is not achieved through inroads into other nations' markets.

It should be noted that this analysis does not conflict in any way with the classical theory of balance of payments maladjustments. It merely applies to an entirely different set of circumstances. Cyclical disturbances of the kind assumed here played little or no part in classical analysis. The error made by later economists—and espe-

[12] In the case of competing oligopolists, the effective demand elasticity is similarly determined by the demand curve for the industry as a whole, rather than by the demand curve which would face any one seller *if* his competitors' prices remained constant.

cially by the "rules of the game" school—was to extend to world-wide, cyclical disturbances an analysis aimed at fundamental maladjustments between *one* economy and the rest of the world. In the latter case, moderate price changes by the deficit country may restore its normal export-import balance and share of world trade without depressing world prices to any significant extent. This is especially true if, as contemplated also in classical theory, its exports are broadly diversified rather than concentrated on one or a few major items. During a global depression, however, simultaneous efforts by many nations at maintaining or increasing their exports in the face of a shrinking world demand merely result in an accelerated fall of prices and reduction of export proceeds.

Gold standard or sterling exchange standard?

A second assumption underlying the classical theory of the gold standard is that of near-perfect competition between many trading nations, more or less coequal in importance. The assumption is obviously unrealistic, and in recent years many writers have empha-sized the central position occupied by Great Britain in the nine-teenth century functioning of the gold standard.[13] It has been suggested that that position "made the prewar gold standard essentially a sterling exchange standard system,"[14] but the concrete implications of that assertion have not been fully drawn. If exam-ined, they may suggest one possible explanation both for the relative success of the gold standard in Britain and for its failure to operate satisfactorily in the least industrialized nations. In many of the latter countries it was adhered to only sporadically, and abandoned in times of crisis. When actually enforced, it may well have retarded rather than accelerated the rate of their economic development. In Great Britain itself the mechanism of balance of payments readjust-ments seems to have operated, in important respects, in a manner directly opposite to that described by gold standard theory. To a very large extent, increases in the London discount rates brought about a readjustment in the British balances of payments, not through their effects on the British economy, but through their effects on the outside world and especially on the agricultural and raw material countries.

[13] See, especially, William Adams Brown, Jr., *The International Gold Standard Reinterpreted* (New York, 1940).

[14] *Idem*, p. xiii.

One of the reasons for this has long been recognized. As early as 1840 it was pointed out by Tooke before a Select Committee of the House of Commons on banks of issue, that: "The effect upon the exchange of a rise in the rate of interest would be that of inducing foreign capitalists to abstain from calling for their funds from this country to the same extent as they otherwise might do, and it would operate at the same time in diminishing the inducements to capitalists in this country to invest in foreign securities or to hold foreign securities, and it might induce them to part with foreign securities in order to invest in British stocks and shares. It would likewise operate in restraining credits from the merchants in this country by advances on shipments outwards, and it would have the effect of causing a larger proportion of the importations into this country to be carried on upon foreign capital." [15]

This shift in international capital movements contributed powerfully to a rapid restoration of equilibrium in the exchange market. However, it tended to relieve rather than accentuate domestic deflationary pressures on the economy, and to that extent to delay or prevent the basic readjustment of fundamental price and cost disparities contemplated by gold standard theorists. It constituted, in a sense, the equivalent of the compensatory monetary policies so strongly condemned by many gold standard theorists.

Similarly, the outflow of capital in periods of favorable balances tended to check surpluses and thus to reduce external expansionary impacts upon the British economy. This again was contrary to the "rules of the game" and tantamount to the opposite policy of sterilization or neutralization of gold movements.

Debtor countries, however, did not have a similar mechanism at their disposal. Capital tended to flow toward them in times of prosperity and away from them in times of depression, irrespective of their discount policy. The effect of such fluctuations in capital movements was to smooth down cyclical monetary and credit fluctuations in the creditor countries, but to accentuate them in the debtor countries. To that extent the financial centers could shift part of the burden of readjustment upon the weaker countries in the world economy. Their only mechanism of defense was the policy consistently followed by the Central Bank of Argentina in the recent past with such remarkable success: to offset external drains from or

[15] Quoted by R.G. Hawtrey, *The Art of Central Banking* (London, 1932), p. 141.

accretions to its reserves through domestic policies of expansion or contraction. This was contrary to classical orthodoxy, but in fact equivalent to the effects of the British discount rate on capital movements to and from Great Britain.

The readjustment of fundamental price disequilibria which changes in the British discount rate were designed to stimulate was thus thwarted and delayed by the effects of such changes on capital movements. It is still contended, however, that those basic readjustments would obtain in the end, capital movements nothwithstanding, through the domestic effects of discount changes on British prices. The discount rate would be raised and credit would be contracted in order to force down excessive British prices to levels more competitive with the level of foreign prices. On the other hand, the discount rate would be lowered and credit would expand when British prices were low relative to foreign prices and tended to disequilibrate the balance of payments in Britain's favor.

It should be noted that, according to this theory, the British deficit would be corrected through a *deterioration* of the British terms of trade (i.e., a decrease in British prices relative to foreign prices), such deterioration being considered necessary to restore the international competitive position of British producers. Logically speaking, however, the opposite assumption is just as plausible. That is to say, the elimination of the deficit might also result from an *improvement* in the British terms of trade, decreasing the unit cost of imports and increasing the returns on exports.[16]

Statistical evidence may be used to support either theory. During the interwar period, the British terms of trade consistently improved in depression and deteriorated during the upswing of the cycle.[17] Before the First World War available data are more difficult to interpret and they reveal, if anything, sharper rises in export prices than in import prices during the crest of the boom. Indexes of export prices for that period, however, give relatively little weight to manu-

---

[16] Reconstruction and statistical verification of balance of payments readjustments would have to distinguish between: (1) the relationship of Britain's prices and costs to competing countries' prices and costs for similar goods; and (2) the relative price movements of non-competing import goods (raw materials and foodstuffs) and export goods (manufactures). Such a discussion, however, would exceed the scope and purpose of this paper.

[17] The ratio of export to import prices, calculated from Board of Trade indexes, declined from 104 in 1923 to 98 in 1929, rose during the ensuing depression to a peak of 122 in 1933, fell to 107 in the relatively prosperous year 1937, and improved again to 116 during the 1938 recession.

factured products and do not appear to be truly representative of British exports in general.

As far as the discount rate is concerned, the interwar period is of minor interest for the elucidation of the problem under consideration. The discount policy had ceased by then to be a major instrument of monetary control and, moreover, Britain was no longer the dominant financial center of the world. In the 30 years prior to the First World War, however, the statistical series fail to confirm the traditional view that an increase in discount rates contributed directly to a lowering of British prices relative to foreign prices. On the contrary, all major rises in the discount rate are associated with an improvement of the British terms of trade, i.e., with an increase in export prices relative to import prices.[18] The declines in the terms of trade followed the increases in the discount rate only after a considerable lag, and actually coincided with decreases in the rate. Their most obvious explanation would seem to lie in depressed business conditions in Britain, associated with the spread of the international cycle, rather than in any direct influence of the discount rate over domestic prices.

This improvement in the British terms of trade in periods of rising discount rates should not be surprising, in view of the special position of Britain as a financial center for world trade. On purely a priori grounds, it would appear at least as probable as the opposite pattern contemplated by the classicists. What was really discussed by them was the case of price disparities between one country and a large number of other countries, equal to the first in importance. Under that assumption, deflation by the first country would force down domestic prices and costs without affecting to any significant extent the level of prices in the rest of the world. The position of Britain in the nineteenth century was, however, a very different one. Britain was the major center of world trade and finance, and British deflationary efforts immediately affected, not only the British economy and prices, but also the economy and prices of other countries, transmitting to them the cyclical fluctuations experienced by Great Britain. Thus, the problem became essentially one, not of disparities

[18] Thus the yearly average of discount rates rose gradually from 2.9 per cent in 1885 to 4.5 per cent in 1890, while the ratio of export to import prices improved from 91 to 106. The next sustained rise in the rate, from 2 per cent in 1895 to 3.9 in 1900, was accompanied by an increase in the ratio from 97 to 114. The same positive correlation between rising rates and better terms of trade continued until the outbreak of war.

between one country and the others, but of a simultaneous upward or downward movement engulfing most other nations along with Great Britain.

We have already seen that the most immediate effect of a rise in the British discount rates was to reverse the normal direction of international capital movements. The outflow of funds from the other countries toward Great Britain exerted an immediate downward pressure on prices and income in those countries. In fact, since the great bulk of foreign exports was financed through London, and since foreign bills far outweighed inland bills in the London discount market, a tightening in discount rates could be expected to affect the prices of foreign goods more drastically and directly than domestic prices in Britain. The reverse would be true in the case of a credit relaxation or expansion in London. These movements would be further magnified by the banking contraction or expansion thus induced in the foreign countries themselves, especially as higher discount rates in those markets would tighten domestic credit without attracting, as they did in London, compensatory capital movements from abroad.

These considerations are reinforced by the fact that a large part of Britain's exports consisted of manufactured industrial products, while the bulk of her imports was composed of foodstuffs and raw materials. Less flexibility of demand and supply conditions could be expected to make the prices of the second category of goods especially sensitive to credit contraction and expansion, as well as to general cyclical fluctuations.

The failure of British discount policy to effect the type of readjustments contemplated in classical theory is thus easily understandable. It was due primarily to the *international* character of the London discount market, whose expansion and contraction affected foreign prices as much as or more than British prices. It is also explainable by the fact that producers of agricultural and raw materials are more vulnerable to cyclical and credit fluctuations than is the British economy.[19]

One main conclusion emerges from the foregoing analysis. The "rules of the game" of the twentieth century gold standard, no

[19] A somewhat similar observation is made by R.G. Hawtrey in *A Century of Bank Rate* (London, 1938), p. 44, but is not systematically related to the general theory of balance of payments readjustments, which it so clearly contradicts.

matter how valid they may be in the case of isolated fundamental disequilibria in one country's or a few countries' international accounts, are totally inappropriate for dealing with world-wide cyclical fluctuations. The main result of "orthodox" gold standard policies under such circumstances was to spread throughout the world at large any cyclical disturbance arising in major industrialized nations. Balance of payments deficits would be corrected in the end, but mostly through a general contraction in income and economic activity, rather than through direct price readjustments. Furthermore, the accompanying price changes would leave in their wake a basically unbalanced structure of international prices when the cyclical depression subsided and more normal conditions were restored.

12. Domestic and International Equilibrium

Ragnar Nurkse

Columbia University

Excerpt from Seymour E. Harris, editor, *The New Economics, Keynes' Influence on Theory and Public Policy* (New York: Copyright 1947 by Alfred A. Knopf, Inc.), pp. 264–292; pp. 264–280, 291–292 excerpted. Reprinted by permission of the author and the publisher.

INTRODUCTION

The impact of Keynesian Economics on the theory of international monetary relations has been powerful. Keynes himself, though he was well aware of the international policy implications of his doctrines, did very little to apply his *General Theory* to the analysis of international equilibrium. But he provided a theoretical framework which subsequent writers had no trouble in adapting to the special case of international relations. From this work of adaptation there emerged a whole system of international economics, set up in terms of the money income and expenditure analysis.

The income approach to international trade was not by any means entirely new. For over a century, writers on international trade had referred occasionally to shifts of purchasing power or changes in relative demand.[1] The Keynesian approach, however, seemed to yield a more comprehensive and consistent account of international monetary relations than had ever been given before. It furnished at one and the same time an explanation of two related matters: (a) the adjustment process of the balance of payments and (b) the international transmission of fluctuations in economic activity and employment. The result has been a fruitful marriage of two subjects that previously led quite separate existences under the conventional names of international trade theory and business cycle theory.

National frontiers as such are basically irrelevant to economic analysis; it is only government policies that make them relevant.

[1] *Cf.* Jacob Viner, *Studies in the Theory of International Trade* (1937), Chapter VI.

239

And yet a political boundary-line may be useful to the economist because it forms, as it were, a zone of light through which economic processes pass and at which at least some of them can best be observed. Customs, immigration and other officials, recording the international movement of goods, people, and money, give us information such as we do not possess for inter-regional movements within the same country. Accordingly, it is often in its international aspects that any monetary or business cycle theory is apt to meet its stiffest test in regard to verification. There have been theories that have not been successful in meeting this test of international application. For example, the traditional price-specie-flow doctrine, which represents the quantity theory of money in its international aspect, was found by one of its last distinguished proponents to be quite unrealistic.[2] Again, the "neutral money" school, when one of its leading authors attempted to apply it to international shifts, led to rather strange results.[3] By contrast, in the income-and-expenditure analysis of the Keynesian type we have a theoretical apparatus which lends itself very simply and naturally to international monetary analysis, and which yields a realistic account of both the adjustment mechanism of the balance of payments and the propagation of economic fluctuations from country to country. The "adjustment problem" and the "propagation problem" appear in this analysis merely as two aspects of the same dynamic process of income change. The former relates

[2] See F.W. Taussig, *International Trade* (1927): "The process which our theory contemplates . . . can hardly be expected to take place smoothly and quickly. Yet no signs of disturbance are to be observed such as the theoretic analysis previses; and some recurring phenomena are of a kind not contemplated by theory at all" (p. 239). Taussig found the facts "baffling" and "puzzling" (pp. 242, 261), and his celebrated statement that "things just happened so" was an honest admission of defeat.

[3] See F.A. von Hayek, *Monetary Nationalism and International Stability* (1937), pp. 25–34. Hayek apparently maintained that, under modern banking conditions, gold movements were bound to cause "monetary disturbances" similar to those which, in *Prices and Production*, he had described for the closed economy: deviations of the "market rate" from the "natural rate" of interest, leading to elongations and contractions in the capital structure of production. That the adjustment of the international balance of payments should necessitate such convulsions is neither plausible *a priori* nor confirmed by the facts. Taussig (*op. cit.*) found the adjustment to work more smoothly and directly than even the price-specie-flow theory had pictured it. So did many other writers, including notably C. Bresciani-Turroni (*Inductive Verification of the Theory of International Payments*, 1932) and Harry D. White (*The French International Accounts, 1880–1913*, 1933).

primarily to the international monetary accounts, while the latter directs attention to fluctuations in domestic income and employment. It is the "propagation" aspect that is mainly significant for the international policy implications of Keynesian economics, though the "accounting" aspect also, as we shall see, imposes itself constantly on any consideration of national policy.

Before taking up the policy implications, we must briefly indicate the nature of the income approach to the mechanics of international equilibrium. A highly simplified account is all that can be attempted in the space available.

NATIONAL INCOME AND THE FOREIGN TRADE MULTIPLIER

There is a two-way relationship between national income and foreign trade. On the one hand, changes in income generally entail changes in the same direction in the demand for imports. On the other, changes in the volume of exports tend to produce changes in domestic income.

If an expansion gets under way in one country, there will be an increase in imports into that country; which means an increase in exports for some other country. It is through this increase in exports that the expansion is transmitted to the other country. Let us see how this happens. The increase in exports will lead directly to an expansion of income and employment in the export industries. Some part of the additional income earned in the export industries may be spent immediately on imported goods, so that an equilibrating tendency toward greater imports to match the increase in exports comes into play at once. But this first increase in imports will usually be far from sufficient to restore an even balance. A part, and presumably the greater part, of the additional receipts of the export industries will be spent on home-produced goods. The increase in incomes spreads to domestic industries. At each step in the sequence of successive spending, a part of the increased money income will be diverted to swell the demand for imports.

To assume that each increment of income is entirely spent, either on imports or on home-made goods, is unrealistic; some part is likely to be saved. If there were no increased investment to absorb this saving, the rise in the total income flow would inevitably be arrested before the point at which imports become equal to the higher exports. In fact, however, the increased flow of spending on home-made goods is likely to have the "acceleration effect" of inducing a higher rate of capital expenditure, which will tend to offset the additional saving.[4]

In short, total money income in the country considered will tend to expand until the increased expenditure on imports equals the original increase in exports. In this way the increase in exports will have generated a multiple expansion in money income at home, and out of the increased income there will be an increased flow of expenditure on imports. The balance of payments comes back into equilibrium at higher levels of both national income and foreign trade.

In this successive-spending analysis, the proportion in which an increment of income is devoted to purchases of imported goods is evidently the central determinant of the process. This proportion is known as the "marginal propensity to import" or the "marginal import ratio." The higher it is, the more rapidly will imports increase after the initial rise in exports, but the smaller will be the expansion of national income associated with the restoration of external equilibrium. The smaller it is, the larger will be the ultimate increase in national income, but the longer will presumably be the time it takes for the balance between imports and exports to be restored. The increment in total income generated by the rise in exports, compared with the increment in the exports itself, gives us the "export multiplier." This is simply the reciprocal of the marginal propensity to import, the reciprocal of the fraction of additional income spent on imports. If this fraction is one-third, for example, the increment in total money income will be equal to three times the increment in exports.[5]

[4] Fritz Machlup in his excellent presentation of the multiplier analysis (*International Trade and the National Income Multiplier*, 1943) excludes such induced investment by assumption. I find no need for this assumption here. The acceleration effect due to induced investment may be unpredictable; but so is the multiplier effect of the successive spending flow, since the marginal propensity to import is not likely to remain constant. In any discussion of general tendencies, both the acceleration and multiplier effects have their place.

[5] This assumes that additional saving is offset by a larger volume of investment, induced in the way just indicated. If increased domestic investment does not provide the necessary offset to the additional saving, the income expansion will be arrested before imports have risen to the new level of exports, and there will remain an export surplus; which means, in effect, that the additional saving is offset by *foreign* investment.

In the event of a decline in foreign demand for the country's exports, the mutliplier mechanism operates in reverse. Equilibrium in the balance of payments will tend to be restored, this time at a lower level of trade, through a reduction in national income by an amount equal to the decrement in exports multiplied by the reciprocal of the marginal import ratio. Total money income will tend to fall to a level at which people's expenditure on imports will balance the diminished receipts from exports.

All these changes—upward in one case, downward in the other— which we have traced in national income, exports, and imports, are changes in terms of money value. To what extent they reflect changes in real volume will depend on the elasticity of supply. At less than full employment, supply is likely to be relatively elastic, so that movements in money value will signify real changes in the same direction. The particular supply conditions for exports and imports may show some elasticity even in a state of general full employment, so long as shifts are possible between production for the home market and for export. They may, on the other hand, be inelastic, if they depend heavily on certain specific factors of production. The extent to which money values reflect real changes need not be the same for exports, imports, and national income. For all three, however, some degree of correspondence between monetary and real changes is likely to exist below the level of general full employment.

The income approach to the study of foreign trade movements, as exemplified in the multiplier technique, is useful mainly in explaining fluctuations in the *volume* of trade. The classical doctrine of comparative costs in its various formulations was primarily concerned with the *composition* of a given volume of trade. In the international sphere, therefore, Keynesian economics has had the effect of shifting our center of attention in a manner analogous to the general shift which it promoted—from the traditional preoccupation with the optimum distribution of a given volume of employment to the analysis of the forces determining the volume of employment itself.

It is true that the multiplier analysis, though always mechanically applicable, is most appropriate, in the sense of most likely to yield significant results in real terms, when changes in total money income come about through changes in the volume of employment rather than through changes in money wage-rates and prices.[6] It is clear that, in the adjustment process, price changes work generally in the right direction for the restoration of equilibrium. But, insofar as they occur at all, they are essentially a by-product of the changes in the volume of employment and productive activity. These latter changes are therefore to be regarded as the primary equilibrating factors.[7]

The multiplier mechanism accounts at the same time for the adjustment of the balance of payments and for the transmission of income and employment fluctuations from country to country. An increase in a country's exports leads to an expansion in the volume of domestic income, expenditure, and employment, so that external equilibrium tends to be restored through an upward shift in the country's demand for imports. We have assumed that the increase in exports is induced by a boom in a foreign country. The expansion initiated in that country is transmitted through the multiplier process, which thus tends to produce a synchronization of economic fluctuations in different countries. It is only in the rather special case of an "autonomous" increase in exports (due, say to devaluation of the home currency, a tariff reduction abroad, or a spontaneous shift of consumer's demand as between home-made and imported goods) that the favorable effect on income and employment at home will be accompanied by an unfavorable effect abroad.

Any expansion or contraction originating in the domestic economy tends to spread abroad through its effects on the demand for imports. A domestic investment boom will "spill over" to other countries since part of the increased money income "leaks out" for the purchase of additional imports. This leakage, while it checks the growth of income at home, is what transmits the expansion process outward. The size of the leakage is determined by the marginal propensity to import; if it is small, the boom at home can go on for a long while before it leads to an import surplus large enough

[6] Machlup's book (op. cit., pp. 19 ff.) proceeds entirely on the assumption that prices remain unchanged. But even Keynes was not so Keynesian as to ignore the price effects of income and employment fluctuations. (See his admirable Chapter 21 in the General Theory.)

[7] "The problem may be synthesized by putting the question: Why should an inflow of gold raise industrial costs and so reduce exports? Surely only by setting up a keener competition for the means of production. . . . The mode of operation through an expansion of activity must therefore be considered the true theory and the phenomena which the classical view tends to stress a by-product." R.F. Harrod. International Economics (1939 edition), page 140.

to stimulate a parallel expansion abroad; if it is large, the boom will not go so far before it "spills over" to other countries.

The special "autonomous" factors tend to produce opposite changes in income and employment in different countries, and so cancel out for the world as a whole. It is in the sphere of domestic expenditure that *general* booms and depressions originate. The propagation mechanism we have described is a passive factor from the world point of view. It is neither expansionist or contractionist in itself, but reflects the balance of forces at play in the domestic economies, and serves to pass on from country to country the expansionist or contractionist influences originating in one place or another.

The relative strength of the expansionist or contractionist impulses which a country imparts to the outside world as a result of domestic income fluctuations is determined by its marginal propensity to import. But the relative amplitude of the fluctuations in its demand for imports may be wider or narrower than that of the corresponding domestic fluctuations. If a given percentage change in national income produces the same percentage change in imports, the "income elasticity of demand for imports" is said to be equal to unity.[8] An elasticity greater or smaller than unity means that expenditure on imports has a wider or closer percentage range of variation than the national income. A country whose national income is relatively variable in itself, and whose imports, in addition, have an income elasticity of demand greater than unity, is particularly troublesome as a source of cyclical change in the world economy. The United States in recent times seems to have corresponded to this description.

The synchronization produced by the multiplier mechanism is naturally imperfect, not only because different countries have different marginal import ratios and income elasticities, but also

---

[8] The "marginal propensity to import" and the "income elasticity of demand for imports" are two distinct concepts, but there is a simple relation between them. The former is defined as $\Delta M/\Delta Y$ while the latter is $\Delta M/M \div \Delta Y/Y$ which can also be written as $\Delta M/\Delta Y \div M/Y$. ($Y$ stands, as usual, for income and M for imports.) Thus the income elasticity of demand is equal to the *marginal* divided by the *average* propensity to import. In the United States, $\Delta M/\Delta Y$ is relatively small, but M/Y is still smaller, and the expression as a whole is therefore large. In England, on the other hand, imports are much greater in relation to income, but they consist more largely of foodstuffs, for which the demand is relatively steady; so that $\Delta M/\Delta Y$, though large, is not as large as M/Y and the whole expression is smaller than unity.

because the successive-spending process of the multiplier analysis takes time. In consequence, fluctuations in one country will lag behind those in the other. The "lags" in the propagation aspect of the mechanism are associated, in the adjustment aspect, with "gaps" in the balance of payments.[9] Transfers of gold, exchange reserves or private short-term funds are needed to *fill* such gaps temporarily; it is the change in domestic income flows that sooner or later *closes* them. In the traditional doctrine, gold movements played a central part as a causally significant factor. In the modern view, they act rather in a passive manner as stop-gaps in the balance of payments, covering discrepancies in foreign receipts and expenditures which, in time, bring about their own adjustment through changes in domestic money incomes.

This explanation of the adjustment process applies, of course, to a system of fixed exchange rates. What it shows is essentially the working of international monetary and cyclical relations in the old days of the automatic gold standard. The gold standard was a system for maintaining equilibrium of external payments among the member countries. It paid no regard to internal equilibrium in any of the member countries, or to the equilibrium of the system as a whole. It required that countries should not seek to control their national money income deliberately by domestic means; it presupposed a laissez faire economy. These prerequisites to its smooth working came to be less and less adequately fulfilled as nations became conscious of a desire for economic stability, and as national policies were framed increasingly with a view to promoting employment and social security. The income approach to international economics would be of purely historical interest if its usefulness consisted merely in a better explanation of the international economy under Queen Victoria. It is useful, more generally, in that it shows what the automatic tendencies of monetary adjustment and cyclical synchronization would be in the absence of governmental or other interferences. Above all, it is useful in any analysis of the external effects of various national policies aimed at internal equilibrium. It is a necessary foundation on which to consider the international policy problems arising from national employment policies.

If internal equilibrium is defined as a level of national income

---

[9] See *Economic Stability in the Post-War World* (League of Nations, 1945), pp. 103 ff. and *International Currency Experience* (League of Nations, 1944), pp. 100 ff.

such that there is neither general unemployment nor an inflationary tendency for prices to rise, while external equilibrium is essentially a balance of payments that maintains itself without the persistent need for monetary "stop-gaps" on the one hand or, to anticipate, increased trade barriers on the other, then the central policy problem is concisely described as that of harmonizing the requirements of internal with those of external equilibrium.

Keynes gave a great deal of thought to the international policy implications of the search for internal equilibrium, but he did not explicitly set out the mechanics of external equilibrium himself. The preceding sketch does not correspond in all particulars to Keynesian doctrine.[10] The multiplier analysis admits, as Machlup has shown, of almost endless variations and refinements in detail. Yet in its essence the application of the income approach to the case of international adjustment is simple and self-evident. It is perhaps for this reason that Keynes did not undertake it himself. In his celebrated controversy with Ohlin (*Economic Journal,* 1929), he had adopted an entirely "un-Keynesian" attitude, stressing the price effects in the transfer process and largely ignoring the income effects. But Keynes never had much difficulty in repudiating his previous views, and it would be hard to believe that the silence he maintained on the international aspects of the *General Theory* was due to a vested interest in his earlier position.

THE PURSUIT OF FULL EMPLOYMENT
IN AN OPEN ECONOMY

Turning to the international policy implications of Keynesian economics, the first general principle is that responsibility for the maintenance of a high and stable level of employment in any given

[10] Thus, we have found no use for the "instantaneous" interpretation of the multiplier as Keynes expounds it in the *General Theory,* and have relied instead on the "serial" interpretation which expressly recognizes the time element in the successive spending process. Also, we have implicitly contradicted Keynes' statement that "the effects of loan expenditure (i.e., home investment) and of the foreign balance are in *pari materia.*" (*The Means to Prosperity,* p. 36.) In our sketch, which follows Machlup's treatment in this respect, the foreign balance arising from an increase in exports leads to a flow of additional income which, so long as exports remain at the higher level, maintains itself even when the foreign balance has fallen back to zero through the induced expansion of imports. In the case of home investment, on the other hand, the net investment expenditure must go on continuously at a steady rate if income is to be maintained at the increased level.

country lies primarily in the field of domestic policy. Nothing can absolve a country from the necessity of taking measures to put its own house in order through the maintenance of a sufficient volume of effective demand at home to keep its productive resources employed at the maximum level that can be continuously sustained without an inflationary rise of prices.

The next point to recognize is that a country in pursuit of this objective—in pursuit, in short, of "full employment"—should never be deterred by difficulties, actual or anticipated, in its balance of external payments. There exists specific methods of influencing the balance of payments so that, regardless of the behavior of its neighbors, and without injuring its neighbors, a country can effectively seek to preserve external equilibrium while pursuing the full employment objective at home.

It is true that these methods can also be resorted to as instruments of a "beggar-my-neighbor" policy, aimed at improving domestic employment by creating external disequilibrium. This policy must for obvious reasons be barred. In fact, no country that knows how to keep up employment by constructive domestic measures will want to adopt it. From the point of view of a national economy, creating employment through an export surplus is just like "digging holes" at home.

The behavior of its neighbors need never deflect a country from the pursuit of full employment. The classical free trade doctrine showed that it was both beneficial and practicable for an individual country to abolish its trade barriers even in the face of a protectionist world. In the same way it is always to some extent possible for a single country to pursue a full employment policy unilaterally. The relative importance of foreign markets, the dependence on imported raw materials, and other similar conditions vary, of course, from country to country. Yet, to some extent, it is always possible for a single country to go ahead with a domestic expansion policy even in a world of depression and unemployment. The expansion will inevitably, under these conditions, produce an adverse balance of payments. So long as there are ample liquid reserves to meet the external deficit, there is no reason to worry about it. When liquid reserves have run out or are not available to start with, there is usually some change in the exchange rate that will preserve external equilibrium. Alternatively, there is the possibility of adopting import restrictions, not in order to reduce imports, but just enough to prevent them from increasing. This will prevent the expansion from "spilling over" abroad, but will not actually hurt the outside world. It is a defensive measure aimed at maintaining the equilibrium of foreign payments, and is to be sharply distinguished from the aggressive and unneighborly policy which operates through a disruption of external equilibrium.

The balance of payments is the test of whether a change in exchange rates or import restrictions is a defensive or an aggressive measure. Nothing is simpler; yet this attitude of "relativity" is repugnant to many laymen and economists alike. People often tend to regard a policy measure as either good or bad in all circumstances. In reality, "it all depends." Devaluation or import restrictions may be justifiable, as in the case of a unilaterally expanding country, when they are intended to close a deficit or preserve equilibrium in the balance of payments. They are not justifiable when their purpose is to create a surplus in the balance of payments or to enlarge a surplus already existing. The distinction was evidently quite clear in Keynes' mind when, in speaking of the Bretton Woods scheme and the U.S. Proposals for the Expansion of World Trade, he said: "Both the currency and the commercial proposals are devised to favour the maintenance of equilibrium by expressly permitting various protective devices when they are required to maintain equilibrium and by forbidding them when they are not so required." [11] The balance-of-payments test is no doubt subject to a great many qualifications in practice; but it is fairly clear in principle.[12] Surpluses and deficits in the balance of payments reflect the external employment effects of economic fluctuations and policies in different countries. The balance-of-payments test may seem a superficial one, but it corresponds in every case to the deeper needs of employment policy. For instance, a country suffering a depression at home is likely to develop automatically a surplus in its balance of payments. Devaluation or import restrictions in these circumstances are the opposite of what is required for

[11] Speech in the House of Lords, Dec. 18, 1945.
[12] The proper criterion is the balance of payments on account of all current transactions and productive capital movements, excluding for obvious reasons gold movements, short-term funds, and hot money flights. I have discussed this more fully in *Conditions of International Monetary Equilibrium* (Princeton University, Essays in International Finance, No. 4, 1945). Compare also *International Currency Experience* (League of Nations, 1944), Chapter IX, Section 3 ("Exchange Adjustments and Exchange Control").

external equilibrium. Nor are they required for internal equilibrium; for it is evident that internal equilibrium, in the sense indicated earlier, can and should be attained by domestic measures of expansion; and its attainment would tend incidentally to restore the equilibrium of external payments as well.

For purposes of employment policy, import restrictions are on a par with exchange devaluation. In their effects on foreign trade, however, the two types of measures are very different. Exchange policy is far preferable to commercial policy, though the latter, being much more effective in emergencies, may have its legitimate uses for temporary purposes. Exchange adjustments and import restrictions alike may serve the ends of a defensive or an aggressive policy. The universal rise of trade barriers in the pre-war decade was due to both these policies and finds its explanation not in the theory of international trade, but in the theory of employment. But to discard permanently the gains from international trade is foolish and, besides, quite unnecessary for internal equilibrium. The case for import restrictions as a defensive measure is sometimes extended far beyond its narrow legitimate scope. It is argued that the domestic policies aimed at full employment can be more easily carried out in a closed economy than in an economy maintaining trade relations with other countries. There are two possible grounds for this proposition. The first is the fear that foreign disturbances may interfere with domestic stability and full employment, and the aim is to lessen the danger of such disturbances by reducing economic intercourse with the outside world to a minimum. This anxiety is groundless. There exists effective methods of offsetting or averting the impact of foreign disturbances by appropriate variations in domestic expenditure combined with the use of external monetary reserves, or by measures designed to protect the equilibrium of external settlements. There is no need to sacrifice the benefits of international trade for the sake of maintaining a stable and satisfactory level of domestic activity.

The second argument for autarky amounts to saying that the employment problem is less serious in a poor community than in a rich one. There is some truth in this. The international division of labor is a labor-saving device. Destroying it, just like destroying machines, may increase the number of jobs in times of unemployment; but it will leave us permanently worse off. Balance-of-payments equilibrium which is obtained by curtailing the international division of labor cannot therefore be regarded as a true equilibrium position. Just as free trade by itself cannot ensure full employment, so the suppression of trade, though it might increase employment numerically, can never bring real prosperity. It is utterly senseless to create employment by reducing the level of economic efficiency. There are other ways of solving the employment problem.

The use of import restrictions may be inevitable when a deficit arises in the balance of payments which cannot be met from liquid reserves, and for which exchange adjustment would be too slow a remedy. Such a deficit may arise from a depression in one of a country's export markets. If the gap is closed by import restrictions, a surplus will develop in the balance of payments as soon as the foreign market recovers. The proper way then to eliminate the surplus is neither exchange appreciation, nor foreign lending, nor anything else except the removal of the import restrictions; it is the only way of restoring balance-of-payments equilibrium together with the pre-existing degree of international specialization.[13]

We have referred earlier to the case of a deficit arising in the balance of payments of a single country trying to raise its level of employment at a time of general depression. The problems of national employment policy may be considered a little more closely in the case of a country which is successfully maintaining both external and internal equilibrium at full employment, but which suddenly finds itself faced with a depression abroad. Here also, a deficit arises, but this time from a fall in exports rather than a rise in imports. The export industries will suffer a depression which, through the multiplier mechanism operating in reverse, will tend to spread to the whole domestic economy. The maintenance of internal equilibrium in these circumstances calls for offsetting the fall in foreign expenditure on the country's products by an increase in the volume of domestic expenditure. This offsetting policy, which is the opposite of what the gold standard rules would require, is subject to limitations; [14] but insofar as total employment depends on total

---

[13] This does not concern import barriers which a country chooses to maintain more or less permanently, for social, military, or other reasons. Starting from his *Means to Prosperity* (p. 25), Keynes repeatedly contrasted these special or structural trade barriers, which we have to take for granted, with the restrictions arising from a general search for employment or from the general state of the balance of payments.

[14] See, e.g., *Economic Stability in the Post-War World* (*op. cit.*), p. 232, or *Conditions of International Monetary Equilibrium* (*op. cit.*), pp. 11–14.

outlay, the compensatory increase in domestic demand will tend to prevent a general depression in the given country. It does nothing, however, to correct the external disequilibrium. The gap in the balance of payments resulting from the fall in exports must be filled by drawing on the country's gold and foreign exchange reserves. How long the offsetting policy can be continued depends entirely on the size of these reserves. If they are ample, the depression abroad may right itself before they run out; it may be followed by an inflationary boom abroad, in which case the country's reserves of international liquidity will be replenished. If, however, the reserves become exhausted or unduly depleted before recovery abroad restores equilibrium in the balance of payments, then resort must be had to other measures: measures designed to correct the balance of payments.

When liquid reserves are inadequate to meet the external deficit, then and only then is the time to take measures to correct the balance of payments. Chief among these measures are exchange depreciation and import restrictions.[15] For the sake of completeness, deflation may also be mentioned here. If it were possible to carry out general wage cuts by government decree overnight, this might be an effective way of righting the foreign balance without adverse effects on domestic employment. The effect of wage reductions in a closed economy are somewhat doubtful, the Keynesian position being that they improve employment, if at all, mainly through their repercussions on the interest rate. In an open economy, by contrast, the efficacy of wage reductions—though not their desirability—is undisputed. Like exchange depreciation, wage reductions act as a beggar-my-neighbor policy of stimulating home employment when their effect is to create a surplus and not, as in the present case, to close a deficit in the balance of payments. In practice, however, it is generally only through unemployment that wage reductions can be brought about. Deflation is a possible means of correcting the balance of payments, but it is destructive of internal equilibrium and therefore out of the question.

We are left with (a) changes in exchange rates and (b) measures of commercial policy. Both operate on the balance of trade either by restricting imports or promoting exports or by a combination of the two. Besides correcting the foreign balance, however, they also

[15] This is not the place to discuss the various types of import restrictions. They include, of course, import quotas and exchange controls as well as tariffs.

contribute on their own account toward offsetting the fall in expenditure and employment which tends to result from the drop in exports abroad. Those measures which operate by restricting imports serve to direct the flow of expenditure from foreign goods to the home market; those which promote exports tend to increase or rather, in the present case, to restore employment and income in the export industries. The effect on aggregate employment and expenditure in the country considered is favorable. But this favorable effect could equally well be obtained by domestic expansion. It is clear, therefore, that these measures are strictly necessary only to correct the balance of payments and are to be judged only in this capacity.

Exchange adjustments or import restrictions should come into play only when the offsetting policy which we have described cannot be continued because of a shortage of liquid reserves. Once they do come into play, however, their effects on domestic employment and expenditure make it necessary, if inflation is to be avoided, to cancel some or all of the compensatory increase in expenditure which characterized the offsetting policy. This may seem an unnecessary theoretical refinement. In practice, the effects of the successive measures can never be observed or judged so closely. Yet even for policy-making there can be no harm in clarity as to the detailed implications of full employment policy in an open economy. The general principle remains: total outlay on the country's output should be kept at a level corresponding to the maximum volume of employment attainable without inflation. The complications introduced by the existence of foreign trade relate, as we have seen, to the need to compensate for changes in foreigners' outlay on the country's products by inverse changes in domestic outlay and, similarly, to offset the incidental effect on total outlay of measures taken primarily to right the balance of payments.

So far we have discussed the problems arising from a depression in the country's export markets abroad. The opposite case, an inflationary boom abroad, has the opposite effects and calls for the opposite policy measures for the maintenance of internal equilibrium. The rise in exports, and also the fall in the marginal propensity to import due to the rise in import prices, will have to be offset by a reduction in domestic expenditure. If gold and exchange reserves become excessive, an appreciation of the currency or a lowering of import barriers is the appropriate remedy. Here again

the secondary adjustments required in domestic expenditure need
not be overlooked. A tariff reduction tends to direct expenditure
from home-made to imported goods; its effect is deflationary; and to
compensate for this, an expansion will be required in domestic
expenditure so as to keep total outlay on the country's output
stable.

Such, in brief, are the rules of conduct which emerge from the
Keynesian system to guide an individual country in search of internal equilibrium at full employment. In the preceding pages some
readers may have missed a discussion of comparative cost structures,
the play of relative prices, the forces of international competition,
the shifts required between production for home needs and for
export, the constant adaptation of a country's export industries to
changing world markets, and other similar topics. All these are valid
subjects of theoretical inquiry and practical concern; they are on a
different level of discourse, but they retain their validity within the
Keynesian system. The classical analysis concerns itself essentially
with the optimum division of labor between countries. It is under
conditions of full employment that this type of analysis comes most
fully into its own. The Keynesian approach demonstrates that any
single country can and should do something to realize these conditions within its borders without hurting its neighbors and without
throwing away the gains from international trade. Speaking for his
own country, Keynes made this resolute statement: "whilst we
intend to prevent inflation at home, we will not accept deflation at
the dictates of influences from outside." [16] And he welcomed the
post-war trade and currency schemes as an attempt to "combine the
advantages of freedom of commerce with safeguards against the disastrous consequences of a laissez faire system which pays no direct
regard to the preservation of equilibrium and merely relies on the
working out of blind forces." [17]

What Keynes sought and, we may hope, achieved, was a multilateral solution to the postwar currency problem. His aim was a
truly international monetary system. It is evident that the bilateral
alternative offers, in essence, not a monetary system at all, but a
system of international barter entirely analogous to inter-personal
barter in a primitive society. Just as inter-personal barter, prefer-

[16] Speech in the House of Lords, May 23, 1944.
[17] Speech in the House of Lords, December 18, 1945.

able though it is to complete self-sufficiency, inhibits that division of labor which money as a medium of exchange makes possible, so the policy of bilateralism cannot but cramp and cripple the international division of labor, especially the more refined and complicated division of labor which the spread of industrial techniques all over the world tends to develop. Keynes was modern enough to see that in the modern world nothing but a multilateral system would do. His distinctive contribution was to equip this system with the controls and safeguards required to make the pursuit of modern full-employment policies compatible with the equilibrium of international settlements. For the operation of these controls and safeguards, he left the necessary criteria—national income, employment, and the balance of payments—and, explicitly or implicitly, a set of general working principles which this essay has tried to indicate. These principles may still seem strange to some, and hard to understand; but they do possess the merit of consistency, seeking in every way to combine the advantages of international trade with the benefits of full employment.

III. *The Adjustment Process: Changes in Prices and Incomes*

COMMENTARY

THE GOLD STANDARD AND THE CUNLIFFE REPORT

The gold standard has been discussed by Graham (selection 6) and Triffin (selection 11) and in the Introduction to Part III. Here we present the view of an English government commission—the famous Cunliffe Report of 1918—on the pre-World War I working of the gold standard.[1]

Under the Bank Charter (Peel's) Act of 1844, the Bank of England could issue notes not backed by gold bullion up to a fixed amount, but beyond this maximum it could issue notes only on the basis of gold.[2] There was free exchange between bullion, notes, and coins, pound for pound, and there were no barriers to the import and export of gold. Thus "there was no means whereby the legal tender currency could be increased except the importation of gold from abroad to form the basis of an increase in the note issue of the Bank of England or to be

[1] First Interim Report of the Cunliffe Committee on Currency and Foreign Exchanges, August 15, 1918, reprinted in T.E. Gregory, editor, *Select Statutes, Documents and Reports Relating to British Banking, 1832–1928* (London: Oxford University Press, 1929), vol. II, pp. 334–365.

[2] The Report recommends that "the principles of the Act of 1844, which has upon the whole been fully justified by experience, should be maintained, namely, that there should be a fixed fiduciary issue beyond which, subject to emergency arrangements . . . , notes should only be issued in exchange for gold." And in general, restoration of the gold standard is considered crucial. "In our opinion it is imperative that after the war the conditions necessary to the maintenance of an effective gold standard should be restored without delay. Unless the machinery which long experience has shown to be the only effective remedy for an adverse balance of trade and an undue growth of credit is once more brought into play, there will be grave danger of a progressive credit expansion which will result in a foreign drain of gold menacing the convertibility of our note issue and so jeopardising the international trade position of the country."

presented to the Mint for coinage, and no means whereby it could be diminished . . . except the export of bullion or sovereigns."

The adjustment mechanism of this "complete and effective gold standard" is described as follows:

When the exchanges were favourable, gold flowed freely into this country and an increase of legal tender money accompanied the development of trade. When the balance of trade was unfavourable and the exchanges were adverse, it became profitable to export gold. The would-be exporter bought his gold from the Bank of England and paid for it by a cheque on his account. The Bank obtained the gold from the Issue Department in exchange for notes taken out of its banking reserve, with the result that its liabilities to depositors and its banking reserve were reduced by an equal amount, and the ratio of reserve to liabilities consequently fell. If the process was repeated sufficiently often to reduce the ratio in a degree considered dangerous, the Bank raised its rate of discount. The raising of the discount rate had the immediate effect of retaining money here which would otherwise have been remitted abroad and of attracting remittances from abroad to take advantage of the higher rate, thus checking the outflow of gold and even reversing the stream.

If the adverse condition of the exchanges was due not merely to seasonal fluctuations, but to circumstances tending to create a permanently adverse trade balance, it is obvious that the procedure above described would not have been sufficient. It would have resulted in the creation of a volume of short-dated indebtedness to foreign countries which would have been in the end disastrous to our credit and the position of London as the financial centre of the world. But the raising of the Bank's discount rate and the steps taken to make it effective in the market necessarily led to a general rise of interest rates and a restriction of credit. New enterprises were therefore postponed and the demand for constructional materials and other capital goods was lessened. The consequent slackening of employment also diminished the demand for consumable goods, while holders of stocks of commodities carried largely with borrowed money, being confronted with an increase of interest charges, if not with actual difficulty in renewing loans, and with the prospect of falling prices, tended to press their goods on a weak market. The result was a decline in general prices in the home market which, by checking imports and stimulating exports, corrected the adverse trade balance which was the primary cause of the difficulty.

When, apart from a foreign drain of gold, credit at home threatened to become unduly expanded, the old currency system tended to restrain the expansion and to prevent the consequent rise in domestic prices which ultimately causes such a drain. The expansion of credit, by forcing up prices, involves an increased demand for legal tender currency both from the banks in order to maintain their normal proportion of cash to liabilities and from the general public for the payment of wages and for retail transactions. In this case also the demand for such currency fell upon the reserve of the Bank of England, and the Bank was thereupon obliged to raise its rate of discount in order to prevent the fall in the proportion of that reserve to its liabilities. The same chain of consequences as we have just described followed and speculative trade activity was similarly restrained. There was therefore an automatic machinery by which the volume of purchasing power in this country was continuously adjusted to world prices of commodities in general. Domestic prices were automatically regulated so as to prevent excessive imports; and the creation of banking credit was so controlled that banking could be safely permitted a freedom from State interference which would not have been possible under a less rigid currency system.

The role of discount rate changes is emphasized:

Under an effective gold standard all export demands for gold must be freely met. A further essential condition of the restoration and maintenance of such a standard is therefore that some machinery shall exist to check foreign drains when they threaten to deplete the gold reserves. The recognised machinery for this purpose is the Bank of England discount rate. Whenever before the war the Bank's reserves were being depleted, the rate of discount was raised. This, as we have already explained, by reacting upon the rates for money generally, acted as a check which operated in two ways. On the one hand, raised money rates tended directly to attract gold to this country or to keep here gold that might have left. On the other hand, by lessening the demands for loans for business purposes, they tended to check expenditure and so to lower prices in this country, with the result that imports were discouraged and exports encouraged, and the exchanges thereby turned in our favour.

The Cunliffe Report may give a rather idealized, unreal version of the pre-World War I gold standard. It has been criticized especially for the conspicuous role which it gives to alterations in the discount rate by the central bank.[3] But the lucidly written Report is of value for reasons other than a completely accurate description of the historical mechanism. First, the pre-war standard in its last years was developing into closer conformity with the system described in the Report. Second, the Report represents an official version at the end of the war of what the gold standard "rules" *should* be, and this version was based on interpretation of history and contained desires and expectations for the future.

ELABORATION OF THE FOREIGN TRADE MULTIPLIER: FOREIGN REPERCUSSIONS

In the Introduction to this Part, it was deduced that k_f, the foreign trade multiplier, is equal to the reciprocal of the sum of the marginal propensities to save and to import: $k_f = 1/(s + m)$. But the simple model employed there omitted the effects of the autonomous exports on foreign incomes and the consequent changes induced in foreign imports, which are the exports of the first nation. We may now incorporate such "foreign repercussions."[4]

The autonomous rise in exports of the country in question (call it country A) represents an autonomous rise in imports

[3] "Over much of the pre-1914 period the instrument of Bank Rate policy was used very warily, and in certain important areas—France is the leading example—it was scarcely used at all. The central banks, far from reacting automatically to gold movements, used all sorts of devices to make Bank Rate changes unnecessary. . . . There was, in general, no serious attempt to keep price movements in different countries in line with each other by using that blunt and laggard instrument Bank Rate. . . ." R.S. Sayers, *Modern Banking* (London: Oxford University Press, 1947, second edition), pp. 184–185. See also P.B. Whale, "The Working of the Pre-War Gold Standard," *Economica*, IV n.s. (February 1937), pp. 18–32, reprinted in T.S. Ashton and R.S. Sayers, editors, *Papers in English Monetary History* (London: Oxford University Press, 1953), pp. 151–164.

[4] The exposition which is most convenient for our review is Fritz Machlup, *International Trade and the National Income Multiplier* (Philadelphia: The Blakiston Co., 1943).

for the rest of the world (country B). When B absorbs an autonomous increase in imports, it must suffer a corresponding autonomous fall in either consumption or saving. Machlup assumes that consumption falls. This autonomous fall in consumption is a disinjection which has a multiplied effect on B's income. The fall in B's income reduces B's imports, which are A's exports. Meanwhile, A's income has been rising, which induces an increase in A's imports, which are B's exports. A's income continues to rise so long as the autonomous increase in the level of A's exports is greater than the rise in A's saving and in A's imports plus the foreign-induced fall in A's exports. Similarly, B's income reaches a lower equilibrium level where the increase in autonomous imports (autonomous decrease in consumption) is matched by the fall in saving and in imports plus the foreign-induced increase in exports.[5]

Table I

Country A: $c = .5$; $s = .2$; $m = .3$

ΔC	ΔS	ΔM	Ind ΔX	Aut ΔX	$\Delta(X - M)$	ΔY
				100	100	100
50	20	30	−20	100	50	130
65	26	39	−25	100	36	140
70	28	42	−25.95	100	32.05	144.05
75.76	30.30	45.46	−24.24	100	30.30	151.52

Country B: $c = .55$; $s = .25$; $m = .2$

ΔC	ΔS	ΔM	Ind ΔX	Aut ΔM	$\Delta(X - M)$	ΔY
−100				100	−100	−100
−155	−25	−20	30	100	− 50	−125
−168.75	−31.25	−25	39	100	− 36	−129.75
−171.36	−32.44	−25.95	42	100	− 32.05	−129.36
−166.67	−30.30	−24.24	45.46	100	− 30.30	−121.21

[5] Table I follows Machlup's procedure except for the ΔC column of country B. Machlup neglects to make explicit in his tables the autonomous fall in B's consumption. It is important to do so, however, for changes in income are determined by changes in expenditure on current *domestic* output. The autonomous change in B's imports does not in itself affect B's income. See William R. Allen, "A Note on the Money Income Effects of Devaluation," *Kyklos*, IX (1956), Fasc. 3, pp. 378–379.

In the two-country case, i.e., when there are foreign repercussions, the income and multiplier equations are more cumbersome, but they are not difficult to derive. The final trade balance of A equals (with opposite sign) that of B, and the final level of saving in each country equals the trade balance. Thus:

$$s_a \Delta Y_a = -s_b \Delta Y_b$$

$$\Delta Y_b = -(s_a/s_b) \Delta Y_a$$

$$\Delta Y_a = \text{aut}\Delta X_a + c_a \Delta Y_a + m_b \Delta Y_b$$

$$= \text{aut}\Delta X_a + c_a \Delta Y_a - m_b(s_a/s_b) \Delta Y_a$$

$$\Delta Y_a - c_a \Delta Y_a + m_b(s_a/s_b) \Delta Y_a = \text{aut}\Delta X_a$$

$$\Delta Y_a[1 - c_a + m_b(s_a/s_b)] = \text{aut}\Delta X_a$$

$$\Delta Y_a = \frac{\text{aut}\Delta X_a}{1 - c_a + m_b(s_a/s_b)} = \frac{\text{aut}\Delta X_a}{s_a + m_a + m_b(s_a/s_b)}$$

And

$$k_a = \frac{1}{s_a + m_a + m_b(s_a/s_b)}.$$

For B, since $-\text{aut}\Delta C_b = \text{aut}\Delta X_a$:

$$Y_b = \frac{-\text{aut}\Delta X_a}{s_b + m_b + m_a(s_b/s_a)} \quad \text{and} \quad k_b = \frac{1}{s_b + m_b + m_a(s_b/s_a)}$$

MODIFICATION: AUTONOMOUS SAVING INSTEAD OF AUTONOMOUS CONSUMPTION

When country B experiences an autonomous rise in imports, the corresponding autonomous change in income disposal may be a fall in saving rather than, as Machlup assumes, in consumption.[6] As we have seen, if consumption is autonomously reduced, the multiplier mechanism leads to a fall in B's income. But if saving, instead of consumption, is decreased autonomously, B's income rises.[7] And with the same marginal pro-

---

[6] See F.D. Holzman and Arnold Zellner, "The Foreign-Trade and Balanced-Budget Multiplier," *American Economic Review*, XLVIII (March 1958), pp. 76 ff.

[7] This is not the only type of circumstances which would lead B's income to change in the same direction with A's. For example, incomes in both countries would rise if we begin the analysis with domestic income expansion in

pensities in Table II as in Table I, in the new income equilibrium there will prevail a larger export-import balance in the saving case than in the consumption case.

Table II

Country A: $c = .5$; $s = .2$; $m = .3$

ΔC	ΔS	ΔM	Ind ΔX	Aut ΔX	$\Delta(X - M)$	ΔY
				100	100	100
50	20	30		100	70	150
75	30	45	6	100	61	181
90.5	36.2	54.3	12.30	100	58	202.8
101.4	40.56	60.84	17.63	100	56.79	219.03
136.37	54.54	81.82	36.36	100	54.54	272.73

Country B: $c = .55$; $s = .25$; $m = .2$

ΔC	ΔS	ΔM	Ind ΔX	Aut ΔM	$\Delta(X - M)$	ΔY
	−100			100	−100	
	−100		30	100	− 70	30
16.50	− 92.50	6	45	100	− 61	61.50
33.83	− 84.62	12.30	54.3	100	− 58	88.13
48.47	− 77.97	17.63	60.84	100	− 56.79	109.31
100.00	− 54.54	36.36	81.82	100	− 54.54	181.82

Again in the new equilibrium, the change in the level of A's savings is equal, with opposite sign, to the change in B's savings. But here the change in B's saving has two components, one autonomous and one induced. Thus:

$$s_a \Delta Y_a = -s_b \Delta Y_b - \text{aut } \Delta S_b$$

And
$$\Delta Y_b = -s_a/s_b (\Delta Y_a) - \text{aut } \Delta S_b/s_b$$

Recalling that $-\text{aut}\Delta S_b = \text{aut}\Delta M_b = \text{aut}\Delta X_a$, we may solve as before for ΔY_a:

A, perhaps because of an autonomous increase in investment; the rise in A's income would induce an increase in imports; A's imports are B's exports, and the rise in B's exports would stimulate B's income; B's imports (A's exports) would increase, and A's income is further expanded; etc.

$$\Delta Y_a = \frac{\text{aut}\Delta X_a(1 + m_b/s_b)}{s_a + m_a + s_a(m_b/s_b)}$$

$$\Delta Y_b = \frac{\text{aut}\Delta X_a(m_a/s_a)}{s_b + m_b + s_b(m_a/s_a)}$$

MODIFICATION: KINDLEBERGER THESIS OF CHRONIC DOLLAR SHORTAGE

Thus far we, like Machlup, have assumed that the marginal propensity to invest is zero. But if we do assume that investment is a function of income, the nature of certain results may be changed. Alternative possible relationships between the marginal propensities to save and to invest in different balance of payments situations have been used as a basis for a theory of "dollar shortage."

Kindleberger, in attempting to account for an alleged tendency toward a chronic world shortage of dollars, has argued that (a) the United States may tend to overcompensate, or overadjust, when confronted with balance of payments deficits, ending in the new income equilibrium with a balance of payments surplus, and also the United States may undercompensate with respect to surpluses, still leaving a surplus in the new income equilibrium, (b) the rest of the world may undercompensate with import balances and overcompensate with export surpluses.[8]

Starting from an initial income and balance of payments equilibrium situation, we may posit an autonomous increase in imports or in exports, and in each case there may be overadjustment or underadjustment. Thus there are four possibilities:

1) underadjustment to increases in exports

[8] C.P. Kindleberger, "International Monetary Stabilization," in Seymour E. Harris, editor, *Postwar Economic Problems* (New York: McGraw-Hill Book Co., 1943), pp. 379–381; *idem*, "The Foreign Trade Multiplier, the Propensity to Import and Balance-of-Payments Equilibrium," *American Economic Review*, XXXIX (March 1949), pp. 491–494; *idem, The Dollar Shortage* (Cambridge: The Technology Press and New York: John Wiley and Sons, Inc., 1950), pp. 98–102.

2) overadjustment to increases in exports
3) overadjustment to increases in imports
4) underadjustment to increases in imports

There will tend to be a persistent dollar shortage, i.e., a United States export surplus, if the United States is characterized by cases (1) and (3) and if the rest of the world follows cases (2) and (4).

If we utilize the income model:

$$\Delta Y = \Delta C + \Delta I + \Delta X$$

$$\Delta Y = \Delta C + \Delta S + \Delta M$$

it follows that:

$$\Delta X + \Delta I = \Delta M + \Delta S$$

$$\Delta X = \Delta M + \Delta S - \Delta I$$

$$= m\Delta Y + s\Delta Y - i\Delta Y$$

$$= \Delta Y(m + s - i)$$

$$\Delta Y = \frac{\Delta X}{m + s - i}$$

For cases of autonomous increases in imports, when accompanied by opposite autonomous changes in consumption:

$$\Delta Y = -\frac{aut\Delta M}{m + s - i}$$

Letting ΔB represent the change in the trade balance, i.e., $\Delta(X - M)$, and noting that $\Delta B = \Delta S - \Delta I$, we have in the case of autonomous increases in exports:

$$\Delta B = \Delta Y(s - i)$$

$$= \frac{\Delta X(s - i)}{m + s - i} = \frac{\Delta X}{[m/(s - i)] + 1}$$

And with autonomous increases in imports:

$$\Delta B = \Delta Y(s - i) = -\frac{aut\Delta M}{[m/(s - i)] + 1}$$

Consider case (1), underadjustment to increases in exports, and suppose that it applies to the U.S. The U.S. begins with an equilibrium level of income and balanced trade, then experiences an autonomous increase in exports, which increases U.S. income, which induces an increase in imports, which reduces but does not eliminate the export surplus. Since $\Delta X + \Delta I = \Delta M + \Delta S$, it follows that $\Delta X - \Delta M = \Delta S - \Delta I$; thus if S increases more than does I, in the new income equilibrium there will be an export balance.

Assume a U.S. export surplus → U.S. income rises → imports and saving rise; investment also rises → if saving rises more than does investment, i.e., if $s > i$ (with rising income), income will not rise sufficiently high for imports to equal the increased level of exports: an excess of X over M will equal the excess of S over I.

Table III

$c = .5; \; s = .2; \; m = .3; \; i = .1$

ΔC	ΔS	ΔM	ΔI	ΔX	$\Delta(X-M)$	ΔY
				100	100	100
50	20	30	10	100	70	160
80	32	48	16	100	52	196
98	39.2	58.8	19.6	100	41.2	217.6
125	50	75	25	100	25	250

Suppose that case (2), overadjustment to increases in exports, characterizes economies other than the United States.

Assume a foreign export surplus to the U.S. → foreign income rises → imports, saving, and investment rise → if ΔI is greater than ΔS, i.e., if $i > s$ (with rising income), income will rise so much that in the new income equilibrium, ΔM will be greater than ΔX.

The reader can verify with his own calculations that if $c = .6$, $s = .1, m = .3, i = .2$, an autonomous increase in exports of 100 will lead to the following income equilibrium values: $\Delta Y = 500$, $\Delta C = 300$, $\Delta S = 50$, $\Delta M = 150$, $\Delta I = 100$, and $\Delta(X - M) = -50$.

With respect to adjustment to increases in imports, case (3) —over-adjustment—pertains to the United States, according to the Kindleberger thesis.

Assume a U.S. import balance → U.S. income falls → imports, saving, and investment fall → if the fall in investment is greater than the fall in saving, i.e., if $i > s$ (with falling income), in the new income equilibrium the induced decrease in imports will be greater than the autonomous increase: the net change in imports is negative, leaving a positive trade balance.

Table IV

$c = .6$; $s = .1$; $m = .3$; $i = .2$

ΔC	ΔS	*Ind* ΔM	ΔI	*Aut* ΔM	$\Delta(X - M)$	ΔY
−100				100	−100	−100
−160	−10	− 30	− 20	100	− 70	−180
−208	−18	− 54	− 36	100	− 46	−244
−246.4	−24.4	− 73.2	− 48.8	100	− 26.8	−295.2
−400	−50	−150	−100	100	50	−500

Case (4) is underadjustment to increases in imports and may apply to foreign economies.

Assume a foreign import surplus from the U.S. → foreign income falls → imports, saving, and investment fall → if investment falls by less than saving, i.e, if $i < s$ (with falling income), in the new income equilibrium there will remain an import balance.

With an autonomous rise in imports of 100, and if $c = .5$, $s = .2$, $m = .3$, and $i = .1$, we will have: $\Delta Y = -250$, $\Delta C = -225$, $\Delta S = -50$, $\Delta M = -75$, $\Delta I = -25$, and $\Delta(X - M) = -25$.

The foregoing analysis illustrates Kindleberger's thesis that "tendencies to overcompensation and undercompensation may exist and are a function of the relationship between the supply of savings at home [presumably the marginal propensity to save] and domestic investment opportunities [marginal propensity to invest]. . . . The existence of persistent disequilibrium in the balance of payments requires that some countries fail to adjust to deficits (or overadjust to surpluses), whereas other countries fail to adjust to surpluses (or overadjust to deficits)." [9] For the United States persistently to have a surplus and the rest of the world a deficit, it would be required that: (a) in the United States, $i < s$ with rising income and $i > s$ with falling income, and (b) in the rest of the world, $i < s$ with falling income and $i > s$ with rising income.

That such a configuration of relative propensities to invest and to save actually exists is an empirical proposition which has not been substantiated. "The real issue involved," as one critic reminds us, "is not whether Kindleberger's particular point is theoretically valid, for if fortified by the appropriate assumptions it would be, but whether or not those assumptions are the most realistic ones to make." [10]

[9] Kindleberger, *The Dollar Shortage,* p. 98
[10] Arthur I. Bloomfield, "Induced Investment, Overcomplete International Adjustment, and Chronic Dollar Shortage," *American Economic Review,* XXXIX (September 1949), p. 971.

IV. The Rate of Exchange and Equilibrium

IV. *The Rate of Exchange and Equilibrium*

INTRODUCTION

The exchange rate is a price, *viz.*, the price of one national currency in terms of another. Being a price, its determination can be analyzed in terms of market forces of demand and supply. However, the market structure within which these forces operate may take myriad forms. The foreign exchange market can be organized in such fashion that exchange rates are free from institutional or public policy constraints to fluctuate freely in accordance with demand and supply pressures. Only rarely has the market been so arranged. Generally the market forces are restricted, channeled, or supplemented by the organization of the market or by discretionary government policy or both. Some of these constraints on the working of the market are generally considered to be compatible with "liberal" economics, i.e., the price system still operates over a wide range, subject only to certain clear, stable, and impersonal organizational restrictions and "rules of the game." This Introduction reviews the determination of exchange rates under such conditions. But some of the constraints on the market, which we may designate generally as "exchange control," aim to restrict more or less severely the freedom of traders and to obviate in large measure the influences of supply and demand. This type of market situation is noted in Part V.

Over the past three-quarters of a century, the major commercial nations have employed a variety of liberal and illiberal foreign exchange arrangements. Speaking very broadly, the period may be characterized as follows: (a) for approximately a third of a century prior to World War I, the "traditional" gold standard was almost universally adopted; (b) during the war, the gold standard was modified in varying degrees in different countries and virtually abandoned as an international monetary system; (c) for several years after the war, the foreign exchange situation was generally chaotic, with most rates freely fluctuating and fitfully depreciating in response to speculative capital movements; (d) during the middle and late 'twenties, there evolved in rather haphazard fashion a gold standard similar in formal appearance to the pre-war standard but quite different in substance; (e) the 'thirties saw the break-up of the revised gold standard, commercial warfare centering on competitive devaluations and exchange controls, exchange rate pegging by stabilization funds, and finally, in 1936, a hesitant step toward international financial cooperation by England, France, and the United States in the Tripartite Monetary Agreement; (f) the International Monetary Fund, which began operations shortly after World War II, was intended to make feasible essentially stable exchange rates over prolonged periods, with provision for occasional rate adjustments without triggering retaliatory devaluations.

These rapid and sometimes violent developments were reflected in evolving official and academic attitudes toward exchange-rate policy and the concept of the equilibrium exchange rate. As Mikesell has summarized the policy issues:

After World War I the major issue for countries that had left the gold standard was the level at which the new gold parity should be established. Conservative opinion tended to favor a return to the pre-1914 gold parity, where its restoration was at all possible, while most economists who had studied the question favored a more scientific determination in terms of a reestablishment of prewar relationships between price levels at home and abroad. When, after 1929, pressures on their balance of payments forced a number of countries off the gold standard, the principal issue for debate among economists interested in foreign exchange was whether rates should be fixed (with currencies tied to gold) or floating (with short-term stability maintained by stabilization operations). Some countries avoided depreciation of their currencies for a time by adopting exchange controls, but such practices were generally frowned upon by economists. Exchange controls were regarded either as short-term expedients to meet emergency conditions or as "Schachtian" weapons in "economic warfare." The techniques of stabilization funds aroused considerable interest. Here the problem was how to distinguish short-term forces from fundamental changes in the demand for, and the supply of, foreign exchange so that the market rate could be supported at an "equilibrium" level.

By the end of the 1930's majority opinion among economists seemed to favor a flexible rate policy as opposed to a rigid link with gold; short-term stability was to be maintained by stabilization fund operations. International cooperation along the lines of the Tripartite Agreement was to be used to avoid competitive exchange depreciation. Economists in both the Western Hemisphere and in Europe developed these ideas further during World War II in the direction of some kind of an international stabilization fund coupled with an agreement for cooperation in exchange rate policies. The product of the deliberations of economists and statesmen was the establishment of the International Monetary Fund.[1]

Before studying the essays of this section it is in order to survey certain basic arrangements under which exchange rates may be determined.

FREELY FLUCTUATING EXCHANGE RATES

Take first the case of freely fluctuating rates. There is no pegging of rates—discretionary or otherwise—and therefore rates are free to move in accordance with market forces. The demand for foreign exchange stems from those who wish to acquire foreign goods, services, and securities; suppliers of exchange are those who sell things to foreigners. The following illustration is in terms of trade in goods and services, but it is simple to superimpose capital transactions later.

In Figure Ia, D_t^{us} is the total demand of the U.S. for a certain "bundle" of goods and services; the U.S. supply of this bundle is indicated by S_t^{us}. The equilibrium price, at which the quan-

---

[1] Raymond F. Mikesell, *Foreign Exchange in the Postwar World* (New York: The Twentieth Century Fund, 1954), pp. 136–137.

tity demanded equals the quantity supplied, is $8. At any price below $8, the quantity demanded is greater than the quantity domestically supplied, and the excess thus constitutes the quantity demanded from abroad. The U.S. demand for im-

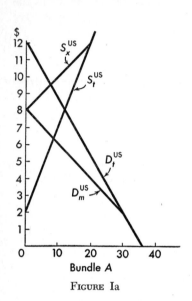

FIGURE Ia

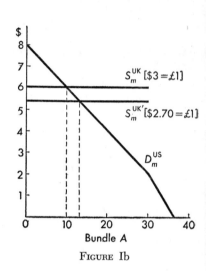

FIGURE Ib

Table I

(a) Price	(b) D_t	(c) S_t	(d) $D_m = D_t - S_t$	(e) $S_x = S_t - D_t$
$12	0	20	—	20
11	3	18	—	15
10	6	16	—	10
9	9	14	—	5
8	12	12	0	0
7	15	10	5	—
6	18	8	10	—
5	21	6	15	—
4	24	4	20	—
3	27	2	25	—
2	30	0	30	—
1	33	—	33	—
0	36	—	36	—

ports is designated by $D_m{}^{us}$ in Figure Ia and is calculated arithmetically in columns (a) through (d) in Table I.

At prices above $8, the quantity of the bundle supplied will be greater than the quantity demanded, and the excess is available for export. The U.S. export supply curve is $S_x{}^{us}$, and it, too, is calculated in the table. We shall assume henceforth that the dollar price of this bundle—call it "bundle *A*"—is never above $8.

The U.S. import demand curve is redrawn in Figure Ib. Now suppose that any quantity of bundle *A* can be imported from the U.K. at an English price of £2. (Admittedly, this is a special case, in which the U.K. supply curve is horizontal. But this special assumption is not unreasonable in principle, and it greatly simplifies calculations.) At a price of £2, what is the equivalent price in dollars? Obviously the answer turns on the rate of exchange. If the rate is $3 = £1 (or $1 = £.333), the U.S. price is $6; at a level of $6, we may draw a horizontal supply curve and label it $S_m{}^{uk}$. At an exchange rate of $2.70 = £1 (or $1 = £.370), the supply curve is shifted to a level of $5.40.

If the U.S. price is $6, the quantity demanded (and supplied) is 10; the dollar expenditure on imports (which is the number of *dollars supplied* on the foreign exchange market) is $60; the equivalent expenditure in terms of pounds (which is the number of *pounds demanded*) is £20. At a price of $5.40, the volume of imports is 13, equal in value to $70.20 and to £26. With a little arithmetic, the reader can verify the following: if the exchange rate is $4 = £1, the supply curve will be at a level of $8, at which price the volume of imports is zero; as the dollar price of the pound falls, the dollar price of imports falls; as the price falls, the quantity of imports and the number of pounds demanded increase, but the number of dollars offered will rise only through the range of prices in which demand is elastic (from $8 to $4) and will fall through the inelastic range ($4 to $0). These calculations are given in columns (a) through (f) of Table II for the range of import prices from $5.40 through $4.60.

Table II

(a) $ Price of U.S. Imports: (c) × 2 or 2 ÷ (e)	(b) Quantity of U.S. Imports	(c) $ per £: (a) ÷ 2 or 1 ÷ (e)	(d) $ Supplied: (a) × (b)	(e) £ per $: 1 ÷ (c) or (g) ÷ 7.5	(f) £ Demanded: (b) × 2, (d) ÷ (c) or (d) × (e)	(g) £ Price of U.K. Imports: 7.5 ÷ (c) or 7.5 × (e)	(h) Quantity of U.K. Imports	(i) £ Supplied: (g) × (h)	(j) $ Demanded: (h) × 7.5, (i) × (c) or (i) ÷ (e)
5.4	13.0	2.70	70.20	.370	26	2.78	10.44	29.02	78.43
5.3	13.5	2.65	71.55	.377	27	2.83	10.34	29.26	77.61
5.2	14.0	2.60	72.80	.385	28	2.89	10.22	29.54	76.73
5.1	14.5	2.55	73.95	.392	29	2.94	10.12	29.75	75.89
5.0	15.0	2.50	75.00	.400	30	3.00	10.00	30.00	75.00
4.9	15.5	2.45	75.95	.408	31	3.06	9.88	30.23	74.09
4.8	16.0	2.40	76.80	.417	32	3.13	9.74	30.49	73.12
4.7	16.5	2.35	77.55	.426	33	3.20	9.60	30.72	72.11
4.6	17.0	2.30	78.20	.435	34	3.26	9.48	30.91	71.06

In Figure IIa we have plotted the demand for pounds ($D_\pounds$) and in Figure IIb the supply of dollars derived through the entire range of $D_m{}^{us}$. $D_\pounds$ slopes downward to the right for alternative dollar prices of the pound; $S_\$$, with reference to pound prices of the dollar, slopes upward to the right through the range corresponding to the elastic portion of $D_\pounds$ (and $D_m{}^{us}$); it bends backward when $D_\pounds$ (and $D_m{}^{us}$) are inelastic.

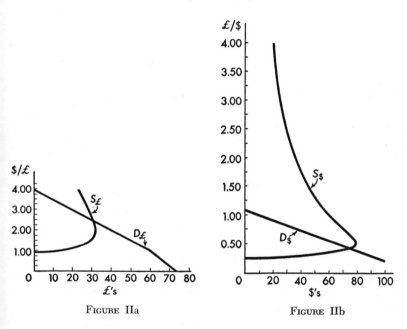

FIGURE IIa   FIGURE IIb

In perfectly analagous fashion, we have, in Figure III, the total U.K. demand for "bundle B" ($D_t{}^{uk}$), the total U.K. supply ($S_t{}^{uk}$), and the derived U.K. import demand ($D_m{}^{uk}$). And suppose that the U.K. can import any quantity of bundle B from the U.S. at a price of \$7.50 per unit. As in Figure Ib, we could draw alternative horizontal U.S. supply curves ($S_m{}^{us}$), each curve at a different pound price and corresponding to a particular rate of exchange. By thus taking different exchange rates and thereby moving $S_m{}^{us}$ up or down $D_m{}^{uk}$, we could calculate the

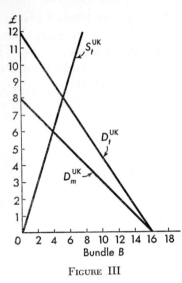

FIGURE III

schedule of *pounds supplied* and *dollars demanded*. Such calculations over a limited range are given in Table II, and the complete schedules are plotted in Figures IIa and IIb.

On the basis of our illustrative data, the equilibrium rate of exchange is $2.50 = £1, at which dollar price of the pound the quantity of pounds demanded equals the quantity of pounds supplied. We can equally well say that the equilibrium rate is $1 = £.4, for at that pound price of the dollar quantities of dollars demanded and supplied will be equal. This is apparent from Table II and from Figures IIa and IIb.[2]

EXCHANGE RATES UNDER THE GOLD STANDARD

For purposes of reviewing the determination of exchange rates under the international gold standard, there are two major characteristics of the gold standard which should be kept in mind: (a) each country on the standard must establish and maintain a domestic-currency free-market price of gold and (b) there must be freedom of import and export of gold.

Again assume a two-country case. Suppose that the U.S. establishes a gold price of $36 per ounce; the U.K. sets the price of an ounce at £15. Since both $36 and £15 are equal to an ounce of gold, they are equal to each other. This rate of exchange, $36 = £15 or $2.40 = £1, is the "mint par."

---

[2] It will be recalled that our calculations were based on bundles of goods and services. If we introduce capital movements, the foreign exchange supply and demand schedules will be affected, and probably the equilibrium exchange rate will be above or below $2.50 = £1. For example, in Figure IIa, if Americans buying British securities increase $D_£$ more than British investment in the U.S. increases $S_£$, the equilibrium rate will be higher than $2.50 = £1.

If there were no cost to shipping gold, the actual, market rate of exchange would never—except in the most extraordinary circumstances—deviate from the mint par. For if there were such deviation, powerful market forces would immediately act to bring the rate back to mint par. If, for example, the market rate were somehow to move to $2.50 = £1, there would ensue "gold arbitrage." People owning pounds would sell them for dollars at the favorable market rate, sell the dollars for gold in the U.S. at the established dollar price of gold, ship the gold to the U.K. and sell the gold for pounds at the established pound price of gold. One pound could purchase $2.50, which could obtain approximately .07 ounces of gold, which could be sold for £1.05. Similarly, owners of dollars would buy gold in the U.S., ship it to the U.K. and obtain pounds, and then convert the pounds into dollars. In the foreign exchange market, we would have an increased supply of pounds (demand for dollars) and a decreased demand for pounds (supply of dollars), and the dollar price of the pound would fall (the pound price of the dollar would rise) to mint par.

However, there are costs in shipping gold. We may suppose that it costs $.02 to ship from the United States to England that amount of gold which sells for $2.40 (or £1). Thus the total cost of transferring gold worth £1 from the U.S. to U.K. is $2.42. So long as the market price of the pound, i.e., the price of a sterling draft, is less than $2.42, anyone wishing to obtain purchasing power in the U.K. will buy pounds directly rather than ship gold. And so long as the market rate is more than $2.38, anyone wanting dollars will buy them directly instead of sending gold. But at rates of $2.42 = £1 and $2.38 = £1, some gold almost certainly will flow. These rates are the "gold points," and normally they are the ceiling and the floor to the dollar price of pounds. No one will pay more than $2.42 for £1, since he can obtain £1 for a maximum price of $2.42 by shipping gold; no one need accept less than $2.38, since he can obtain $2.38 by shipping gold.

In Figure IV we have redrawn the segments of the $S_£$ and $D_£$ curves of Figure IIa corresponding to the data of Table II.

The equilibrium rate is $2.50 = £1, but $2.42 = £1 is the maximum market rate. The actual rate will, therefore, be $2.42
= £1, but at that rate the quantity of pounds demanded (31.60)
is greater than the quantity supplied (30.38). The supply deficiency (1.22) will be filled by shipment of gold from the
U.S. to the U.K., for with the rate at $2.42 = £1, it is a matter of

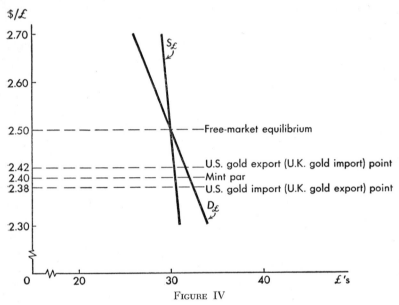

FIGURE IV

indifference pricewise to demanders of pounds whether they
buy pounds directly or export gold.

It is apparent, then, that exchange rates under the gold
standard are substantially stable, but they are free to fluctuate
in accordance with forces of demand and supply within the
narrow limits of the gold points. The rate of exchange will not
go beyond the gold points, for at those rates a buyer or seller
of foreign exchange will deal in gold rather than in drafts at
less favorable rates.

EXCHANGE RATE PEGGING BY
STABILIZATION FUNDS

During the 1930's, all of the major nations attempted limited
management of exchange rates through buying and selling

activities in the foreign exchange market. Stabilization funds were established for this purpose, the first being the British Exchange Equalization Account, begun in 1932; the American Exchange Stabilization Fund was set up in 1934. "An Exchange Stabilization Fund is a collection of assets segregated under a central control for the purpose of intervention in the exchange market to prevent undesirable fluctuations in exchange rates." While stabilization was the general aim, "exchange stability as an objective of practical policy has had no precise and generally accepted meaning."

An early and often repeated formulation of the aims of the British Exchange Equalization Account was that the Account was designed, without resisting general trends, to iron out undue fluctuations in the exchanges caused by erratic movements of capital and the disturbing activities of speculators. This objective was extended to include combatting seasonal exchange fluctuations. In practice, however, it proved impossible to confine the effects of Exchange Fund activity within such limits. . . . The major purposes of other Exchange Funds was to establish and defend "appropriate" levels, that is, to resist general trends in the exchanges. . . .

The aim of the American Fund like that of the British Fund was to promote greater exchange stability. But the theory of non-resistance to general trends was conspicuously absent from the American conception of exchange stability. The smoothing out of "undue" fluctuations due to temporary causes was indeed an important objective, but it was subordinate to the "defence" of the dollar against any general movement in other major currencies, sterling in particular, to levels that were not satisfactory to the United States. The defence of the dollar was conceived of primarily as a defence against competitive exchange depreciation, and the American Stabilization Fund was established as an instrument for preventing the dollar from rising in value in terms of other currencies.[3]

There were two types of funds. (1) "Credit" funds, such as the British Account, originally had assets of government securities which could be sold for domestic currency. (2) "Gold" funds, represented by the American Fund, were initiated with

---

[3] William Adams Brown, Jr., in Ragnar Nurkse, *International Currency Experience* (League of Nations, 1944), pp. 143–144.

assets of gold obtained from revaluations of monetary gold reserves; when the dollar price of gold was raised in 1933–34, the government acquired a $2.8 billion "profit," $2 billion of which was allotted to the Fund.

The foreign exchange activities of a credit fund can be illustrated as follows:

I. Depreciate (or prevent appreciation of) domestic currency on foreign exchange market (e.g., in face of capital inflow).

Fund buys inflowing foreign exchange with domestic money → foreign investor deposits domestic money: demand deposits and reserves of commercial banks are increased → Fund sells treasury bills in money market and replenishes its deposit in central bank, reducing commercial bank reserves → Fund uses newly acquired foreign exchange to import gold and hold it.

Commercial *bank reserves* first rise and then fall: on balance, bank reserves are unaffected. The *money supply,* i.e., demand deposits, may or may not increase on balance: foreign-owned deposits rise, but domestically owned deposits may remain constant or fall, depending on whether the treasury bills bought from the Fund are purchased with money newly borrowed from banks or with already existing money. Even if the money supply remains unchanged, the *volume and pattern of expenditure* on goods and services may be affected by the capital inflow, for the expenditure of the new foreign-owned deposits may well be different from the expenditure which would have been made with the domestically-owned funds now used to purchase treasury bills. However, despite the probability that the effects on the domestic economy will be only damped and not completely neutralized, the Fund will have raised the domestic-currency demand for foreign exchange and the supply of domestic currency, thus supporting the price of foreign currency and depressing the price of domestic currency.

II. Appreciate (or prevent depreciation of) domestic currency (e.g., in face of capital outflow).

Fund sells foreign currency in exchange for domestic: demand deposits and reserves of commercial banks are decreased → Fund

buys treasury bills in money market, increasing bank reserves →
Fund exports gold to replenish stock of foreign exchange.

There is no net effect on bank reserves; the money supply
tends to remain unchanged but could rise if capital exporters
acquire foreign exchange with funds newly borrowed from
banks; and the pattern and volume of general expenditure will
surely be affected to some degree. But the Fund has increased
the demand for domestic currency and the supply of foreign
currency in the foreign exchange market.

The gold-type fund could operate in substantially the same
manner. To support the domestic currency, the Fund could
export gold and obtain foreign currency, sell the foreign currency against domestic, use the domestic currency to buy
domestic securities and thus at least partially neutralize the
original capital outflow that caused (or threatened) depreciation of the domestic currency. To depress the domestic currency, buy foreign currency with domestic, convert foreign
currency into gold and import it, sell gold to the central bank
for domestic currency with which the Fund can continue its
operations.

It is apparent that a fund must possess gold or foreign exchange to support the domestic currency and have command
over domestic currency to depress it (i.e., support foreign currency). In supporting the domestic currency, the gold fund
could be preferable to the credit fund, for it has gold with
which to acquire foreign currency and enable it to increase
the demand for domestic currency in the exchange market.
By contrast, the credit fund would have no "ammunition" with
which to start operations—unless gold or foreign exchange had
been previously accumulated in opposite transactions. But in
depressing the domestic currency to counteract a capital inflow—which was the problem of the American fund in the
1930's—the gold fund may be at a disadvantage for two reasons:
it may have no securities which can be converted into domestic
currency for purposes of buying foreign currency; the importation of gold will be inflationary.

EXCHANGE RATE PEGGING UNDER THE INTERNATIONAL MONETARY FUND

With respect to the determination and behavior of exchange rates (but not in all other respects), the I.M.F. has similarity to both the gold standard and stabilization funds. Exchange rates under the Fund are essentially stable over indefinitely long periods, free to fluctuate only within limits closely analogous to "gold points"; this stability is achieved through governmental pegging operations, even using the stabilization funds established in the 1930's. Provision is made for altering exchange rates (in order to correct "fundamental disequilibria"), but any appreciation or depreciation of a currency supposedly is to be made only after consultation with and approval of the Fund.

We may illustrate the pegging procedure with reference to the dollar-pound exchange rate.

The "par" value of the pound is $2.80. "Gold points" above and below this par value are established by the prices at which the respective central banks will buy and sell gold and (in the case of the Bank of England) dollars. Under the I.M.F. agreement, the market rate may not diverge from the par value by more than 1 per cent in either direction, i.e., the permissible limits are $2.828 and $2.772 per pound. In practice, the Bank of England has established a somewhat narrower range of $2.82 and $2.78. This spread is sufficient to cover the costs of transporting gold from one country to the other. Sterling is pegged within this range.

Broadly speaking, the rate is free to fluctuate between $2.82 and $2.78 according to market supply and demand forces, but the Bank of England (on behalf of the Exchange Equalization Account, which technically is under the control of the Treasury and holds title to the U.K. reserves) may intervene in the market at any point to influence the supply or demand position. In fact, the authorities intervene before the dollar rate on the pound reaches the limits of 2.82/2.78, and the rate has never hit either limit. The Federal Reserve Bank of New York does not intervene in the market on its own account to influence the rate.

Operation of the lower "peg." With, for example, a heavy U.K. import balance from the U.S., the market demand for dollars against sterling may depress the rate toward $2.78. But the rate cannot fall below this level, since the Bank of England stands ready to supply dollars against sterling to the market without limit at a price of $2.78. No buyer of dollars will, therefore, pay more than £0.36 for $1 (equivalent to £1 = $2.78). Following are examples:

(a) Where the U.K. importer initiates the financing (e.g., by paying with a bankers' bill of exchange [4]), he will not pay more than £1 for $2.78. If U.K. exchange dealers' dollar balances are low, they will buy dollars from the Bank of England—in effect, the Bank is entering the market in a pegging operation. If, in turn, the Bank's dollar balances are low, it may replenish them by selling gold earmarked for its account in New York or by exporting gold to New York. Finally, if the Bank is short of dollars and of gold, it may arrange to borrow dollars, e.g., by purchasing dollars against sterling from the I.M.F.

(b) Where the financing initiative is taken by the U.S. exporter (who draws a commercial draft against the U.K. importer), he will not sell the bill to a U.S. exchange dealer for less than $2.78 per £1 for two reasons: (1) the U.S. dealer can sell sterling (acquired when the U.K. importer pays the bill) to U.K. dealers (or to the Bank of England operating through the New York Federal Reserve Bank) for not less than $2.78, and competition among U.S. dealers ensures that the dollar rate on the pound to American exporters does not fall below this rate; (2) the exporter can sell sterling directly

[4] A legal definition of a bill of exchange, or draft, is "an unconditional order in writing addressed by one person to another, signed by the person giving it, and requiring the person to whom it is addressed, to pay on demand or at a fixed or determinable future time, a certain sum of money to, or to the order of, a specfic person or bearer." The essence of this definition can be stated simply: A (drawer) orders B (drawee and payer) to pay—on demand or in the future—C (payee, who may be also the drawer). "Bankers'" bills are drawn in foreign currency by a bank on its account in a foreign bank—both drawer and drawee are banks—and sold to persons having obligations to pay abroad. "Commercial" bills are drawn by exporters (or others to whom foreign funds are due) on importers.

to U.K. dealers at not less than $2.78. In both cases, competition among U.K. dealers ensures that the rate does not fall below $2.78, for they can acquire dollars at that rate from the Bank of England.

Operation of the upper "peg." With, for example, a large U.K. export surplus to the U.S., market demand for sterling against dollars may force the rate up toward $2.82. But the rate cannot rise above this level, since the Bank of England stands ready to supply sterling against dollars to the market without limit at a price of $2.82. Therefore, no buyer of sterling will pay more than $2.82 for £1.

(a) Where the U.K. exporter draws a commercial bill against the U.S. importer, he will not accept less than £1 for $2.82. As U.K. dealers' dollar balances increase and their sterling balances fall, they may sell dollars to the Bank of England. As the Bank's dollar balances increase, it may buy gold for its account in New York or import gold from New York.

(b) Where the U.S. importer pays with a bankers' draft, he will not pay the U.S. dealer more than $2.82 per £1 for two reasons: (1) the U.S. dealer can buy sterling against dollars from U.K. dealers for not more than $2.82, and competition among U.S. dealers ensures that the U.S. rate does not rise above this rate; (2) the U.K. exporter can buy sterling directly from U.K. dealers (who in turn have recourse, if necessary, to the Bank of England) at not more than $2.82. In both cases, competition among U.K. dealers prevents the rate from rising above the level at which they can sell dollars for sterling to the Bank of England.

13. Exchange Rates and Prices

Lloyd A. Metzler

University of Chicago

Excerpt from "Exchange Rates and the International Monetary Fund," *International Monetary Policies*, Postwar Economic Studies No. 7 (Washington: Board of Governors of the Federal Reserve System, September 1947), pp. 1–45; pp. 16–24 excerpted. Reprinted by permission of the author and the Board of Governors.

THE PURCHASING POWER PARITY THEORY

One of the factors which must be taken into account in any discussion of present currency values is the general rise in prices and costs which was brought about by the war. Even in countries where price controls were maintained throughout the war years, the inflationary effects of large government purchases of goods and services could not be entirely avoided. If these price increases had been uniform throughout all countries, no particular difficulties would have arisen as far as foreign trade is concerned. A casual glance at a few statistics of prices, however, will convince the reader of the enormous disparity which has developed between the price changes in one country and those in another. In France, for example, wholesale prices have increased about 700 per cent above the prewar level, compared with increases of 200 per cent in Czechoslovakia, 185 per cent in Mexico, and 45 per cent in Australia. In view of these discrepancies, it is obvious that relative changes in the internal purchasing power of different currencies will have substantial effects on the course of international trade unless they are offset by corresponding changes in exchange rates.

After the First World War, the descrepancies between movements of price levels in different countries were equally great, and since exchange rates in many countries were uncontrolled, these changes in relative purchasing power exerted a considerable influence on exchange rates. Indeed the changes in prices and costs were so striking by comparison with other economic changes that there was a tendency to explain the observed movement of exchange rates entirely in terms of changes in relative purchasing power. This was the doctrine of purchasing power parity which enjoyed a considerable popularity among economists in the 1920's. The theory of purchasing power parity, in its simplest form, may be illustrated by means of a numerical example.

Suppose that in some initial period, when international payments are in a balanced condition, the exchange rate between the dollar and the pound sterling is $4.50 = £1. And suppose that as a result of a war, prices and costs in the United States increase uniformly to a level just twice their former level, while prices and costs in the United Kingdom rise to three times their former level; in other words, the index of prices in the United States increases to 200 while the index in the United Kingdom increases to 300. According to the purchasing power parity doctrine the internal purchasing power of the dollar at the close of the war is one-half of its former level, and the internal purchasing power of the pound is one-third its former level. Hence, it is argued, in order to preserve balanced trade relations between the two countries, the price of the pound, in terms of dollars, must drop to two-thirds of the old price, or to $3 = £1. More generally, the so-called parity exchange rate is equal to the price of the pound in the base year, in terms of dollars, multiplied by the ratio of the price index in the United States to the price index in the United Kingdom.

The virtue of the parity rate is that it preserves the earlier real exchange ratio between the goods and services of one country and the goods and services of another. To see why this is true, suppose in the above example that an American product, X, before the war sold for $1.50, while a British product, Y, sold for £1. At the old exchange rate, American purchasers of Y would have had to pay $4.50 per unit, and the price per unit in the United States would thus have been three times the price of a unit of the American product, X. We may assume, now, that as a result of the war inflation the cost of production and the price of each commodity, in the currency of the selling country, rises according to the general price rise. In other words, the selling price of X, the American product, is doubled while the price of Y, the British product, is tripled; the new price of X is $4.00, and the new price of Y is £3. At the parity exchange rate of $3 = £1, the American price of the British product is thus $9. Once again, therefore, the unit price of the British product, in dollars, is three times the unit price of the American product.

Since the relative price of British goods, compared with the price of American goods, is the same after the inflation as before, the general rise in prices will not affect the import of British goods; unless tastes or conditions of production and trade have changed, the physical volume of British imports will be the same as in the prewar situation, and only the monetary units in which these imports are measured will have changed. Likewise, in the United Kingdom the sterling price of United States goods, relative to the price of British goods, will remain the same as before the inflation, and a presumption exists that the physical volume of British imports will be unchanged.

CRITICISMS OF PURCHASING POWER PARITY

While adoption of the parity rate is desirable in the solution of some problems, it may be quite undesirable in the solution of others, for in some circumstances it may be necessary to change the real terms of trade between countries in order to restore a balanced condition in international trade. If this is true, the so-called "equilibrium" rate of exchange will differ from the parity rate. Suppose, for example, that the base period chosen for the calculation of a parity rate in the numerical example above had been a period in which the United States had a deficit in its balance of payments. Other things being equal, the parity rate between the dollar and the pound, by perpetuating the real terms of exchange between British and American goods, will likewise perpetuate the deficit. Only the money units in which the deficit is measured will have changed. In order to restore a balanced condition, exports of the United States must be encouraged, and imports reduced, by means of a depreciation in the value of the dollar below the parity rate. Thus, if the base period is one of disequilibrium, the parity rate, after the price rise has taken place, will not be the same as the rate which will establish equilibrium in a country's balance of payments.[1]

Other factors will also create a disparity between the parity rate and the equilibrium rate. Consider, for example, the effects of capital movements. Suppose that in the prewar base period there were no capital movements, and that after the rise in prices has taken

[1] On all of these criticisms of parity calculations cf. Gottfried Haberler, "The Choice of Exchange Rates after the War," *American Economic Review*, June 1945, pp. 311–15.

place the United States expects to make extensive loans to the United Kingdom. Assuming that the base period was one of balanced trade without capital movements, the parity rate will also establish a balanced condition, in the absence of capital movements, after the price rise has taken place. But if the United States is to make large foreign loans an export surplus can and should be allowed to develop in the United States balance of trade, and in order to bring about such an export surplus, the exchange rate for the dollar must be depreciated below the parity rate. Accordingly, we find once more a difference between the parity rate and the equilibrium rate. Changes in tastes or in methods of production will create a similar difference between the two rates. If, because of such changes, the American demand for British goods has increased during the time interval between the base period and the period of comparison, the parity rate, by re-establishing the earlier ratio of exchange between British and American goods, will lead to a deficit in the United States balance even though the initial period was one of equilibrium. In order to make the supply of foreign exchange equal to the demand, the value of the dollar in this case must again be depreciated below the purchasing power parity rate.

Movements of output and employment are also important in judging the validity of parity calculation, for these movements bring with them substantial changes in the demand for imports. In times of comparative economic stability, the effects of changes in employment upon the equilibrium level of exchange rates can perhaps be neglected, but in a period such as the prewar decade of the thirties, when movements of output and employment were the dominant feature of economic activity, large discrepancies may develop between the parity exchange rates and the rates which would restore equilibrium in a country's balance of payments. To see why this is true, suppose that international trade is initially in equilibrium, and that the level of output in a single country is increased while output in other countries remains unchanged. As a result of the higher output in the expanding country, the demand for imports rises; a greater volume of imported materials is required to produce the higher level of output and, at the same time, consumers with higher incomes increase their purchases of foreign commodities. The expanding country is faced with a deficit in its balance of payments which will normally lead to a depreciation of its currency even if there are no changes in sellers' prices either at home or abroad. In other words, a relative expansion of output in one country alters the equilibrium exchange rate in a way which does not correspond to the movement of prices; in extreme examples the equilibrium exchange rate can be altered with no changes in prices at all.

The foregoing criticisms of purchasing power parity have all considered the most favorable case for the parity theory in which prices and costs rise or fall uniformly within any given country. Although this implied assumption may be justified, to a considerable extent, in periods of hyper-inflation, the practical application of the parity doctrine is usually complicated by differences in the degree of price rise or fall within each country. When some prices or costs rise more rapidly than others within the same country, no simple comparison between price movements in different countries can be made. The best that can be done is to use an average or index number of price changes, and if the discrepancies in price movements as between different commodities in the same country are large, such an index number, at best, is only a rough indication of the change in the value of the monetary unit. Moreover, since several types of price-index numbers are usually available, the calculation of parity rates is not a simple procedure, but involves a considerable element of judgment as to what prices and costs are important for a country's balance of payments.

Considering this element of judgment, it is not surprising that the selection of an appropriate price index has been one of the most controversial topics concerning purchasing power parity. Indeed, in some cases the difficulty of selecting an index has been the most important single cause for the disrepute into which the parity theory has fallen. It has been said, on the one hand, that the prices of commodities which do not enter into international trade are irrelevant, since these prices, at most, have only an indirect influence on a country's balance of payments. And on the other hand, it has been argued that international prices, or the prices of goods which enter into international trade, cannot be used because these prices necessarily adjust themselves to changes in exchange rates. In other words, it has been argued that prices for commodities which have a world market, such as many agricultural products and raw materials, necessarily adjust themselves, within a given country, to any change in that country's exchange rate.

To clarify this point, suppose that Canada is an exporter of such a product, Z, to the United Kingdom. If the exchange rate between

Canada and the United Kingdom is $4 = £1, and if the British price of Z is one-fourth pound per unit, the Canadian price will necessarily be $1.00, since Canada is an exporter of Z, and its price is governed by the world price. Now suppose the exchange rate is altered to $5 = £1. If the British price of Z were to remain unchanged, the price in Canadian currency would rise to $1.25, and the relative change in the price of Z between the two countries would conform exactly to the change in the exchange rate. Since this type of behavior is characteristic of many commodities which are sold in competitive international markets, it has been said that the prices of internationally traded goods cannot be used in parity calculations. To include such prices, it is said, imparts a bias in the parity calculations, which tends to justify the existing exchange rate, whatever it may be. If prices of domestic goods cannot be used in the calculations because they are irrelevant, and if prices of international goods cannot be used because they always adjust themselves to movements of exchange rates, it must seem, as it did to some economists, that the theory of parity has little substance, and must be replaced by other methods of judging exchange rates.

One proposed solution of the price dilemma is a substitution of data on unit costs of production for price data. In other words, it has been suggested that parity rates might be computed from indexes of costs rather than price indexes. If adequate information concerning costs were available this would no doubt be a useful approach, for the cost figures would be free, to a considerable extent, of some of the most glaring logical problems which beset the use of price indexes. Unlike some price comparisons, it could hardly be said that parity calculations based upon costs of internationally traded goods would inevitably justify existing exchange rates, for costs of production do not adjust themselves as quickly or as completely to a change in exchange rates as do the prices of some international goods.

Although cost comparisons would obviously be preferable to price comparisons in some respects, it is clear that the use of cost data in the parity calculations could also present some new difficulties. If costs of production for a given product vary as between different firms, for example, which firms' costs are to be included in the index of general costs? And if the costs for a particular firm vary according to the level of output, at what level of output should the parity calculations be made? These questions will be recognized as the same difficult questions as those which arose in connection with the tariff to equalize costs of production at home and abroad, and the answers are no less difficult to find now than they were with regard to the tariff.

The selection of cost data for parity calculations, like the selection of price index numbers, involves a more or less arbitrary judgment, and the resulting parity rates are thus to be regarded as rough approximations to the effects of monetary inflation or currency values, and not as final answers to the problem of exchange rates.

Perhaps the principal advantage of cost comparisons over price comparisons is that costs are likely to represent more or less permanent changes in monetary values whereas prices may reflect the transitory effects of inflation. At the close of a period of general inflation, it is possible that prices may have increased considerably more than wage rates and other costs. In this event a short recession may cause a significant reduction in prices without a corresponding reduction in costs. In many instances, the permanent effects of inflation on the value of a currency will accordingly be measured more accurately by cost changes than by price movements.

Accurate and comprehensive data of unit costs of production are seldom published even in countries with as much economic data as the United States and the United Kingdom possess, and in other countries having less advanced statistical services cost information is virtually nonexistent. Changes in wage rates, the most important element of unit costs, might be substituted for the unavailable unit cost figures, but here again the investigation is confronted with a lack of data, for general indexes of wages are much less common than are general price indexes.

PARITY RATES IN PEACE AND IN WAR

The arguments against purchasing power parity appeared to be so overwhelming during the interwar period that many economists abandoned the theory entirely. It is a curious fact, nevertheless, that despite its abandonment in principle the theory continues to be widely used in practice as a means of judging the pattern of postwar exchange rates. What are the reasons for this divergence between theory and practice? Why is the purchasing power parity doctrine generally discredited and at the same time widely employed? The explanation of this inconsistency, the writer believes, is in the fact that the parity theory is not a *general* theory of exchange rates, and that it has been applied, in the past, to conditions for which it was not intended. The parity doctrine was used primarily for the purpose of explaining the movements of exchange rates after the First World War, and as a theory of postwar exchange rates it retains much validity notwithstanding the arguments against it. The theory was discredited not because it was unimportant or irrelevant in the explanation of exchange rates after the war, but because attempts were later made to use it in the explanation of exchange rates under more normal conditions for which it was not appropriate.

The factors which should be taken into account in setting exchange rates after a period of war-induced inflation are obviously quite different from those which affect exchange rates under more normal conditions. In particular, wartime movements in prices and costs are unusually large, and the discrepancies in price movements between different countries are likewise large. Examples of these discrepancies, taken from wholesale price statistics, were presented at the beginning of the present discussion of prices and exchange rates. Equally great discrepancies appeared during the war in retail prices. Although retail price movements did not always agree with wholesale price movements in any particular country, the order of magnitude of the two types of price change was in most instances roughly comparable, and the changes in prices, whether measured by one index or the other, were so large and so different as between one country and another that they immediately impress the observer as one of the most important influences on relative currency values.

Perhaps even more important than the amplitude of the price and cost movements is the fact that such movements, in times of war, tend to be more or less independent of changes in output and employment. Indeed, the really large price changes do not occur until output has approached the limits of a country's capacity. In contrast to these war developments, price and cost changes in normal years of peace are smaller and much more closely related to rising and falling output and employment. The disturbances in a country's balance of payments during non-war periods are therefore largely attributable to factors other than price change, and parity calculations have a correspondingly small significance. This was particularly true during the thirties when international payments throughout the world were disrupted by large and divergent movements of output and employment as well as by large and rapidly changing capital movements. Under these circumstances, it is not surprising that a method of estimating equilibrium exchange rates which was reasonably satisfactory for conditions of war and postwar inflation should have been quite inapplicable to the depressed and unstable conditions of the early thirties. It is unfortunate, however, that the inappropriateness of the parity doctrine to the conditions of the thirties should have led to a complete condemnation of purchasing power parity under all conditions. Despite the limitations of parity calculations, it ought to be recognized that a comparison of price movements in different countries, in times of war inflation, provides much useful information regarding exchange rates and international equilibrium. In other words, war-induced movements of prices and costs should be recognized as an independent influence on the flow of foreign payments and receipts.

14. Conditions of International Monetary Equilibrium

Ragnar Nurkse

Columbia University

Excerpt from "Conditions of International Monetary Equilibrium," *Essays in International Finance* (International Finance Section, Department of Economics and Sociology, Princeton University), Spring 1945; pp. 1–14 excerpted. Reprinted by permission of the author and the publisher from Howard S. Ellis and Lloyd A. Metzler, editors, *Readings in the Theory of International Trade* (Philadelphia: The Blakiston Co., 1949, now published by Richard D. Irwin, Inc.), pp. 3–21.

The purpose of this essay is to consider some of the central issues of international monetary policy in the light both of pre-war experience and of the post-war plans concerning foreign exchange and finance. For the facts of recent history and the conclusions to which they point, our principal source is a League of Nations report entitled *International Currency Experience: Lessons of the Inter-War Period.*[1] For the post-war plans, reference will be made to the agreements adopted at the Bretton Woods Conference.[2]

Our discussion is concerned with relations between independent national currencies. It may be well to state at the outset that the system of relations here envisaged is not of the gold-standard type if that means immutable exchange rates with domestic monetary and economic policies subordinated to the balance of payments. Changes in exchange rates are accepted as a legitimate method of adjustment, and the conditions in which such changes are appropriate will be our first topic (Sections I and II). We shall then comment on "cyclical" fluctuations in the balance of payments for which the method of exchange adjustment is unsuitable (Section III). One of our main preoccupations will be to determine the international

[1] Columbia University Press (International Document Service), New York, 1944.

[2] United Nations Monetary and Financial Conference, *Final Act and Related Documents,* U.S. Government Printing Office, Washington, 1944.

monetary framework compatible, on the one hand, with the pursuit of national policies for the maintenance of employment and, on the other, with the fullest possible development of international trade.

I. THE EQUILIBRIUM RATE OF EXCHANGE

Let us begin with the concept of the equilibrium rate of exchange. This, to be sure, is a rather hackneyed subject; but it is of considerable practical importance and, despite all the attention it has received, still remains in need of clarification.

A notable feature of the constitution of the International Monetary Fund as drawn up at Bretton Woods is that it provides for agreed and orderly changes in the exchange rates of member countries whenever a change is considered necessary to correct a "fundamental disequilibrium." While certain other terms in the Fund's charter are defined and explained at some length, no attempt is made to give a definite meaning to the phrase "fundamental disequilibrium." From a tactical point of view, it may have been wise to leave the interpretation of this phrase to the managers of the Fund or to the member countries concerned in each particular case; the statutes of the Fund may not be a suitable place for the definition of so abstruse and perhaps controversial a subject. But if the machinery of the Fund is to operate successfully, there should be some more or less generally accepted notion as to what constitutes "equilibrium" or "disequilibrium" in regard to international exchange rates.

At the various monetary conferences after the first world war, the late Gustav Cassel campaigned vigorously for the theory of "purchasing power parity." He and his followers were under the impression that this theory furnished all that was needed for a definition of the equilibrium rate of exchange. Today it is realized that the purchasing-power-parity theory cannot provide a definition of the equilibrium rate; that it can provide only a pseudo-definition in terms which themselves require definition and, indeed, turn out to be incapable of precise interpretation.

The only satisfactory way of defining the equilibrium rate of exchange is to define it as that rate which, over a certain period of time, keeps the balance of payments in equilibrium. This seems very simple. Indeed, for any practical use, it is much too simple. We must carefully examine the component elements of this definition.

Take, first of all, the phrase "over a certain period." What is the length of the period over which payments have to be balanced? Is it a day, a month, a year, or ten years? If, for the purposes of this definition, the balance has to be in equilibrium every hour, every day, or even every week, then we have in effect a constantly fluctuating exchange rate. The rate is left free to vary in order to secure equilibrium in the balance of payments over these very short periods. Now experience has shown that freely fluctuating exchanges are apt to give rise to speculation of a disequilibrating kind, including disequilibrating movements not only of capital but also of commodity exports and imports. Under a system of freely fluctuating exchanges there may be little or nothing to limit people's "elasticity of expectations," at least in the short run. Any change in the rate is likely to create anticipations of a further change in the same direction. Thus exchange depreciation may well occasion a flight of capital, leading to further depreciation, and, if the prices of commodities exported and imported also come to be affected by disequilibrating anticipations, exports will fall instead of rise and imports rise instead of fall, so that the result is still further depreciation. Such self-aggravating processes make it impossible to achieve equilibrium in the balance of payments even in very short periods such as a day or a week.

Moreover, there are reasons why freely fluctuating exchanges would be undesirable even if they *could* secure continuous equilibrium in the balance of payments. For one thing, they create considerable exchange risks, which tend to discourage international trade. For another, they call for constant shifts of domestic factors of production between export and home-market industries, shifts which may be disturbing and wasteful. No country has shown any desire for a system of wholly uninhibited fluctuations in exchange rates, and a prime objective of the International Monetary Fund is to make such a system unnecessary.

The period which we contemplate in the definition of the equilibrium rate of exchange cannot, therefore, be as short as a day or a week. Even if it were a month, exchange rates in most countries would be subject to seasonal fluctuations within each year. The period, therefore, should certainly not be less than a year. But if we make it long enough to eliminate seasonal fluctuations, why not make it long enough to eliminate "cyclical" fluctuations as well? This would give us a period of between five and ten years. If, that is to say, a country's external accounts, at a given rate of exchange, attain an even balance over a period of five to ten years, then that exchange rate would be regarded as an equilibrium rate.

Some countries—especially those exporting primary commodities —have often shown a wide cyclical movement in their balance of payments, and here it is particularly desirable to strike the balance for a period long enough to cover a whole cycle. There are, however, countries (such as France or even England) in which the balance of payments normally shows no very marked cyclical behavior, and, in these cases, it might be safe enough to take the balance over a shorter period—say, two or three years—as an indication of equilibrium or disequilibrium.

But as soon as we turn away from the imaginary system of freely fluctuating exchanges, in which the balance is kept in equilibrium every hour or every day, we must assume that there exists some medium to settle the discrepancies arising within the standard period. To act as such a medium is the most elementary function of the central reserves of international means of payment held by each country in the form of gold, foreign exchange, or international borrowing facilities. Later in this article there will be more to say on the functions of international liquidity. For the present, it is clear that, if we wish, we can alter the wording of our definition and describe the equilibrium rate as that rate at which, over a certain period, there would be no net change in a country's reserve of international means of payment. The longer we make the standard period the larger is the amount that is likely to be needed for settling the intervening discrepancies. As a rule, it takes a larger reserve to even out cyclical fluctuations than it takes to meet seasonal fluctuations. The larger the stock of international means of payment held by any country, and by countries in the aggregate, the less will be the need for changes in exchange rates. It is, therefore, natural that the International Monetary Fund agreement should contain more liberal provisions for exchange adjustments than the British scheme for an International Clearing Union (the "Keynes Plan" of 1943) since the latter proposed to create an amount of international liquidity more than three times as large as the resources of the Fund.

So much for the period over which we consider the balance of payments for the purpose of defining the equilibrium rate. We must now look at the balance of payments itself. What shall we include in the balance of payments for the purpose of this definition? Or rather, is there anything we do not wish to include? There is at least one thing that must be excluded, namely, the transfer of gold or other liquid reserves which may be necessary to balance a country's external accounts. Otherwise these accounts would always be in balance and there would never be any disequilibrium. A net change in any country's international currency reserve is, in fact, our criterion of disequilibrium.[3]

Another item that should be excluded is short-term capital movements. Such capital movements may be of two kinds. They may be of the equilibrating kind, such as used to occur in the gold standard mechanism in response to temporary changes in discount rates or to movements in exchange rates within the gold points. In that case they merely take the place of—and fulfill the same function as—transfers of gold or foreign exchange reserves. A country with a deficit in its balance of payments can cover the deficit either by an outflow of gold or an inflow of foreign short-term funds, if it is able to attract such funds by raising its bank rate or otherwise. These funds are equivalent to a loan by foreigners and should be regarded as a draft on the recipient country's stock of international reserves. Whether there is an outflow of gold or an inflow of foreign short-term loans, the country's net international liquidity will be reduced. The foreign short-term funds are a liability, can be withdrawn at any moment, and must be treated as a negative gold reserve.

Short-term capital movements of the *dis*equilibrating kind should also be excluded from the balance of payments which we wish to use as a standard of the equilibrium rate. Such capital movements became very familiar during the 'thirties, in the form of capital flight and "hot money," and were due mainly to fear of exchange depreciation and of war. They gave rise to large discrepancies in balances of payments which it proved impossible or undesirable to meet by means of adjustments in trade and other normal items and which, therefore, were generally settled by large gold movements. In considering the balance of payments as a criterion of exchange equilibrium it is desirable, as a rule, to exclude all discrepancies which are due to such abnormal factors. There is now almost general agreement that, in the future, capital movements of this type

---

[3] If there are changes in the world total of international currency reserves (as a result, for example, of new gold production), this criterion should of course be applied not literally but rather in the sense of the *relationship* between the reserves held by the several countries.

had better be prevented, or at least curbed, by some form of control.

Apart from international currency transfers and short-term capital movements, no exclusions are necessary or desirable for the purpose of our definition. We must include all other international transactions entering into the balance of payments. In particular, we must include all capital movements relating to international investment. A certain rate of exchange may be an equilibrium rate with a certain flow of foreign investment. With a different flow of foreign investment, this rate is not likely to be an equilibrium rate. After the first world war, the exchange rates which were established during the 'twenties may have been appropriate so long as there was a certain average annual export of capital from the United States. The fact that during the 'thirties the currencies of many debtor countries depreciated below their previous parities with the United States dollar was no doubt partly due to the complete cessation of capital exports from the United States; some depreciation of these currencies in relation to the dollar may well have been necessary to the restoration of equilibrium in the international accounts under the new conditions in the capital market.

Having examined the "standard period" and the "balance of payments" to be used for the purpose of our definition we come now to a third element that needs clarification. The balance of payments is said to be "in equilibrium" when payments are equal to receipts (apart from the items which, for the reasons given, must be excluded). But payments can be made equal to receipts by artificial restrictions on imports.[4] If a deficit appears in the balance of payments, and the deficit is closed by cutting down imports, are we to conclude that the rate is now at the equilibrium level? The answer is clearly in the negative. To use our definition properly, we must take the structure of trade barriers existing at a given starting-point. If subsequently a certain exchange rate can be maintained, or a balance-of-payments deficit closed, only by means of an increase

---

[4] Artificial stimulation of exports by means of subsidies has, for fiscal reasons, been much less common, but it may obviously achieve the same result. We should observe, however, that a *combination* of uniform *ad valorem* import duties with uniform *ad valorem* export subsidies can be exactly equivalent to a devaluation of the exchange. If a deficit in the balance of payments is closed by means of such a combination, then the exchange will, in effect, already have been devalued. In practice, of course, the distinguishing feature of import duties and export subsidies is that they are not uniform but selective and discriminating.

in trade barriers, then the rate cannot be accepted as the equilibrium rate. The true equilibrium rate is that rate at which payments and receipts are equalized without additional restrictions on trade.

This point has been of great practical importance without having always been clearly apprehended. Germany had no balance-of-payments deficit and suffered no loss of gold after 1934. Nevertheless the reichsmark was rightly regarded as overvalued. At the given exchange rate, Germany's external accounts were balanced only by means of additional import restrictions, which took mainly the form of drastic exchange controls. In the same way France, though failing to close her balance-of-payments deficit, certainly managed to reduce it by means of import quotas.

When a currency is kept far above its equilibrium level, and especially when the country's gold and exchange reserves run out— as they did in Germany—import restrictions become practically inevitable, and the result is a sharp cut in the volume of foreign trade. A country with an overvalued currency suffers a loss in its competitive power to export and, as exports decline, imports must be cut down correspondingly if the external accounts are to be balanced. The methods by which the cut is brought about are of secondary interest: they may be exchange controls, import quotas, prohibitions, licenses, or merely increased import duties. Exchange control, in particular, was often blamed for the contraction of world trade in the 'thirties. The underlying casual condition was rather the extreme dislocation of exchange rates.

The mere equality of a country's foreign receipts and payments is not, then, an acceptable criterion of the equilibrium rate of exchange if the equality must be enforced by restrictions on imports. There is another important case in which such equality is not a sufficient criterion. It is conceivable that a country may keep its balance of payments in equilibrium by reducing the demand for imports through a depressed level of aggregate domestic money income in relation to productive capacity; and if wage rates and prices are rigid, this contraction in money income will manifest itself in large-scale unemployment in that country. The balance of payments is in equilibrium; yet it is hardly proper to call the exchange rate a true equilibrium rate if it can be maintained only by means of depression and unemployment at home.

Great Britain in the years 1925–1930 affords a good illustration of this point. There was little sign of disequilibrium in the British balance of payments, yet the pound was rightly regarded as overvalued. There was practically no net change in the British gold reserve during that period. An inflow of foreign short-term funds, however, would have been equivalent to an outflow of gold. What happened before 1927 is largely a matter of guesswork, though some inflow undoubtedly occurred, especially as a result of capital flight from France and of speculative anticipation of the pound's return to its former gold parity in the spring of 1925. But for the period from the end of 1927 to the end of March 1931 we have the estimates of the Macmillan Committee, and these show no increase in London's net foreign short-term liabilities.[5] On the contrary, they show a slight reduction which, however, was matched by a slight reduction in the gold reserve, so that, on balance, no change seems to have taken place in Great Britain's international liquidity over those years. If we apply our definition of the equilibrium rate literally, the pound cannot be said to have been overvalued. The British balance of payments was kept in equilibrium, however, only at the cost of depressed conditions at home compared with conditions in the outside world.

Just as the German case led us to conclude that balance-of-payments equilibrium is not a sufficient criterion of an equilibrium exchange rate in the presence of special or additional import restrictions necessitated by the maintenance of the actual rate, so the British case suggests that it is not a sufficient criterion in the presence of a special or additional depression necessitated by the maintenance of the actual rate. At different levels of national income and employment in a given country, equilibrium in the balance of payments can be secured at different rates of exchange. It would seem better therefore to define the true equilibrium rate of exchange as one that maintains a country's external accounts in equilibrium without the need for wholesale unemployment at home. And if we extend our view from the position of a single country to the whole network of international exchange rates, this would lead us to define an ideal system of equilibrium rates as one that maintains the accounts of all countries simultaneously in equilibrium when all countries

[5] The fact that the estimates were incomplete can scarcely invalidate the evidence they afford in the present context. For we are concerned with the *movement* in the total over a period of time, and we have no reason to suppose that the amounts not covered by the Macmillan estimates moved in an entirely different manner from the amounts covered, which certainly formed the greater part of the true total.

simultaneously are free from mass unemployment on the one hand and inflation on the other.

A country which, at a level of full employment, has a deficit in its balance of payments must reduce its national income below the level corresponding to full employment if balance-of-payments equilibrium is to be restored at the existing exchange rate. Of course, by depressing still further its national income and hence its demand for imports, the country in question may actually produce a surplus in its balance of payments and an increase in its international currency reserve. But this would be needless self-torture. Even to depress the national income to the point at which the balance of payments is in equilibrium is necessary only if the country's reserve is not adequate to meet the deficit.

One might argue that Great Britain in the late 'twenties should have expanded her domestic income and employment to a normal or satisfactory level; at that level she would have had a deficit in her balance of payments; this deficit would have been conclusive proof that her currency was overvalued; and only after furnishing this proof should the pound have been permitted to depreciate. This would be an excellent general rule; but it does not work in the case of a country whose margin of international liquidity is so small that it cannot afford to incur a deficit. The British gold reserve of about 150 million pounds in the late 'twenties was in itself rather a small margin; and if we take into account Britain's net foreign short-term liabilities at that time (about 275 million pounds, according to the incomplete estimate of the Macmillan Committee), there would seem to have been no margin at all. A lowering of money rates in England might have led immediately to an outflow of foreign short-term funds and a corresponding loss of gold. This gold would then, of course, not have been available for meeting the rise in imports and the consequent deficit in the balance of payments (exclusive of short-term capital movements) which would have tended to result from Great Britain's domestic expansion.

As a general rule, however, so long as its liquid international reserves are adequate, a country should be expected to make use of these reserves to meet an actual deficit in its balance of payments before a downward adjustment of its exchange rate can be approved. This principle was embodied in the "Keynes Plan," which provided for devaluation only after a country had used up a certain proportion of its quota in the International Clearing Union.

A publicly recognized and recognizable criterion of exchange adjustment has, it is true, the disadvantage that it may act as a signal for speculative capital transfers in anticipation of changes in exchange rates. It may be partly for this reason that such a criterion was not included in the Bretton Woods agreement. But the absence of an objective criterion does not by any means ensure absence of "speculation" and of speculative capital movements. Theoretically such capital movements could be offset, but for this purpose the Fund would need enormous additional resources. The limited resources with which, in fact, it is endowed had certainly better be devoted to the balancing of normal international transactions, including trade, services, and productive investment. Since, in any case, the Fund wisely provides for restrictions on capital movements that might drain its resources for speculative purposes, it is doubtful what force remains in the objection to an agreed and recognizable criterion of exchange adjustment.

II. PRINCIPLES OF EXCHANGE ADJUSTMENT

In spite of the qualifications we have discussed, our general conclusion is that the balance of payments must be the chief criterion for any changes in exchange rates. A country with a surplus in its balance of payments should never resort to devaluation; on the contrary, it might be asked to appreciate its currency. Only when a country's balance shows a persistent deficit can devaluation be approved, though in special cases, as we have seen, it may be desirable to permit devaluation even if the balance of payments is apparently in equilibrium.

This simple code is sufficient to regulate the use of devaluation as a means whereby an individual country may seek to influence total demand for its output in the interest of its domestic employment situation. As an anti-depression measure, devaluation can represent either a beggar-my-neighbor policy or a buffer policy. The case of a beggar-my-neighbor policy of devaluation arises when a country that suffers from a depression of mainly domestic origin seeks to cure that depression by improving its balance of payments through devaluation; that is, in effect, by securing for its own national output a larger share of the existing world demand at the expense of other countries. Even without any devaluation such a country is likely to develop a surplus in its balance of payments as an automatic consequence of the fall in its demand for imports and possibly also as a result of a fall in its export prices with a more than corresponding increase in sales. The simple code just mentioned will generally not authorize a country in these circumstances to devalue, since the circumstances themselves will already have given a favorable turn to its balance of payments. Thus the beggar-my-neighbor policy of exchange depreciation would be effectively ruled out. This alone would be a gain, for otherwise any country suffering a depression in its domestic market might claim that such depression constitutes a "fundamental disequilibrium" justifying exchange depreciation. As long as the term is not defined, it may not be easy to reject such a claim. Yet the claim is obviously groundless, since any country that suffers a depression as a result of a fall in domestic investment can and should cure its depression by domestic measures. When depression at home creates a surplus in the balance of payments, there is nothing in the international monetary position to prevent the country in question from adopting a policy of domestic expansion.

The case is quite different when the purpose of devaluation is to act as a protective buffer against a depression originating abroad. If a given country is faced with a depression in one of its foreign markets, this depression will tend to spread to its domestic economy through an adverse balance of payments resulting from a fall in its exports and, if prices abroad are reduced, a rise in the volume of its imports. According to our definition of the equilibrium rate, the deficit in the balance of payments would in this case justify a certain measure of devaluation. Thus it is clear that the definition, if applied in practice, would, on the one hand, exclude devaluation of the "beggar-my-neighbor" type and, on the other, permit the type of devaluation which serves the purpose of a "buffer" policy designed to prevent the spread of depression from country to country.

Devaluation for buffer purposes is defensible, but it should not, in general, be necessary. The first and most desirable method of checking the spread of cyclical depressions is the policy of "offsetting," coupled with the use of international currency reserves for meeting cyclical balance-of-payments discrepancies in a manner presently to be considered. Another possible instrument that might help to insulate a certain area of depression would be the apportionment of scarce currencies, contemplated under the Bretton Woods agreement, which would tend to have the effect of discriminating against the exports of any country that allows its national income, and hence its imports, to decline far below the level corresponding to full employment. The method of exchange-rate adjustment constitutes only a third line of defense. Exchange adjustments for cyclical purposes are likely to be comparatively ineffective. Cyclical shifts in demand schedules may be so wide and violent that it is difficult, or even impossible, to determine precisely what alteration in exchange rates would secure balance-of-payments equilibrium in the short run. Besides, it is generally not worth while to create all the disturbances attending an alteration in exchange rates—including the shifts induced in the structure of production as between export and home-market industries—if the change is required for only short-term reasons; and cyclical factors must certainly be regarded as short-term reasons in this context. As we have seen, the standard period over which the balance of payments is to be balanced as a test of exchange-rate equilibrium should be long enough to permit any cyclical changes to cancel out. This presupposes a volume of international liquidity adequate to settle any temporary deficits within the standard period. It should be the function of international currency reserves, and not of exchange-rate adjustments, to meet cyclical and other short-term discrepancies in the balance of payments.

Exchange-rate adjustments are appropriate mainly in cases of chronic or structural disequilibria in the balance of payments. As a remedy for such persistent strains, they can scarcely fail, given time, to produce the desired effect. It is sometimes objected that the demand for imports on the part of an individual country, as well as the foreign demand for that country's exports, may be so inelastic with respect to price changes that a depreciation of the exchange would increase instead of reduce a deficit in the balance of payments. But even in this case exchange adjustment might still be capable of securing equilibrium though it would then have to take the form of an *appreciation* of the exchange.

III. THE FUNCTIONS OF INTERNATIONAL LIQUIDITY

In a world in which economic activity is subject to fluctuations but in which there is a growing demand for stability, the basic function of international currency reserves is to serve as a "buffer" giving each country some leeway for the regulation of its national income and employment and providing it with a means to soften the impact of economic fluctuations arising outside its borders.

This buffer function of international liquidity can be made clear by a simple example. Imagine a country whose monetary authorities are intent on keeping the national income at a level compatible with good employment at the given wage structure. Suppose a depression occurs abroad. The country's exports will fall as a result of the fall in foreign demand. There will be a loss of income and employment in the export industries. If nothing is done, the depression in the export industries is likely to lead, through the familiar "multiplier" mechanism, to a general and cumulative depression in the home-market industries as well. The depression at home will automatically tend to bring about a reduction in imports to the level of the reduced exports. Equilibrium will have been restored in the balance of payments, but only by rendering the depression general.

In order to prevent the spread of depression, the country we are considering must endeavor to offset the fall in foreign expenditure on its exports by an increase in domestic expenditure. Though a local or partial depression in its export industries may be inevitable, a general and cumulative depression of the whole economy can undoubtedly be averted by such a policy of "offsetting." In so far as the volume of employment depends on total expenditure, it is essential that total expenditure be maintained, which means in this case that the flow of domestic spending must be increased so as to compensate for the decline in foreign expenditure on the country's exports.

This is the policy required for domestic stability; but it does nothing to remove the deficit in the balance of payments resulting from the fall in exports. The deficit will tend to persist so long as the depression abroad continues. The country pursuing an offsetting policy must be prepared to give up temporarily some of its international currency reserve in order to meet this deficit. Only with an adequate reserve of international means of settlement will a country in this situation be able to avoid exchange depreciation or import restrictions.

The policy of offsetting is intended not to raise total expenditure, but to prevent it from falling. Since, therefore, the national income is not raised above its previous level, this policy does not necessarily lead to an increase in imports above their previous level. Yet the amount of imports, and hence the gap in the balance of payments, will certainly be greater than if the country allowed depression to spread to its whole domestic economy. This means that the volume of international liquidity required is larger, with a compensatory national income policy of the type described, than it would be if a country left things to take their "natural" course.

Under the gold standard, not only were things expected to take their natural course but a country in the situation described was expected even to accelerate the spread of depression by pushing up discount rates and contracting credit as gold flowed out. No doubt the gold standard "rules of the game" tended to reduce the loss of gold to a minimum; but they did so only by speeding up the propagation of depressions.

The offsetting procedure described is precisely the opposite of that which would be called for under the gold-standard rules of the game. The essential principle is that any deflationary or inflationary shock entering from abroad and threatening a country's economic stability is to be offset rather than reinforced; and the resulting discrepancy in the balance of payments is to be settled through a transfer of international liquidity. The example just discussed was that of a deflationary shock; but, with the signs reversed, the discussion applies in exactly the same way to the case of an inflationary disturbance.[6]

Even in the best days of the gold standard, the rules of the game were not always very strictly observed. There is some statistical evidence of "neutralization," for example, on the part of the Bank of France and the Bank of England in the nineteenth century.[7] In the inter-war period neutralization of gold movements by central banks became, in fact, the rule rather than the exception. Neutralization of this type was concerned primarily with the cash base of the banking system; any change in a central bank's gold and foreign exchange reserve was usually accompanied by a change *in the opposite direction* in the bank's domestic loans and securities. This tended, no doubt, to stabilize the volume of money in a country. It certainly went some way, though only a small part of the way,

[6] See *International Currency Experience: Lessons of the Inter-War Period, op. cit.*, pp. 214ff.

[7] See Harry D. White. *The French International Accounts 1880–1913* (Harvard Economic Studies, vol. XL, 1933, p. 198); and Elmer Wood, *English Theories of Central Banking Control 1819–1858* (Harvard Economic Studies, vol. LXIV, 1939, p. 216).

towards the more comprehensive policy of offsetting designed to give stability not merely to the money supply but to the national income.

Though neutralization by central banks was very common in the inter-war period it was nearly always frowned upon; it was widely regarded as wicked and disreputable behavior. The hold which the orthodox rules of the game had on people's minds was evidently strong—much stronger than the hold they had in practice. It is time to recognize that for any country aiming at some stability in its national economy, the policy of offsetting—which of course includes "neutralization" in the narrow sense—is the natural method of making use of its international currency reserves: it is time to accept it as a normal and respectable procedure.

The main function of the International Monetary Fund will be to create an addition, and quite a substantial addition, to aggregate international liquidity. Without this function, the Fund might still be a useful institution; in particular, it could still serve as a center for international consultations concerning the fixing and adjustment of exchange rates. But even as regards exchange rates, the Fund's effectiveness is likely to rest to some extent on its power to provide countries with additional liquidity.

The additional liquidity furnished by the Fund would no doubt make it easier for countries to pursue what we have called "offsetting" policies in the interests of domestic economic stability. The statutes of the Fund, however, are not very explicit as to the way countries are expected to use the Fund's resources. In regard to the contrast we have discussed between the buffer function of international liquidity and the orthodox rules of the gold standard game, the Bretton Woods agreement gives little or no indication of what will be the attitude in the administration of the Fund, though here again, as in the case of "fundamental disequilibrium," any attempt to lay down a hard-and-fast doctrine would perhaps have been out of place in a document of this kind. In Article I of the agreement there is a general statement of objectives according to which one of the purposes of the Fund is "to shorten the duration and lessen the degree of disequilibrium in the international balances of payments." This may be variously interpreted; but it sounds rather like the orthodox rules which placed all the emphasis on countries keeping in step with one another, and removing as rapidly as possible any discrepancies in the balance of payments among them, no matter what happened to production and employment. In fact, production and employment were left free to move up and down in all countries more or less simultaneously, and a deflationary process in any important country was communicated to the others.

All this is no longer practical politics. In a system of generally stable and unrestricted exchanges the only way to "shorten the duration and lessen the degree of disequilibrium" in balances of payments is to establish close co-ordination between the domestic policies of the different countries with a view to keeping prices in harmony and national incomes at a level corresponding to good employment in all the countries concerned.

Under such conditions any single country pursuing, or at least aiming at, a policy of good and steady employment without inflation will find some reserve of international liquidity indispensable if, without resort to either exchange depreciation or import restrictions, it wishes to offset external disturbances of a cyclical character affecting its balance of payments. What a country pursuing this policy must do is simple; it must endeavor to keep total expenditure on its current national output at a level corresponding as nearly as possible to full employment. But a part of the total expenditure on its output is expenditure by foreigners on its exports. Over that part, the country can have no control. It must therefore be prepared to offset variations in its own domestic expenditure in order to keep the total flow of spending at the optimum level.

This offsetting policy has its limitations. As stated before, it cannot as a rule prevent booms and depressions in the export industries. It can prevent them only if the export goods are storable and are actually stored by the country in bad years for release in boom years. In this ideal case the compensatory domestic expenditure would be directed to the same goods that are affected by the change in foreign expenditure, so that even local and frictional unemployment would be kept to a minimum. This may not usually be practicable; and just as a road-building program, for example, owing to the imperfect mobility of labor, is not likely to remove all unemployment in, say, the textile industry, so a compensatory increase in domestic spending is not likely to be a complete remedy for depression in the export industries. But the offsetting policy should at least be able to prevent the wide and cumulative fluctuations throughout the domestic economy which might otherwise result from fluctuations in foreign demand.

This seems to be the kind of system for which the world was groping in the inter-war period, and it seems the only one that is compatible at once with a national full employment policy and with a reasonable stability of exchange rates and freedom from severe exchange restrictions.

15. The Case for Flexible Exchange Rates

Milton Friedman

University of Chicago

Excerpt reprinted from "The Case for Flexible Exchange Rates" in *Essays in Positive Economics* by Milton Friedman by permission of the author and of The University of Chicago Press; pp. 157–187, 196–203 excerpted. Copyright 1953 by The University of Chicago Press.

This paper had its origin in a memorandum written in the fall of 1950 when I was a consultant to the Finance and Trade Division of the Office of Special Representative for Europe, United States Economic Cooperation Administration. Needless to say, the views it expresses are entirely my own. I am grateful to Joel Bernstein and Maxwell Obst for criticism of the original memorandum and to Earl J. Hamilton and Lloyd A. Metzler for criticism of a subsequent draft. The paper owes much, also, to extensive discussion of the general problem with a number of friends, particularly Aaron Director, James Meade, Lloyd Mints, and Lionel Robbins. Unfortunately, these discussions failed to produce sufficient agreement to make a disclaimer of their responsibility unnecessary.

The Western nations seem committed to a system of international payments based on exchange rates between their national currencies fixed by governments and maintained rigid except for occasional changes to new levels. This system is embodied in the statutes of the International Monetary Fund, which provides for changes in exchange rates of less than 10 per cent by individual governments without approval of the Fund and for larger changes only with approval; it is implicit in the European Payments Union; and it is taken for granted in almost all discussions of international economic policy.

Whatever may have been the merits of this system for another day, it is ill suited to current economic and political conditions. These conditions make a system of flexible or floating exchange rates—exchange rates freely determined in an open market primarily by private dealings and, like other market prices, varying from day to day—absolutely essential for the fulfilment of our basic economic

313

objective: the achievement and maintenance of a free and prosperous world community engaging in unrestricted multilateral trade. There is scarcely a facet of international economic policy for which the implicit acceptance of a system of rigid exchange rate does not create serious and unnecessary difficulties. Promotion of rearmament, liberalization of trade, avoidance of allocations and other direct controls both internal and external, harmonization of internal monetary and fiscal policies—all these problems take on a different cast and become far easier to solve in a world of flexible exchange rates and its corollary, free convertibility of currencies. The sooner a system of flexible exchange rates is established, the sooner unrestricted multilateral trade will become a real possibility. And it will become one without in any way interfering with the pursuit by each nation of domestic economic stability according to its own lights.[1]

Before proceeding to defend this thesis in detail, I should perhaps emphasize two points to avoid misunderstanding. First, advocacy of flexible exchange rates is *not* equivalent to advocacy of unstable exchange rates. The ultimate objective is a world in which exchange rates, while *free* to vary, are in fact highly stable. Instability of exchange rates is a symptom of instability in the underlying economic structure. Elimination of this symptom by administrative freezing of exchange rates cures none of the underlying difficulties and only makes adjustment to them more painful. Second, by unrestricted multilateral trade, I shall mean a system in which there are no direct quantitative controls over imports or exports, in which any tariffs or export bounties are reasonably stable and nondiscriminatory and are not subject to manipulation to affect the balance of payments, and in which a substantial fraction of international trade is in private (nongovernmental) hands. Though admittedly vague and subject to considerable ambiguity, this definition will do for our purposes. I shall take for granted without detailed examination that unrestricted multilateral trade in this sense [2] is a desirable objective

---

[1] Indeed, I have elsewhere argued that flexible exchange rates are the logical international counterpart of the monetary and fiscal framework for economic stability that seems to me the most promising. See "A Monetary and Fiscal Framework for Economic Stabilty," *American Economic Review*, XXXVIII (June 1948), pp. 245–264, reprinted in *Essays in Positive Economics*, pp. 133–156.

[2] And indeed in the even more extreme sense of trade free from all barriers, including tariffs and export bounties.

of economic policy.[3] However, many of the arguments for flexible exchange rates remain valid even if this premise is not accepted.

I. ALTERNATIVE METHODS OF ADJUSTING TO CHANGES AFFECTING INTERNATIONAL PAYMENTS

Changes affecting the international trade and the balance of payments of various countries are always occurring. Some are in the "real" conditions determining international trade, such as the weather, technical conditions of production, consumer tastes, and the like. Some are in monetary conditions, such as divergent degrees of inflation or deflation in various countries.

These changes affect some commodities more than others and so tend to produce changes in the structure of relative prices—for example, rearmament by the United States impinges particularly on selected raw materials and tends to raise their prices relatively to other prices. Such effects on the relative price structure are likely to be much the same whether exchange rates are rigid or flexible and to raise much the same problem of adjustment in either case and so will receive little attention in what follows.

But, over and above these effects on particular commodities and prices, the changes in question affect each country's balance of payments, taken as a whole. Holders of foreign currencies want to exchange them for the currency of a particular country in order to purchase commodities produced in that country, or to purchase securities or other capital assets in that country, or to pay interest on or repay debts to that country, or to make gifts to citizens of that country, or simply to hold for one of these uses or for resale. The amount of currency of a particular country that is demanded per unit of time for each of these purposes will, of course, depend in the first instance on the exchange rate—the number of units of a foreign currency that must be paid to acquire one unit of the domestic currency. Other things the same, the more expensive a given cur-

[3] In brief, it is desirable in its own right as one of the basic freedoms we cherish; it promotes the efficient use of resources through an appropriate international division of labor and increases consumer welfare by maximizing the range of alternatives on which consumers can spend their incomes; it facilitates international political amity by removing potent sources of conflict between governments.

rency, that is, the higher the exchange rate, the less of that currency will in general be demanded for each of these purposes. Similarly, holders of the currency of the country in question want to exchange that currency for foreign currencies for the corresponding purposes; and, again, the amount they want to exchange depends, in the first instance, on the price which they can get. The changes continuously taking place in the conditions of international trade alter the "other things" and so the desirability of using the currencies of various countries for each of the purposes listed. The aggregate effect is at one time to increase, at another to decrease, the amount of a country's currency demanded at any given rate of exchange relative to the amount offered for sale at that rate. Of course, after the event, the amount of a particular currency purchased must equal the amount sold—this is a question simply of double-entry bookkeeping. But, in advance, the amount people want to buy need not equal the amount people want to sell. The *ex post* equality involves a reconciliation of these divergent desires, either through changes in the desires themselves or through their frustration.

There is no way of avoiding this reconciliation; inconsistent desires cannot simultaneously be satisfied. The crucial question of policy is the mechanism whereby this reconciliation is brought about. Suppose the aggregate effect of changes in the conditions affecting international payments has been to increase the amount of a country's currency people want to buy with foreign currency relatively to the amount other people want to sell for foreign currency at the pre-existing exchange rate—to create an incipient surplus in the balance of payments. How can these inconsistent desires be reconciled? (1) The country's currency may be bid up, or put up, in price. This increase in the exchange rate will tend to make the currency less desirable relative to the currency of other countries and so eliminate the excess demand at the pre-existing rate.[4]

_____

[4] It is conceivable that, under some conditions and for some range of exchange rates, a rise in exchange rates would increase the excess demand. Though this possibility has received considerable attention, it will be neglected in what follows as of little practical relevance. As a purely theoretical matter, there will always be some set or sets of rates that will clear the market, and, in the neighborhood of at least one of these sets of rates a rise in the rate will mean a decline in excess demand (i.e., a negative excess demand); a fall, a rise in excess demand. Exchange rates can remain in a region in which this is not true only if they are not free to move and if some nonprice mechanism is used to ration domestic or foreign currency. As a practical matter, the conditions necessary for any relevant range of rates to have the property that a rise

(2) Prices within the country may rise, thus making its goods less desirable relative to goods in other countries, or incomes within the country may rise, thus increasing the demand for foreign currencies. (3) Direct controls over transactions involving foreign exchange may prevent holders of foreign balances from acquiring as much domestic exchange as they would otherwise like to; for example, they may be prevented from buying domestic goods by the inability to get a required export license. (4) The excess amount of domestic currency desired may be provided out of monetary reserves, the foreign currency acquired being added to reserves of foreign currencies—the monetary authorities (or exchange equalization fund or the like) may step in with a "desire" to buy or sell the difference between the amounts demanded and supplied by others.

Each of these four methods has its obvious counterpart if the effect of the changes is to create an incipient deficit. Aside from purely frictional frustrations of desires (the inability of a buyer to find a seller because of imperfections of the market), these are fundamentally the only four ways in which an *ex ante* divergence between the amount of a country's currency demanded and the amount supplied can be converted into the *ex post* equality that necessarily prevails. Let us consider each in turn.

A. Changes in exchange rates

Two different mechanisms whereby exchange-rate changes may be used to maintain equilibrium in the balance of payments must be sharply distinguished: (1) flexible exchange rates as defined above and (2) official changes in temporarily rigid rates.

1. Flexible exchange rates. Under flexible exchange rates freely determined in open markets, the first impact of any tendency toward a surplus or deficit in the balance of payments is on the exchange rate. If a country has an incipient surplus of receipts over payments —an excess demand for its currency—the exchange rate will tend to rise. If it has an incipient deficit, the exchange rate will tend to fall. If the conditions responsible for the rise or the fall in the exchange rate are generally regarded as temporary, actual or potential holders

---

increases excess demand seem to me highly unlikely to occur. But, if they should occur, it would merely mean that there might be two possible positions of equilibrium, one above, the other below, the existing controlled rate. If the higher is regarded as preferable, the implication for policy would be first to appreciate the controlled rate and then to set it free.

of the country's currency will tend to change their holdings in such a way as to moderate the movement in the exchange rate. If a rise in the exchange rate, for example, is expected to be temporary, there is an incentive for holders of the country's currency to sell some of their holdings for foreign currency in order to buy the currency back later on at a lower price. By doing so, they provide the additional domestic currency to meet part of the excess demand responsible for the initial rise in the exchange rate; that is, they absorb some of what would have been surplus receipts of foreign currency at the former exchange rate. Conversely, if a decline is expected to be temporary, there is an incentive to buy domestic currency for resale at a higher price. Such purchases of domestic currency provide the foreign currency to meet some of what would have been a deficit of foreign currency at the former exchange rate. In this way, such "speculative" transactions in effect provide the country with reserves to absorb temporary surpluses or to meet temporary deficits. On the other hand, if the change in the exchange rate is generally regarded as produced by fundamental factors that are likely to be permanent, the incentives are the reverse of those listed above, and speculative transactions will speed up the rise or decline in the exchange rate and thus hasten its approach to its final position.

This final position depends on the effect that changes in exchange rates have on the demand for and supply of a country's currency, not to hold as balances, but for other purposes. A rise in the exchange rate produced by a tendency toward a surplus makes foreign goods cheaper in terms of domestic currency, even though their prices are unchanged in terms of their own currency, and domestic goods more expensive in terms of foreign currency, even though their prices are unchanged in terms of domestic currency. This tends to increase imports, reduce exports, and so offset the incipient surplus. Conversely, a decline in the exchange rate produced by a tendency toward a deficit makes imports more expensive to home consumers, and exports less expensive to foreigners, and so tends to offset the incipient deficit.

Because money imparts general purchasing power and is used for such a wide variety of purposes abroad as well as at home, the demand for and supply of any one country's currency is widely spread and comes from many sources. In consequence, broad, active, and nearly perfect markets have developed in foreign exchange whenever they have been permitted—and usually even when they have not been. The exchange rate is therefore potentially an extremely sensitive price. Changes in it occur rapidly, automatically, and continuously and so tend to produce corrective movements before tensions can accumulate and a crisis develop. For example, if Germany had had a flexible exchange rate in 1950, the crisis in the fall of that year would never have followed the course it did. The exchange rate would have been affected not later than July and would have started to produce corrective adaptations at once. The whole affair would never have assumed large proportions and would have shown up as a relatively minor ripple in exchange rates. As it was, with a rigid exchange rate, the warning of impending trouble was indirect and delayed, and the government took no action until three months later, by which time the disequilibrium had grown to crisis dimensions, requiring drastic action at home, international consultation, and help from abroad.

The recurrent foreign-exchange crises of the United Kingdom in the postwar period are perhaps an even more dramatic example of the kind of crises that could not develop under a system of flexible exchange rates. In each case no significant corrective action was taken until large disequilibriums had been allowed to cumulate, and then the action had to be drastic. The rigidities and discontinuities introduced by substituting administrative action for automatic market forces have seldom been demonstrated so clearly or more impressively.

2. *Official changes in exchange rates.* These examples suggest the sharp difference between flexible exchange rates and exchange rates held temporarily rigid but subject to change by government action to meet substantial difficulties. While these exchange-rate changes have the same kind of effect on commodity trade and the like as those produced automatically under a system of flexible exchange rates, they have very different effects on speculative transactions. Partly for this reason, partly because of their innate discontinuity, each exchange-rate change tends to become the occasion for a crisis. There is no mechanism for producing changes in exchange rates of the required magnitude or for correcting mistakes, and some other mechanism must be used to maintain equilibrium during the period between exchange-rate changes—either internal price or income changes, direct controls, or monetary reserves.

Even though an exchange-rate change would not otherwise be the occasion for a crisis, speculative movements are highly likely to convert it into one, for this system practically insures a maximum of destabilizing speculation. Because the exchange rate is changed infrequently and only to meet substantial difficulties, a change tends to come well after the onset of difficulty, to be postponed as long as possible, and to be made only after substantial pressure on the exchange rate has accumulated. In consequence, there is seldom any doubt about the direction in which an exchange rate will be changed, if it is changed. In the interim between the suspicion of a possible change in the rate and the actual change, there is every incentive to sell the country's currency if devaluation is expected (to export "capital" from the country) or to buy it if an appreciation is expected (to bring in "capital"); either can be done without an exchange loss and will mean an exchange gain when and if the rate is changed. This is in sharp contrast with the situation under flexible exchange rates when the decline in the exchange rate takes place along with, and as a consequence of, the sales of a currency and so discourages or penalizes sales, and conversely for purchases. With rigid rates, if the exchange rate is not changed, the only cost to the speculators is a possible loss of interest earnings from an interest-rate differential. It is no answer to this argument to say that capital flows can be restricted by direct controls, since our ultimate objective in using this method is precisely to avoid such restrictions.

In short, the system of occasional changes in temporarily rigid exchange rates seems to me the worst of two worlds: it provides neither the stability of expectations that a genuinely rigid and stable exchange rate could provide in a world of unrestricted trade and willingness and ability to adjust the internal price structure to external conditions nor the continuous sensitivity of a flexible exchange rate.

B. Changes in internal prices or income

In principle, changes in internal prices could produce the same effects on trade as changes in the exchange rate. For example, a decline of 10 per cent in every internal price in Germany (including wages, rents, etc.) with an unchanged dollar price of the mark would clearly have identically the same effects on the relative costs of domestic and foreign goods as a decline of 10 per cent in the dollar price of the mark, with all internal prices unchanged. Similarly, such price changes could have the same effects on speculative transactions. If expected to be temporary, a decline in prices would stimulate speculative purchases of goods to avoid future higher prices, thus moderating the price movement.

If internal prices were as flexible as exchange rates, it would make little economic difference whether adjustments were brought about by changes in exchange rates or by equivalent changes in internal prices. But this condition is clearly not fulfilled. The exchange rate is potentially flexible in the absence of administrative action to freeze it. At least in the modern world, internal prices are highly inflexible. They are more flexible upward than downward, but even on the upswing all prices are not equally flexible. The inflexibility of prices, or different degrees of flexibility, means a distortion of adjustments in response to changes in external conditions. The adjustment takes the form primarily of price changes in some sectors, primarily of output changes in others.

Wage rates tend to be among the less flexible prices. In consequence, an incipient deficit that is countered by a policy of permitting or forcing prices to decline is likely to produce unemployment rather than, or in addition to, wage decreases. The consequent decline in real income reduces the domestic demand for foreign goods and thus the demand for foreign currency with which to purchase these goods. In this way, it offsets the incipient deficit. But this is clearly a highly inefficient method of adjusting to external changes. If the external changes are deep-seated and persistent, the unemployment produces steady downward pressure on prices and wages, and the adjustment will not have been completed until the deflation has run its sorry course.

Despite these difficulties, the use of changes in internal prices might not be undesirable if they were called for only rarely and only as a result of changes in the real underlying conditions of trade. Such changes in underlying conditions are likely in any event to require considerable changes in relative prices of particular goods and services and only changes of a much smaller order of magnitude in the general level of internal prices. But neither condition is likely to be satisfied in the modern world. Adjustments are required continuously, and many are called for by essentially monetary phenomena, which, if promptly offset by a movement in the exchange rate, would require no change in the actual allocation of resources.

Changes in interest rates are perhaps best classified under this heading of changes in internal prices. Interest-rate changes have in the past played a particularly important role in adjustment to external changes, partly because they have been susceptible to direct influence by the monetary authorities, and partly because, under a gold standard, the initial impact of a tendency toward a deficit or surplus was a loss or gain of gold and a consequent tightening or ease in the money market. The rise in the interest rate produced in this way by an incipient deficit increased the demand for the currency for capital purposes and so offset part or all of the deficit. This reduced the rate at which the deficit had to be met by a decline in internal prices, which was itself set in motion by the loss of gold and associated decrease in the stock of money responsible for the rise in interest rates. Conversely, an incipient surplus increased the stock of gold and eased the money market. The resulting decline in the interest rate reduced the demand for the currency for capital purposes and so offset part or all of the surplus, reducing the rate at which the surplus had to be met by the rise in internal prices set in motion by the gain of gold and associated rise in the stock of money.

These interest-induced capital movements are a desirable part of a system relying primarily on changes in internal prices, since they tend to smooth out the adjustment process. They cannot, however, be relied on alone, since they come into operation only incidentally to the adjustment of internal prices.

Primary reliance on changes in internal prices and incomes was tolerable in the nineteenth century partly because the key countries of the Western world placed much heavier emphasis on freedom from government interference at home and unrestricted multilateral trade abroad than on domestic stability; thus they were willing to allow domestic economic policy to be dominated by the requirements of fixed exchange rates and free convertibility of currencies. But, equally important, this very emphasis gave holders of balances confidence in the maintenance of the system and so made them willing to let small differences in interest rates determine the currency in which they held their balances. Furthermore, the emphasis on freedom from government interference at home gave less scope to internal monetary management and so meant that most changes affecting international trade reflected real changes in underlying conditions, or else monetary changes, such as gold discoveries, more or less common to the major nations. Modern conditions, with the widespread emphasis on full employment at home and the extensive intervention of government into economic affairs, are clearly very different and much less favorable to this method of adjustment.

C. Direct controls

In principle, direct controls on imports, exports, and capital movements could bring about the same effects on trade and the balance of payments as changes in exchange rates or in internal prices and incomes. The final adjustment will, after all, involve a change in the composition of imports and exports, along with specifiable capital transactions. If these could be predicted in advance, and if it were technically possible to control selectively each category of imports, exports, and capital transactions, direct controls could be used to produce the required adjustment.

It is clear, however, that the changes in imports and exports and the required capital transactions cannot be predicted; the fact that each new foreign-exchange crisis in a country like Britain is officially regarded as a bolt from the blue is ample evidence for this proposition. Even if they could be predicted, direct control of imports, exports, and capital transactions by techniques other than the price system [5] necessarily means extending such control to many internal matters and interfering with the efficiency of the distribution and production of goods—some means must be found for rationing imports that are being held down in amount or disposing of increased imports and for allocating reduced exports or getting increased exports.

Aside from the many unfortunate results of such a process which are by now abundantly clear, it has a perverse effect on the foreign-payments problem itself, particularly when direct controls are used, as they have been primarily, to counter an actual or incipient deficit. The apparent deficit that has to be closed by direct controls is larger than the deficit that would emerge at the same exchange rate without the direct controls and, indeed, might be eliminated entirely or converted into a surplus if the direct controls on imports and exports and their inevitable domestic accompaniments were removed. The mere existence of the direct controls makes the currency less desirable for many purposes because of the limitations it places on what

[5] Note that a tariff of a uniform percentage on all imports used to pay a subsidy of a uniform percentage on all exports is equivalent to a depreciation in the exchange rate by the corresponding percentage; and, similarly, a subsidy of a uniform percentage on all imports financed by a tax of a uniform percentage on all exports is equivalent to an appreciation in the exchange rate by the corresponding percentage. Thus devices such as these should be classified under exchange-rate changes rather than direct controls.

holders of the currency may do with it, and this is likely to reduce the demand for the currency more than it would be reduced by the fluctuations in exchange rates or other adaptive mechanisms substituted for the direct controls. In addition, permitted imports are generally distributed at prices lower than those that would clear the market and so are used wastefully and in the wrong places, increasing apparent import "requirements"; similarly, the composition of imports is determined by administrative decisions that tend to have the same effect. Both of these are particularly important in hindering exports, because export industries are not likely to get so large a fraction of the imports as they would bid away in a free market, even if the government supposedly favors export industries, and cannot make their influence fully felt in determining the composition of imports; and the direct controls have a tendency to make the incentive to export lower than it would otherwise be.[6]

The considerations mentioned in the preceding paragraph may help to reconcile—and, indeed, their elaboration was stimulated by my own need to reconcile—the impression of casual visitors to England, and the conclusions of some careful students of the subject, that the pound is currently (1952) undervalued in purchasing power terms with the recurrent pressures on the pound and the restrictive measures that seem to be required to maintain the pound at its present rate. They show that there is no necessary inconsistency between the following two assertions: (1) the market value of the pound would be higher than $2.80 if all exchange restrictions and associated controls were removed and the exchange rate were allowed to be determined by primarily private dealings in a free market; (2) given the retention of an official exchange rate and of the existing *system* of exchange restrictions and associated internal controls, an *easing* of restrictions would produce pressure on the exchange rate and require a rate lower than $2.80 to keep exchange reserves from being depleted. Both statements may not, in fact, be

---

[6] Selling import licenses at a price that would clear the market would eliminate the first effect; it would not eliminate the second and third unless the permits were not for specific commodities but for foreign exchange to be used in any way desired. Even this would not eliminate the fourth unless the proceeds were used to pay a percentage subsidy to exports and other transactions leading to the acquisition of foreign exchange. This final system is, as indicated in the preceeding note, identical with a change in the exchange rate. If the price of permits to use foreign exchange and the subsidy for acquiring it were determined in a free market so as to make total receipts equal total payments, the result is equivalent to or identical with a system of flexible exchange rates.

correct; but there is no such obvious contradiction between them as there appears to be at first sight.

Finally, whatever the desirability of direct controls, there are political and administrative limits to the extent to which it is possible to impose and enforce such controls. These limits are narrower in some countries than in others, but they are present in all. Given sufficient incentive to do so, ways will be found to evade or avoid the controls. A race develops between officials seeking to plug legal loopholes and to discover and punish illegal evasions of the controls and the ever numerous individuals whose inventive talents are directed toward discovering or opening up new loopholes by the opportunities for large returns or whose respect for law and fear of punishment are overcome by the same opportunities. And the race is by no means always to the officials, even when they are honest and able. In particular, it has proved extremely difficult in all countries to prevent capital movements by direct controls.

D. Use of monetary reserves

Given adequate reserves, tendencies toward a surplus or a deficit can be allowed to produce an actual surplus or deficit in transactions other than those of the monetary authority (or exchange equalization fund, or whatever the name may be) without a change in exchange rates, internal prices or incomes, or direct controls, the additional domestic or foreign currency demanded being supplied by the monetary authority. This device is feasible and not undesirable for movements that are small and temporary, though, if it is clear that the movements are small and temporary, it is largely unnecessary, since, with flexible exchange rates, private speculative transactions will provide the additional domestic or foreign currency demanded with only minor movements in exchange rates.

The exclusive use of reserves is much less desirable, if possible at all, for movements of large magnitude and long duration. If the problem is a deficit, the ability of the monetary authorities to meet the deficit is immediately limited by the size of their reserves of foreign currency or the equivalent plus whatever additional sums they can or are willing to borrow or acquire in other ways from holders of foreign currency. Moreover, if the internal price level (or level of employment) is to be kept stable, the proceeds from the sales of foreign-exchange reserves must not be impounded or used in other deflationary ways. This assumes, of course, that the deficit is not itself produced by internal inflationary policies but occurs despite a stable internal price level. The proceeds must be used to retire debt or to finance a deficit in the budget to whatever extent is necessary to prevent a price decline.

If the problem is a surplus, the monetary authorities must be prepared to accumulate foreign exchange indefinitely, providing all the domestic currency that is demanded. Moreover, if the internal price level is to be maintained constant, it must obtain the domestic currency it sells for foreign currency in noninflationary ways. It can print or create the currency only to the extent that is consistent with stable prices. For the rest it must get the amount required by borrowing at whatever interest rates are necessary to keep domestic prices stable or from a surplus of the appropriate amount in the government budget. Entirely aside from the technical problem of monetary management involved, the community is unlikely to be willing to exchange indefinitely part of its product for unproductive currency hoards, particularly if the source of the surplus is monetary inflation abroad, and thus the foreign currency is decreasing in real value.

Traditionally, of course, monetary reserves have not been used as the primary method of adjusting to changes in external conditions but as a shock absorber pending changes in internal prices and incomes. A deficit has been met out of monetary reserves in the first instance, but the proceeds or even a multiple of the proceeds have been, as it were, impounded; that is, the stock of money has been allowed or made to decrease as a result of the decline of monetary reserves, with a consequent rise in interest rates and downward pressure on internal prices. Similarly, the domestic currency exchanged for a surplus of foreign currency has, as it were, been created and allowed to or made to increase the stock of money by the same amount or a multiple of that amount, with a consequent decline in interest rates and upward pressure on internal prices.[7]

Since the end of the first World War, nations have become increasingly unwilling to use reserves in this way and to allow the effect to be transmitted directly and immediately to internal monetary conditions and prices. Already during the 1920's the United States, to cite one outstanding and critical example, refused to allow

---

[7] Under a pure gold standard, these effects follow automatically, since any international claims not settled otherwise are settled by gold, which, in case of a deficit, is bodily extracted from the monetary stock and, in case of a surplus, bodily added to it.

its surplus, which took the form of gold imports, to raise domestic prices in the way the supposed rules of the gold standard demanded; instead, it "sterilized" gold imports. Especially after the Great Depression completed the elevation of full employment to the primary goal of economic policy, nations have been unwilling to allow deficits to exert any deflationary effect.

The use of monetary reserves as the sole reliance to meet small and temporary strains on balances of payments and of other devices to meet larger and more extended or more basic strains is an understandable objective of economic policy and comes close to summarizing the philosophy underlying the International Monetary Fund. Unfortunately, it is not a realistic, feasible, or desirable policy. It is seldom possible to know in advance or even soon after the event whether any given strain in the balance of payments is likely to be reversed rapidly or not; that is, whether it is a result of temporary or permanent factors. Reserves must be very large indeed if they are to be the sole reliance in meeting changes in external conditions until the magnitude and probable duration of the changes can be diagnosed with confidence and more fundamental correctives undertaken in light of the diagnosis, far larger than if they serve the function they did under the classical gold standard. Except perhaps for the United States, and even for the United States only so long as gold is freely acceptable as an international currency, reserves are nothing like this large. Under the circumstances there is a strong tendency to rely on reserves too long for comfort yet not long enough for confident diagnosis and reasoned action. Corrective steps are postponed in the hope that things will right themselves until the state of the reserves forces drastic and frequently ill-advised action.

E. A comparison

One or another of the methods of adjustment just described must in fact be used to meet changes in conditions affecting external trade; there is no avoiding this necessity short of the complete elimination of external trade, and even this would be an extreme form of direct controls over imports and exports. On the basis of the analysis so far, flexible exchange rates seem clearly the technique of adjustment best suited to current conditions: the use of reserves is not by itself a feasible device; direct controls are cumbrous and inefficient and, I venture to predict, will ultimately prove ineffective in a free society; changes in internal prices and incomes are undesirable because of rigidities in internal prices, especially wages, and the emergence of full employment—or independence of internal monetary policy—as a major goal of policy.

The argument for flexible exchange rates is, strange to say, very nearly identical with the argument for daylight saving time. Isn't it absurd to change the clock in summer when exactly the same result could be achieved by having each individual change his habits? All that is required is that everyone decide to come to his office an hour earlier, have lunch an hour earlier, etc. But obviously it is much simpler to change the clock that guides all than to have each individual separately change his pattern of reaction to the clock, even though all want to do so. The situation is exactly the same in the exchange market. It is far simpler to allow one price to change, namely, the price of foreign exchange, than to rely upon changes in the multitude of prices that together constitute the internal price structure.

II. OBJECTIONS TO FLEXIBLE EXCHANGE RATES

Three major criticisms have been made of the proposal to establish a system of flexible exchange rates: first, that flexible exchange rates may increase the degree of uncertainty in the economic scene; second, that flexible exchange rates will not work because they will produce offsetting changes in domestic prices; and, third, that flexible exchange rates will not produce the best attainable timing or pace of adjustment. The first objection takes many different forms, and it will promote clarity to deal with some of these separately, even though this means considerable overlapping.

A. Flexible Exchange Rates and Uncertainty

1. Flexible exchange rates mean instability rather than stability. On the naïve level on which this objection is frequently made, it involves the already-mentioned mistake of confusing the symptom of difficulties with the difficulties themselves. A flexible exchange rate need not be an unstable exchange rate. If it is, it is primarily because there is underlying instability in the economic conditions governing international trade. And a rigid exchange rate may, while itself nominally stable, perpetuate and accentuate other elements of instability in the economy. The mere fact that a rigid official exchange rate does not change while a flexible rate does is no evidence that the former means greater stability in any more fundamental sense. If it does, it is for one or more of the reasons considered in the points that follow.

2. *Flexible exchange rates make it impossible for exporters and importers to be certain about the price they will have to pay or receive for foreign exchange.* Under flexible exchange rates traders can almost always protect themselves against changes in the rate by hedging in a futures market. Such futures markets in foreign currency readily develop when exchange rates are flexible. Any uncertainty about returns will then be borne by speculators. The most that can be said for this argument, therefore, is that flexible exchange rates impose a cost of hedging on traders, namely, the price that must be paid to speculators for assuming the risk of future changes in exchange rates. But this is saying too much. The substitution of flexible for rigid exchange rates changes the form in which uncertainty in the foreign-exchange market is manifested; it may not change the extent of uncertainty at all and, indeed, may even decrease uncertainty. For example, conditions that would tend to produce a decline in a flexible exchange rate will produce a shortage of exchange with a rigid exchange rate. This in turn will produce either internal adjustments of uncertain character or administrative allocation of exchange. Traders will then be certain about the rate but uncertain about either internal conditions or the availability of exchange. The uncertainty can be removed for some transactions by advance commitments by the authorities dispensing exchange; it clearly cannot be removed for all transactions in view of the uncertainty about the total amount of exchange available; the reduction in uncertainty for some transactions therefore involves increased uncertainty for others, since all the risk is now concentrated on them. Further, such administrative allocation of exchange is always surrounded by uncertainty about the policy that will be followed. It is by no means clear whether the uncertainty associated with a flexible rate or the uncertainty associated with a rigid rate is likely to be more disruptive to trade.

3. *Speculation in foreign-exchange markets tends to be destabilizing.* This point is, of course, closely related to the preceding one. It is said that speculators will take a decline in the exchange rate as a signal for a further decline and will thus tend to make the movements in the exchange rate sharper than they would be in the absence of speculation. The special fear in this connection is of capital

flight in response to political uncertainty or simply to movements in the exchange rate. Despite the prevailing opinion to the contrary, I am very dubious that in fact speculation in foreign exchange would be destabilizing. Evidence from some earlier experiences and from current free markets in currency in Switzerland, Tangiers, and elsewhere seems to me to suggest that, in general, speculation is stabilizing rather than the reverse, though the evidence has not yet been analyzed in sufficient detail to establish this conclusion with any confidence. People who argue that speculation is generally destabilizing seldom realize that this is largely equivalent to saying that speculators lose money, since speculation can be destabilizing in general only if speculators on the average sell when the currency is low in price and buy when it is high.[8] It does not, of course, follow that speculation is not destabilizing; professional speculators might on the average make money while a changing body of amateurs regularly lost larger sums. But, while this may happen, it is hard to see why there is any presumption that it will; the presumption is rather the opposite. To put the same point differently, if speculation were persistently destabilizing, a government body like the Exchange Equalization Fund in England in the 1930's could make a good deal of money by speculating in exchange and in the process almost certainly eliminate the destabilizing speculation. But to suppose that speculation by governments would generally be profitable is in most cases equivalent to supposing that government officials risking funds that they do not themselves own are better judges of the likely movements in foreign-exchange markets than private individuals risking their own funds.

The widespread belief that speculation is likely to be destabilizing is doubtless a major factor accounting for the cavalier rejection of a system of flexible exchange rates in the immediate postwar period. Yet this belief does not seem to be founded on any systematic analysis of the available empirical evidence.[9] It rests rather, I believe,

[8] A warning is perhaps in order that this is a simplified generalization on a complex problem. A full analysis encounters difficulties in separating "speculative" from other transactions, defining precisely and satisfactorily "destabilizing speculation," and taking account of the effects of the mere existence of a system of flexible rates as contrasted with the effects of actual speculative transactions under such a system.

[9] Perhaps the most ambitious attempt to summarize the evidence is that by Ragnar Nurkse, *International Currency Experience* (Geneva: League of Nations, 1944), pp. 117–22. Nurkse concludes from interwar experience that speculation can be expected in general to be destabilizing. However, the evi-

primarily on an oversimplified interpretation of the movements of so-called "hot" money during the 1930's. At the time, any speculative movements which threatened a depreciation of a currency (i.e., which threatened a *change* in an exchange rate) were regarded as destabilizing, and hence these movements were so considered. In retrospect, it is clear that the speculators were "right"; that forces were at work making for depreciation in the value of most European currencies relative to the dollar independently of speculative activity; that the speculative movements were anticipating this change; and, hence, that there is at least as much reason to call them "stabilizing" as to call them "destabilizing."

In addition, the interpretation of this evidence has been marred by a failure to distinguish between a system of exchange rates held temporarily rigid but subject to change from time to time by government action and a system of flexible exchange rates. Many of the capital movements regarded as demonstrating that foreign-exchange speculation is destabilizing were stimulated by the existence of rigid rates subject to change by government action and are to be attributed primarily to the absence of flexibility of rates and hence of any incentive to avoid the capital movements. This is equally true of post-World War II experience with wide swings in foreign-payments positions. For reasons noted earlier, this experience has little direct

---

dence he cites is by itself inadequate to justify any conclusion. Nurske examines only one episode in anything approaching the required detail, the depreciation of the French franc from 1922 to 1926. For the rest, he simply lists episodes during which exchange rates were flexible and asserts that in each case speculation was destabilizing. These episodes may or may not support his conclusion; it is impossible to tell from his discussion of them; and the list is clearly highly selective, excluding some cases that seem prima facie to point in the opposite direction.

Even for the French episode, the evidence given by Nurkse does not justify any firm conclusion. Indeed, so far as it goes, it seems to me clearly less favorable to the conclusion Nurkse draws, that speculation was destabilizing, than to the opposite conclusion, that speculation was stabilizing.

In general, Nurkse's discussion of the effects of speculation is thoroughly unsatisfactory. At times, he seems to regard any transactions which threaten the existing value of a currency as destabilizing even if underlying forces would produce a changed value in the absence of speculation. At another point, he asserts that destabilizing transactions may occur on *both* capital and current account simultaneously, in a context in which these two accounts exhaust the balance of payments, so that his statement is an arithmetical impossibility (pp. 210–11). It is a sorry reflection on the scientific basis for generally held economic beliefs that Nurkse's analysis is so often cited as "the" basis or "proof" of the belief in destabilizing speculation.

bearing on the character of the speculative movements to be expected under a regime of genuinely flexible exchange rates.

4. *Flexible exchange rates involve increased uncertainty in the internal economy.* It is argued that in many countries there is a great fear of inflation and that people have come to regard the exchange rate as an indicator of inflation and are highly sensitive to variations in it. Exchange crises, such as would tend to occur under rigid exchange rates, will pass unnoticed, it is argued, except by people directly connected with international trade, whereas a decline in the exchange rate would attract much attention, be taken as a signal of a future inflation, and produce anticipatory movements by the public at large. In this way a flexible exchange rate might produce additional uncertainty rather than merely change the form in which uncertainty is manifested. There is some merit to this argument, but it does not seem to me to be a substantial reason for avoiding a flexible exchange rate. Its implication is rather that it would be desirable, if possible, to make the transition to a flexible rate at a time when exchange rates of European countries relative to the dollar would be likely to move moderately and some to rise. It further would be desirable to accompany the transition by willingness to take prompt monetary action to counter any internal reactions. A fear of inflation has little or no chance of producing inflation, except in a favorable monetary environment. A demonstration that fears of inflation are groundless, and some experience with the absence of any direct and immediate connection between the day-to-day movements in the exchange rate and internal prices would very shortly reduce to negligible proportions any increase in uncertainty on purely domestic markets, as a result of flexible yet not highly unstable exchange rates. Further, public recognition that a substantial decline in the exchange rate is a symptom of or portends internal inflation is by no means an unmixed evil. It means that a flexible exchange rate would provide something of a barrier to a highly inflationary domestic policy.

Very nearly the opposite of this argument is also sometimes made against flexible exchange rates. It is said that, with a flexible exchange rate, governments will have less incentive and be in a less strong position to take firm internal action to prevent inflation. A rigid exchange rate, it is said, gives the government a symbol to fight for—it can nail its flag to the mast of a specified exchange rate and resist political pressure to take action that would be inflationary in the name of defending the exchange rate. Dramatic foreign-exchange crises establish an atmosphere in which drastic if unpopular action is possible. On the other hand, it is said, with a flexible exchange rate, there is no definite sticking point; inflationary action will simply mean a decline in the exchange rate but no dramatic crisis, and people are little affected by a change in a price, the exchange rate, in a market in which relatively few have direct dealings.

Of course, it is not impossible for both these arguments to be valid—the first in countries like Germany, which have recently experienced hyperinflations and violently fluctuating exchange rates, the second in countries like Great Britain, which have not. But, even in countries like Britain, it is far from clear that a rigid exchange rate is more conducive under present conditions to noninflationary internal economic policy than a flexible exchange rate. A rigid exchange rate thwarts any immediate manifestation of a deterioration in the foreign-payments position as a result of inflationary internal policy. With an independent monetary standard, the loss of exchange reserves does not automatically reduce the stock of money or prevent its continued increase; yet it does temporarily reduce domestic inflationary pressure by providing goods in return for the foreign-exchange reserves without any simultaneous creation of domestic income. The deterioration shows up only sometime later, in the dull tables of statistics summarizing the state of foreign-exchange reserves. Even then, the authorities in the modern world have the alternative—or think they have—of suppressing a deficit by more stringent direct controls and thus postponing still longer the necessity for taking the appropriate internal measures; and they can always find any number of special reasons for the particular deterioration other than their internal policy. While the possibilities of using direct controls and of finding plausible excuses are present equally with flexible exchange rates, at least the deterioration in the foreign-payments position shows up promptly in the more readily understandable and simpler form of a decline in the exchange rates, and there is no emergency, no suddenly discovered decline in monetary reserves to dangerous levels, to force the imposition of supposedly unavoidable direct controls.

These arguments are modern versions of an argument that no longer has much merit but was at one time a valid and potent objection to flexible exchange rates, namely, the greater scope they give for government "tampering" with the currency. When rigid exchange rates were taken seriously, and when the armory of direct controls over international trade had not yet been resurrected, the maintenance of rigid rates left little scope for independent domestic monetary policy. This was the great virtue of the gold standard and the basic, albeit hidden, source of its emotional appeal; it provided an effective defense against hyperinflation, against government intervention of a kind that had time and again led to the debasement and depreciation of once-proud currencies. This argument may still be a source of emotional resistance to flexible exchange rates; it is clear that it does not deserve to be. Governments of "advanced" nations are no longer willing to submit themselves to the harsh discipline of the gold standard or any other standard involving rigid exchange rates. They will evade its discipline by direct controls over trade if that will suffice and will change exchange rates before they will surrender control over domestic monetary policy. Perhaps a few modern inflations will establish a climate in which such behavior does not qualify as "advanced"; in the meantime we had best recognize the necessity of allowing exchange rates to adjust to internal policies rather than the reverse.

B. Flexible exchange rates and internal prices

While I have just used the primacy of internal policy as an argument for flexible exchange rates, it has also been used as an argument against flexible exchange rates. As we have seen, flexible exchange rates promote adjustments to changes in internal circumstances by producing changes in the relation between the prices of foreign and domestic goods. A decline in an exchange rate produced by a tendency toward a deficit in the balance of payments tends to make the prices of foreign goods higher in terms of domestic currency than they would otherwise have been. If domestic prices are unaffected—or affected less—this means a higher price of foreign goods relative to domestic goods, which stimulates exports and discourage imports.

The rise in prices of foreign goods will, it is argued, mean a rise in the cost of living, and this, in turn, will give rise to a demand for wage increases, setting off what is typically referred to as a "wage-price spiral"—a term that is impressive enough to conceal the emptiness of the argument that it generally adorns. In consequence, so the argument continues, prices of domestic goods rise as much as prices of foreign goods, relative prices remain unchanged, there are no market forces working toward the elimination of the deficit that initially caused the decline in the exchange rate, and so further declines in the exchange rate are inevitable until nonmarket forces are brought into play. But these might as well have been used before as after the decline in the exchange rate.

This argument clearly applies only to rather special circumstances. At most, it may be an objection to a particular country at a particular time allowing its currency to go free; it is not a general objection to a *system* of flexible exchange rates as a long-run structure. It does not apply to circumstances making for the appreciation of a currency and applies only to some circumstances making for depreciation. Suppose, for example, that the tendency toward a deficit were produced by monetary deflations in other countries. The depreciation of the currency would then prevent the fall in external prices from being transmitted to the country in question; it would prevent prices of foreign goods from being forced down in terms of domestic currency. There is no way of eliminating the effect of the lowered "real" income of other countries; flexible exchange rates prevent this effect from being magnified by monetary disturbances. Similarly, the argument has little relevance if the decline in exchange rates reflects an open inflationary movement at home; the depreciation is then an obvious result of inflation rather than a cause. The argument has perhaps most relevance in either of two cases: an inflationary situation being repressed by direct controls or a depreciation produced by a change in the "real" conditions of trade.

Even in these cases, however, the argument cannot be fully granted. The crucial fallacy is the so-called "wage-price spiral." The rise in prices of foreign goods may add to the always plentiful list of excuses for wage increases; it does not in and of itself provide the economic conditions for a wage rise—or, at any rate, for a wage rise without unemployment. A general wage rise—or a general rise in domestic prices—becomes possible only if the monetary authorities create the additional money to finance the higher level of prices.[10] But if the monetary authorities are ready to do so to validate any rise in particular prices or wages, then the situation is fundamentally unstable without a change in the exchange rate, since a wage rise for any other excuse would lead to similar consequences.

---

[10] In principle, there are other possibilities related to the "velocity of circulation" of money that I neglect to simplify the argument; they do not change its essence.

The assumption is that to him who asks will be given, and there is never a shortage of willingness to ask under such circumstances.

It will be answered that this innate instability is held in check by some sort of political compromise and that this compromise would be disturbed by the change in the exchange rate. This is a special case of the general argument considered earlier that the government is more likely to resist political pressure to take inflationary action if it nails its flag to the mast of a rigid exchange rate than if it lets the exchange rate fluctuate. But note that the forces leading to a changed exchange rate are not eliminated by freezing the rate; foreign exchange will have to be acquired or economized somehow. The "real" adjustment must be made in one way or another; the question is only how. Why should this way of making the adjustment destroy the compromise while other ways do not? Or, if this is true for a time, can it be expected to continue to be true? If, as we have argued, flexible exchange rates are the least costly way of making the adjustment, will not other methods be even more likely to destroy a tenuous political compromise?

C. Flexible exchange rates and the timing of adjustment

The ultimate adjustment to a change in external circumstances will consist of a change in the allocation of productive resources and in the composition of the goods available for consumption and investment. But this ultimate change will not be achieved immediately. It takes time to shift from the production of goods for domestic consumption to the production of goods for export, or conversely; it takes time to establish new markets abroad or to persuade consumers to substitute a foreign for a domestic good to which they have been accustomed; and so on in endless variety. The time required will vary widely: some types of adaptations can take place instantaneously (e.g., curtailment by a high price of the purchase of imported cheese, though even here the price rise required to achieve a given curtailment will be higher at first than after a time when people have had a chance to adapt their habitual pattern of consumption to the new price); other types of adaptation may take a generation (e.g., the development of a new domestic industry to produce goods formerly imported).

Suppose a substantial change in (real) external circumstances to occur and, to keep matters simple, circumstances thereafter to remain essentially unchanged for a lengthy period, so that we can (conceptually) isolate the adaptation to this one change. Suppose, further, that exchange rates are flexible and that international "capital" or "speculative" transactions are impossible, so that payments on current accounts must balance—a condition it is admittedly difficult to define precisely in any way susceptible to observation. It is clear that the initial change in exchange rates will be greater than the ultimate change required, for, to begin with, all the adjustment will have to be borne in those directions in which prompt adjustment is possible and relatively easy. As time passes, the slower-moving adjustments will take over part of the burden, permitting exchange rates to rebound toward a final position which is between the position prior to the external change and the position shortly thereafter. This is, of course, a highly oversimplified picture: the actual path of adjustment may involve repeated overshooting and undershooting of the final position, giving rise to a series of cycles around it or to a variety of other patterns. We are here entering into an area of economics about which we know very little, so it is fortunate that a precise discussion of the path is not essential for our purposes.

Under these circumstances it clearly might be in the interests of the community to pay something to avoid some of the initial temporary adjustments: if the exchange rate depreciates, to borrow from abroad at the going interest rate to pay for an excess of imports while the slower-moving adjustments take place rather than making the full immediate adjustment by curtailing those imports that can be readily curtailed and forcing out those exports that can be readily increased; if the exchange rate appreciates, to lend abroad at the going interest rate to finance an excess of exports while the slower-moving adjustments take place rather than making the full immediate adjustment by expanding those imports that can be readily expanded and curtailing those exports that can be readily curtailed. It would not, however, be worth doing this indefinitely, even if it were possible. For, if it were carried to the point at which the exchange rate remained unchanged, no other adjustments at all would take place. Yet the change in external circumstances makes a new allocation of resources and composition of goods optimal for the country concerned. That is, there is some optimum pace and timing of adjustment through exchange-rate-induced changes in the allocation of resources which is neither at the extreme of full immediate adjustment in this way alone nor at the other extreme of complete avoidance of adjustment.

Under a flexible exchange-rate system with a reasonably broad
and free market in foreign exchange and with correct foresight on
the part of speculators, just such an intermediate pace and timing of
adjustment is produced even if there is no explicit negotiation of
foreign loans. If the exchange rate depreciates, for example, the
tendency for the exchange rate to fall further initially than ultimately
offers an opportunity to make a profit by buying the currency now
and reselling it later at a higher price. But this is precisely equivalent to lending by speculators to the country whose currency has
depreciated. The return to the speculators is equal to the rate at
which the currency they hold appreciates. In a free market with
correct foresight, this will tend, aside from the minor costs of buying
or selling the foreign exchange, to approach the interest rate that
speculators could earn in other ways. If the currency appreciates at
more than this rate, speculators still have an incentive to add to
their holdings; if it appreciates at less than this rate, it is costing the
speculators more in foregone interest to hold the balances than they
are gaining in the appreciation of the exchange rate. In this way,
speculation with a flexible exchange rate produces the same effect
as explicit borrowing by a country whose currency has depreciated
or explicit lending by one whose currency has appreciated. In practice, of course, there will be both explicit lending or borrowing and
implicit lending or borrowing through exchange speculation. Moreover, the prospect of appreciation of a currency is equivalent to a
higher interest rate for loans to the country and thus serves the same
function in attracting capital to that country as the rises in interest
rate that took place under the gold standard when a country was
losing gold. There is, however, this important difference: under
flexible exchange rates the inducement to foreign lenders need involve no change in the interest rate on domestic loans; under the
gold standard, it did—a particular example of the independence of
domestic monetary policy under flexible exchange rates.

But is the pace and timing of adjustment achieved in this way
under flexible exchange rates an approximation to the optimum?
This is an exceedingly difficult question to answer, depending as it
does on whether the interest rate implicitly paid in the form of the
appreciation or depreciation of the currency reflects the full relevant costs of too rapid or too slow adjustment. About all one can
say without much more extensive analysis, and perhaps even with
such analysis, is that there seems no reason to expect the timing or

pace of adjustment under the assumed conditions to be systematically biased in one direction or the other from the optimum or
to expect that other techniques of adaptation—through internal
price changes, direct controls, and the use of monetary reserves with
rigid exchange rates—would lead to a more nearly optimum pace and
timing of adjustment.

This much would probably be granted by most persons who argue
that flexible exchange rates lead to an undesirable pace and timing
of adjustment. But, they would maintain, the foreign-exchange market is not nearly so perfect, or the foresight of speculators so good,
as has been assumed to this point. The argument already considered,
that speculation in foreign exchanges is destabilizing, is an extreme
form of this objection. For, in that case, the immediate change in the
foreign-exchange rate must go far enough to produce an immediate
adaptation sufficient not only to balance current transactions but also
to provide payment in foreign currencies for the balances of domestic currency that speculators perversely insist on liquidating when
the exchange rate falls, or to provide the domestic currency for the
balances speculators perversely insist on accumulating when the
exchange rate rises. The country lends, as it were, when it should be
borrowing and borrows when it should be lending.

But one need not go this far. Speculation may be stabilizing on
balance, yet the market for foreign exchange, it can be said, is so
narrow, foresight so imperfect, and private speculation so dominated
by socially irrelevant political considerations that there is an insufficient smoothing-out of the adjustment process. For this to be a valid
argument against flexible exchange rates, even if true, there must be
some alternative that promises a better pace and timing of adjustment. We have already considered several other possibilities. We
have seen that direct controls with a rigid exchange rate and the
official use of monetary reserves have striking defects of their own,
at least under modern conditions; they are likely to produce a highly
erratic pace and timing of adjustment with alternate fits of unduly
slow and unduly rapid adjustments, and direct controls are besides
likely to produce the wrong kind of adjustments. Private capital
movements in response to interest-rate differentials were at one time
a real alternative but have been rendered largely unavailable by the
unwillingness of monetary authorities to permit the required changes
in interest rates, by the loss of confidence in the indefinite maintenance of the fixed exchange rates, and by the fear of restrictions on

the use of exchange. In any event, such capital movements are, as we have seen, available and at least as likely to take place under flexible exchange rates.

The plausibility of the view that private exchange speculation produces too little smoothing of exchange-rate fluctuations derives, I believe, primarily from an implicit tendency to regard any slowing-down of the adjustment process as an improvement; that is, implicitly to regard no adjustment at all or an indefinitely prolonged one as the ideal.[11] This is the counterpart of the tendency to believe that internal monetary policy can and should avoid all internal adjustments in the level of income.[12] And both, I suspect, are a manifestation of the urge for security that is so outstanding a feature of the modern world and that is itself a major source of insecurity by promoting measures that reduce the adaptability of our economic systems to change without eliminating the changes themselves.

III. SOME EXAMPLES OF THE IMPORTANCE OF A SYSTEM OF FLEXIBLE EXCHANGE RATES

It cannot be too strongly emphasized that the structure and method of determining exchange rates have a vital bearing on almost every problem of international economic relations. It will illustrate this basic proposition and at the same time help to bring out some of the implications of the preceding analysis if we consider the rela-

[11] An interesting example is provided by an argument for 100 per cent banking reserves under a gold standard given by James E. Meade, *The Balance of Payments,* Vol. I of *The Theory of International Economic Policy* (Oxford: Oxford University Press, 1951), p. 185. Meade argues correctly that with 100 per cent reserves the internal adaptations consequent on an external change of any given size will be at a slower rate than with a lower reserve ratio. On this ground, he says, 100 per cent reserves are better than fractional reserves. But this conclusion follows only if any slowing-down in the rate of internal adaptation is an improvement, in which case 200 per cent reserves or their equivalent ("sterilization" of gold imports and exports) would be better than 100 per cent, and so on indefinitely. Given that there is some optimum rate of adjustment, all one can say is that there exists some reserve ratio that would tend to produce this rate of adjustment and so be optimal on these grounds alone; I see no way of knowing on the basis of the considerations Meade presents whether this ratio would be 5 per cent or 500 per cent.

[12] See "The Effects of a Full-Employment Policy on Economic Stability: A Formal Analysis," *Économie appliquée,* IV (July–December 1951), pp. 441–456, reprinted in *Essays in Positive Economics,* pp. 117–132, for a more detailed consideration of the formal problem involved in both internal and external policy and for some examples of this tendency.

tion of flexible exchange rates to three specific problems of great current importance: (*a*) the promotion of unrestricted multilateral trade; (*b*) the harmonization of internal monetary and fiscal policies; and (*c*) the rearmament drive.

A. Unrestricted international trade

We have seen that flexible exchange rates are entirely consistent with unrestricted multilateral trade. On the other hand, the absence of flexible exchange rates is almost certain to be incompatible with unrestricted multilateral trade. With rigid exchange rates, any changes in conditions of trade can be met only by changes in reserves, internal prices and monetary conditions, or direct controls over imports, exports, and other exchange transactions. With few exceptions, reserves of European countries are small, and, in any event, the use of reserves is a feasible device only for mild and temporary movements. Primary reliance on changes in the internal price level is undesirable, and, largely for this reason, there is great political reluctance to rely on such changes. Germany, Belgium, and Italy might perhaps be willing to go some way in this direction. England, France, Norway, and some other countries would almost certainly be completely unwilling to allow the level of prices and employment at home to be determined primarily by the vagaries of foreign trade.

The only other alternative to movements in exchange rates is direct control of foreign trade. Such control is therefore almost certain to be the primary technique adopted to meet substantial movements in conditions of international trade so long as exchange rates are maintained rigid. The implicit or explicit recognition of this fact is clearly one of the chief sources of difficulty in attempts to achieve a greater degree of liberalization of trade in Europe; it is reflected in the extensive escape clauses of all recent international agreements; it is dramatically demonstrated by the ultimately successful pressure on the Germans to use direct controls in the exchange crisis of the fall of 1950, despite the general belief that the crisis was temporary and would be over in a matter of months. It is part of the explanation of the pressures for direct controls produced by the rearmament drive.

Suppose that, by some fortunate turn of events, complete liberalization of trade and convertibility of currencies were achieved tomorrow and resulted in equilibrium in the balance of payments of all European countries at existing exchange rates without American aid. Suppose, in consequence, American aid and pressure were permanently removed. I have no hesitancy in predicting that, given the existing system of determination of exchange rates and the present general political and economic environment, direct controls over exports and imports would be reimposed on a large scale within two or three years at the most.

But even this understates the problem raised by fixed exchange rates. Not only is ultimate liberalization of trade almost certain to be inconsistent with rigid and fixed exchange rates in the present state of the world; equally important, the process of moving toward this objective is rendered unduly difficult. There is no way of predicting in advance the precise economic effects of meaningful reductions of trade barriers. All that is clear is that the impact of such reductions will vary from country to country and industry to industry and that many of the impacts will be highly indirect and not at all in the particular areas liberalized. The very process of liberalization will therefore add substantial and unpredictable pressures on balances of payments over and above those that would occur in any event. These pressures would make any system of rigid exchange rates appropriate to the initial position almost certainly inappropriate to the final position and to intermediate positions. And there seems no way to decide on the appropriate final exchange rates in advance; they must be reached by trial and error. Thus, even if the ultimate goal were a new system of rigid exchange rates, it seems almost essential to have flexibility in the interim period. In the absence of such flexibility, liberalization is likely to be brought to an untimely end by the very consequences of any initial successes.

The current political reluctance to use changes in internal price levels and employment to meet external changes is matched by a political reluctance to use changes in exchange rates. But I submit that the reluctance to use changes in exchange rates is on a different level and has a different basis than the reluctance to use internal changes. The reluctance to use changes in exchange rates reflects a cultural lag, the survival of a belief the bases for which have disappeared; it is a consequence of tradition and lack of understanding. The reluctance to use changes in internal price levels and employment, on the other hand, is a new development, a product of harsh experience of the recent past and, for the moment at least, in tune with current economic conditions.

B. Harmonization of internal monetary and fiscal policies

The positive side of the reluctance to use changes in internal price levels and employment to meet external changes is the promotion of internal monetary stability—the avoidance of either inflation or deflation. This is clearly a highly desirable objective for each country separately. But, under a system of rigid exchange rates and unrestricted trade, no country can attain this objective unless *every* other important country with which it is linked directly or indirectly by trade does so as well. If any one country inflates, for example, this tends to increase its imports and reduce its exports. Other countries now start to accumulate currency balances of the inflating country. They must either be willing to accumulate such balances indefinitely—which means they must be willing to continue shipping out goods without a return flow and thus in effect subsidize the inflating country—or they must follow the inflation themselves (or impose import controls). Hence the strong pressure to achieve harmonization of internal monetary policies.

But this pressure has understandably not been matched by a willingness of all countries to submit their internal policy to external control. Why should a country do so when the failure of any one country to co-operate or to behave "properly" would destroy the whole structure and permit it to transmit its difficulties to its neighbors? Really effective "co-ordination" would require essentially either that nations adopt a common commodity monetary standard like gold and agree to submit unwaveringly to its discipline or that some international body control the supply of money in each country, which in turn implies control over at least interest-rate policy and budgetary policy. The first alternative is neither currently feasible nor particularly desirable in the light of our past experience with the gold standard.[13] As to the second alternative, whether feasible or not, is it desirable that such far-reaching powers be surrendered to any authority other than an effective federal government democratically elected and responsible to the electorate?

A system of flexible exchange rates eliminates the necessity for such far-reaching co-ordination of internal monetary and fiscal policy

---

[13] See my "Commodity-Reserve Currency," *Journal of Political Economy,* LIX (June 1951), pp. 203–232, reprinted in *Essays in Positive Economics,* pp. 204–250, for a more extensive discussion of the advantages and disadvantages of a commodity standard.

in order for any country separately to follow a stable internal monetary policy. If, under such a system, any one country inflates, the primary effect is a depreciation in its exchange rate. This offsets the effect of internal inflation on its international trade position and weakens or eliminates the tendency for the inflation to be transmitted to its neighbors; and conversely with deflation. Inflation and deflation in any one country will then affect other countries primarily in so far as it affects the real income position of the initial country; there will be little or no effect through purely monetary channels.

In effect, flexible exchange rates are a means of combining interdependence among countries through trade with a maximum of internal monetary independence; they are a means of permitting each country to seek for monetary stability according to its own lights, without either imposing its mistakes on its neighbors or having their mistakes imposed on it. If all countries succeeded, the result would be a system of reasonably stable exchange rates; the substance of effective harmonization would be attained without the risks of formal but ineffective harmonization.

The chance that all countries would succeed is far greater with flexible exchange rates than with a system of rigid exchange rates that is not also a strict commodity standard. For not only do the laggards tend to call the tune under rigid exchange rates by infecting the other countries with which they are linked but also the very existence of this link gives each country an incentive to engage in inflationary action that it would not otherwise have. For, at least in the initial stages, inflationary currency issue enables the issuers to acquire resources not only from within the country but also from without: the rigid rates mean, as we have seen, that other countries accumulate balances of the currency of the inflating country. Under reasonably stable but not rigid rates, this incentive is largely removed, since the rates will remain stable only so long as countries avoid inflationary action. Once they embark on it, a decline in the exchange rates for their currency will replace the accumulation of balances that would have to take place to keep the rates rigid.

C. The current rearmament drive

A particular example of the preceding problem is provided by the present rearmament drive. A really serious rearmament drive is almost certain to produce inflationary pressure, differing in degree from country to country because of differences in fiscal structures, monetary systems, temper of the people, the size of the rearmament effort, etc. With rigid exchange rates, these divergent pressures introduce strains and stresses that are likely to interfere with the armament effort. Country *A*, let us say, has more inflationary pressure than *B*, and *B* more than *C*. *B* will tend to find its exports to *A* expanding at the same time that its exports to *C* are falling and its imports from *C* expanding. Over all it may be in balance, but it is not in particular industries. It will be under strong pressure to impose export controls on products that it tends to export to *A* and at the same time import controls on products it imports from *C*. Under flexible exchange rates neither might have been necessary; its currency would appreciate relative to *A*'s currency and depreciate relative to *B*'s, thus offsetting both distortions in its trade patterns—distortions because by assumption the changes were produced primarily by differences in the rate of monetary expansion.

This kind of phenomenon is, I believe, one of the important factors that has made for resistance to the removal of import controls and for renewed pressure for export controls, though clearly there are other factors involved as well.

Of course, the rearmament drive will require changes in the structure of trade for technical and physical reasons and not merely for monetary reasons. It is essential for the efficiency of the armament effort that such changes be permitted. Under flexible exchange rates they would tend to be the primary ones. Monetary expansion in any country produces a general increase in demand for imports and a general reduction in supply of exports and so, with flexible exchange rates, is reflected primarily in exchange rates. On the other hand, the rearmament effort involves a shift of demand from some products to others and need involve no change in aggregate money demand. In consequence, particular prices rise relative to other prices, thereby providing the incentive for the required changes in production and trade. Even if the rearmament effort is financed by means that involve an increased aggregate money demand, it will mean a much greater increase in demand for some products than others and so can still lead to the required changes in *relative* prices.

IV. CONCLUSION

The nations of the world cannot prevent changes from occurring in the circumstances affecting international transactions. And they would not if they could. For many changes reflect natural changes in weather conditions and the like; others arise from the freedom of countless individuals to order their lives as they will, which it is our ultimate goal to preserve and widen; and yet others contain the seeds of progress and development. The prison and the graveyard alone provide even a close approximation to certainty.

The major aim of policy is not to prevent such changes from occurring but to develop an efficient system of adapting to them—of using their potentialities for good while minimizing their disruptive effects. There is widespread agreement, at least in the Western world, that relatively free and unrestricted multilateral trade is a major component of such a system, besides having political advantages of a rather different kind. Yet resounding failure has so far marked repeated attempts to eliminate or reduce the extensive and complex restrictions on international trade that proliferated during and immediately after World War II. Failure will continue to mark such attempts so long as we allow implicit acceptance of an essentially minor goal—rigid exchange rates—to prevent simultaneous attainment of two major goals: unrestricted multilateral trade and freedom of each country to pursue internal stability after its own lights.

There are, after all, only four ways in which the pressures on balances of payments produced by changes in the circumstances affecting international transactions can be met: (1) by counterbalancing changes in currency reserves; (2) by adjustments in the general level of internal prices and incomes; (3) by adjustments in exchange rates; and (4) by direct controls over transactions involving foreign exchange.

The paucity of existing currency reserves makes the first impractical for all but very minor changes unless some means can be found to increase the currency reserves of the world enormously. The failure of several noble experiments in this direction is testimony to the difficulty of this solution.

The primacy everywhere attached to internal stability makes the second method one that would not be permitted to operate; the institutional rigidities in internal price structures make it undesirable that it should be the major means of adjustment.

The third—at least in the form of a thoroughgoing system of flexible rates—has been ruled out in recent years without extensive explicit consideration, partly because of a questionable interpretation of limited historical evidence; partly, I believe, because it was condemned alike by traditionalists, whose ideal was a gold standard that either ran itself or was run by international central bankers but in either case determined internal policy, and by the dominant strain of reformers, who distrusted the price system in all its manifestations—a curious coalition of the most unreconstructed believers in the price system, in all its other roles, and its most extreme opponents.

The fourth method—direct controls over transactions involving foreign exchange—has in this way, by default rather than intention, been left the only avenue whereby pressures on balances of payments can be met. Little wonder that these controls have so stubbornly resisted elimination despite the repeated protestations that they would be eliminated. Yet this method is, in my view, by all odds the least desirable of the four.

There are no major economic difficulties to prevent the prompt establishment by countries separately or jointly of a system of exchange rates freely determined in open markets, primarily by private transactions, and the simultaneous abandonment of direct controls over exchange transactions. A move in this direction is the fundamental prerequisite for the economic integration of the free world through multilateral trade.

16. Stable and Unstable Equilibria in the Foreign Exchanges

William R. Allen

University of California, Los Angeles

Reprinted from *Kyklos*, VII (1954), Fasc. 4, pp. 395–408, slightly modified, by permission of the publisher.

Of the several friends who have read one draft or another of this note, special thanks are due L.W. MacKenzie, K. Brunner, and N.V. Breckner. Much of the approach stems from lectures of L.A. Metzler and C.L. Allen.

A number of writers have expounded in detail the price effects of a domestic currency devaluation on the country's balance of payments position. Formulas have been derived to show that these effects depend upon the foreign and domestic elasticities of supply and of demand for exports and imports.[1] It is possible for the elasticities to be such that a depreciation or devaluation would worsen,

[1] For a history of the stability discussion, see L.A. Metzler, "The Theory of International Trade," in H.S. Ellis, ed., *A Survey of Contemporary Economics*, The Blakiston Co., Philadelphia 1948, vol. I, p. 228–32. For recent discussions, see A.O. Hirschman, "Devaluation and the Trade Balance: A Note," *Review of Economics and Statistics*, XXXI (1949), p. 50–53; G. Haberler, "The Market for Foreign Exchange and the Stability of the Balance of Payments," *Kyklos*, III (1949), p. 193–218; P.T. Ellsworth, "Exchange Rates and Exchange Stability," *Review of Economics and Statistics*, XXXII (1950), p. 1–12, and M. Bronfenbrenner, "Mathematical Supplement," p. 12–16; A.C. Harberger, "Currency Depreciation, Income, and the Balance of Trade," *Journal of Political Economy*, LVIII (1950), p. 47–60; A.C.L. Day, "Devaluation and the Balance of Payments," *Economica*, N.S. XVII (1950), p. 431–37; J.E. Meade, *The Balance of Payments*, Oxford University Press, New York 1951, esp. p. 68–73, 232–47; G. Stuvel, *The Exchange Stability Problem*, Augustus M. Kelley, Inc., New York 1951; S. S. Alexander, "Devaluation versus Import Restriction as an Instrument for Improving Foreign Trade Balance," *International Monetary Fund Staff Papers*, I (1951), p. 379–96; J.J. Polak and Ta-Chung Liu, "Stability of the Exchange Rate Mechanism in a Multi-Country System," *Econometrica*, XX (1954), p. 360–89. See also S.S. Alexander, "Effects of a Devaluation on a Trade Balance," *International Monetary Fund Staff Papers*, II (1952), p. 263–78, and H. Brems, "Foreign Exchange Rates and Monopolistic Competition," *Economic Journal*, LXIII (1953), p. 289–94, which are not based on the conventional elasticities approach.

instead of improve, the payments situation, in which case appreciation has been recommended as appropriate policy.

There is, however, an asymmetry in the alternatives of depreciation and appreciation that can readily be demonstrated geometrically. The asymmetry, which is a corollary of the familiar Hicksian stability conditions, can be stated: (a) if a country can improve its balance of payments position by depreciation, the equilibrium exchange rate must be a *stable* equilibrium; (b) if in order to improve its balance of payments position a country must appreciate, this must be a situation of *unstable* exchange equilibrium.[2]

Section I will lay the analytical framework by considering the demand and supply conditions for the imports and exports of a country depreciating its currency. The diagrams of section I will be used to construct different diagrams in section II, which will illustrate the conditions of exchange stability. Section III will consider the stability conditions in terms of elasticities. And section IV will discuss the elasticity of the balance of payments. Metzler has remarked on the complexity of exchange stability theory.[3] It is hoped that this exposition, built upon mathematics less esoteric and more fully presented than that which characterizes the literature, will simplify the crux of existing theory.

I

In figure I, consider the U.K. as the devaluing country and the U.S. as the only other country in question.[4] With a given dollar-pound exchange rate, we may translate pound prices into dollars and measure vertically in terms of dollar prices. Now, assume that

[2] The following analysis is of the usual "partial" type which assumes that there is a single equilibrium exchange rate, even in the unstable case. That is, we are not concerned here with the problem of the limits of possible divergence from the equilibrium rate.

This analysis, like others, is "partial" in another sense: our consideration is the direct price effects of altering the exchange rate, and we omit money income effects, speculative activity in anticipation of exchange fluctuations, government monetary and fiscal policies, and other variables pertinent to a comprehensive treatment. J. Viner (*International Trade and Economic Development* [The Free Press, Glencoe 1952], chap. 2) has criticised such severe abstraction in the literature on this topic; see also A.C. Harberger, "Pitfalls in Mathematical Model-Building," *American Economic Review*, XLII (1952), p. 855–61. We can plead only that our purpose of clarifying some basic aspects of present theory is not inconsequential.

[3] Metzler, *op. cit.*, p. 226.

[4] Cf. Haberler, *op. cit.*, p. 196–99.

the pound is devalued, from a rate of, say, $5 = £1 to $4 = £1.•In our diagrams, the U.S. curves, which are stated domestically (i.e., in the U.S.) in dollar terms, are unaffected. But the U.K. curves, which remain constant in terms of pounds, fall by twenty per cent in dollar figures.[5]

As a result of the pound devaluation, dollar expenditures by the U.K. on imports will normally decline: the quantity of imports falls,

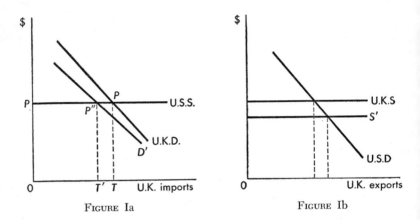

Figure Ia   Figure Ib

and the price falls or, as in the diagram, remains constant.[6] However, dollar receipts from U.K. exports may increase, remain constant, or decrease, as the equilibrium supply-demand intersection moves down the demand curve.[7]

It is the purpose of section II to demonstrate that if dollar receipts increase, or if they decrease less than do dollar expenditures, we have a case of stable equilibrium. If dollar receipts decline more than

---

[5] It is not essential to the analysis that the supply curves be perfectly elastic. If these curves are drawn sloping upward to the right, it is convenient to assume that they are (or are derived from) long-run industry supply curves, and therefore do not fluctuate with changes in output.

[6] We are assuming that a normally shaped U.S. supply curve is accompanied by a U.K. demand curve of normal slope. U.K. expenditures will fall also if the supply curve has a negative slope and elasticity of supply (e_s) is less than one (ignoring signs), and elasticity of demand (e_d) is greater than e_s; or if S has a negative slope with $e_s > 1$, and $e_d < e_s$; or if with D of positive slope, S slopes negatively with $e_s < 1$.

[7] Of course, it is possible also to measure prices in terms of pounds. Then, a depreciation of the pound would involve *raising* the U.S. supply of imports (pound expenditures could increase, decrease, or remain the same) and *raising* the U.S. demand for U.K. exports (pound receipts would increase).

expenditures, so that the U.K. balance of payments position is worse as a result of devaluation, it is a case of unstable equilibrium.

II

The U.K. demand and U.S. supply curves in the import diagram (figure Ia) can be utilized to construct a "demand" curve for dollars in a diagram (figure II) measuring dollars on the horizontal axis and pounds vertically, with the exchange rate indicated by the tangent (or cotangent) of the angle formed by the X-axis and a line through the origin. For example, with exchange rate line OE, the pound price of the dollar is MN/OM, and OM, the number of dollars expended on imports, equals $OPP'T$ in figure Ia. Line OE' represents a depreciated pound, i.e., the pound price of the dollar is higher, and OM' equals $OPP''T'$ in figure Ia. Thus, the commodity import demand and supply curves in figure I are assumed not to shift (except by construction as a result of the devaluation); given these curves, the dollar expenditure will be determined by the exchange rate; the dollar demand curve of figure II is constructed by plotting the appropriate quantities of dollars for alternative exchange rates.[8]

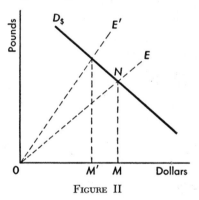

FIGURE II

More generally, a depreciation (appreciation) of the pound will decrease (increase) or leave unchanged import expenditures in terms of dollars; expenditures in terms of pounds may increase, decrease, or remain the same. The normal limiting slopes of the dollar demand curve are, therefore, vertical and that of any line through the origin. (See figure IIIa; the arrows indicate the directions along the curves which one follows in tracing a depreciation of the pound.)

Similarly, a "supply" curve of dollars may be constructed from the U.K. export diagram (figure Ib), showing the effects of pound devaluation upon dollar receipts.[9] A depreciation (appreciation) of

[8] Some may object to calling this a "demand" curve. But the difference between this construction and the usual curve is not conceptually significant. In both types of diagram, three things are shown or derivable: quantity demanded, total expenditure, and the exchange ratio (price).

[9] It should be noted that the dollar-demand curve is also pound-supply, and

the pound will increase (decrease) export receipts in terms of pounds; but the quantity of dollars supplied may increase, decrease, or remain constant. Normally, the limiting slopes of the dollar supply curve are horizontal and that of a curve passing through the origin (figure IIIb).[10]

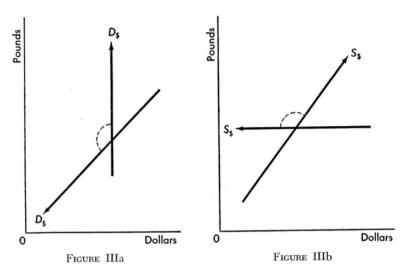

FIGURE IIIa   FIGURE IIIb

Assume, in figure IV, that the exchange rate is indicated by OE, which is below the equilibrium pound price of the dollar, OE'. At

dollar-supply is pound-demand. The schedule derived from the U.K. import diagram is a demand for dollars (needed to pay for the imports) and also a supply of pounds (given in the exchange market, according to the exchange rate, for the dollars); the schedule derived from the U.K. export diagram is a supply of dollars (export receipts) and a demand for pounds (for conversion of foreign currency into domestic).

[10] Haberler employs a diagram (*op. cit.*, p. 195) in which the price of one currency in terms of the other is measured vertically and quantities of the first currency are measured horizontally. This sort of figure has the advantage of familiarity. Our diagrams resemble the reciprocal demand figures common in international trade theory. The major reason for using diagrams measuring quantities of respective currencies on both axes is that it is thereby convenient to measure directly the effects of devaluation (or appreciation) on receipts and expenditures in *either* currency. Our analysis is couched in terms of amounts of the foreign currency. But, as Haberler notes (*ibid.*, p. 197–99), for some purposes one may be interested primarily in the effects in terms of domestic currency. For a discussion comparing these two types of construction in a different context, see my "The Effects on Trade of Shifting Reciprocal Demand Schedules," *American Economic Review*, XLII (1952), p. 135–40.

this low price, the quantity of dollars demanded is greater than the quantity supplied: $OM > OM'$. We should therefore expect that starting with ratio OE in a free market, the ratio would move toward OE', which represents a depreciation of the pound. (If we started with a pound price of the dollar above equilibrium, it would tend to fall.) Depreciation of the pound would improve the U.K.'s balance of payments position; and this is a case of *stable* equilibrium.

In figure V, the slope of the supply curve is algebraically greater than that of the demand curve. Assume again that the exchange rate

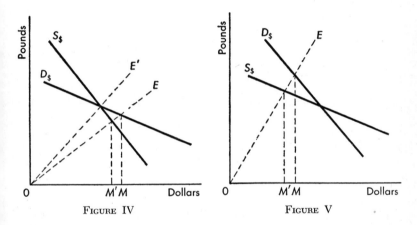

FIGURE IV   FIGURE V

is such that the quantity of dollars demanded is greater than the quantity supplied: $OM > OM'$. But in this case, depreciation of the pound would increase the gap between the quantities demanded and supplied. Appreciation is in order. However, in a free market we should expect the pound to depreciate: this is a situation of *unstable* equilibrium. (Similarly, if we begin with the rate on the dollar below equilibrium, market forces would tend to move the rate still further from equilibrium.) Improving a balance of payments position in a case of unstable equilibrium would involve *setting* the exchange rate at the desired level (i.e., lowering the domestic-currency price of the foreign currency in the illustration, despite the fact that at the original exchange rate the quantity of foreign exchange demanded is greater than the quantity supplied) and *pegging* that level in some fashion.

With normally shaped schedules, we may summarize the slope properties of stable equilibrium as follows: (a) if both the dollar demand and the dollar supply curves have negative slopes, the slope of the latter must be algebraically smaller, with respect to the dollar (horizontal) axis; (b) if the dollar supply curve has a positive slope, the slope of the demand curve, within its normal limits, is immaterial; and (c) if the dollar demand curve has a positive slope, the slope of the supply curve is immaterial. These conditions may be stated more briefly:

slope of $S_{\$} >$ slope of $D_{\$}$ when slope of $S_{\$}$ is positive

slope of $S_{\$} <$ slope of $D_{\$}$ when slope of $S_{\$}$ is negative

III

It is not difficult to demonstrate the stability conditions in terms of the elasticities of the currency supply and demand curves. For this purpose, we define "elasticity" of either the dollar supply-pound demand schedule or the dollar demand-pound supply schedule as the proportionate change in pounds traded corresponding to a proportionate change in dollars.

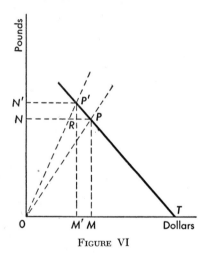

FIGURE VI

In figure VI, P is the point at which we wish to measure elasticity. The original quantities are OM dollars and ON pounds; with a decrease in the dollar price of the pound, the quantities become OM' and ON'.

$$
E_p = \frac{\Delta £}{\Delta \$} \cdot \frac{\$}{£} = \frac{NN'}{MM'} \cdot \frac{OM}{ON} = \frac{RP'}{RP} \cdot \frac{OM}{MP} = \frac{MP}{MT} \cdot \frac{OM}{MP} = \frac{OM}{MT}.
$$

Elasticity will be measured by OM/MT for any slope of either currency schedule if the figures are appropriately labelled, i.e., O is the origin, T is the X-axis intercept of the schedule, and M is on the X-axis directly below the point where elasticity is measured.[11]

[11] This elasticity measure is not identical with that presented by A. Marshall (*Money, Credit and Commerce*, Macmillan and Co., Ltd., London 1923, p. 337, note 1) and others. Marshall's measure, derived for commodity reciprocal demand schedules, indicated the elasticity of import demand with respect to the terms of trade and in our figure would be OM/OT.

With this measure of elasticity, and letting E_s represent elasticity of the dollar supply curve and E_d be elasticity of dollar demand, we have the following stability conditions: (a) when both schedules have negative slopes, E_s and E_d are negative, and *algebraically* $E_s < E_d$; (b) if E_s is positive and E_d is negative, $E_s > E_d$; (c) if E_d is positive and E_s is negative, $E_s < E_d$; and (d) if both E_s and E_d are positive, $E_s > E_d$. This may be more concisely summarized:

$$E_s > E_d \text{ when } E_s > 0$$

$$E_s < E_d \text{ when } E_s < 0$$

These results are consistent with, and add little to, the conclusions reached through the slope analysis of the preceding section. However, it is convenient to deal with elasticities in order to demonstrate relations between the currency supply and demand schedules and the basic "import-export behavior functions" with which we started (figure I).

The following can be derived:[12]

$$E_d = \frac{1 - 1/\epsilon_1}{1 + 1/\eta_2}$$

$$E_s = \frac{1 + 1/\eta_1}{1 - 1/\epsilon_2}$$

where ϵ_1 is the elasticity of U.K. demand for imports with respect to their dollar price; η_2 is the elasticity of U.S. supply; η_1 is the elasticity of U.K. supply; and ϵ_2 is the elasticity of U.S. demand.

On the basis of these formulas for E_d and E_s, we may state exchange stability conditions in terms of elasticities of the commodity supply and demand schedules.

(1) $\epsilon_2 > 1$. In this case, $(1 - 1/\epsilon_2)$ is a positive fraction, and $E_s > 1$; thus, necessarily $E_s > E_d$, for E_d can be no larger than 1. And for stability $E_s > E_d$ if $E_s > 0$.

(2) $\epsilon_1 > 1$. Here, $(1 - 1/\epsilon_1)$ is a positive fraction, and E_d is a positive fraction. If $\epsilon_2 > 1$, then $E_s > 1$, and $E_s > E_d$; if $\epsilon_2 < 1$, then $E_s < 0$, and $E_s < E_d$.

(3) $\epsilon_1 + \epsilon_2 > 1$ in the supply-limiting case when $\eta_1 = \infty = \eta_2$. If $\epsilon_2 < 1$, then $E_s < 0$, and if $\epsilon_1 < 1$, then $E_d < 0$. With both E_s and E_d negative, in the stable case *arithmetically* $E_d < E_s$. And when supply elasticities are infinite, $E_d = 1 - 1/\epsilon_1$ and

[12] See Part A of the Appendix.

$$E_s = \frac{1}{1 - 1/\epsilon_2}.$$

Thus:
$$1 - \frac{1}{\epsilon_1} < \frac{1}{1 - 1/\epsilon_2}$$

$$1 < \frac{\epsilon_2}{\epsilon_2 - 1} + \frac{1}{\epsilon_1}$$

$$1 < \frac{\epsilon_2\epsilon_1 + \epsilon_2 - 1}{\epsilon_1\epsilon_2 - \epsilon_1}$$

$$\epsilon_1\epsilon_2 - \epsilon_1 < \epsilon_2\epsilon_1 + \epsilon_2 - 1$$

$$\epsilon_1 + \epsilon_2 > 1$$

(4) $\epsilon_1\epsilon_2(\eta_2 + \eta_1 + 1) > \eta_2\eta_1(1 - \epsilon_1 - \epsilon_2)$ in the intermediate case in which $\epsilon_1 < 1 > \epsilon_2$ and $\epsilon_1 + \epsilon_2 < 1$ and also in which $\eta_1 > 0 < \eta_2$ but $\eta_1 < \infty > \eta_2$. E_s and E_d are both negative, so arithmetically $E_d < E_s$ in a stable situation.

$$\frac{1 - 1/\epsilon_1}{1 + 1/\eta_2} < \frac{1 + 1/\eta_1}{1 - 1/\epsilon_2}$$

$$\frac{\epsilon_1 - 1}{\epsilon_1} \frac{\eta_2}{\eta_2 + 1} < \frac{\eta_1 + 1}{\eta_1} \frac{\epsilon_2}{\epsilon_2 - 1}$$

$$\frac{\eta_2\epsilon_1 - \eta_2}{\epsilon_1\eta_2 + \epsilon_1} - \frac{\epsilon_2\eta_1 + \epsilon_2}{\eta_1\epsilon_2 - \eta_1} < 0$$

$$\eta_2\epsilon_1\eta_1\epsilon_2 - \eta_2\epsilon_1\eta_1 - \eta_2\eta_1\epsilon_2 + \eta_2\eta_1 - \epsilon_1\eta_2\epsilon_2\eta_1 - \epsilon_1\eta_1\epsilon_2 - \epsilon_1\epsilon_2\eta_2 - \epsilon_1\epsilon_2 < 0$$

$$\eta_2\eta_1(1 - \epsilon_1 - \epsilon_2) - \epsilon_1\epsilon_2(\eta_1 + \eta_2 + 1) < 0$$

$$\epsilon_1\epsilon_2(\eta_1 + \eta_2 + 1) > \eta_2\eta_1(1 - \epsilon_1 - \epsilon_2)$$

(5) $\eta_1 = 0 = \eta_2$. It is apparent from condition (4) that if the supply elasticities are zero—or if either of the supply elasticities is zero—the situation is stable provided only that the demand elasticities are anything greater than zero, for then $\epsilon_1\epsilon_2(\eta_1 + \eta_2 + 1) > \eta_2\eta_1(1 - \epsilon_1 - \epsilon_2)$.

IV

We may extend the analysis to incorporate an explicit formulation of the elasticity of the balance of payments (expressed in dollars, the foreign currency), defined as the proportionate (net) change in dollar receipts (or expenditures) as a result of a proportionate change in the exchange rate.

Refer again to figure I. The elasticity of demand for dollars ($e_\$$) and the elasticity of supply of dollars ($\eta_\$$) *with respect to the exchange rate* can be derived:[13]

$$e_\$ = - \frac{\epsilon_1(\eta_2 + 1)}{\eta_2 + \epsilon_1}$$

$$\eta_\$ = \frac{\eta_1(\epsilon_2 - 1)}{\eta_1 + \epsilon_2}$$

where, as before, ϵ_1 is the elasticity of U.K. demand, η_2 is the elasticity of U.S. supply, η_1 is the elasticity of U.K. supply, and ϵ_2 is the elasticity of U.S. demand. By subtracting $e_\$$ from $\eta_\$$, we obtain the elasticity of the balance of payments (E_{bp}), showing the rate of (net) change in dollars with respect to the rate of change in the pound price of the dollar: [14]

$$E_{bp} = \eta_\$ - e_\$ = \frac{\eta_1(\epsilon_2 - 1)}{\eta_1 + \epsilon_2} + \frac{\epsilon_1(\eta_2 + 1)}{\eta_2 + \epsilon_1}$$

$$= \frac{\epsilon_1\epsilon_2(\eta_1 + \eta_2 + 1) + \eta_1\eta_2(\epsilon_2 + \epsilon_1 - 1)}{(\eta_1 + \epsilon_2)(\eta_2 + \epsilon_1)}$$

In figure IV, a stable equilibrium situation, if we start from equilibrium exchange rate OE' and continuously raise the pound price of the dollar, the excess of dollars supplied over dollars demanded will, at least up to a point, increase; with linear $S_\$$ and $D_\$$, the gap will finally grow smaller and become zero when OE' becomes vertical; with nonlinear $S_\$$ and $D_\$$, the gap need never reach a maximum (until OE' is vertical) nor decrease, but likely the typical case would be first an increase and then a decrease in the gap. There can be similar relationships between the excess of pounds demanded over pounds supplied and depreciation of the pound, but in the linear case the gap would grow ever larger. In any event, with a stable equilibrium case, the excesses of dollars supplied and of pounds demanded will both be positive.

[13] See Part B of the Appendix. These results—but not their derivation—are given in Haberler, *op. cit.*, p. 201, n. Unfortunately, the minus sign in the equation for $e_\$$ is omitted there.

[14] Strictly, this formula is accurate only when there is no net balance in dollars before the exchange rate is altered.

In figure VIIa, horizontally from the origin to the right, we plot excess of dollars supplied; to the left, excess of dollars demanded; vertically upward, excess of pounds demanded; downward, excess of pounds supplied. *OE* represents the equilibrium exchange rate, and *OB* indicates the net changes in dollars supplied and pounds demanded as the pound is depreciated. If the pound is appreciated, we trace *OB'* in the third quadrant. As noted above, *BOB'* may take many shapes (always lying "above" *EOE'*, as in the diagram), but

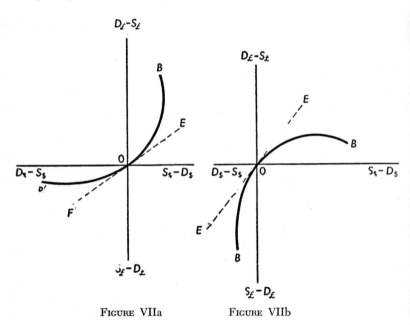

Figure VIIa   Figure VIIb

this general sort of configuration will obtain with $D_\$$ and $S_\$$ curves which are linear or roughly approximate linearity.

For the unstable case (see figure V), we measure pound appreciation in the first quadrant and depreciation in the third. *BOB'* will lie "below" *EOE'*, as in figure VIIb. For example, appreciation will reduce the slope of *OE*, and we move to the right on *OB*, showing a greater increase of dollars supplied over dollars demanded.

Finally, by measuring the elasticity of *OB* (or *OB'*), we are measuring the elasticity of the balance of payments. In figure VIII, consider the solid straight line a tangent to *OB* in figure VIIa at point *T*. Our problem is to measure the elasticity of *OB* (i.e., *VT*) at *T*. An exchange rate line from the origin goes through T; another, representing an appreciation of the pound, passes through X. $\Delta\$/\$ = MN/OM$.

$$\frac{\Delta(£/\$)}{£/\$} = XS/MS = BX/OM.$$

$$E_{bp} = MN/OM \cdot OM/BX = MN/BX = XY/BX = VN/OV.$$

It is apparent that $E_{bp} = \infty$ at the equilibrium exchange rate, falls to zero when OB is vertical, and then becomes negative as OB bends backward. The "optimum" adjustment of the exchange rate, where the excess of dollars supplied is maximized, is established at the level at which "point" elasticity of the balance of payments is zero. But while point E_{bp} may be positive, zero, or negative, "arc" E_{bp}, with the initial exchange rate OE (where $S_\$ - D_\$ = 0$), will be positive in the stable case (unless OE moves all the way to a vertical position, in which case arc E_{bp} is zero).

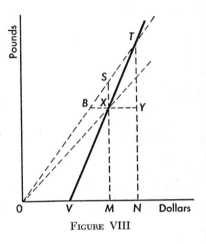

FIGURE VIII

APPENDIX *

A

Consider the U.K. import situation, with equilibrium price and quantity of P and Q before devaluation, and we shall derive the equation for the elasticity of the U.K. demand for dollars, where

$$E_d = \frac{d£/£}{d\$/\$}.$$

Let the price of dollars in pounds be K_0 and then change to K. Define $\rho = K_0/K$, so that $K = K_0/\rho$.

The original import demand function f and supply function g may be approximated near (P, Q) as

* The form of this appendix is a contribution mainly of L.W. MacKenzie.

$$P_d = P + f'dQ$$

$$P_s = P + g'dQ$$

When K_0 becomes $K = K_0/\rho$, the demand function changes from D to D', or f becomes

$$P'_d = \rho P + \rho f'dQ.$$

Put $P'_d = P_s$ and solve for dQ:

$$\rho P + \rho f'dQ = P + g'dQ$$

$$(\rho - 1)P = (g' - \rho f')dQ$$

$$dQ = \frac{\rho - 1}{g' - \rho f'} P \tag{1}$$

The supply function has not moved, so

$$dP = g'dQ = g'\left(\frac{\rho - 1}{g' - \rho f'}\right)P. \tag{2}$$

The rest follows without difficulty:

$$d\$ = d(PQ) = PdQ + QdP$$

$$= \frac{\rho - 1}{g' - \rho f'} P^2 + g'\left(\frac{\rho - 1}{g' - \rho f'}\right)QP \text{ by } (1) \text{ and } (2)$$

$$d\$ = \frac{\rho - 1}{g' - \rho f'} P(P + g'Q)$$

$$d\pounds = K_0/\rho\,(\$ + d\$) - K_0\$$$

$$= K_0(1/\rho - 1)\$ + 1/\rho\, K_0 d\$$$

$$= K_0(1/\rho - 1)PQ + 1/\rho\, K_0 d\$$$

Therefore:

$$\frac{d\pounds}{d\$} = \frac{K_0(1/\rho - 1)PQ}{d\$} + \frac{1}{\rho}K_0$$

And:

$$\frac{1}{K_0}\frac{d\pounds}{d\$} = \frac{(1/\rho - 1)PQ}{d\$} + \frac{1}{\rho}$$

$$= \frac{(1 - \rho)PQ}{\rho\left(\dfrac{\rho - 1}{g' - \rho f'}\right)P(P + g'Q)} + 1/\rho$$

$$= 1/\rho \left(\frac{-Q(g' - \rho f')}{P + g'Q} + 1 \right)$$

$$= \frac{1}{\rho} \frac{P + Q\rho f'}{P + Qg'} \tag{3}$$

Since $£/\$ = K_0$ and thus $\frac{1}{K_0} \frac{d£}{d\$} = \frac{\$}{£} \frac{d£}{d\$}$, equation (3) gives E_d.

Let η be elasticity of supply and e be elasticity of demand. Then:

$$\eta = \frac{P}{Q} \left(\frac{dQ}{dP} \right)_s = \frac{P}{Q} \frac{1}{g'}$$

$$e = \frac{P}{Q} \left(\frac{dQ}{dP} \right)_d = \frac{P}{Q} \frac{1}{f'}$$

And by equation (3):

$$E_d = \frac{1}{\rho} \frac{1 + Q/P \, \rho f'}{1 + Q/Pg'} \text{ dividing numerator and denominator by } P$$

$$= \frac{1}{\rho} \frac{1 + \rho \, 1/e}{1 + 1/\eta} = \frac{1}{\rho} \frac{\eta(\rho + e)}{e(1 + \eta)}$$

Let $\rho \to 1$. Then $E_d \to \dfrac{1}{1} \dfrac{1 + 1/e}{1 + 1/\eta} = \dfrac{\eta(1 + e)}{e(1 + \eta)}$ $\qquad (4)$

Finally, we alter our conclusion by introducing certain economic content, *viz.*, the negative value of the elasticity of demand. By assuming that $e = -\epsilon$, we can later insert the arithmetic values of the demand elasticity in equation (4) without further reference to their (minus) sign. Equation (4) thus becomes:

$$E_d = \frac{1 - 1/\epsilon}{1 + 1/\eta} = \frac{\eta(\epsilon - 1)}{\epsilon(1 + \eta)}$$

B

Our objective here is to obtain an expression for the elasticity of the demand for dollars with respect to the exchange rate, i.e.,

$$e_\$ = \frac{d\$}{\$} \div \frac{d(£/\$)}{£/\$}.$$

Following Part A of the Appendix,

$$d\$ = \frac{\rho - 1}{g' - \rho f'} P(P + g'Q).$$

And $\$ = PQ$. Further,

$$\frac{d(\pounds/\$)}{\pounds/\$} = \frac{K - K_0}{K_0} = \frac{1}{\rho} - 1 = \frac{1 - \rho}{\rho}.$$

$$e_\$ = \frac{\dfrac{\rho - 1}{g' - \rho f'} P(P + g'Q)}{PQ} \div \frac{1 - \rho}{\rho}$$

$$= \frac{\rho - 1}{g' - \rho f'} \frac{1}{Q} (P + g'Q) \frac{\rho}{1 - \rho}$$

$$= \frac{1}{Q} (P + g'Q) \frac{-\rho}{g' - \rho f'}$$

$$= -\rho \frac{P + g'Q}{-Q\rho f' + g'Q} \qquad (1)$$

Recalling that $\eta = (P/Q)(1/g')$ and $e = (P/Q)(1/f')$, and dividing numerator and denominator of equation (1) by P, we obtain:

$$e_\$ = -\rho \frac{1 + 1/\eta}{-\rho 1/e + 1/\eta} = \rho \frac{1 + 1/\eta}{\rho 1/e - 1/\eta}$$

$$= \rho \frac{\eta + 1}{\eta} \frac{e\eta}{\rho\eta - e} = \rho \frac{e(\eta + 1)}{\rho\eta - e}$$

Letting $\rho \to 1$, $e_\$ \to \dfrac{e(\eta + 1)}{\eta - e}$ \qquad (2)

Again defining $e = -\epsilon$, equation (2) becomes:

$$e_\$ = \frac{-\epsilon(\eta + 1)}{\eta + \epsilon}.$$

17. BALANCE-OF-PAYMENTS POLICY AT FULL EMPLOYMENT

Ragnar Nurkse

Columbia University

Excerpt reprinted by permission of the author and of the Harvard University Press from "The Relation Between Home Investment and External Balance in the Light of British Experience, 1945-1955," *The Review of Economics and Statistics*, XXXVIII (May 1956), pp. 121-150; pp. 137-142 excerpted. Copyright, 1956, by the President and Fellows of Harvard College.

At a given level of productivity, a fully employed economy has no possible way of closing a deficit in its foreign balance unless it can cut down its absorption of resources for domestic purposes—that is, for consumption, investment, and government use. A country's net foreign balance on account of goods and services (exports less imports, or $X - M$) necessarily reflects the difference between its aggregate income (Y), derived from its production of goods and services for all purposes, and its aggregate expenditure (E), the volume of goods and services which the country absorbs from all sources for its own uses. The formula $X - M = Y - E$ is an accounting identity and holds true at all times. It acquires pragmatic interest when we impose constraints on it: postulating that $X - M$ be reduced to zero and that Y be kept at the level corresponding to full employment. An improvement in the foreign balance not only implies in logic, but requires in policy terms, a reduction in domestic expenditure relatively to income.

In short, if a country is to live within its export earnings on foreign exchange account it must keep its total expenditure within its income. In an open economy income and expenditure are not necessarily equal. An excess of expenditure over income can persist and will express itself in an external deficit so long as reserves or other means of financing it exist. If action is taken focusing narrowly on closing the external gap alone, excess expenditure may go on but, when thus confined to the home economy, will force up money incomes and prices. A trade deficit constitutes a leakage of purchasing power. If the external escape valve is shut off, the increased pressure in the system cannot fail to affect the home economy in such a way as to reopen the external gap.

Balance-of-payments measures such as import restrictions or exchange-rate changes cannot be relied upon as automatic means of bringing about the required adjustment in aggregate expenditure or, in real terms, of keeping a country's absorption of goods and services within the limits of its total production. Consider import restrictions first. When expenditures on foreign goods are forcibly curtailed it is possible that (a) the money income which consumers spent on them is spent instead on domestic goods and services. In this case the result will be a tendency toward increased pressure of demand in the home market encroaching directly or indirectly on supplies available for export. Some temporary relief may come, it is true, to the extent that the increased demand in the home market is met out of stocks. If these are stocks of imported goods the diversion we have assumed can be postponed as long as they last. If they are home-made goods, action taken to arrest and reverse the unintended inventory drop will spread and possibly reinforce the inflationary pressure. Only in conjunction with some deliberate measure of restraint on total spending can the restriction of imports in this case bring any lasting relief to the balance of payments.

It is conceivable, however, that (b) consumers save that part of their income which they used to spend on imports. If so, the reduction in total spending that is necessary for correcting the trade balance comes about directly as a result of the import controls. Here the balance-of-payments measure produces "automatically" the right effect on the income-absorption relation as well. This is possible; but how likely is it? How much can we expect from it? The answer depends on a great many circumstances rarely considered in the popular discussion of balance-of-payments restrictions on imports. It is easy to see, for example, that if spending on home-produced goods and services is widely restricted by rationing and other physical controls, money previously spent on imports may, as a consequence of import restrictions, now remain unspent.[1] But

---

[1] It may also be confined to spending on various services where, despite full employment, it may not do much harm. But still the foreign balance can improve only in so far as the additional income so created is saved. As a practical matter

when there is freedom from controls in the domestic economy, import controls are much less likely to have any effect on total spending. We may note that this was the case in Britain in 1954–55, when the authorities repeatedly expressed their determination to avoid resort to import restrictions to deal with the setback which then occurred in the payments balance.

In the popular argument, an increase in domestic production of import substitutes is almost invariably presented as a means of improving the foreign balance. Such a shift in production is indeed a common result of balance-of-payments restrictions on imports; but, at full employment, it can only happen by increasing the pressure of demand and weakening the capacity to export. And it is just the wrong result if what is needed is increased saving induced by import cuts. Why this is needed is clear: external balance cannot be attained without bringing aggregate outlay and income into line. The efficacy of import restrictions as a means to this end is limited and uncertain.

Next let us turn to exchange-rate adjustment. However favorable the price elasticities, a devaluation at full employment can be of no use unless in the field of domestic expenditure an act of retrenchment is enforced that serves to make room for an improvement in the foreign balance. (A possible secondary burden due to a worsening of the terms of trade would entail some additional retrenchment.) This does not mean deflation; it means counteracting the inflationary effects of devaluation. If this is done, total money income corresponding to the full-employment level will tend to remain unchanged (and if it does, income elasticities and propensities, when strictly defined in relation to income changes, will be irrelevant). If the inflationary effects of devaluation are not counteracted, any increase in exports or decrease in imports resulting from devaluation must cause inflation of money incomes and prices, leading to renewed weakness in the balance of payments.

This is the so-called "absorption approach" to balance-of-payments analysis. There is nothing new about it: the notion that a country's net foreign balance is necessarily equal to what the country produces *less* what it "absorbs" for its own uses forms a central theme in

---

British experience suggests that not much reliance can be placed on the supply elasticity of dog-racing and other entertainments furnished from a given stock of factors engaged in such activities.

Isaac Gervaise's *System or Theory of the Trade of the World* (London, 1720).[2] Some writers have opposed the "absorption approach" to the "elasticity approach." The opposition seems to me unreal; both are needed. We find, however, one prominent advocate of the absorption approach devoting an excellent paper to a search for *automatic* effects of devaluation on domestic absorption; and these, admittedly, prove to be tenuous, if not actually perverse.[3] But why assume that some self-regulating mechanism of international adjustment *must* exist, if only we could discover it? The conclusion is unavoidable that domestic expenditure must form an essential *policy variable* for the maintenance of external balance.

If contractual income payments such as wages can be kept unchanged, the rise in import and export prices following a devaluation will cut the real purchasing power of these incomes. (The "if" is a big one, though British wage restraint in 1950 is a notable case where the condition was met.) But even this does not guarantee the "disabsorption" necessary for an increase in the trade balance. The income-receivers affected may seek to maintain their consumption by reducing their saving or by dissaving, and moreover they are likely to do so. This possibility figured prominently in the Laursen-Metzler analysis of the terms-of-trade effects of devaluation,[4] but it is not necessarily dependent on any change in terms of trade: it may happen even when export prices rise as much as import prices.

On the other hand, the necessary disabsorption *may* come about even if wage rates are fully adjusted. A wage-price spiral incorporating a wage lag and a shift to profits may after a while grind out enough forced saving to satisfy the income-absorption relationship. But this is likely to spoil the international price adjustment which

[2] See J.M. Letiche, "Isaac Gervaise on the International Mechanism of Adjustment," *Journal of Political Economy*, LX (February 1952). A reprint of Gervaise's pamphlet is now available (Baltimore, 1954).

[3] These are the "cash balance effect," the income redistribution, money illusion, and other direct effects on absorption, which S.S. Alexander discusses in his paper, "Effects of a Devaluation on a Trade Balance," I.M.F. *Staff Papers*, April 1952. "Tenuous" is the adjective which Alexander himself applies to them (page 268), and possibilities of perverse reaction are also recognized (page 273). G. Stuvel's *The Exchange Stability Problem* (New York, 1951), is another work in which an exhaustive search for automatic effects on expenditure proves, on the whole, fruitless: the outcome depends on "the way home demand reacts to changes in incomes and prices" (page 231).

[4] "Flexible Exchange Rates and the Theory of Employment," this REVIEW, XXXII (November 1950).

devaluation was intended to achieve and which remains a prerequisite for its success.

The income-absorption analysis, though its practical emphasis may be on the problem of "living within one's means," is readily applicable to surplus as well as deficit countries—countries that underspend their income as well as those that overspend it. The manner of its application will depend to some extent on the pattern of international balances—on whether, for example, there is a dominant surplus country facing a great number of deficit countries, or one large deficit confronted by many small surpluses. Similarly the analysis can take account of international investment, which in a borrowing country creates a margin for "overabsorption" and "over-importing" and which calls only for a modified definition of external equilibrium (not simply as $X - M$ reduced to zero, but $X - M$ *plus* the foreign borrowing).

The initial assumption of a given level of productivity simplifies discussion but is easily dropped. The secular growth of output due to rising productivity can be substantial even in the short run, from year to year. In Britain it is something that Chancellors of the Exchequer count upon in their annual budget statements. It renders the conditions of external balance less stringent and makes it possible for the income-absorption equation to be satisfied by altering the proportions in which different claimants share in output increments. At a given wage and price level the aggregate money income corresponding to full employment is increased and the deficit country's problem may reduce itself to checking the concurrent growth of domestic expenditure.

H.G. Johnson's recent analysis of the effect of increasing productivity on a country's trade balance [5] has pessimistic implications that seem at variance with those suggested by J.R. Hicks.[6] Clearly, different results are possible, depending on varying circumstances and, more particularly, on the assumptions made as to whether productivity gains are taken out in rising money incomes or in falling prices. I have myself been inclined to think that, apart from the rate of its change, the *level* of productivity and hence of real income per head has also a bearing on the balance of payments.[7] Other things being the same, it should be easier for a country to live within

[5] *Economic Journal*, LXIV (September 1954).
[6] *Oxford Economic Papers*, June 1953.
[7] *Economia Internazionale*, February 1954.

its income if that income is high in relation to (a) past peaks experienced at home (the ratchet effect) and (b) current levels observed elsewhere (the demonstration effect). While other things cannot be relied upon to remain the same, these two factors nevertheless provide grounds for believing that greater productivity tends fundamentally to help rather than hinder a country in maintaining external balance. Yet some control over domestic absorption remains an essential condition.

Reliance on exchange-rate adjustment alone does not fulfill this condition. In particular, exclusive reliance on freely fluctuating exchanges as an automatic means of equilibration seems for this reason mistaken.[8] It does not meet the need for a domestic expenditure policy. But this need arises when there are no idle resources. In an economy in which, by contrast, ample slack exists there may be room for *increasing* domestic absorption and improving the foreign balance simultaneously. In such circumstances the income effects of exchange adjustment, though they generally reduce the power of devaluation to improve the trade balance, need not by any means destroy its efficacy. The frequent neglect of the absorption aspects in postwar discussions of exchange adjustment may be a hangover from prewar depression economics, but such neglect is not permissible in the economics of full employment, in which classical doctrine in more than one respect comes back into its own. In the same way the classical tendency to deny that import restrictions are capable of improving the trade balance is seen to have some validity in an economy at full activity.

It is sometimes argued that a high level of employment means low supply elasticities and therefore tends to make exchange-rate adjustments ineffective. There is no doubt that inelastic supply, though it may be good for the terms of trade of the depreciating country, limits the extent to which international price adjustment can take advantage of elastic demand conditions for the correction of international imbalance. In the analysis of exchange variation a number of

[8] See L. Robbins, *The Economist in the Twentieth Century* (London, 1954), 97-101. A similar view expressed by C.F. Carter with reference to the dollar problem is worth quoting in this connection: "The dollar problem is linked to the desire of non-dollar countries to maintain a standard of living not justified by their productivity. As long as this remains the case, changes in exchange rates do not solve the underlying problem, but shift its stress to a different place." ("The International and Domestic Financial Policy of the United Kingdom," *Public Finance*, No. 3, 1953, 229.)

writers have equated full employment with low elasticity of supply.[9]
But this need not be the case when devaluation is accompanied by
the necessary domestic policies acting on the volume of absorption.
How are we to take these policies into account? How, in fact, are the
two approaches—elasticity and absorption—to be combined on this
point? It cannot be right to suggest, as one writer does,[10] that in the
depreciating country these measures will serve to increase the elasticity of export supply. Elasticity is a functional relationship that
cannot properly take account of policy measures designed to cut

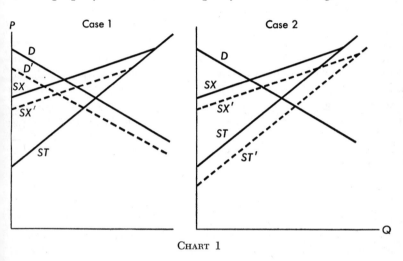

CHART 1

down domestic spending. It is surely better to regard these measures
as tending to lower the country's supply *schedule* of goods available
for export. There are two ways in which this downward shift of
export supply curves can come about (see Chart 1).

1. If the policy cut in domestic expenditure affects directly an
exportable commodity, this means a downward shift in the domestic
demand schedule for this commodity (from *D* to *D'*). The supply
schedule for exports (*SX*) is the total supply of that commodity
forthcoming at any given price (*ST*) *minus* the amount sold at home

[9] A.J. Brown, "The Fundamental Elasticities in International Trade," in
Oxford Studies in the Price Mechanism (ed. T. Wilson and P.W.S. Andrews,
Oxford, 1951), 103–104; W.L. Smith, "Effects of Exchange Rate Adjustments
on the Standard of Living," *American Economic Review*, XLIV (December
1954), 822; G. Stuvel, *op. cit.*, 204–208.
[10] W.L. Smith, *op. cit.*, 822.

at that price (D). The lowering of the domestic demand curve implies necessarily a downward shift in the derived supply schedule of exports (from SX to SX'). At any given price more can now be sold abroad.

2. If the expenditure cut affects home-produced goods that do not enter into the export trade, factors will be released in the domestic industries and will seek re-employment in export industries, for whose products the home demand (D) has not decreased. This forces a downward shift in the total supply schedule of exportable goods (from ST to ST'), and hence also in the export supply schedule of these goods (from SX to SX').

Neither case 1 nor case 2 includes effects of devaluation proper, which will in addition bring upward shifts in foreign demand schedules expressed in domestic currency. For this reason alone it should not be assumed that case 2 must mean an intolerable volume of unemployment; there is a pull as well as a push of resources into export industries. Conceptually, apart from structural maladjustments, a proper combination of devaluation and "disabsorption" can preserve any given degree of employment that may be deemed desirable.

But in reality it is impossible to abstract from the problem of structural adjustment. The lowering of export supply schedules is incomparably easier in case 1 than in case 2. In the latter it depends on inter-industrial mobility of resources and, if mobility is inadequate, will certainly involve some frictional unemployment. It is a considerable advantage for a country like Britain to be able to rely largely on the method of case 1, even though this happens to affect, in the main, the domestic investment sector.

In short, exchange depreciation at full employment when combined with the appropriate absorption measures will cause a shift of demand and supply schedules, and in these circumstances there is no general reason to be afraid of supply difficulties. One arm of the combined operation makes room for the change in commodity flows, the other sets up incentives for the exchange to go ahead. Exchange depreciation under full-employment conditions *without* the complementary expenditure policies is likely to be disruptive of domestic stability and powerless to secure external equilibrium. Reliance on exchange fluctuation alone courts disappointment.

Reliance on domestic expenditure policy alone is liable to conflict with the maintenance of employment. If nothing else happens, the reduction of home expenditure is bound to lower national income below the full-employment mark. External equilibrium could be achieved in this way, but only by sacrificing internal balance. It is clear, therefore, that in general *two* policy handles are required for the simultaneous attainment of the two policy goals of internal and external balance. On the one hand there is need for instruments such as exchange-rate variation, import restrictions, export subsidies, or domestic price reduction. On the other, there must be an appropriate change in domestic outlay.

Here we encounter a fruitful application of J. Tinbergen's theory of economic policy, centering on his distinction between target variables and instrument variables, and on his demonstration that "if more than one target is set, then a like number of instruments will be required." [11] Since in the present case we have two targets—a high level of employment and a net foreign balance of zero—we must make use of two policy instruments, one apparently designed to induce (or force) a change in external transactions, the other to keep domestic expenditure in line with the full-employment level of income. But although we may not be able to avoid using teleological terms and may be strongly tempted to link up each instrument with one particular target, all we can really say is that two policy variables are necessary for the simultaneous attainment of the two goals. As Tinbergen emphasizes, it is not strictly possible to hold the view that each instrument serves one of the goals.[12] In a system with an equal number of target variables and instrument variables a unique solution can be found, but there is complete interdependence between all individual targets pursued and instruments employed.

[11] J. Tinbergen, "The Relation between Internal Inflation and the Balance of Payments," Banca Nazionale del Lavoro (Rome), *Quarterly Review,* October–December 1952. For his general treatment of the subject see J. Tinbergen, *On the Theory of Economic Policy* (Amsterdam, 1952).

[12] As a matter of labelling and classification such measures as exchange adjustment and import restriction can of course be classed as "external," if only because in a closed economy they would be non-existent and pointless. But in an open economy they do affect internal conditions and indeed have sometimes been used for this purpose.

COMMENTARY

The essays in this Part are concerned with the equilibrium rate of exchange—its nature, its measurement, its prerequisites, the mechanisms and policies by which it may be achieved, the consequences of not attaining or maintaining it. Therefore, they consider the exchange rate, not as an isolated phenomenon, but in connection with the balance of payments and in the context of the entire international adjustment mechanism.

PURCHASING POWER PARITY

One approach to both the concept and the measurement of the equilibrium rate of exchange is "purchasing power parity." It is most commonly associated with Gustav Cassel, who expounded the notion in the 1920's. One of Cassel's early statements runs in part as follows:

Our willingness to pay a certain price for a foreign money must ultimately and essentially depend on the fact that this money has a purchasing power as against commodities and services in the foreign country. On the other hand, when we offer so and so much of our own money we offer, in fact, a purchasing power against commodities and services in our own country. Our valuation of a foreign money will, therefore, essentially depend on the relative purchasing power of the currencies of both countries.

Given a normal freedom of trade between two countries, A and B, a rate of exchange will establish itself between them and this rate will, smaller fluctuations apart, remain unaltered as long as no alteration in the purchasing power of either currency is made and no special hindrances are imposed upon the trade. But as soon as an inflation takes place in the money of A, and the purchasing power of this money is, therefore, diminished, the value of the A-money in

B must necessarily be reduced in the same proportion. And if the *B*-money is inflated and its purchasing power is lowered, the valuation of the *A*-money in *B* will clearly increase in the same proportion. . . . Hence the following rule: When two currencies have been inflated, the new normal rate of exchange will be equal to the old rate multiplied by the quotient between the degrees of inflation of both countries. . . . The rate calculated in the way indicated must be regarded as the new parity between the currencies. This parity may be called the *purchasing power parity*, as it is determined by the quotient of the purchasing powers of the different currencies.[1]

It is possible to have a certain amount of deviation from the purchasing power parity:

If trade between two countries is more hampered in one direction than in the other, the value of the money of the country whose export is relatively more restricted will fall, in the other country, beneath the purchasing power parity. This result is only in accordance with our general conception of the rate of exchange as an expression of the valuation of a means of securing the supply of foreign commodities; if this supply is made artificially difficult, the actual value of the foreign currency must sink in proportion.[2]

The Metzler essay (selection 13) notes numerous empirical difficulties and conceptual inadequacies of the purchasing power parity doctrine. The major difficulty is the price data to use, e.g., whether the price indices should include only "domestic" goods or "international" goods or both. The crucial conceptual problem is that the change in the *equilibrium* rate over time may not be accurately indicated by the *parity* calculations: "The virtue of the parity rate," as Metzler puts it, "is that it preserves the earlier real exchange ratio between the goods and services of one country and the goods and services of another. . . . [However] in some circumstances it may be necessary to *change* the real terms of trade between countries

---

[1] Gustav Cassel, *The World's Monetary Problems* (New York: E.P. Dutton and Co., 1921), pp. 36–37; originally written as a memorandum on invitation of the League of Nations for the International Financial Conference in Brussels, 1920.

[2] *Ibid.*, p. 39.

in order to restore a balanced condition in international trade. If this is true, the so-called 'equilibrium' rate of exchange will differ from the parity rate" [our italics]. Nevertheless, as Metzler concludes, despite the serious deficiencies of the purchasing power parity approach, it is useful in special circumstances, notably after a major war during which price levels have drastically changed.

THE "ADJUSTABLE PEG" AND THE INTERNATIONAL MONETARY FUND

Nurkse (selection 14) advocates a system of non-freely fluctuating exchange rates. His proposal is essentially the I.M.F. system of the "adjustable peg."[3]

According to this approach, exchange rates are pegged for indefinite periods, and they are not allowed to change appreciably to correct temporary and cyclical balance of payments disturbances. If the rate is not permitted to fluctuate in such cases and if national income is maintained at a full employment level and also if the price level is kept substantially constant, then a balance of payments deficit must necessitate either (a) drawing down of international reserves or (b) imposing trade restrictions, probably including exchange controls. The avoidance of using exchange controls rests, therefore, on reserves adequate to finance a (short-lived) deficit. But a nation may not be compelled to rely solely on its own reserves: it may borrow from the I.M.F. Thus the Fund is to increase international liquidity and make feasible basically stable exchange rates without undue fluctuations in national incomes and prices or increases in trade barriers.

However, the I.M.F. is not intended to support exchange rates when the balance of payments problem is one of "fundamental disequilibrium." The Fund Agreement does not define

[3] For a recent, brief comment on the Nurkse conception of the equilibrium rate of exchange, see Fritz Machlup, "Equilibrium and Disequilibrium: Misplaced Concreteness and Disguised Politics," *Economic Journal*, LXVIII (March 1958), pp. 15–17.

"fundamental disequilibrium." But presumably a balance of payments deficit which is sizable and persistent can justify devaluation.[4]

Officials of the I.M.F. have explained that "stability of exchange rates does not mean rigidity of exchange rates."

A fixed exchange rate is desirable as long as a country is able to adjust its economy to changes in its real international economic position. But when the adjustments needed in face of a radical change in a country's international economic position cannot be made through home prices and costs, it may be necessary to change the exchange rate. Such a change should not be regarded as meaning the abandonment of the policy of exchange stability but rather the focusing of this policy on a different parity better suited to the new conditions.

The Fund Agreement recognizes that changes in exchange rates can, and under appropriate conditions should, be an instrument of economic policy. It may be preferable for a country to change an unsuitable exchange rate through the machinery of Fund consultation rather than to subject its economy to the risks of serious deflation and unemployment or to impose restrictions that keep imports so low as to endanger its well-being and efficiency.[5]

PEGGED VERSUS FREELY FLUCTUATING RATES

Why stabilize exchange rates in the first place? If rates are free to move in accordance with market forces of supply and

[4] For discussions of the concept of "fundamental disequilibrium," see Alvin H. Hansen, "Fundamental Disequilibrium," pp. 379–383, and Gottfried Haberler, "Currency Depreciation and the International Monetary Fund," pp. 384–396, both in Seymour E. Harris, editor, *Foreign Economic Policy for the United States* (Cambridge: Harvard University Press, 1948). "The fact that the monetary authorities must engage in compensatory financing at a given moment does not mean that fundamental disequilibrium exists. The situation may be temporary. Similarly, the absence of compensatory financing does not mean that there is no fundamental disequilibrium. There may be a strong tendency toward deficit held in check by the imposition of direct controls; or there may be a genuine balance at the moment, but the developing situation may be such that, as it unfolds, the prospects are for large and sustained deficits. Questions of fundamental disequilibrium must by their very nature revolve around prospects rather than a static cross-section of the past." International Monetary Fund, *Balance of Payments Yearbook, 1938, 1946, 1947* (Washington, 1949), p. 23.

[5] *International Monetary Fund Annual Report*, April 30, 1949, pp. 21–22.

demand, we do not have to determine an appropriate rate to peg or distinguish temporary and cyclical balance of payments strains from fundamental disequilibria.

We shall not review the debate between Nurkse and Friedman (selections 14 and 15). However, it may be useful to comment on a few selected points.

In another place, Nurkse states that "it might seem that in practice nothing would be easier than to leave international payments and receipts to adjust themselves through uncontrolled exchange variations in response to the play of demand and supply. Yet nothing would be more at variance with the lessons of the past."

Freely fluctuating exchanges involve three serious disadvantages. In the first place, they create an element of risk which tends to discourage international trade. The risk may be covered by "hedging" operations where a forward exchange market exists; but such insurance, if obtainable at all, is obtainable only at a price and therefore generally adds to the cost of trading. . . .

Secondly, as a means of adjusting the balance of payments, exchange fluctuations involve constant shifts of labour and other resources between production for the home market and production for export. Such shifts may be costly and disturbing; they tend to create frictional unemployment, and are obviously wasteful if the exchange-market conditions that call for them are temporary. The resources would have to be shifted back again once a temporary disequilibrium has been removed.

Thirdly, experience has shown that fluctuating exchanges cannot always be relied upon to promote adjustment. Any considerable or continuous movement of the exchange rate is liable to generate anticipations of a further movement in the same direction, thus giving rise to speculative capital transfers of a disequilibrating kind tending greatly to accentuate any change that may be required for the balancing of normal transactions. Moreover, the normal transactions also may come to be affected by speculative anticipations: a fall in the exchange value of a country's currency may lead to a rise in imports and a decline in exports if traders at home expect the prices of foreign goods to be still higher in the future and if foreign buyers hold off in anticipation of still lower prices as a result of an expected further decline in the exchange. Self-aggravating movements of this kind, instead of promoting adjustment in the balance of payments, are apt to intensify any initial disequilibrium. . . .

Stability of exchange rates has proved essential not only for international economic intercourse but for domestic stability as well. But this does not mean that exchange rates must be kept permanently fixed at all costs. . . .

The general interest may call for an occasional revision of currency values so as to eliminate as far as possible any chronic and structural disparity between price levels and exchange rates in different countries.[6]

Meade agrees that "a serious argument against a system of fluctuating exchange rates is that it adds to the risks and uncertainties of foreign trade." But to say only this

completely ignores the risks to trade which are removed by the adoption of a system of fluctuating exchange rates. If my basic argument is right, we must regard fluctuating exchange rates as an alternative to policies of exchange control and import restriction. For example, in 1951, when the United Kingdom had a balance-of-payments problem, continental producers of many products for our markets suddenly found themselves debarred from sales to us, because we were restricting imports on balance-of-payments grounds. The sterling-franc exchange rate was stable enough, but

---

[6] Ragnar Nurkse, *International Currency Experience* (League of Nations, 1944), pp. 210–212. Cf. *International Monetary Fund Annual Report, 1951*, p. 38: "Those who advocate allowing rates to find their 'natural' level, permitting market forces to determine a rate of exchange that will be stabilized, seek to provide a simple solution for a very complex problem. There is no such thing as a 'natural' level for the rate of exchange of a currency. The proper rate will, in each case, depend upon the economic, financial and monetary policies followed by the country concerned and by other countries with whom it has important economic relationships. If the economy of a country is to adapt itself to a given exchange rate, there must be time for the producers, sellers and buyers of goods and services to respond to the new set of price and cost relationships to which the rate gives rise. This means that in the short run changes in the exchange rate are either no test or a very poor test of basic economic inter-relationships. It also means that whether a given exchange rate is at the 'correct' level can be determined only after there has been time to observe the course of the balance of payments in response to that rate. Moreover, past experience with fluctuating rates of exchange has proved that movements in the rate are significantly affected by large speculative transfers of capital. Consequently countries prefer to make adjustments in their rates of exchange in a manner that will minimize distortions through speculation."

ask the French exporters of tinned peas whether there were any
risks involved in the export trade which they had rather laboriously
built up with this country.[7]

In addition, Meade will not concede that the problem of
exchange speculation necessarily constitutes an argument *for*
pegged rates.

The adjustable peg cannot be operated without exchange controls,
import restrictions, and the rest of the paraphernalia of direct controls, unless the countries concerned have exceptionally large
reserves of gold or foreign currencies. . . .

[In addition to other reasons] very large reserves will be required
because of the pernicious effect which this system is likely to have
on the speculative movements of capital. A country runs into
balance-of-payments difficulties; it looks as if these are likely to be
lasting; it becomes clear that the currency may be depreciated—
perhaps by 20, 30, or even 40 per cent at one fell swoop; it is quite
certain that it will not be appreciated; speculators have every incentive to move out of this currency into others; if the depreciation does
take place they will make a very large profit overnight; if it does not
take place, they will not lose. Meanwhile, the authorities of the
country in question will have to finance this speculative outflow of
funds by a loss of reserves additional to that which is necessary to
finance the current deficit which is the basic cause of the whole
problem. If the depreciation takes place and the speculators bring
back their funds, the monetary authorities buy them back at a much
higher price. No useful purpose has been served by the movement,
which has merely enriched the private speculator at the expense of
the monetary authority.[8]

It may be well to pursue the topic of speculation a bit

[7] J.E. Meade, "The Case for Variable Exchange Rates," *Three Banks Review,*
September 1955, pp. 15–16. Another writer adds: "It should, furthermore, be
stressed that the effects of hedging costs, like those of an increase in transportation costs, are *marginal.* Trade is cut in the least disadvantageous way:
the reduction affects the imports of the commodities whose home-producing
costs are relatively lowest, and the exports of those commodities whose production costs in the export countries are comparatively highest. The same cannot
be said of alternative methods of restricting international trade." Roger Dehem,
"Exchange Rate Policy: Experience and Theory Reconsidered," *Economia internazionale,* V (August 1952), p. 569.
[8] Meade, *op. cit.,* pp. 12–13.

further.[9] Assume that the U.K. balance of payments is in equilibrium with an exchange rate of $4 = £1. Now the equilibrium is upset by a drastic fall in U.S. demand for U.K. goods. The demand for pounds falls, and the rate becomes $2 = £1. But the elasticity of demand for pounds will likely be larger in the long run than in the short: any given fall in the price of the pound will induce a greater increase in the quantity of pounds demanded per time period after some while than is effectuated immediately. In Figure I, D_s is the short run demand curve for pounds; D_l is the (more elastic) long run curve. For any price of the pound lower than $4, the quantity of pounds demanded is greater in the long run.

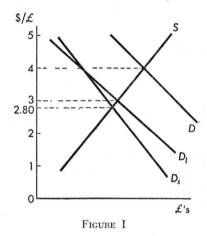

FIGURE I

The exchange rate may quickly fall to $2 = £1, but assume that the long run equilibrium rate is $3 = £1, as indicated in the diagram. *If* foreign exchange speculators feel that eventually the rate on the pound will rise from $2 to $3, they will buy pounds with dollars. Indeed, this speculative demand for pounds could prevent the price of the pound falling as low as $2 in the first place: as soon as it falls appreciably below $3, "it is realized that the value of the pound is abnormally low and that it will recover towards $3 = £1 when the forces of readjustment have had time to operate." [10] Speculators start buying pounds, and the price may be prevented from going below, say, $2.80. Then as time proceeds and the pound depreciation begins to take full effect in adjusting the balance of payments, the rate starts to rise toward $3. The speculators cannot know what the long run equilibrium rate is exactly, so probably be-

[9] The following discussion is based on J.E. Meade, *The Balance of Payments* (London: Oxford University Press, 1951), pp. 218–223.
[10] *Ibid.*, p. 221.

fore the rate reaches $3, they will begin their disinvestment of
pounds, converting back into dollars. This later increased
supply of pounds will slow the movement of the rate to the
long run equilibrium level.

The speculative activity has done three things: (a) it has
reduced the extent of the fluctuation in the rate of exchange,
checking the initial fall in the price of the pound at $2.80
instead of the price reaching $2; (b) it has made the exchange
rate adjustment relatively gradual in moving back up over
time to $3; (c) the original shock to the balance of payments,
when U.S. demand for U.K. goods fell, is eased by the speculative purchase of pounds, for this purchase constituted a "balancing" capital movement to the U.K. Speculation

has greatly eased the balance-of-payments problems of B [the
U.K.]. Capital funds have been temporarily lent from A to B
during the period when there was the maximum strain on B's balance of payments, so that B did not need in that period to generate
so favourable a balance of trade as would have been necessary in the
absence of speculation. This loan has been repaid at a later date
when the mechanism of price adjustment has had time to operate
and when it is, therefore, easier for B to develop the necessary
favourable balance of trade.[11]

Obviously these benefits derive from activities of well-in-
formed speculators. Meade concedes that speculation can be
harmful according to the criteria used above. (a) Speculation
may be "perverse," i.e., operate in the wrong direction. After
the rate on the pound falls from $4 to $2, if speculators feel
that it will continue to move downward they will sell, rather
than buy, pounds. This will, indeed, temporarily push the price
still lower. Speculators will gain if they reconvert from dollars
to pounds before the rate rises—contrary to Friedman's admittedly simplified suggestion (selection 15), it *is* possible for
destabilizing speculative activity to be profitable—but they have
hindered long-run adjustment, increased the degree of fluctuation, and added to the balance of payments strain. (b) Specu-

[11] *Ibid.*, p. 222.

lation may be "grossly excessive," i.e., operate in the right direction but at an inappropriate stage of developments or level of the exchange rate. If, for example, speculators started buying pounds prematurely, before the rate had fallen below $3, the balance of payments adjustment is postponed. Only after the bulk of the speculative "ammunition" had been squandered could the rate fall—and it would fall initially at least to the $2 level which would have been reached in the absence of speculation.

DEVALUATION

With an international monetary arrangement under which exchange rates are essentially stable—as with the gold standard or the I.M.F.—the exchange rate can be a discretionary policy variable to combat balance of payments disequilibria.

The conventional alteration in the exchange rate by a country in (typically deficit) disequilibrium would be devaluation of the domestic currency in the foreign exchange market. Under what circumstances would devaluation be effective, i.e., reduce the deficit (or create a surplus or enlarge an already existing surplus)? It is a temptation to assert simply that the necessary condition for "stability" in the exchange market is that the foreign demand for the country's exports be elastic. If, for example, the English devalue the pound from $4 = £1 to $3 = £1, assuming that pound prices of commodities in England do not rise (or rise proportionately less than the pound itself is devalued), English goods are now cheaper in terms of dollars. And if the U.S. demand for English goods is elastic, American dollar expenditure (English dollar earnings) will increase as the dollar price falls.

An elastic U.S. demand for English goods is, indeed, a *sufficient* condition for stability, but it is not *necessary*. A complete statement of the elasticity conditions of stability must include the English import side of the picture and the supply conditions in the two countries. As the Allen article (selection 16) points out, there are thus four elasticities involved: the elasticities of U.K. supply of (η_x) and U.S. demand for (ϵ_x) English exports, and the elasticities of U.K. demand for (ϵ_m) and U.S. supply of (η_m) English imports.

We have already noted that a sufficient condition for stability is that $\epsilon_x > 1$. Similarly it is sufficient that $\epsilon_m > 1$. Another sufficient (and less exacting) condition is that $\epsilon_x + \epsilon_m > 1$. This is a necessary condition only in the limiting case of horizontal (perfectly elastic) supply curves. Suppose we have the situation of Figure II. When prices are measured in terms of

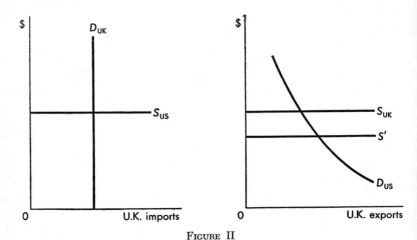

FIGURE II

dollars, the U.S. curves are not affected by devaluation; but the curves of the devaluing country fall at every quantity by the percentage of the devaluation. Since D_{uk} is vertical ($\epsilon_m = 0$), it cannot be shifted downward: the import diagram is unaffected, and the dollar value of U.K. imports remains the same. In the export diagram, the value of exports will increase if the elasticity of U.S. demand (ϵ_x) is greater than one, fall if elasticity is less than one, and remain unchanged if elasticity equals one. For the balance of payments to be improved, the value of exports must rise, i.e., $\epsilon_x + \epsilon_m > 1$.

Devaluation will improve the balance of payments even if $\epsilon_x + \epsilon_m < 1$, provided that supply elasticities are appropriate. To take the simplest type of situation, devaluation will be helpful—as the reader can readily verify by drawing his own diagrams—if *either* of the supply elasticities is zero, and if both demand elasticities are greater than zero. When both demand curves are negatively sloped and both supply curves are positively sloped, the statement of the stability condition is $\epsilon_m \epsilon_x (\eta_m + \eta_x + 1) > \eta_m \eta_x (1 - \epsilon_m - \epsilon_x)$.

These stability conditions are implicit in the equation for the "elasticity of the balance of payments." We may define the elasticity of the U.K. balance of payments in terms of dollars ($E_{bp\$}$) as the proportionate net change in dollar receipts as a result of a proportionate change in the exchange rate. Let $\$_s$ represent dollars supplied (from U.K. exports), $\$_d$ be dollars demanded (to pay for U.K. imports), $\eta_\$$ be elasticity of dollar supply and $e_\$$ be elasticity of dollar demand with respect to the exchange rate, and £/$ be the pound price of the dollar; and assume an initial zero balance on current account.

$$E_{bp\$} = \frac{\Delta(\$_s - \$_d)/\$}{\Delta(\pounds/\$)/(\pounds/\$)} = \eta_\$ - e_\$ = \frac{\eta_x(\epsilon_x - 1)}{\eta_x + \epsilon_x} + \frac{\epsilon_m(\eta_m + 1)}{\eta_m + \epsilon_m}$$

$$= \frac{\epsilon_m \epsilon_x (\eta_x + \eta_m + 1) + \eta_m \eta_x (\epsilon_x + \epsilon_m - 1)}{(\eta_x + \epsilon_x)(\eta_m + \epsilon_m)}$$

Thus, assuming that $\$_s = \$_d$ before the devaluation and letting $K = \Delta(\pounds/\$)/(\pounds/\$)$, a small proportionate change in the exchange rate will result in a proportionate change in the balance of payments equal to $K \times E_{bp\$}$.

The "elasticities" approach is concerned with the direct price, or "impact," effects of devaluation, for it assumes that the commodity supply and demand curves of the two countries remain unchanged in terms of the respective domestic-currency prices. But the immediate effects of devaluation will be modified by repercussions on national money incomes.[12]

---

[12] The following discussion closely follows William R. Allen, "A Note on the Money Income Effects of Devaluation," *Kyklos*, IX (1956), Fasc. 3, pp. 372–382. The article calls attention to the problem of simply adding national income changes to the completed price effects of devaluation when, in actual fact, the price and income effects would be evolving simultaneously and probably modifying each other in the process.

Suppose that supply and demand elasticities are such that devaluation will help the U.K. balance of payments in terms of *pound* values. (If, as we have been assuming, the current account is balanced before devaluation, an improvement in the balance of payments in dollar terms will be improvement in terms of pounds as well.) Then the excess of pounds demanded (by U.K. exporters who wish to convert acquired foreign currency into domestic) over pounds supplied (by U.K. importers in purchasing foreign exchange) represents an "injection" which will induce—in the absence of governmental compensatory policies—a multiplied expansion of U.K. income.

We may use again a model in which $Y = C + I + X$, from the standpoint of income determination, and $Y = C + S + M$, with respect to income disposition. Assume that the marginal propensity to invest is zero, and let ΔX and ΔM be autonomous changes in export and import values resulting directly from the devaluation. Then

$$\Delta Y_{uk} = \frac{\Delta X_{uk} - \Delta M_{uk}}{s_{uk} + m_{uk} + m_{us}\,(s_{uk}/s_{us})},$$

and the multiplier is

$$k = \frac{1}{s_{uk} + m_{uk} + m_{us}\,(s_{uk}/s_{us})}.$$

Assume the following propensities for the two countries:

U.K.: $c = .4$; $s = .3$; $m = .3$
U.S.: $c = .7$; $s = .2$; $m = .1$

Assume further that the pound-devaluation results in an autonomous increase in U.K. exports of 6 and an autonomous decrease in imports (giving rise, it is assumed, to an autonomous increase in consumption) of 4. There is, then, an initial positive trade balance for the U.K. and a negative balance for the U.S. of 10.

The assumed propensities give the U.K. a multiplier of 1⅔ and the U.S. a multiplier of 2. With multiplicands of 10, the new equilibrium income of the U.K. will show an increase of

Table I

Ind ΔC	Ind ΔS	Ind ΔM	Ind ΔX	Aut ΔX	Aut ΔM	Net Δ(X − M)	ΔY
U.K.: $c = .4$; $s = .3$; $m = .3$							
4.000				6	−4	10.000	10.000
8.000	3.000	3.000	−1.000	6	−4	6.000	13.000
9.200	3.900	3.900	−1.400	6	−4	4.700	13.800
9.520	4.140	4.140	−1.590	6	−4	4.270	13.930
9.572	4.179	4.179	−1.699	6	−4	4.122	13.873
9.333	4.000	4.000	−2.000	6	−4	4.000	13.333
U.S.: $c = .7$; $s = .2$; $m = .1$							
− 6.000				−4	6	−10.000	−10.000
−13.000	−2.000	−1.000	3.000	−4	6	− 6.000	−14.000
−15.800	−2.800	−1.400	3.900	−4	6	− 4.700	−15.900
−17.130	−3.180	−1.590	4.140	−4	6	− 4.270	−16.990
−17.893	−3.398	−1.699	4.179	−4	6	− 4.122	−17.714
−20.000	−4.000	−2.000	4.000	−4	6	− 4.000	−20.000

13.333; the income of the U.S. falls by 20. Table I illustrates the paths of expansion and of contraction for several periods plus the final equilibrium values.

With a rise in U.K. income and a fall in U.S. income, the U.K. experiences an increase in induced imports and a decrease in induced exports, thereby reducing her trade balance from the value obtaining directly from the devaluation. The balance falls from 10 to 4 in terms of pounds; the balance in terms of dollars would fall also by 60 per cent.

THE "ABSORPTION" APPROACH TO BALANCE OF PAYMENTS ANALYSIS

The conventional "elasticities," or "supply and demand," analysis of devaluation has been strongly criticized by some. Alexander, who has stirred interest in the "absorption" approach, thus condemns the traditional analysis:

> While supply and demand curves are very useful tools for analyzing the factors that determine price and output for a single good, their value is much more questionable when applied to imports and exports as a whole. . . . The elasticities for which the conventional formulas are valid must be defined as total elasticities and not as partial elasticities.
> Partial elasticities measure the effect of a change of price on the quantity supplied or demanded when all other things remain equal. Total elasticities relevant to a devaluation measure the corresponding relationship when the other things have changed that are likely to change as a result of the devaluation. Accordingly, a total elasticity does not measure the direct effects of price changes on quantity, but the covariation of price and quantity as the whole economic system seeks a new equilibrium. A total elasticity is the ratio of a percentage change in quantity to a percentage change in price. But the percentage change in quantity is the result not only of the price change to which it is related, but also of many other price and income changes which are themselves direct and indirect effects of devaluation. . . . Therefore the total elasticities appropriate for the analysis of the effects of a devaluation depend on the behavior of the whole economic system, and the statement that the effect of a

devaluation depends on the elasticities boils down to the statement that it depends on how the economic system behaves.[13]

Nurkse—who feels (see selection 17) that the opposition between the "elasticity" and "absorption" approaches is "unreal; both are needed"—has furnished us with an excellent introduction to the nature and application of the latter approach.[14] The following remarks illustrate parts of the Nurkse article.

First we may set up a national income model (in which G is government spending and T is tax collections).[15]

If	$Y = C + I + G + X$	
and	$Y = C + S + T + M$	
then	$I + G + X = S + T + M$	
and	$I + G - S - T = M - X$	
or	$S + T - I - G = X - M$	(1)

If	$E = C + I + G + M$	
then	$Y = E + X - M$	
and	$Y - E = X - M$	
or	$Y - C - I - G - M = X - M$	(2)

Between them, equations (1) and (2) give $X - M$ in terms

[13] Sidney S. Alexander, "Effects of a Devaluation on a Trade Balance," *International Monetary Fund Staff Papers*, II (April 1952), p. 264.

[14] For an attempt to join the two approaches in wedlock—although some would claim that the relationship is at best still one of courtship and perhaps one of sinful cohabitation—see Hans Brems, "Devaluation, A Marriage of the Elasticity and the Absorption Approaches," *Economic Journal*, LXVII (March 1957), pp. 49–64.

[15] Nurkse employs the following model:

$$Y = C' + I + G + X - M$$
$$Y = C' + S + T$$

If	$E = C' + I + G$
then	$Y = E + X - M$
and	$Y - E = X - M$

In national income accounting, e.g., by the Department of Commerce, "sources" of national income include *net* exports $(X - M)$. C, I, G, and X are "gross," inclusive of imports, and then M must be explicitly subtracted. For convenience, we assume here that all imports are "consumption" imports: $C' = C + M$. In either the model in the text or the Nurkse model, $Y - E = X - M$. But for purely abstract, as compared to empirical, work, the model in the text appears more straight-forward.

of C, S, T, I, and G. It would be helpful to have C, S, and T in one equation, as we have C, I, and G in equation (2).

Since $\quad C + I + G + X = C + S + T + M$
then $\quad\;\; C + I + G + M = C + S + T + 2M - X$
Since $\quad Y - C - I - G - M = X - M$
then $\quad\;\; Y - C - S - T - 2M + X = X - M$

Assume the following values: [16]

$$Y = C + I + G + X$$
$$160 = 100 + 15 + 25 + 20$$

$$Y = C + S + T + M$$
$$160 = 100 + 10 + 20 + 30$$

Assume that we wish to increase $X - M$ to 0, i.e., eliminate the deficit. We can (a) increase X to 30, (b) reduce M to 20, or (c) alter both X and M so that the combined change is $+10$, where increases (decreases) in exports and decreases (increases) in imports are considered plus (minus) variables.

(a) $\quad Y - C - I - G - M = X - M$
$\qquad 160 - (\quad 130 \quad) - 30 = 30 - 30 = 0$

$\qquad Y - C - S - T - 2M + X = X - M$
$\qquad 160 - (\quad 130 \quad) - 60 + 30 = 30 - 30 = 0$

With Y and M constant, when $X = 30$, the aggregate of $C + I + G$ must fall from 140 to 130. If the decrease in $C + I + G$ falls to any extent on C, to that degree $S + T$ must rise, for $C + S + T$ remains constant at 130; if the entire decrease falls on I and G, S and T (as well as C) remain constant.

(b) $\quad Y - C - I - G - M = X - M$
$\qquad 160 - (\quad 140 \quad) - 20 = 20 - 20 = 0$

$\qquad Y - C - S - T - 2M + X = X - M$
$\qquad 160 - (\quad 140 \quad) - 40 + 20 = 20 - 20 = 0$

[16] In the Nurkse model, we would have:

$$Y = C' + I + G + X - M$$
$$160 = 130 + 15 + 25 + 20 - 30$$

$$Y = C' + S + T$$
$$160 = 130 + 10 + 20$$

When $M = 20$, with Y and X constant, the sum of $C + I + G$ remains unchanged at 140. But $C + S + T$ must increase from 130 to 140. If some of the increase in $C + S + T$ takes the form of consumption, to that extent $I + G$ must fall; if C does not rise, $S + T$ must increase by 10.

(c) $Y \; - \; C - I - G - M = \; X - \;\; M$
       $160 - (\quad 134 \quad) - 26 = \;\; 26 - \;\; 26 = 0$

       $Y \; - \;\; C - S - T - 2M + \; X = X - \;\; M$
       $160 - (\quad 134 \quad) - 52 \; + 26 = 26 - \;\; 26 = 0$

The fall in M requires that $C + S + T$ rise from 130 to 134; the increase in X requires that $C + I + G$ fall from 140 to 134. If C is unaffected, the changes take place entirely in $S + T$ and $I + G$. If C rises, $S + T$ rises by that much less, and $I + G$ falls by that much more; if C falls, $S + T$ rises by that much more, and $I + G$ falls by that much less.

Nurkse postulates that "Y be kept at the level corresponding to full employment." This is logically acceptable and policy-wise highly desirable, but with respect to neither logic nor policy is it necessary in order to improve the balance of payments to some extent. The initial improvement in the trade balance may not be accompanied by adjustments in S, T, I, and G required to keep Y constant. If inflation results, induced changes in imports and possibly in exports will reduce the improvement in the trade balance—but need not eliminate it. Table I illustrates such a case, in which ΔT, ΔI, and ΔG are zero. As in case (c), where (aut) $\Delta X = 6$ and (aut) $\Delta M = -4$, the trade balance is (initially) improved by 10. In case (c), Y is held constant, so there are no income-induced changes in imports and in exports, and the change in the final trade balance is not different from the initial change. But in Table I, income is allowed to rise, and the improvement in the final balance is only a fraction of the initial change. Thus the trade balance can be improved even if inflation is not prevented, but the improvement is smaller, given the initial change, if inflation is allowed.[17]

[17] "For exchange adjustment to be successful, it is essential that the expected

Consider one other matter. The figures we have been using are in terms of the domestic currency, say, pounds. But the relevant export and import figures for balance of payments analysis are in terms of foreign money, say, dollars. An improvement of the trade balance expressed in pounds may or may not be an improvement in dollar value; and even if the balance improves in both currencies, it may or may not improve by the same proportion in both currencies.

This is illustrated in Table II. There we assume that the policy in question is devaluation of the pound. (If the exchange

Table II

	$X_£$	−	$M_£$	=	$B_£$	$X_\$$	−	$M_\$$	=	$B_\$$
1. \$3 = £1	30	−	30	=	0	90	−	90	=	0
\$2 = £1	40	−	25	=	15	80	−	50	=	30
2. \$3 = £1	20	−	30	=	−10	60	−	90	=	−30
\$2 = £1	30	−	30	=	0	60	−	60	=	0
3. \$3 = £1	20	−	30	=	−10	60	−	90	=	−30
\$2 = £1	21	−	29	=	− 8	42	−	58	=	−16
4. \$3 = £1	20	−	30	=	−10	60	−	90	=	−30
\$2 = £1	28	−	38	=	−10	56	−	76	=	−20
5. \$3 = £1	20	−	30	=	−10	60	−	90	=	−30
\$2 = £1	21	−	34	=	−13	42	−	68	=	−26
6. \$3 = £1	30	−	20	=	10	90	−	60	=	30
\$2 = £1	40	−	15	=	25	80	−	30	=	50
7. \$3 = £1	30	−	20	=	10	90	−	60	=	30
\$2 = £1	31	−	18	=	13	62	−	36	=	26

benefits should not be dissipated by an offsetting rise in local prices and costs. It must, therefore, have public support and be accompanied by appropriate fiscal and credit policies. . . . Even if an exchange adjustment is accompanied without a significant rise in prices and costs, it would be futile if the greater demand abroad were not matched by an equivalent supply of exports. Unless home demand is restrained, the expansion of exports, which alone can justify an exchange adjustment, will not be achieved." *International Monetary Fund Annual Report,* April 30, 1949, p. 15.

rate is not altered, i.e., the balance of payments policy is implemented by means other than devaluation, the trade balance will change in the same direction and in the same proportion in terms of both currencies.) It is apparent in case (1) in Table II that if $X = M$ before devaluation and if devaluation creates a surplus in terms of pounds, it creates a surplus also in dollars. Similarly, as illustrated in case (2), if an initial deficit in pounds is eliminated, the same is true in dollars. Also a reduction (but not elimination) of a deficit in pounds will mean a reduction of the deficit in dollars (case 3). However, the converse is not always the case: decreasing the deficit in dollars can mean that the deficit in pounds decreases (case 3), remains the same (case 4), or increases (case 5).[18] Finally, if a surplus in pounds already exists and is then increased by devaluation, the surplus in dollars may increase (case 6) or decrease (case 7).[19]

[18] The devaluation involves an increase in the pound price of the dollar from £1/3 to £1/2, a 50 per cent increase. If the deficit in dollars falls by 50 per cent (as in case 4), the deficit in pounds is unaffected. If the deficit in dollars falls by more than 50 per cent (case 3), the deficit in pounds falls; if the deficit in dollars falls by less than 50 per cent (case 5), the deficit in dollars increases.

[19] The devaluation lowers the dollar price of the pound by 50 per cent. In this instance, if the surplus in pounds increases by more than 50 per cent (case 6), the surplus in dollars also increases; if the surplus increase in pounds is less than 50 per cent (case 7), the surplus in dollars decreases.

V. Multilateralism
and Capital Movements

INTRODUCTION

The first three essays of this Part (by Frisch, Hilgerdt, and Haberler) consider the closely related topics of direct trade controls and discrimination, multilateral exchange, and currency convertibility. The following selections (by Buchanan, Salter, and Nurkse) discuss capital movements—their mechanics, British and American experience, and modern problems and prospects.

EXCHANGE CONTROL

"In a broad sense," Ellis has written, "exchange control embraces all measures directed toward stabilizing the market in foreign exchange."[1] However, the activities of exchange stabilization funds do not involve channeling private foreign exchange transactions through official agencies and are very different in both mechanics and philosophy from the usual conception of "exchange control."

Exchange control, as the term is generally used, involves a government monopoly of dealings in foreign exchange, which may be only an arrangement for centralization and not necessarily result in discriminatory or restrictive action. More severe than a monopoly over the current flow of foreign exchange earnings is government disposition over accumulated private holdings of foreign exchange and assets. As a means of international adjustment—or, more accurately, as a means of avoiding adjustment by repressing some of the consequences of disequilibrium—exchange control "suspends the free market," as Machlup (selection 5) puts it. Exporters may be required

[1] Howard S. Ellis, *Exchange Control in Central Europe* (Cambridge: Harvard University Press, 1941), p. 1.

to surrender receipts of foreign exchange to the government, and foreign exchange is rationed in some (frequently discriminatory) fashion to importers. The government sets official exchange rates and makes transactions at other rates illegal. It may set a number of rates for some foreign currencies, the rate differentials being based on commodities or on nations or both. Sometimes pairs of domestic exchange control systems are linked through bilateral clearing arrangements.

Exchange control may be used in part as an instrument of domestic policy, e.g., to affect the level of economic activity, to protect domestic producers from foreign competition, to obtain government revenue, to extend the general scope of state economic planning. Typically, exchange control has been utilized to "defend" a disequilibrium (generally overvalued) rate of exchange. Ellis generalizes that enforcement of a disequilibrium rate "is almost as ubiquitous a feature of exchange control as the state monopoly in exchange dealing. Indeed, it is difficult to find an example of the latter which does not have as its purpose the maintenance of a rate from which the market would tend to diverge." [2]

Although most systems of exchange control which began in the early 1930's were intended as short-run devices to protect foreign exchange reserves from depletion and exchange rates from "excessive" fluctuations due to withdrawals or "flight" of capital (an outward movement of funds inspired by fear of, say, approaching war or impending domestic economic catastrophe), they tended to degenerate into persistent and less innocuous schemes. Not only may an overvalued rate be defended for essentially "monetary" reasons, including avoidance of inflation, but controls may be extended in scope and purpose as a weapon of commercial warfare affecting the composition or direction of trade. Human ingenuity is well nigh unlimited in devising methods for direct control over foreign trade and investment.

[2] Howard S. Ellis, "Exchange Control and Discrimination," *American Economic Review*, XXXVII (December 1947), p. 879. This article (pp. 877–888) gives a brief survey of the instruments and purposes of exchange control.

It was seen in Part IV (particularly selection 17 and the Commentary) that analysis of balance of payments policy necessitates inclusion of domestic relationships and repercussions. Consider again the following initial situation:

$$(1) \quad Y - C - I - G - M = X - M$$
$$160 - 100 - 15 - 25 - 30 = 20 - 30 = -10$$

$$(2) \quad Y - C - S - T - 2M + X = X - M$$
$$160 - 100 - 10 - 20 - 60 + 20 = 20 - 30 = -10$$

Once more we wish to equate X and M, this time by the imposition of exchange controls and thereby cutting the value of M to 20. We may assume that the controls are effective in thus reducing M. But from this point on in the analysis, there are several possibilities: the reduction in expenditure on imports by 10 may (a) be saved or drained off in taxes, or (b) spent on domestic consumption; and if consumption rises, we may specify that national income either (a) remains the same or (b) rises.

In the first income-disposal alternative, equation (2) becomes:

$$(2') \quad Y - C - S - T - 2M + X = X - M$$
$$160 - 100 - (\ 40\ ) - 40 + 20 = 20 - 20 = 0$$

In the second case, equation (2) becomes:

$$(2'') \quad Y - C - S - T - 2M + X = X - M$$
$$160 - 110 - 10 - 20 - 40 + 20 = 20 - 20 = 0$$

But if now $C = 110$, equation (1) also is affected. If national income is to be held constant (i.e., on the assumption of full employment initially and if inflation is to be avoided), the increase in C must be offset by an equal fall in $I + G$:

$$(1') \quad Y - C - I - G - M = X - M$$
$$160 - 110 - (\ 30\ ) - 20 = 20 - 20 = 0$$

If, however, money income is allowed to rise, equation (1) could—with a consumption multiplier of unity—be:

$$(1'') \qquad Y - C - I - G - M = X - M$$
$$170 - 110 - 15 - 25 - 20 = 20 - 20 = 0$$

And, correspondingly, equation (2) would look as follows:

$$(2''') \qquad Y - C - S - T - 2M + X = X - M$$
$$170 - 110 - (\quad 40 \quad) - 40 + 20 = 20 - 20 = 0$$

Which of these alternatives is fulfilled is scarcely a matter of indifference. Assuming that Y is to be held constant when M is reduced, total absorption in the form of $C + I + G$ must not be allowed to rise. If the money not now spent on imports is saved or taxed away, the fall in imports has no further direct repercussions. But if the cut in imports leads to an increase in consumption, income can be held constant only by an equal reduction in investment plus government expenditure. Probably public authorities did not desire, and possibly did not anticipate, that the import "belt-tightening" would eventuate in a curtailment of capital accumulation or government activity.

We may allow C to rise without a concommitant restriction of I and G, but only by allowing Y to rise. If idle resources exist, this rise in money income will tend to induce a rise in real income. But idle resources did not characterize most economies after World War II, when exchange controls were widely utilized. If the increase in Y is a manifestation of inflation, in itself undesirable, X—which heretofore we have assumed to be constant—will tend to fall, at least in volume. Finally, whether or not inflation occurs, the reduction in imports will possibly discourage exports through induced income effects abroad: reduction of one country's imports is a reduction in exports of other countries, which tends to reduce incomes and thus imports abroad, and a fall in imports by other countries will probably reduce to some extent exports of the first country.

The moral seems apparent that the imposition of exchange control, whatever defense may be made for such policy, is not a conceptually simple operation (and no one claims that it is administratively simple) which is confined in its effects to the foreign trade and exchange markets. The "liberal" or "free market" methods of international adjustment involve the whole domestic economy, and this doubtlessly is the basis for much of the sentiment in favor of exchange control. Such sentiment might be less strong if it were fully appreciated that exchange control, too, involves the whole economy.

It is not inferred that no defensible case can be made in support of quantitative controls on imports.[3] Suppose a nation strives to improve its balance of payments position, i.e., increase the foreign-currency value of its exports relative to its imports, and it has the alternative policies of devaluation and of directly restricting imports. Either policy will hurt, for the volume of goods and services available for domestic use will fall, but it may be that the cost of one policy will be less than the cost of the other.

Figure I gives the U.K. import-export situation in terms of dollar prices. Originally the exchange rate is $5 = £1; now the pound is devalued to $4 = £1, and D_{uk} and S_{uk} fall at each quantity by the proportion of the devaluation. If the elasticity of U.S. demand for U.K. exports (ϵ_x) is unity, the value of exports remains unchanged; the value of imports falls, for the dollar price is constant and quantity is now only OM'.[4] Since the entire balance of payments adjustment is made in terms of imports, we could achieve the same quantitative adjustment simply by restricting imports to a level of OM'. With both devaluation and controls, export value is unaffected, and imports are restricted to OM' at an unchanged price. But there is one difference which provides a basis for preferring controls over devaluation: under controls, the *volume* of exports is unaffected, and under devaluation it increases.

If $\epsilon_x < 1$, the argument is still stronger in favor of controls.

[3] The following discussion is an interpretation of portions of Sidney S. Alexander, "Devaluation Versus Import Restriction as an Instrument for Improving Foreign Trade Balance," *International Monetary Fund Staff Papers*, I (April 1951), pp. 379–396.

[4] Suppose that the elasticity of the U.K. demand for imports (ϵ_m) is one throughout the analysis—although any value greater than zero and less than infinity would do for our purposes. The general equation of elasticity, $\epsilon = dQ/Q \cdot P/dP$, may be written as $\epsilon = dQ/Q \cdot 1/K$, where K is the degree of devaluation and is equal to dP/P. Then $\epsilon K = dQ/Q$. That is, the proportionate change in quantity, $M'M/OM$ in the figure, equals the elasticity of demand multiplied by the degree of devaluation.

Devaluation then would reduce the value of exports, which offsets to that extent the effect on the trade balance of the reduction in import value. Therefore, if the same net effect on the balance of payments were to be achieved through controls, imports could be allowed in a greater volume than under devaluation, e.g., OQ_1 in contrast to only OM'. Controls enable the nation to achieve the same balance of payments improvement as under devaluation, but with a greater volume of imports and a smaller volume of exports.

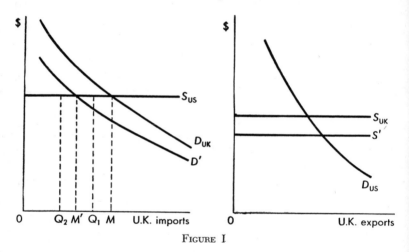

FIGURE I

The situation is ambiguous when $\epsilon_x > 1$. The increase in export value obtained with devaluation must be offset under controls by an equal decrease in import value, i.e., imports must be held to a level below that obtainable under devaluation— $OQ_2 < OM'$.

Table I illustrates these relationships with a series of alternative cases.[5] In each case, the initial situation is one of balanced trade; $\epsilon_m = 1$ throughout, and thus we have the same import situation under devaluation in each case; it is assumed that exports are unaffected under a policy of controls; finally, im-

[5] For purposes of numerical calculation, it is assumed that $\epsilon_x = (Q_2 - Q_1)/Q_1 \div (P_2 - P_1)/P_2$, where Q_1 is the original quantity, Q_2 the new quantity after devaluation, P_1 the original price, and P_2 the new price.

ports are restricted by controls to just that level which will give the same trade balance as could be obtained by devaluation. When $\epsilon_x < 1$ (cases 2 and 3), import volume is greater under controls than under devaluation, and export volume is less (except in case 2, when $\epsilon_x = 0$); with $\epsilon_x = 1$ (case 1), the import picture is the same under both devaluation and controls, but export volume is less under controls; when $\epsilon_x > 1$ (cases 4 and 5), both import and export volumes are less under controls.

Table I

	Imports ($\epsilon_m = 1$)	*Exports*	
1. Initial situation	50 @ \$10 = \$500	100 @ \$5 = \$500	
Devaluation alternative	40 @ \$10 = \$400	125 @ \$4 = \$500	($\epsilon_x = 1$)
Control alternative	40 @ \$10 = \$400	100 @ \$5 = \$500	
2. Initial situation	50 @ \$10 = \$500	100 @ \$5 = \$500	
Devaluation alternative	40 @ \$10 = \$400	100 @ \$4 = \$400	($\epsilon_x = 0$)
Control alternative	50 @ \$10 = \$500	100 @ \$5 = \$500	
3. Initial situation	50 @ \$10 = \$500	100 @ \$5 = \$500	
Devaluation alternative	40 @ \$10 = \$400	110 @ \$4 = \$440	($\epsilon_x = .4$)
Control alternative	46 @ \$10 = \$460	100 @ \$5 = \$500	
4. Initial situation	50 @ \$10 = \$500	100 @ \$5 = \$500	
Devaluation alternative	40 @ \$10 = \$400	150 @ \$4 = \$600	($\epsilon_x = 2$)
Control alternative	30 @ \$10 = \$300	100 @ \$5 = \$500	
5. Initial situation	50 @ \$10 = \$500	100 @ \$5 = \$500	
Devaluation alternative	40 @ \$10 = \$400	225 @ \$4 = \$900	($\epsilon_x = 5$)
Control alternative	0 @ \$10 = 0	100 @ \$5 = \$500	

In cases 4 and 5, the choice between devaluation and controls is clouded, for it consists of choosing between fewer-imports-but-smaller-export-drain (when controls are accepted) and more-imports-but-larger-export-drain (under devaluation). Without further information on preference patterns, we cannot determine which choice is preferable.

We might assume that the initial situation is one of equilibrium in the sense that one dollar's worth of imports is equal in "welfare" terms to one dollar's worth of exports, i.e., the U.K. is indifferent in choosing between one physical unit of imports and two of exports. *If* the $1M = 2X$ welfare ratio remained constant irrespective of changes in trade, then controls would always be preferred to devaluation. For example, in case 4, if we shift from devaluation to controls, 10 more units of imports must be sacrificed, but exports are reduced by 50; if the loss of $10M$ can be compensated by only $20X$, the shift to controls is advantageous. But there is no warrant for assuming that the welfare, or indifference, ratio will remain constant. If, with the trade situation of case 4, the ratio is $1M = 6X$, and thus $10M = 60X$, devaluation is the preferable policy.

Even in cases of inelastic foreign demand ($\epsilon_x < 1$), controls are preferable over devaluation only with respect to certain criteria. We have used the criterion of import and export volumes. According to other criteria, devaluation seems clearly better—particularly the consideration of avoiding bureaucratic direction, minimizing interferences with individual choice (the criterion of maximizing trade *volume* neglects trade *composition*), and, in short, allowing the price mechanism to continue to operate.[6]

CONVERTIBILITY

Traditionally, "convertibility" has referred to the freedom to exchange a currency for gold. Freedom to buy and sell and export gold in any quantity characterized the pre-World War I gold standard, but it does not now prevail. In modern discussions, "convertibility" generally has reference not to conversion between currency and gold, but rather directly between one national currency and another. Thus Ellis speaks of convertibility being "the freedom of any holder of any national currency to exchange it at will at the ruling rate of exchange for any other currency." [7]

[6] *Cf.* Alexander, *op. cit.*, pp. 380, 392.

[7] Howard S. Ellis, "Changing Concepts of Convertibility and the Future of Currencies," *Journal of Finance*, X (May 1955), p. 181. Similarly, convertibility of a currency has been termed "the right of resident and nonresident holders of the currency freely to convert it into any other currency for any purpose whatsoever." "Currency Convertibility," *Staff Papers, Commission on Foreign Economic Policy* (Washington, D.C.: February 1954), p. 466.

Perfectly free, or full, convertibility is basically inconsistent with quantitative restrictions on international payments (exchange control) and incompatible with quantitative restrictions on international trade (import quotas).[8] Free international exchange of goods, services, and securities will manifest itself in a multilateral, not bilateral, trade pattern. By its nature, multilateral exchange requires that a nation use the receipts of its export balances with some trading partners to finance its import balances with others; but for country *A* to use currency earned by exports to country *B* to pay for imports from country *C* necessitates convertibility between the currencies of *B* and of *C*.[9]

Convertibility may be less than "full" and yet exist for some purposes and some traders. Without attempting an exhaustive classification, we can illustrate some of the possible types of convertibility: [10]

[8] "Currency convertibility in the sense of transferability of a currency into all others should never be considered in isolation from the liberalisation of imports. This is not to say that it does not serve any useful purpose unless it is combined with the abolition of quantitative import controls. Even if such controls are in existence, currency convertibility at least permits traders to buy in the cheapest market those commodities which may be imported. Nevertheless the full benefits of convertibility can only be realized if import controls are abolished, so that every importer can buy any amount of goods and services anywhere in the world." Bank for International Settlements, *Twenty-Seventh Annual Report* (Basle: June 1957), p. 205. But it has been argued that if convertibility and the abolition of quantitative restrictions on imports are not to be introduced simultaneously, it may be strategic to achieve the abolition of restrictions first: (a) the elimination of restrictions after convertibility is restored might impose balance of payments strains which would endanger the maintenance of convertibility; (b) restrictions should be early relaxed or abolished so that they may be tightened or restored at a later date in order to protect the balance of payments without cancelling convertibility. See Albert O. Hirschman, "Types of Convertibility," *Review of Economics and Statistics,* XXXIII (February 1951), p. 61.

[9] "Absence of convertibility implies that the surpluses cannot be utilized for the financing of the deficits. Since one country's bilateral deficit is another's surplus, the blocking of a balance somewhere along the line tends to affect settlement within the whole circuit of multilateral payment. Accordingly, instead of having to deal with national payment disequilibria which can be overcome one at a time, this situation presents one indivisible international disequilibrium which is not readily subject to national solution." Willard L. Thorp, *Trade, Aid or What?* (Baltimore: The Johns Hopkins Press, 1954), p. 128.

[10] Hirschman, *op. cit.,* pp. 60–62; Raymond F. Mikesell, *Foreign Exchange in the Postwar World* (New York: The Twentieth Century Fund, 1954), pp. 479–481.

1. Convertibility may be general, or it may pertain to only current account transactions. Many economists favor, at least in principle, the restriction of some kinds of capital movements—especially "disequilibrating" movements and "capital flights"—which they deem undesirable or inconvenient.

2. The convertibility of foreign-owned balances may be general or restricted to current transactions, while domestically-owned balances are inconvertible. Or there may be general convertibility for non-residents and only current-transaction convertibility for residents.

3. Only certain foreign-owned balances may be convertible, e.g., those held by foreign central banks and treasuries, as opposed to foreign residents in general. And the convertibility of foreign official balances may be general or restricted to current transactions.

THE UNITED STATES FOREIGN INVESTMENT POSITION

To accompany the essays by Salter and by Nurkse (selections 22 and 23), we present selected historical data on United States foreign investments. It appears in Table II that the United States international net debtor position steadily grew during the nineteenth century, up to World War I. During the war, the United States shifted from a debtor of nearly $4 billion to a creditor of $3 billion. The decade of the 'twenties saw a further increase of almost $6 billion in the United States net creditor position. The 'thirties brought a severe reversal of this trend; not until 1947 did America regain the dollar net creditor standing of 1930. In Table III, the jump in United States investments and in the United States net creditor position from 1946 to 1947 was mainly in the form of increased government credits and claims. From 1948 through 1957, increases in private investments, particularly direct investments,[11] were the

---

[11] Speaking generally, direct investment is (a) equity capital in foreign enterprises in sufficient volume to give an important voice in management to the investors and (b) foreign branches of domestic companies. Portfolio invest-

major element. But the increase in the United States net creditor position in the post-war period has come about with considerable backing and filling. And while American private investment has not been inconsequential, American foreign lending clearly has not played the conspicuous role since World War II—or at any other time, including even the 'twenties— which was filled by British lending prior to World War I. However, it is worth noting that the *net* creditor position of the U.S. has been determined in large measure by foreign investment in the U.S., which has doubled since 1946 and more than tripled since 1939.

The data of Table IV indicate that American investments in Western Europe, Canada (by far the most important single nation), and Latin America represent over three-fourths of its total, but this is a fall from the 86 per cent of 1946. Investments in the United States from these three areas constitute four-fifths of the total foreign investments in the United States, about the same proportion as obtained in 1946. As seen in Table V, approximately two-thirds of United States direct investments are in petroleum (which has grown dramatically since 1946) and in manufacturing.

---

ment, directed to income and not to control, consists of holdings of securities and other assets which do not confer an important voice in management.

Table II

INTERNATIONAL INVESTMENT POSITION OF THE UNITED STATES, SELECTED YEARS, 1843–1957

(Billions of dollars)

	1843	1869	1897	1914	1919	1930	1939	1946	1956	1957 ᵖ
U.S. Investments Abroad, total	neg	.1	.7	3.5	7.0	17.2	11.4	18.7	49.5	54.2
Private Investments	neg	.1	.7	3.5	7.0	17.2	11.4	13.5	33.0	36.8
Long Term	na	.1	.7	3.5	6.5	15.2	10.8	12.3	30.1	33.6
Direct	na	na	.6	2.6	3.9	8.0	7.0	7.2	22.2	25.3
Portfolio	na	na	.1§	.9	2.6	7.2	3.8	5.1	7.9	8.3
Short Term	na			na	.5	2.0	.6	1.3	2.9	3.2
U.S. Government Credits and Claims*								5.2	16.5	17.4
Long Term								5.0	15.2	15.5
Short Term								.2	1.3	1.9
Foreign Assets and Investments in U.S., total	.2	1.5	3.4	7.2	4.0	8.4	9.6	15.9	31.6	31.4
Long Term	na	1.4	3.2	6.7	3.2	5.7	6.3	7.0	13.4	12.8
Direct	na	na	na	1.3	.9	1.4	2.0	2.5	4.5	4.8
Portfolio	na	na	na	5.4	2.3	4.3	4.3	4.5	8.8	8.0
Short Term†	na	.2	.3	.5	.8	2.7	3.3	8.9	18.3	18.5
U.S. Net Creditor Position	−.2	−1.5	−2.7	−3.7	3.0	8.8	1.8	2.8	17.9	22.8
Net Long Term	na	−1.3	−2.5	−3.2	3.3	9.5	4.5	10.3	31.9	36.3
Net Short Term	na	− .2	− .3	− .5	− .3	−.7	−2.7	−7.4	−14.1	−13.4

ᵖ Preliminary.

* Excludes World War I loans.

† Includes U.S. government obligations in 1946, 1956, and 1957.

§ Given as .5; presumably should be .05.

Sources: United States Department of Commerce, *Historical Statistics of the United States 1789–1945* (Washington, D.C.: Government Printing Office, 1949), p. 242; *idem*, *Survey of Current Business*, August 1956, p. 15; *ibid*., August 1957, p. 23; *ibid*.,

Table III

INTERNATIONAL INVESTMENT POSITION OF THE UNITED STATES, 1946–1957
(Billions of dollars)

	1946	1947	1948	1949	1950	1951	1952	1953	1954	1955	1956	1957 p
U.S. Investments Abroad, total	18.7	27.0	29.4	30.7	32.8	35.0	37.3	39.6	42.2	45.0	49.5	54.2
Foreign Assets and Investments in U.S., total	15.9	16.1	16.5	16.9	19.5	20.6	22.5	23.7	26.8	29.6	31.6	31.4
Net Creditor Position	2.8	10.9	12.9	13.8	13.4	14.4	14.7	15.9	15.4	15.4	17.9	22.8

p Preliminary

Sources: United States Department of Commerce, *Survey of Current Business,* May 1954, p. 12; *ibid.,* August 1955, p. 12; *ibid.,* August 1956, p. 18; *ibid.,* August 1957, p. 23; *ibid.,* September 1958, p. 16.

Table IV

INTERNATIONAL INVESTMENT POSITION OF THE UNITED STATES,
BY AREA, 1946 AND 1957

(Billions of dollars)

	Western Europe		Canada		Latin American Republics	
	1946	1957 p	1946	1957 p	1946	1957 p
U.S. Investments Abroad, total	6.2	16.8	5.6	12.9	4.3	12.3
Private Investments	2.7	6.8	5.6	12.9	4.0	11.0
Long Term	2.3	5.8	5.5	12.5	3.6	9.7
Direct	1.0	4.0	2.5	8.3	3.1	8.8
Portfolio	1.3	1.8	3.0	4.2	.5	.9
Short Term	.5	1.0	.2	.3	.4	1.3
U.S. Government Credits and Claims	3.5	10.0	neg	neg	.3	1.2
Long Term	3.4	9.1			.3	1.1
Short Term	.1	.9				.1
Foreign Assets and Investments in U.S., total	8.3	16.9	2.3	4.8	1.9	3.8
Long Term	4.8	8.7	1.2	2.6	.6	.9
Direct	1.7	3.0	.6	1.6	.1	.1
Portfolio	3.1	5.7	.6	1.0	.5	.8
Short Term *	3.5	8.2	1.1	2.2	1.3	2.9
U.S. Net Creditor Position	−2.1	−.1	3.3	8.1	2.4	8.5
Net Long Term	.9	6.2	4.3	9.9	3.3	9.9
Net Short Term	−2.9	−6.3	−.9	−1.9	−.9	−1.5

p Preliminary
* Includes U.S. government obligations.

Table V

VALUE OF UNITED STATES DIRECT INVESTMENTS
SELECTED AREAS AND MAJOR INDUSTRIES, 1946 AND 1957
(Billions of dollars)

	Total		Mining and Smelting		Petroleum		Manufacturing		Public Utilities		Trade	
	'46	'57	'46	'57	'46	'57	'46	'57	'46	'57	'46	'57
All Areas	8.9	25.3	1.1	2.6	1.8	9.0	2.9	7.9	1.3	1.8	.7	1.6
Canada	2.7	8.3	.5	1.0	.2	2.2	1.2	3.5	.4	.4	.2	.5
Latin American Republics	3.1	8.8	.4	1.2	.8	3.2	.5	1.7	.8	1.3	.2	.5
Brazil		1.3				.2		.7		.2		.2
Venezuela		2.7				2.2		.1		.1		.1
Western Europe	1.8	4.0	.1	.1	.3	1.2	.9	2.1	neg	.1	.3	.3
U.K.		1.9		neg		.4		1.2		neg		.2
Other Countries	1.3	4.1	.1	.3	.6	2.4	.3	.6	.1	.1	.1	.2

Sources: United States Department of Commerce, *Survey of Current Business*, January 1951, p. 22; *ibid.,* September 1958, p. 18.

18. On the Need for Forecasting a Multilateral Balance of Payments

Ragnar Frisch

University of Oslo

Reprinted from *The American Economic Review*, XXXVII (September 1947), pp. 535–551, considerably shortened, by permission of the author and the American Economic Association.

I. THE PROBLEM

In the years immediately following 1929 a spectacular contraction took place in the aggregate volume of world trade. To quote only a single example: In the period 1929–1932 the volume of imports into the United States of crude materials was reduced to something in the neighbourhood of one half, and at the same time the volume of exports of finished manufactures fell to about one-third.[1]

During this period of depression the forms and methods of world trade underwent a significant change. The national governments began to intervene in the affairs of world trade to a much greater extent than before and through new forms and systems. Currency questions were handled with a view to influencing the position of a given country in world trade. Various systems of import and export regulations, many of them in the form of quantitative restrictions, were introduced, and systems of bilateral arrangements based on quotas were developed. At the same time there was a marked tendency toward economic autarchy in a number of countries.

The fact that this element of regulation and restriction occurred simultaneously with the great contraction in world trade, together with the fact that it must, of course, be apparent to each individual exporter or importer that his particular business could be carried on more speedily and more easily if regulations did not exist, is responsible, it seems, for the development of a widespread belief that these

[1] League of Nations, *World Economic Survey 1935–36,* p. 171.

various forms of regulation in themselves are, more or less, the cause of the contraction in world trade, and that therefore the abolition of these regulations is the crucial factor on which maintenance of world trade on a high level will depend.

This conception of the problem is, I believe, fundamentally wrong. It confuses cause and effect. Undoubtedly there are certain types of restrictions which are undesirable from the viewpoint of increased world trade, and some advantage may be gained through negotiations with a view to abolishing them. But such negotiations do not go to the bottom of the problem, and there is a real danger of losing sight of the essence of the problem of world trade if too much energy and effort are concentrated on the abolition of the regulation aspect of the problem.

The problem has also another equally important aspect that must be brought into the foreground and must be faced squarely if the International Trade Organization is to have any chance of achieving a lasting success. The object of the present memorandum is to draw attention to certain points of principle which are pertinent in this connection.

II. THE DEFINITION OF A BALANCE OF PAYMENTS

It will be well to start by making quite clear what is meant in international trade by "payment," "balance of payments" and in particular by "balance-of-payments difficulties." Some of the remarks I am going to make will be more or less familiar to everyone who has been thinking about economics along modern lines, but for the sake of systematization it may be well to state them explicitly.

Barring unilateral transactions such as gifts, deliveries according to lend-lease arrangements and payments of indemnities, any given international transaction may be looked upon as an exchange of two equal values, one moving in one direction and the other in the opposite direction. These values may be of very different sorts: goods, services (of persons, capital goods or financial capital), gold, monetary notes, credit documents or sundry claims whose transfer is technically performed in some other way than by the sending of a credit document.

Therefore, if at any given moment or during any given period, all transactions are included (except the specified unilateral ones), their aggregate for any given country and consequently for any

larger region or for the world as a whole must by definition always
be in balance.

When it is possible at all to arrive at the concept of a "balance"
which for any given country may be either positive, negative or zero,
it is because certain items are purposely omitted from inclusion in
that list of transactions for which the question of balance is raised.
The line of demarcation between what should and what should not
be included must of course to a certain extent be conventional. But
it is fair to say, I think, that in all cases the underlying criterion involved is the degree of liquidity of the things that move. The things
that possess the highest degree of liquidity are excluded. They are
instead considered separately and taken to define "means of payments." Thus, the change that takes place in the holding of such
means of payment becomes the exact counter-picture of the balance
of the aggregate of all the other transactions. In other words, any
of the other transactions that do not pay for one another are to be
"paid for" out of the liquid means.

This being so, the presence of adequate holdings of such means
and a reliable process of replenishing them in due time become
questions of the greatest concern to any country partaking in world
trade. If the holdings are not replenished rapidly enough, the country runs into "balance-of-payments difficulties."

III. THE SPECIALIZATION EFFECT AND THE
PAYMENT EFFECT

The big argument in favour of an extensive world trade is, of
course, that it increases productivity through specialization amongst
countries. Undoubtedly this is a fundamental thing which must be
given due recognition. We may speak of it as the specialization
effect.

Alongside of this we must consider the payment effect. Its nature
may be explained as follows. If Say's famous "law of the markets"
had been true and in particular if it had been valid in international
trade, that is to say if supply in the international market had always
created its own demand, then the specialization effect would have
been the only fundamental factor to consider. But to proceed on this
assumption would be abstractionism beyond excuse. Say's law may
hold good in a barter economy, but it is certainly far from being
true in a world where the system of trading is essentially based on

the distinction between two kinds of value-streams: one that represents something which has "to be paid for" and another that represents the "payment," the latter stream being to a large extent beyond the control of the prospective buyer. Here the balance-of-payments problem emerges in all its seriousness. In this case demand does not come into being spontaneously but is controlled by the concern about how to acquire the liquid values which by definition constitute "payment."

This concern creates a peculiar kind of mechanism which is of paramount importance in determining the ebb and flow in international trade. Under certain conditions it may lead to the monstrous situation where each of the parties in self-defence must refrain from buying the goods and services of the others, because the others in self-defence must refrain from buying the goods and services produced by the first.

This applies both to debtor and creditor countries. When the tension has reached a certain point, the debtor countries (or debtor groups) will try to consolidate their financial position by attempting to pay off debts. And the creditor countries will want to safeguard their financial position by demanding cash reimbursement as loans fall due, or at least, they will want to switch to more liquid investments. At the same time they will try to maintain home employment by impeding imports. All this will create the paradoxical downward spiral where each country, through its efforts to strengthen its own financial position, makes that of the others worse and gradually makes the international flow of goods and services dwindle. This is the "payment effect" in its extreme form.

At the present moment these depressive factors in world economy do not show up to any great extent, because they are counteracted by other factors, particularly by the fact that there is now a shortage of goods and excess demand nearly everywhere as a consequence of the war. But history shows that such periods always give place to periods of excess supply, and then the depressive effects of the maladjustments in international trade will manifest themselves in full if they are not forestalled by appropriate action.

It is no use blaming the individual countries for acting as they do under the influence of the payment effect. Each of them acts as it has to act and it is its duty to act to protect the interest of its nationals. The evil resides in the system itself, in the rules of the game. The main point of issue is not to persuade any particular country or group of countries to make sacrifices for the benefit of the others. But the point is to introduce rationalized methods of transaction that can eliminate as much of the payment effect as possible and thus be of benefit to all parties. To achieve this, the first thing needed is bold and constructive thinking in the light of fundamental principles, and the second is international action based on such thinking.

To approach the problem from this angle consider for a moment what is achieved by a bilateral trade agreement. In order to pass a fair judgment on such an agreement one must keep in mind the payment effect, not only the specialization effect. The bilateral trade agreement has the unquestionable merit of eliminating entirely the strangulation on foreign trade which is caused by the payment effect. This is the *raison d'être* of the bilateral trade agreement. And there can be no doubt about the fact that in the impossible situation that existed in the period previous to World War II the bilateral trade agreements helped to salvage something that would otherwise have been lost.

So far as the specialization effect is concerned the bilateral agreement compares, of course, unfavourably with a multilateral system. But here it must be remembered that we are not interested in the merits of a system with respect to any single one of the two effects, but in its merits with respect to the composite effect. What is desperately needed is a system that is not only multilateral, but at the same time such that it will eliminate as much as possible of the payment effect.

The last qualification is absolutely essential and goes to the very root of the principles on which an international trade organization must be built. It is chimerical to believe that the strangulation produced by the payment effect will be eliminated by lowering tariff barriers and restoring a freer organization of world trade. It is safe to predict that such measures will not have any sizeable influence on the mechanism through which the payment effect operates. With tariff reductions or without such reductions the payment effect will be unfailingly at work and will continue to dominate the whole problem of international trade. From time to time it will continue to create the same kind of bottle neck that it has created in the past. True, some countries will be more susceptible to the effect than others, but all will suffer. To attack the payment effect at the root one must approach the problem from a different angle.

IV. THE TRADE MATRIX

The balance-of-payments problem occupies, and rightly so, an important position in the system of rules that govern the activities of the special agencies connected with the United Nations such as the already existing Monetary Fund and the planned International Trade Organization.

Article 7, Section 3 (a) of the articles of agreement of the Fund provides that the Fund may declare a currency scarce and Section 3 (b) provides that in this case a member country may impose limitations on the freedom of exchange operations in the scarce currency.

Alongside of this should be considered Paragraph 1 of Article 26 of the draft Charter of the ITO which provides that a country that has a deficit in its balance of payments may impose import restrictions. In the subsequent paragraphs and in Article 27 a number of more or less complicated rules are formulated regarding the way in which these import restrictions shall be applied.

The intention back of these provisions is highly commendable. It has obviously been to eliminate the worst manifestations of the payment effect. But the way in which the intention is carried out is not very fortunate. The provisions as now formulated are not only inadequate for the purpose of eliminating the payment effect, but they are worked out on a principle that may intensify this undesirable effect. They treat the problem too much in the one-country-at-a-time manner while the only way in which a basic solution can be found is to treat it as one unified problem concerning the simultaneous adjustment between all countries. In other words, the problem and its solution must essentially be formulated in multilateral terms.

To be specific: The criteria on which a given country should be authorized to apply restrictions on exchange operations or on imports ought not to refer solely to the payment or trade situation of that particular country, leaving the effects of these restrictions to be distributed over the other countries according to some crude proportionality principle. In Article 7, Section 3 (b) of the articles of agreement of the Fund it is stated explicitly that the nature of the limitations shall be no more restrictive than is necessary to limit the demand for the scarce currency to the supply held by or accruing to

Table I

MERCHANDISE TRADE, 1928

(Based on export figures not including transport costs. Tens of millions of dollars according to the parities in force, 1928)

	Importing Country							
	1	2	3	4	5	6		
Exporting Country	Tropics	United States	Regions of Recent Settlement	Continental Europe	Non-Continental Europe	Rest of World	Total	Surplus
1 Tropics	80	165	24	142	75	50	536	133
2 United States	87	0	138	150	86	55	516	121
3 Regions of recent settlement	18	74	22	135	115	17	381	50
4 Continental Europe	91	76	53	663	173	83	1139	
5 Non-Continental Europe	95	23	89	100	39	29	375	
6 Rest of world	32	57	5	81	33	106	314	
Total	403	395	331	1271	521	340	3261	
Deficit				132	146	26		304

Source: the League of Nations publication, The Network of World Trade, 1942 (mainly the work of Mr. Folke Hilgerdt). The figures are arranged differently to bring out the essence of the multilateral balancing problem.

the member in question. And in Article 27 of the ITO draft Charter the proportionality principle is accepted and elaborated upon.

If the restrictions are carried through according to such one-country-at-a-time principles, the result may simply be to shift the difficulty from one point of the system to others. Import restrictions carried out in such a way may throw a previously balanced country out of balance, or worse still, they may deal a blow to some country that is already a deficit country or is striving to repay a previously contracted debt through an export surplus. In other words, international trade would be run directly into a situation where the payment effect was working full blast.

This situation must be faced when the rules and provisions of the ITO Charter are worked out in their final form. The problem of how to construct them is undoubtedly a difficult one but the task must be taken up and at least an approximation to a formulation in terms of multilateral criteria must be attempted.

The work must be based on a thorough study of the structure of the maladjustments as they appear from the multilateral viewpoint. In order to bring out this aspect of the balancing problem it is desirable—one could almost say necessary—to use a particular analytical device, namely the multilateral balance of payments, or, as it may be termed, the *trade matrix* (taking the term "trade" in a broad sense). This matrix is simply a multilateral balance sheet of the form illustrated in Table I.

The figures of Table I represent merchandise movements. This is an important item, but from the viewpoint of multilateral balancing other items must be considered as well. This leads, for instance, to a matrix involving the aggregate of goods and services or to a matrix of total transactions (except the transfer of liquid means of payment). For many purposes a much more detailed geographical classification must, of course, be used than that in Table I. As a rough indication of the international economic structure and as an example of the technique of exhibiting it, Table I may, however, suffice.

If the sum of the elements in a row of Table I is larger than the sum of the elements in the corresponding column, the country (group) in question may be called a surplus country (group). The difference between the sum of the row and the sum of the column for each surplus country has been entered to the right in the table. In the opposite case the country (group) may be called a deficit

country (group): the corresponding difference is then entered at the
bottom of the table. These differences entered to the right or at the
bottom of the table may be called the net marginals of the table, or
for short, the marginals. The sum of the righthand marginals must
obviously be equal to the sum of the bottom marginals. The total of
these sums—in the example, 304—may be called the skewness of the
matrix. More precisely it may be called the absolute skewness. The
ratio of the absolute skewness to the aggregate volume of the table
—that is, to 3261—is the relative skewness, in the example 304/3261
= 9.3 per cent. In a table consisting exclusively of non-negative
numbers (as is the case for a trade matrix) the relative skewness
must be a number between 0 and 100 per cent. It is 0 when and only
when the table is completely balanced, that is when each country
(group) considered as part of the multilateral system is in balance.

A similar table may be put up for the import figures (including
transport costs). It is remarkable that although the elements of the
two tables show considerable differences, the marginals are not very
different.

The skewness as here defined also expresses the amount of outside
value movements that is needed in order to make possible the trade
of the matrix in question. In particular, when the figures in the matrix
pertain to the total of goods and services, the skewness is an expression for the amount of liquid transfers or international lending that
is needed. This is another point which suggests the fruitfulness of
the parameter designated as the skewness, and more generally, the
fruitfulness of a set-up such as the one exemplified in Table I.

A few words may be in order regarding international lending as
a means of making up for the skewness of a matrix of goods and
services. On the one hand there may, of course, be circumstances
under which sizeable international loans may be highly profitable
both to the lending and to the borrowing country. This may, in particular, apply to well-founded long-term developments. The economic history of the United States is an example in point.

On the other hand, there may be circumstances under which there
is less reason for optimism regarding the wholesome effects of
international lending on a large scale. This applies particularly to
the employment problem that confronts us in a world of several
nations wanting to conduct their affairs to a considerable extent on
the *laissez-faire* principle. Even in this case the intervention of international credit will, of course, smooth out a skewness of the trade

matrix and thus temporarily keep things going without trouble. But if the trade skewness is not compensated within a reasonable time by a movement in the opposite direction, the tension is, through the credit system, allowed to accumulate, thus intensifying the difficulties.

Once started, such accumulated tensions will, through their psychological and other effects, tend to create a situation where downward spirals and disastrous payment effects may develop. Such situations one must be prepared to meet, and preparations must be made in advance because the problem of counteracting the vacuum of depression is so much more difficult than the problem of keeping the driving force of an expansion under control.

The essential point to be remembered in this connection is that international lending, if it is to be sound in the sense of not carrying in it the germ of an internationally contagious contraction, must be expressible in terms of a planned timeshift in the import-export balance (or a highly probable forecast thereof). Any amount of skewness in the trade matrix that is accepted must be justified by such considerations. Otherwise it cannot be considered a sound phenomenon. From the viewpoint of a lending country, lending must correspond to an excess capacity to export at the time of lending, and the paying back must correspond to an excess capacity and willingness to import at the time of paying back. And *vice versa* for the borrowing country. When due account is taken of planned or forecasted timeshifts of this sort—barring outright gifts or lend-lease arrangements—a reasonable degree of consistency between demand and supply of goods and services among countries must be achieved. That is to say if we enter such planned or forecasted sound movements of financial capital as items in the matrix, any amount of residual skewness must be considered a danger signal and ought to give rise to efforts at eliminating it.

The balancing of the trade matrix in this sense is a necessary condition for the successful application of a world policy of high and productive employment and of economic expansion. True enough, if sensible counter-depressive policies are applied *within* a given country, the situation within that country—and to some extent, the world situation—may be alleviated. But this can only be a partial measure when substantial maladjustments between the power and willingness to export and the power and willingness to import are allowed to exist. The nature of the maladjustments that may exist multilaterally between the figures expressing these exports and imports is therefore a very essential fact from the viewpoint of economic stability and development, and the structure of the maladjustments in such figures is an important field of study.

V. THE BALANCING OF THE TRADE MATRIX

If a world trade situation, even one of considerable skewness, is left to itself, it will always have a tendency to regress in its own way to a balanced state. And if one is willing to let it do so by the time-honoured method of the downward spiral, there is no need to bother about it. But if this solution is not considered desirable—and the Charter of the United Nations states clearly that it is not considered desirable—then definite regulatory measures must be taken with a view to bringing the trade matrix into balance in such a way as to produce the smallest possible reduction in welfare.

For obvious reasons it will be no easy task to agree upon how welfare is to be measured on an international scale. In the absence of a definite scale of such measurements one will have to be satisfied with a rough indicator of the welfare created by the international trade. The *total* volume of international transactions in goods and services seems to be the nearest one can come to a useful indicator at the present time. The condition of balancing would be then to carry it through in such a way as to maximize total volume of world trade. At least it will be useful to ascertain the main consequences of such a formulation of the problem.

The most desirable solution of the balancing problem is, of course, to find ways and means of making such increases in some of the elements of the matrix as will achieve the balancing. But in many cases increases of sufficient magnitude are not feasible, at least not in the short run, and even if some elements can be substantially increased, such a change may not harmonize with what is needed for a complete balancing of the matrix. That is to say, increasing some of the elements would simply mean changing some of the data of the problem. Having taken account of this change one would again be facing exactly the same type of problem as originally, namely, the problem of balancing a trade matrix by reducing some of its elements. It will therefore always be of considerable interest to study the principles and methods of this kind of balancing.

In practice one would have to consider all sorts of special relations that connect the elements in a given trade matrix. For instance, an import element into a given country may be only a small item so far as value or tonnage is concerned, but it may have a vital bearing on the whole productive activity of the country in question because it represents an indispensable means of production, say lubricating oil. It is outside the scope of this note to go into detail concerning forms and methods of taking due regard of such special relations. But there are certain general principles—one could almost say certain mathematical propositions—regarding the nature of the skewness in trade matrices of aggregate figures that I am greatly concerned in bringing to light. These principles must be kept in mind. They must, in a sense, form the intellectual framework within which the practical solutions are worked out.

The nature of these general principles can best be explained by means of some purposely simplified numerical examples. Consider three countries whose trade matrix is as indicated in Table II.

Table II

UNBALANCED MATRIX
(Global sum 20)

Importing Country

Exporting Country	1	2	3	
1	0	5	1	
2	3	0	2	
3	8	1	0	6
	5	1		6

In this example, countries No. 1 and 2 have deficits in their balance of payments amounting to 5 and 1 respectively, while country No. 3 has a surplus of 6.

In a trade matrix it is always possible to solve the balancing problem simultaneously for all the countries by an application of import restrictions on a proportionality basis. In the example this means that it is possible to find three positive coefficients, less than or at most equal to unity, and such that if all the import figures of country No. 1 are multiplied by the first of these coefficients, all the import figures of country No. 2 are multiplied by the second of the coefficients, and all those of country No. 3 by the third, then the matrix will be brought into complete balance.

The absolute magnitudes of the multipliers are obviously immaterial because if a certain set of them brings the matrix into balance, any set—that is, say, twice the former—must also give a balanced matrix. But if none of the elements is to be increased, this establishes obviously an upper bound for the multipliers. In the example 16/51, 25/51 and 1 form a set of such multipliers. Indeed, if the figures in the first column of Table II are multiplied by 16/51, those in the second by 25/51 and those in the third by 1, we get the matrix of Table III. It can be proved that regardless of how many rows (and corresponding columns) a matrix has, and regardless of how the numbers in it are distributed, if only the elements are non-negative numbers, then a solution of this sort exists.[2]

Table III

MATRIX BROUGHT INTO BALANCE BY USING THE PROPORTIONALITY PRINCIPLE
(Global sum 9.39)

0	$\dfrac{125}{51}$	$\dfrac{51}{51}$		0	2.45	1.00
$\dfrac{48}{51}$	0	$\dfrac{102}{51}$	or in decimal figures:	0.94	0	2.00
$\dfrac{125}{51}$	$\dfrac{25}{51}$	0		2.51	0.49	0

But this method of bringing the matrix into balance may be a very expensive one in the sense that the total volume of transactions is brought substantially down from what it was originally. In the example the total volume of transactions is reduced from 20 in Table II to 9.39 in Table III.

Looking at the figures in Table II, it is easily seen that if we give up the condition of proportionality, we may adjust the matrix in such a way that the total volume of transactions is reduced by a much smaller amount, namely by the total skewness which is contained in the original matrix, that is, by 6. This can be done, for instance,

[2] *Econometrica*, 1934, pp. 275–77. A similar adjustment when account is taken of *priority coefficients* is discussed (under simplifying assumptions), pp. 293–320.

by reducing the figure 8 by 5 and the lower figure 1 by 1. This gives the result shown in Table IV, which is balanced.

Table IV

MATRIX BROUGHT INTO BALANCE WITHOUT IMPOSING THE PROPORTIONALITY CONDITION
(Global sum 14)

$$
\begin{array}{ccc}
0 & 5 & 1 \\
3 & 0 & 2 \\
3 & 0 & 0
\end{array}
$$

In Table IV the reduction in total trade is much less than in Table III. But country No. 3 (the surplus country) may perhaps find it "unjust" that in this case its exports have been drastically reduced while those of the other countries have not been reduced at all. The fundamental answer to this is the following: Even if the proportionality principle had been applied throughout, country No. 3 would have suffered the same total reduction in exports. This is seen by comparing the last row of Table IV with that of Table III. The only "advantage" which the surplus country could have gained by insisting on the proportionality principle would have consisted in the pleasure of also seeing the *others* suffer. Its own fate—at least so far as the *aggregate* export is concerned—would have been the same.

The above example is a very simple one. In particular it is simple in the sense that the balancing can here be carried completely through by what may be called *first order* adjustments, that is to say, by reducing only such elements as have the property of being at the same time an export item for a surplus country and an import item for a deficit country. In this case the skewness of the matrix is reduced by the same amount as the elements themselves. In more complicated cases the situation may be such that this is not possible. Table V is an example of this. In Table V there does not exist any positive item which is at the same time an export item for a surplus country and an import item for a deficit country. Therefore, if the condition is imposed that the matrix shall be brought into balance and no item increased, then it is necessary to reduce one or more of the items for a country which is already in balance.

If one item pertaining to a balanced country is changed, it becomes necessary to change correspondingly one or more of the other items pertaining to that country in order that it shall be kept in

Table V

Importing Country

Exporting Country	No. 1	2	3	4	5	
No. 1	0	30	60	0	100	0
2	30	0	20	0	0	5
3	75	10	0	0	0	0
4	60	5	5	0	5	0
5	25	0	0	75	0	
	0		0	0	5	5

balance. In other words, the kind of operation now to be considered is to reduce *pari passu* both an import item and an export item (or several) of a country which is already in balance, the import item in question being one that comes from a surplus country and the export item in question being one that goes to a deficit country. This is a *second-order* operation. Here the elimination of one unit of skewness in the matrix entails a reduction of aggregate trade by two units. Such a method of carrying the trade matrix towards balance may not be very appealing, but it is necessary if none of the items is to be increased (as will be the case when the possibilities of expansion and sound lending are already taken into account). The question is not whether one likes this way of bringing the matrix into balance or not, but whether the balancing shall be brought about by such a rational measure or whether one shall leave it to be done by the time-honored method of the freely working downward spiral, which may bring the aggregate trade down by a still more considerable amount. As an example of second-order operations Table V may be adjusted in the following way: The export from the surplus country 2 into the balanced country 1 (which in the table is equal to 30) is reduced by 5 and at the same time the export from the balanced country 1 into the deficit country 5 (which is 100) is reduced by the same amount, 5. This will bring the matrix into complete balance, and the aggregate trade is reduced by 10.

Incidentally, Table V shows also another thing, namely that the scarce currency clause may not be sufficient to cover an unbalanced situation. In Table V it was indeed necessary to adjust also a country whose "currency" is not scarce.

In still more difficult cases we may need to go to third-order operations. That is, operations where we reduce *pari passu* three items, a first item being the export from a surplus country into one of two balanced countries, the second being the export from the first of the balanced countries into the other, and the third being the export from the second balanced country into a deficit country. In this case aggregate trade will be brought down by an amount which is three times as large as the amount by which the skewness is brought down. Similarly, higher-order operations may be needed.

Without going into further details it is clear that one cannot, as is frequently done, pass a general and sweeping judgment to the effect that discrimination is always something reprehensible. In particular, one must in many cases admit import restrictions of a non-proportional character. This is necessary in order to assure that the reduction in world trade be rendered as small as possible. To adopt a more flexible attitude towards the problem of how to define permissible import restrictions is, it seems, desirable also for the immediate practical reason that many countries would at the present time probably not be ready to accept the type of rules contained in Article 27 of the ITO draft charter. The very concept of discrimination ought really to be changed. It should be given a multilateral meaning: Those, and only those, operations should be considered discriminatory which tend to work counter to the maximization of total world trade, this maximization being considered in the light of the principles developed above.

In view of the fact that a trade matrix may display many peculiarities so far as its skewness is concerned, and of the further fact that these peculiarities may, each of them, have important consequences for what sort of situation is likely to develop in international trade, it seems that everybody ought to be able to agree upon the desirability of instituting a continuous study—both factual and analytical—of trade matrices of appropriate forms and a regular world-wide dissemination of information regarding the results of this study.[3]

[3] [Note added in the spring of 1958.] The developments of the last years show, I believe, that a study of the trade relations *as a matrix* is more needed than ever before. And action on this basis is vitally important. We are facing a downward spiral and an international scramble for liquidity that cannot be eliminated by conventional monetary weapons. International coordinated action of a new type is immediately needed.

19. The Case for Multilateral Trade

Folke Hilgerdt

Reprinted from *The American Economic Review, Supplement,*
XXXIII (March 1943), pp. 393–407, slightly shortened, by permission of the American Economic Association. At the time of
original publication the author was with the League of Nations.

A WORLD SYSTEM OF MULTILATERAL TRADE

The case for multilateral trade has frequently been argued in
vague and general terms. It is easy enough to point out that the
requirements of any two countries for each other's products cannot
be expected to be equal, and that, accordingly, certain advantages
gained from international trade depend upon triangular or multilateral settlement. But this truth—or shall we call it truism—does not
carry us very far. Nor do the tools of deductive reasoning to which
economists usually have recourse.

In fact, multilateral trade is a subject which can best be approached by statistical research. When we have explored the multilateral pattern or patterns according to which payments among
nations are normally settled, we may be able to consider the case for
multilateral trade in specific terms and with an understanding of the
subject that cannot be acquired otherwise.

Such a study presents no easy task. Each country as a rule exports
on balance to certain countries and imports on balance from others.
As there are some 200 "countries" (or statistical areas) to consider,
the student is faced with what may appear a most confused and involved network of bilateral trade balances. The difficulties of
analysis are increased by statistical imperfections of various kinds,
including the lack of adequate information concerning international
transactions other than trade in goods.

Without pretending that all these difficulties have been overcome,
I am happy to present a few details of an inquiry on multilateral
trade that has been pursued over years.[1] The figures I am going to

---

[1] For more detailed information, see *The Network of World Trade* issued
recently by the League of Nations. It should be observed, however, that the
following pages give certain particulars not included in *The Network of World
Trade.*

show refer to merchandise trade alone, the importance of which in international business transactions is overwhelming; but they give a clue to the manner in which payments on account of other transactions are settled.

One of the chief results of the inquiry was the fact that normally almost all the bilateral balances of trade of almost all countries are involved in what may be called the world system of multilateral trade. When the work started, it did not seem necessary that this should be the case; it was thought possible that the chief balances of trade might be accounted for by triangular or multilateral settlement within smaller groups of countries and that only minor balances might have served settlement among the groups. The fact that all but a few countries partook directly in a world-wide system of settlement naturally stresses the importance of international interdependence so frequently overlooked in the past.

The outline of this system became clear when it was found that almost all countries could be arranged in the order of the direction of their balances of trade, so that each country had an import balance from practically all countries that preceded it in the list and an export balance to practically all countries that succeeded it.

At the beginning of this list we find the tropical debtor countries with export balances in almost all directions, and at the end of it the European creditor countries with import balances from almost all countries, the United Kingdom being the most typical case. But between these two extremes the countries arrange themselves in an order that is not necessarily determined by the absolute or relative magnitude of their total balances of trade.

A synoptical view is afforded by Chart 1, in which countries representing nine-tenths of the world's trade have been arranged in the order just referred to. Only the three largest trading countries—the United Kingdom, the United States, and Germany—are shown separately; the other countries are grouped in three categories: the Tropics, the regions of recent settlement in the temperate belts (including the British dominions, the Argentine, Uruguay, and Paraguay), and Europe with the exception of the United Kingdom and Germany. The year considered is 1928, since in the thirties the system was disturbed by factors which we shall consider later.

The figures in the chart represent the balances of trade, in millions of dollars, among the six specified countries or groups, after the trade values had been adjusted so as to represent "frontier values" in cases where imports are not recorded c.i.f., and certain other minor adjustments made. Of the two amounts shown on the arrow between any two groups, the smaller represents the export balance of the group from which the arrow emerges, and the larger the import balance of the group to which the arrow points. Obviously the inclusion of freight in imports tends to increase the import balances and to reduce the export balances; if freight between the areas concerned were excluded throughout (as, for instance, in United States trade returns) the balance of trade would be about midway between the two amounts shown.

Naturally, the real network of trade balances is more involved than the chart suggests. If we had not grouped numerous countries into

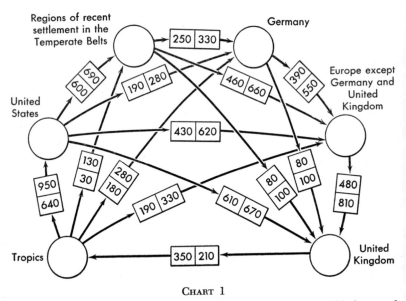

CHART 1

The system of multilateral trade, as reflected by the orientation of balances of merchandise in 1928.

Note. Balances in millions of dollars, calculated from adjusted frontier values of trade (imports valued c.i.f., exports f.o.b.). Both import and export balances are shown; the smaller of the two figures in each square represents the export balance of the group from which the arrows emerge, and the larger figure the import balance of the group to which the arrows point. The difference between the amounts in question is due largely to the inclusion in imports of transport costs between the frontiers of the exporting and importing countries.

three composite categories but shown them separately, the picture would have been more complicated; but it would have afforded the same general impression.

The chief countries omitted from the chart are the U.S.S.R., which in fact entered the system between the "regions of recent settlement" and Germany; China, which if account is taken of "invisible" items and certain imperfections in the Chinese trade statistics, is found to fit in between the Tropics and the United States; and Japan whose international accounts appear to have been settled according to a more complicated multilateral pattern than that of most other countries.[2]

An interesting feature in the system is the manner in which the three principal trading and industrial countries were sandwiched between groups of less important trading countries—the United States between the Tropics and recently settled temperate countries, Germany between that group and the lesser countries of continental Europe, and the United Kingdom between these countries and the Tropics.

The order in which the various countries enter into the system is not due to chance but determined by their climate, stage of economic development, financial position, and consumption habits deeply embedded in their economic structure. If we follow the arrows of the outer rim of the chart, we find that the United States had a big net import from the tropics, due to purchase of products such as jute, rubber, and coffee from countries not very dependent upon United States goods and indeed not able to carry on a bilateral trade with the United States as they required an export surplus to that country in order to pay interest and dividends due to European creditor countries. The United States import balance from the tropics was more than offset by export balances to other countries, particularly the "regions of recent settlement in the temperate belts"— sparsely populated areas, "white man's country," generally rich in mineral wealth, with vast plains suitable for argicultural production and in the process of industrial development. The United States does not import very much from these countries, as in fact she is herself a "recently settled" country with similar natural conditions; but as she is more advanced industrially, she is able to supply them with

[2] Other nontropical countries of Asia and the North-African countries are also omitted from the chart.

motor cars, machinery, etc., required for their development along the same lines as the United States. The regions of recent settlement thus had a net import from the United States and, indeed, from the tropics, paid for by a net export of foodstuffs and raw materials to Germany and other industrial European countries. Germany paid for her net imports from overseas by a net export to the rest of Europe; she was, of course, a net importer of primary goods and net exporter of manufactures of which four-fifths was absorbed by Europe. Other countries of Continental Europe, and particularly northwestern Europe, financed their net imports from Germany and from overseas in part by interest and dividends on oversea investments, but in part by net exports to the United Kingdom, which was a principal market for French fashion textile products, Danish bacon and butter, Swedish paper and timber, etc. It was in the form of such goods that the United Kingdom collected a large portion of the yield of her investment outside Europe and her income from shipping in oversea traffic.[3] Such income from tropical countries was transferred in part by net imports from the United States; on the other hand, the United Kingdom had a net export to tropical countries, as her export industry had adjusted itself to the requirements of these countries during the long period of British capital exports to them.

Most of the trade balances entering into the system served the transfer, along roundabout routes, of payments due to European creditor countries on account of their oversea investments and shipping services performed. But the countries which neither made nor received such payments but were only intermediaries in the transfer were also well served: they found extensive export markets in countries where their own purchases were limited, and they could use the export balances resulting from such trade to finance indispensable imports from countries in which the market for their own export products was limited.

The United States occupies a rather unique position in the system. As the chart shows, her aggregate export balances to nontropical countries far exceeded her import balance from the tropics. This is due in part to capital exports, and in part to the fact that a considerable portion of the export balances to Europe was offset by the expenditures of United States tourists and by immigrants' remittances. In other words, the export balances of the United States tend

---

[3] Or rather, the amount by which such yield and shipping income exceeded net capital exports to oversea countries.

to exaggerate the importance of multilateral settlement.[4] But the direction of the net payments entering into such settlement is correctly depicted in the chart.

HOW THE SYSTEM DEVELOPED

To understand the nature of the system, we must know something of its history. Multilateral transactions probably began as soon as trade developed beyond the stage of primitive barter. But the particular world-wide system just described is not very old. It arose during the last few decades of the nineteenth century and was from the beginning linked up with the transfer of the yield of British investments. As these investments increased and the yield began greatly to exceed new British capital exports, the amounts due by the debtor countries began to be transferred in part through Europe and the United States. Industrial growth in these areas rendered them dependent upon a net import of primary products from overseas, paid for by the excess of exports to the United Kingdom that arose when their dependence upon British manufactures declined. There were rising import balances of the United Kingdom from Europe and the United States from the late sixties to the first World War, in contrast to falling balances from the rest of the world, which had absorbed the bulk of the British oversea investments. The British investments in Europe and, later, in the United States tended to decline and by the twenties represented less than a tenth of the total. The income from oversea investments thus tended to be transferred by net imports from countries other than those in which the investments were made.

During the early years of this development trade became triangular rather than bilateral. The multilateral features of trade appear not to have developed until later. Thus, from the eighties Germany emerges as a separate link in the transfer chain leading to the United Kingdom. The rapid growth of German industry and the ensuing increase in German net imports from continents other than Europe were accompanied by an increase in German net exports, not to the United Kingdom, but to other European countries which in their turn had a net export to the United Kingdom.

[4] The same may be true of the trade balances of certain other countries, particularly Germany. In certain cases, however, the inclusion of "invisible" items would add to the amount liable to multilateral settlement.

A few years after Germany had entered into the system the
"regions of recent settlement in the temperate belts" emerge as a
separate group and enter between the United States and Germany.
Certain of these regions in the Southern Hemisphere—the Argentine,
Australia, New Zealand—profited greatly from the development of
refrigeration rendering it possible to transport fresh meat across the
equator to Europe. But while these countries replaced the United
States as meat exporters to Europe, they used their export surpluses
with Europe for financing a growing import balance of iron and
steel, machinery, etc., from the United States. A similar development took place in Canada—another member of the "recent settlement" group—where the wheat belt was colonized. There arose a
growing United States export surplus to Canada on account of the
sale of railway equipment and other capital goods, though Canada
financed these imports less by the export surpluses resulting from
the sale of wheat to Europe than by capital put at her disposal by
the United Kingdom.

Industry in the United States naturally profited from the acquisition of these new export markets. The United States became a net
exporter of manufactured goods from 1897 and, about the same
time, a net importer of industrial raw materials. The export balance
with the countries of recent settlement thus became largely offset
by an import balance with the tropics. It continued after World
War I and was an outstanding factor in the system of multilateral
trade during the twenties. United States capital exports during that
decade also contributed greatly to the growth of multilateral trade,
as they supplied foreign currency to countries experiencing difficulties in the settlement of their accounts and thus strengthened the
weakest links in the transfer chains depicted in Chart 1.

The development of the system of multilateral trade, accomplished
over a period of a few decades, was similar to the unfolding of a
fan: more and more countries became involved, and their insertion
took place in a given order, each country being further away from
the United Kingdom on the transfer routes to that country from
its debtors. This development was undoubtedly as important to the
growth of modern economy as it was neglected by economists. It is
not by chance that we usually think of this economy as beginning to
develop around 1870—the time when, as we have seen, the system of
multilateral trade came into being—or that it agrees with our notions
that international economy had reached a stage of maturity in the

early years of our century, when the multilateral system had assumed the shape, if not the quantitative growth, that it retained until the early thirties.

During the thirties the system was largely disorganized. Debt service payments were in part "shortcircuited"; the previous export balance of the United Kingdom to the tropical group was replaced by an import balance, and the whole superstructure of roundabout transfer was radically reduced. It is usual to attribute the disorganization of trade to the restrictive commercial policy, to clearing agreements, and to other devices aiming at bilateralism. Apparently the depreciation of sterling and the introduction of protective tariffs in the United Kingdom caused a change in commercial policy the world over, for no sooner had these measures been taken than there sprang up, almost overnight, a rich vegetation of trade restrictions in almost all countries directly or indirectly affected by the decline in the British import surplus from Europe.

But let us make no mistake about the causation. The changes in monetary and commercial policy were not causes; they were *results* of disturbances in international finance that culminated in the financial crisis of 1931. The economic and monetary instability after World War I had given rise to big international movements of "hot money" either seeking speculative gain or simply seeking to avoid loss. French funds alone, invested in the big international money markets and re-lent through them to debtor countries all over the world, equaled several billion dollars. A large-scale withdrawal of these funds was initiated when the French franc was legally stabilized in June, 1928, and continued unabated until the crisis occurred in 1931. Let us consider what takes place when short-term capital is being rapidly withdrawn from a country. The currency derived from that country's export surpluses in certain directions is being transferred abroad in the liquidation of debt and thus cannot fulfill its usual function of financing import balances in other directions. The currency situation thus tightens both in the country in question and in those from which it used to derive its net imports. In such a situation it is customary to have recourse to measures of commercial policy. But because of fear of retaliation, countries usually avoid imposing import restrictions on manufactured goods or foodstuffs from a country with which they enjoy an export surplus. If a country A reduces its import balance from country B, the latter cannot retaliate but must reduce its imports from country C, with which it has an import balance, and so on. Thus, the restrictions, spreading like wildfire, aim directly at reducing bilateral balances, and countries tie each other by ties which they cannot loosen by either unilateral or bilateral action. Equalization of trade balances in one direction entails equilization in others. This was, briefly, what happened during the early thirties, and there resulted a general economic warfare which lasted until the war broke out.

THE CASE FOR MULTILATERAL TRADE

So much about the system of multilateral trade, its organization, its development and decay. Even the short summary made permits of drawing significant conclusions concerning the case for multilateral trade.

One thing is obvious from the outset. The problem that confronts us is not concerned primarily with the necessity of multilateral trade for any particular country, for the supply of any particular article, or for the satisfaction of any particular demand. Nor do we wish to discuss the desirability of multilateral transactions in general terms, but rather the case for a well-defined system of multilateral settlement embracing all important trading countries. Briefly, the problem is one of world economic equilibrium. The history of the thirties has given us a clear example of the effects upon monetary, financial, economic, and political relationships among nations that occur when the system of multilateral trade is disturbed. I shall deal briefly with these various aspects.

MONETARY ASPECT

The minimum required for international monetary equilibrium, besides a certain degree of exchange stability, is a uniform valuation of each currency in all foreign markets; that is, local differences in the supply of and demand for each currency should be overcome through arbitrage transactions. But we must always keep in mind that currency arbitrage is only apparently a question of banking operations. Let us suppose that there is an excess of A currency in country B and a deficiency of the same magnitude in country C. Normally, the exchange value of A currency will nevertheless be the same in B and C, for B is likely to sell its surplus to C, *provided,* however, that *C* can pay by a net export of goods, services, gold, or securities to *B* or to other countries which, in their turn, export on balance to *B*. Currency transactions, if they are not compensatory, do not settle anything; they are only the reflection of the parallel exchange of goods or other wealth.

Our argument thus runs as follows: (1) uniform valuation in different markets of each currency is a primary condition for international monetary equilibrium; (2) such valuation is possible only if each currency can be freely turned into any other currency at nondiscriminatory rates of exchange; (3) but such currency operations are possible only through the multilateral exchange of goods, services, etc., of which they form the counterpart.

Thus, the blocking of the channels of multilateral trade is not compatible with the application of a world-wide system of nondiscriminatory exchange rates for all currencies; it implies, for instance, the sort of chaos in international monetary relationships that existed in the thirties, when countries applying exchange control in fact, if not always in form, maintained different rates of exchange for different types of transactions or even for trade with different countries. It is easy to see why certain countries should have recourse to exchange control when their currency is exposed to pressure. Given that the natural tendency of each country is to have export balances in certain directions offset by import balances (or debt service obligations) in others, such pressure is likely to be felt only in their business relations with certain countries. This is just a situation in which nondiscriminatory currency depreciation, as an alternative to exchange control, may appear uneconomical.

In view of what has been said, it is no wonder that the world-wide application of the gold standard—which we are accustomed to associate not only with exchange stability but also with the feasibility of free transfer from one currency to another—covers the same period as the world system of multilateral trade which we have examined; namely from the early seventies [5] to 1931, with the exception of World War I and the years immediately following it.

Exchange stability is not a prerequisite for international monetary equilibrium of the same kind as uniformity of exchange rates applied in different markets. Its importance is more indirect but

[5] More exactly, 1873; cf. William Adams Brown, Jr., *The International Gold Standard Reinterpreted*, 1914–34, Vol. I, p. xv.

may be as great, as we saw from our historical analysis. The lack of exchange stability is likely to lead to the formation of speculative migratory funds the withdrawal of which may disturb the system of multilateral trade, as it did around 1930.

FINANCIAL ASPECT

As we have seen, interest and dividends due from overseas to European creditor countries are normally transferred through multilateral trade. Blocking of such trade accordingly hinders the transfer of capital yields, except insofar as trade channels can be diverted so as to permit of transfer in bilateral transactions between debtor and creditor country. To achieve this, the creditor country may endeavor to increase its import from the debtor country, or to reduce its export to it. An increase in imports is generally limited, for the investments had generally served the development of the debtor country's export to the world market. With the best will in the world, the United Kingdom and the Netherlands, for example, would not have been able to absorb more than a fraction of the rubber exported by the Netherlands Indies and British Malaya, two-thirds of which normally went to the United States. But even a reduction in exports from creditor to debtor country has its limits, besides being of great concern to the export industry. From the experience gained during the thirties, we know that creditor countries are by no means willing to sacrifice their export industry; rather, in the conflict between financial and economic interests, they are likely to sacrifice the financial. But even if they do not, the transferable yield of investments is likely to decline.

When such a decline occurs, the market value of direct investments decreases, and investments in bonds are likely to be repudiated, as happened on a large scale in the thirties. Consequently, it does not pay to make new investments, and a tendency arises to liquidate outstanding investments, even at a loss. The development of world resources by means of capital from the wealthier countries ceases, a condition which, sooner or later, will affect all countries. The rapid and general economic progress of the period 1870–1930 would not have been possible had not the system of multilateral trade facilitated the development of production in economically young countries with the aid of foreign capital.

ECONOMIC ASPECTS

We just mentioned that in the creditor countries not only finance but also the export industry is affected by the disorganization of the system of mutlilateral trade. More obvious, however, are the effects upon the economies of several countries situated along the round-about transfer routes between debtor and creditor countries. As their export balances towards the countries on the right of Chart I are reduced or disappear they can no longer finance their import balances from countries shown to the left. As the latter countries (particularly the tropics and the "regions of recent settlement in the temperate belts") are the chief suppliers of primary products, there arises the problem of commercial access to raw materials which overshadowed commercial and political relations during the thirties. In the light of our analysis this problem is reduced simply to one of maintaining a working system of multilateral trade.

As the monetary demand for primary products which many countries can exercise in the world market is thus reduced, the prices of such goods decline and unsalable stocks pile up in the exporting countries. This increase in stocks and the inability of other countries to buy are two sides of the same phenomenon. The price fall naturally spreads from international to national markets. As long as only primary goods decline in price, a boom tendency may be released in industrial countries, owing to the widening producer's margin between the cost of raw materials and the price of the finished product. But when the price fall spreads to finished goods, an industrial depression is likely to set in, and all branches of economic and financial life are affected. In such a situation countries are likely to protect their national price level by means of import restrictions.

SOME ASPECTS OF COMMERCIAL AND GENERAL POLICY

If world-wide settlement of payments breaks down, nations will try, in their foreign transactions, to bring about settlement that is bilateral or confined to a limited group of countries. Such a policy involves discrimination, the establishment of empire preferences, the end of the policy of "the open door." Almost all the "empires" applied discriminatory policies intensifying their internal trade in the thirties; and the previous export balances of mother countries to their oversea territories were reversed as capital yields could not be transferred in multilateral trade. Countries outside empires and complementary to each other in their economy are under these circumstances induced to increase their mutual trade, and this to an extent and in a way that easily endangers the economic and political independence of the weaker party in this relationship. Meanwhile the "world market" to which previously all countries, great or small, developed or undeveloped, had access on equal terms as buyers or sellers disintegrates or is being confined to one sector of the world; outside that sector the exchange of goods is taking place at prices that are higher, calculated in terms of the currencies which, by means of exchange control, are held at a level exceeding that which would otherwise have established itself. Exchange control, however, necessitates a wasteful administrative apparatus and is even so never watertight.

CONCLUDING REMARKS

It is legitimate to ask whether all these disturbances, which at least over a limited period have a tendency to grow increasingly grave, are really of a permanent character. The multilateral trading system was a result of historical growth. May we not expect that conditions of production, after a more or less difficult adjustment process, will adapt themselves to bilateral or empire exchange so that a new equilibrium will finally arise without the need for a world system of settlement? Or to put it otherwise, were not the international economic difficulties of the thirties only the painful experiences of a period of transition to a new world in which multilateral settlement will be outmoded?

We can, I believe, reply to this question in the negative. True, conditions of production can be adjusted to a certain extent in each area; but climate, soil, and geographical position cannot be changed. These natural conditions vary to such an extent that a high degree of specialization of production for world distribution will always be extremely advantageous; and such specialization is possible only if trade follows a multilateral pattern. Failing this, there will always be a strong incentive for each country to increase the efficiency of its economy by including foreign areas under its domination. To ascertain the functioning of the multilateral trading system is therefore not only an economic task, it is also an object of general policy, as it reduces tensions of the kind that are instrumental in bringing about war.

What has been said may be enough to show that there is hardly any important aspect of modern economy that is not adversely affected by the breakdown of the system of multilateral trade. This is due less to the fact that all economic phenomena are interrelated than to the very central importance which multilateral settlement on a world-wide basis occupies in peacetime economy. We can no longer afford to ignore a factor exercising a determinant influence on international monetary equilibrium, on international finance, on the level of prices formed in the world market (and, through them, in national markets), and accordingly on production, employment, and the course of the business cycle.

When considering the future, we must be on our guard against the common misconception that the chief obstacles to international settlement lie in the field of monetary transfer. In recent years, several ingenious schemes of what in practice amount to universal clearing have been invented with a view to compelling each country to make immediate use of the foreign currency accruing to it from its foreign transactions and thus preventing the formation of heavy short-term debts repayable on call. Our problem, however, is not so easily solved. If we force international settlement of payments (for example, by allowing unused claims resulting from exports to depreciate or become valueless), we force a corresponding multilateral exchange of goods and services which does not reflect each country's true requirements of foreign products and accordingly does not agree with the pattern of multilateral trade that would have been determined by economic factors. We naturally wish that trade—and accordingly the monetary settlement which only reflects trade movements—should be established in agreement with this multilateral pattern, or with a pattern very close to it. Our main object is not the settlement of monetary claims but the multilateral exchange of goods and services that provides for the international economic integration of countries in a manner profitable to all. If this can be achieved, there will be no reason to replace the traditional forms of monetary settlement with multilateral clearing, at least in a world where there is a reasonable degree of monetary and political security and where there is thus no particular reason for exporters in any country to pile up short-term assets abroad.

The international integration we have in mind will have to be achieved by co-ordination of national economic policies, particularly in the field of foreign trade. We have already found that the trade restrictions imposed since the early thirties cannot easily be removed by unilateral or bilateral action; and the changes in world economy taking place during the present war afford additional reason for believing that the restoration of multilateralism on sound principles will require international planning on an extensive scale. It may prove necessary to invent new instruments of commercial policy to open up the channels of multilateral trade. But to go deeper into this matter would fall outside the scope of a paper which aims only at contributing to the understanding of such trade.

20. CURRENCY CONVERTIBILITY

Gottfried Haberler

Harvard University

Excerpt from *Currency Convertibility* (Washington: American Enterprise Association, Inc., 1954), pp. 5–15, 22–30. Reprinted by permission of the author and the publisher.

INTRODUCTION

Currency convertibility is not merely a much debated international economic problem; it is also an issue that has divided the "Free World." Advocates of planning in Great Britain in particular have denounced the quest for convertibility of the world's currencies as the "old adoration of blind deities."[1] On the other hand, truly liberal economists have always regarded convertibility as an indispensable condition of a multi-lateral trading system that is compatible with a free enterprise economy based on a freely working price mechanism, and on the forces of demand and supply.

As Europe in particular and the world economy at large recovered from the war, and as the postwar wave of economic chaos and planning gradually receded, the gap between advocates and opponents of convertibility has progressively narrowed, although it is by no means yet completely bridged. Now almost everybody who writes on these matters pays lip service to less fettered international trade and, therefore, to currency convertibility as an ultimate goal. But many who profess the ideal stipulate exacting conditions which either imply an indefinite delay or would jeopardize the benefits from convertibility. Moreover the meaning of convertibility has undergone great changes. It is no longer a clear cut, unambiguous concept. Many varieties and degrees of convertibility must now be distinguished, some so restricted as to raise serious doubt whether that kind of convertibility would mark a significant step towards freer, nondiscriminatory trade.

[1] Barbara Ward, formerly on the editorial staff of *The Economist* who frequently writes in the *New York Times*. The quotation comes from the *New York Times* Magazine, July 30, 1950, p. 38.

Convertibility is closely related to several other issues in the area of international economic policy. Obviously, it is a part of the task of freeing trade of the shackles of exchange control (payments restrictions). Convertibility is also intimately connected with the problem of discrimination in international trade inasmuch as inconvertibility always implies discrimination and favoritism. Furthermore, for at least two reasons convertibility is connected with the question of tariffs and other methods of import restriction. On the one hand, relaxation of import restrictions by the United States and other countries with convertible ("hard") currencies is often listed as an indispensable condition for making Sterling and other "soft" currencies convertible. On the other hand, it is now occasionally suggested that convertibility may indeed be a good thing *provided* it is accompanied by a tightening of import restrictions in the countries with inconvertible currencies. This highly dubious suggestion, of course, makes a mockery of the ideal of really free convertibility.

Still another related issue is that of fixed vs. variable exchange rates. The restoration of convertibility may require changes in the relative values of some currencies—changes which cannot possibly be figured out beforehand. Hence, it may be necessary to set exchanges free, at least for some time, so that market forces of demand and supply can determine the equilibrium rate pattern characteristic of general convertibility.

These different issues will be explored. But first the meaning of convertibility in its various forms should be clarified, to show why currency convertibility is so important and desirable.

MEANINGS AND FORMS OF CONVERTIBILTY

Prior to August, 1914, and even until the advent of the Great Depression in 1929, convertibility was generally understood to mean the right to convert a currency freely and at a constant rate into gold. In that sense not even the U.S. dollar is fully convertible any more. True, any holder of dollars can walk into any U.S. bank and buy almost any foreign currency. But only foreign central banks, not private individuals, can obtain gold for their dollars. Convertibility of currency into gold is undoubtedly an important matter. But it is not convertibility in the sense in which it is now debated.

What is now meant by full convertibility is that any holder of any national currency should be free to exchange it at the ruling rate of exchange (which may be either constant or variable) into any other currency. I shall confine myself to convertibility in this sense and shall not discuss free convertibility into gold.

Even within this limitation, few of those who advocate convertibility now or for the near future think of unrestricted convertibility. Various types of more or less stringent qualifications are proposed—restrictions with respect to (a) who holds the balances, (b) the origin of the balances, (c) the purposes for which conversion into foreign currency is desired. Moreover, as to holders of balances a double distinction is made: first between residents and non-residents; second, among the latter, between foreign Central Banks and other non-residents.

In current discussions convertibility is often deemed applicable only to foreign holders of the currency. For example, if Sterling were to be made convertible into dollars, it would not be intended that Englishmen should be permitted to buy dollars as they please; but that *foreign* holders of Sterling should be allowed to convert pounds freely into dollars. Some proposals would reserve to foreign Central banks the right to convert Sterling balances freely into dollars. Theoretically, members of the Sterling Area at present possess "Central Bank Convertibility"; that is to say, the Commonwealth Central Banks have access to the Sterling Area Dollar pool in London. But it is certain that there exists a gentleman's agreement whereby the Commonwealth Central banks use great caution in exercising their right of demanding dollars from the central dollar reserve in exchange for their Sterling balances.

Convertibility distinctions in respect to the origin of balances differentiate between "old" and "new." When convertibility is envisaged it usually excludes "old," that is war or pre-war debts. Old debts (e.g., the case of what Britain owes to India for wartime supplies, or the case of the German pre-war debts) are subject to special arrangement. Old balances, when large, have been a stumbling block for convertibility. But in the case of Britain this burden has been greatly reduced by repayment and by depreciation of the real value of these balances through the rise in prices. And Western Germany has been able to make settlement with pre-war German creditors. Henceforth when speaking of convertibility we shall refer to "new" balances, assuming that "old" ones have been somehow funded. While the border line between old and new may be hazy in a few cases, it is usually quite well defined.

With respect to the purpose for which foreign currencies (dollars) are sought by holders of sterling, a distinction is made between current transactions and capital transfers. Convertibility is often restricted to current account purposes, that is to say to payments for goods and services (merchandise, shipping charges, commissions, fees, tourist expenditures and the like) as well as for interest and dividend payments. This type of current account, as distinguished from capital convertibility, is envisaged by the Bretton Woods agreements, which expressly permit (and under certain conditions even require) the maintenance of payment restrictions on capital transfers.

A further distinction is made between capital transfers to repay existing debt, which extinguish an existing claim on the paying country, and transfers of investment capital which establish a claim by the paying country. For practical purposes current account may perhaps be defined in the wider sense, including scheduled or authorized repayment of debts.

It should be observed, however, that the distinction between current account convertibility and capital convertibility makes sense only for balances owned by residents. With respect to foreign holders the *origin* of the balance is important, whether "old" or "new" or whether it resulted from capital or current transactions. The *purpose* of the transfer, however, does not or should not concern the authorities of the debtor country. For example, whether a French exporter to Britain wants U.S. dollars to pay for American cotton ("current transaction") or for repaying a debt in the U.S. or buying American securities ("capital transaction") is his own (or the French Government's) business and should be of no concern to the British authorities.

On the basis of these distinctions an elaborate classification of different types of convertibility could be worked out. For the specialist it might be useful. But for most purposes it will be sufficient to distinguish between (a) full, unlimited convertibility applicable to residents and non-residents alike, irrespective of the purpose, for current as well as for capital transactions and (b) limited convertibility—confined to current transactions, including governmentally authorized debt repayments. Under (b) the British national could buy as many dollars, Swiss francs, etc., as needed to pay for imports, travel, interest and authorized repayment of old debts. He would not be permitted to convert his pounds into dollars for the purpose of buying U.S. securities, as this would be a form of capital export.

It must be stressed, however, that current account convertibility (limited or unlimited) loses sense and economic value to the extent that trade restrictions (by tariffs, quotas, state trading or by any other method) and travel restrictions become tight and discriminatory. When consumers are dissuaded or prevented from importing what they want and whence they want by any of the many methods in the modern arsenal of protective and discriminatory devices, then formal convertibility, i.e., the right to obtain foreign currency for the purpose of paying for imports, will not of itself serve to promote multilateral trade.

This fact is being increasingly recognized. Thus the European Payments Union, which has established non-resident convertibility (also called "external" convertibility) among its members, has tried at the same time to liberalize trade by reducing quota restrictions on imports. This effort at liberalization, which has had more than negligible success, was, however, confined to trade between the members of E.P.U., thus discriminating against imports from the U.S. and other outsiders. On the continent of Europe, convertibility for residents (sometimes called "internal" convertibility) is now often so defined as to imply absence of quantitative import restrictions by quotas.

It certainly is important to recognize the mutual substitutability of trade and payments restrictions and it is all to the good that quota restrictions be eliminated and that attempts at emasculating convertibility by substituting other types of trade control be forestalled. But it would be absurd to speak of "internal" convertibility only if other quantitative restrictions are entirely absent; for in that case we would have to declare the U.S. dollar and Swiss franc as inconvertible currencies! [2]

[2] It is misleading to distinguish as it is now occasionally done (see for example the note on "The Swiss Concept of Convertibility" in *Swiss Review of World Affairs*, November 1953) between the Swiss and British concept of convertibility. The Swiss are said to have "internal" convertibility while the British are interested only in "external" convertibility.

It is more correct to describe the Swiss currency as fully convertible with certain exceptions (for residents as well as non-residents) the purpose of which is to retaliate against or prevent discrimination against Switzerland. It is technically correct to say that the Swiss franc is inconvertible as far as the trade with countries with which Switzerland has special payments arrangements is concerned. For example, an exporter from an EPU country to Switzer-

THE IMPORTANCE OF FULL CONVERTIBILITY

The first and basic advantage of freely convertible currencies for the world at large is that it enables producers and consumers everywhere to buy from the cheapest sources and sell at the highest prices, i.e., where the need for each commodity is most urgent. As a consequence every country and region can specialize on those lines of production where it has the greatest comparative efficiency and can import those commodities which other countries can in turn produce more efficiently. Convertibility is thus an indispensable condition for the attainment of maximum world output.

This is, of course, the familiar argument for free trade. True, currency convertibility does not imply free trade in an absolute sense, because there are other trade barriers such as tariffs, quotas, state trading monopolies, bulk purchasing schemes, and administrative protectionism. But currency inconvertibility, and the exchange control which it entails, have proved one of the most formidable obstacles to international movement of goods and services.

Closely connected with the basic advantage of full convertibility is the elimination of red tape which would be achieved. Inconvertibility necessitates rigid exchange control, which means in effect a close official supervision not only of international payments, but of every kind of international transaction. All shipments of commodities across the border must be carefully scrutinized to make sure that there is no evasion of payment restrictions. If commodity exports and export prices were not checked and if exporters were not com-

---

land cannot ask for payment in U.S. dollars, nor is the Swiss importer allowed to pay him in dollars (or convertible Swiss francs); the payment has to be cleared through EPU channels. But these are exceptions which apply only to countries that in the absence of such arrangements would discriminate against Switzerland; they do not apply to convertible currency countries like the U.S. or Canada.

The Swiss policy is different from the American. While we let our exporters fend for themselves (occasionally we bail them out through a special loan from the Export-Import Bank), Switzerland, being a tiny country for which foreign trade is a matter of life and death, cannot afford to take discriminatory treatment of its exports on the chin without trying to defend itself.

It is incorrect to say that Great Britain is interested only in "external" convertibility. The proposal made by some British economists that formal convertibility should be introduced only after quota restrictions have been perfected to such a degree that they take over all the discriminatory functions of an inconvertible currency, has never been espoused by the British Government.

pelled to surrender foreign money for exchange at the official rate, illegal capital flight would take place. The whole or part of the proceeds from exports, including proceeds from the export of services (e.g., receipts from foreign tourists), would be likely to stay abroad.

Currency inconvertibility has produced an infinite variety of exchange control systems, ranging from those that rely largely on moral suasion to extremely rigid systems requiring detailed supervision and control. The degree of severity of the restrictions depends on several factors. One is the strength of inflationary pressures. Another is the self-discipline and patriotism of the population and the degree of confidence in the economic future of the country. A third factor is the efficiency and incorruptibility of the administrative officials. Experience has shown that even mild systems of exchange control provide a constant temptation to use them for other than the avowed purposes of preventing capital flight.

Moreover, in countries where international trade constitutes a large fraction of total income, Government trade control constantly threatens to spread its vicious effects. If a country has not already embarked on a policy of widespread regimentation in a vain attempt to repress the symptoms of inflation by direct controls, then exchange control (and to a lesser extent a quota system of import restriction) is likely to be the wedge through which excessive Government intervention or even central planning is introduced. Only full, unlimited convertibility, can completely vanish these dangers. Limited convertibility, in the sense explained earlier, does not fully eliminate the dangers mentioned, because it requires the maintenance of an extensive apparatus of control.

Are there any countervailing considerations that could justify the maintenance of inconvertible currencies and exchange control and invalidate the presumption that convertibility will benefit everybody?

Planners and interventionists hostile to the free enterprise economy are naturally opposed to convertibility. It would play havoc with their programs of regimentation. But some who cannot possibly be called "starry-eyed planners" nevertheless regard inconvertibility as a necessary evil, at least for the time being. It is also believed that countries with inconvertible currency, if cleverly managed, attain certain advantages although it is generally admitted that this must be at the expense of countries with convertible currencies.

In later sections we shall consider the view that convertibility would be feasible only under conditions not likely to be fulfilled in the near future—such as "a quasi revolution in U.S. commercial policy" as one prominent economist puts it.[3]

The advantage which a skillfully managed system of exchange control, especially if practiced by a group of countries such as the Sterling area or the European Payments Union, in discriminiation against U.S. and other dollar countries' exports, is supposed to be capable of yielding, consists of an improvement in the so-called "terms of trade"—the ratio of export to import prices—for the inconvertible group. By the same token this implies a deterioration of the terms of trade for countries without exchange controls. It is at best a "beggar-my-neighbor" policy, assuming that it is possible for a group of countries acting in concert to reduce the price of the things they import relatively to the prices of the things they export.

This discriminatory exploitation of the dollar countries can be achieved by different methods: by preferential tariff arrangements, such as the British Commonwealth preferential tariff system; by preferential quota manipulation, as now practiced by the members of the European Payments Union; or by keeping currencies inconvertible *vis à vis* the dollar while making them freely convertible among the members of a group (E.P.U. and Sterling Area). It is argued that the abandonment of such discriminatory schemes would result in a deterioration of the terms of trade for countries with inconvertible currencies.

It is widely conceded, even by liberal, free trade economists that there is in theory a possibility for any country or group of countries to derive such benefits from cleverly contrived discriminatory practices at the expense of others. But certain conditions are necessary: (a) the cartel of countries must be large enough to have an appreciable influence on prices; (b) retaliation by the outside countries must be avoided; (c) the right dose of discrimination must be applied at the right time and place.[4]

These conditions and limitations are not likely to be fulfilled; they are not generally understood even by economic experts, let alone

[3] Professor Sir Dennis Robertson of Cambridge University in his speech before the International Chamber of Commerce, Vienna, May, 1953.

[4] It must not be assumed that the benefit is the larger, the more severe the import restriction. There is an optimum degree of import restriction (e.g., an optimum tariff) which depends upon the elasticities of demand and supply of the commodities concerned.

by those who formulate and administer foreign trade policy. The most probable, if not practically certain, outcome of the general adoption of such policies is that everybody will be worse off in the end, except perhaps some special interests here or there.

For Great Britain, moreover, it is necessary to balance such manipulated advantages against losses due to the fact that this discriminatory system undermines her traditional position as international trader and banker. If London is again to become the world's financial and commercial center, exchange control must be avoided; Sterling must be made impregnably convertible; its value in dollars and gold must be as stable as is compatible with continued convertibility.

In summary: Currency convertibility is highly desirable to maximize world output; to minimize red tape in international trade; to check Governmental intervention in the free market economy. Limited or partial convertibility, although much better than none at all, seriously reduces and dilutes the benefits of convertibility.

CONVERTIBILITY, INFLATION AND EXCHANGE RATES

It cannot be repeated too often that any form of open or repressed inflation is incompatible with convertibility and stable exchange rates. More precisely, if any country inflates faster than its trade partners do, it cannot hope to maintain equilibrium in its balance of payments without either introducing *ad hoc* restrictions on imports and payments *or* letting its currency depreciate; in other words without abandoning either convertibility or stability of its currency. Therefore, easy money policies, budgetary deficits, lax credit policies, are all incompatible with convertibility and stability of the currency.

But even if inflation is scrupulously avoided, the budget balanced and bona fide price and cost levels kept stable (without recourse to price control, rationing and other methods of concealing and suppressing the symptoms of inflation), we cannot be sure that after convertibility is restored equilibrium in the balance of payments will be maintained at the present exchange rates. A country can get into balance of payments difficulties, even if it avoids inflation, for the following reasons:

First, the pre-existent value of a country's currency may prove to be too high under convertibility, even if there is no visible pressure on the exchange rate under present conditions of inconvertibility.

Second, if the currency is not overvalued when convertibility is restored, troubles can arise later for a variety of reasons other than renewed inflationary pressure. There may be a recession in the United States or elsewhere. A country may lose major export markets due to technological change or foreign competition or protectionist policies abroad. A country may require larger imports because of bad harvests. In the past, under the rule of the Gold Standard, such conditions were dealt with by deflation, that is by a reduction of price and cost levels (including wages). With wages, and hence to a lesser extent prices, as rigid as they are nowadays, deflation must immediately lead to general unemployment. This effectively excludes deflation from the realm of practical policy.

This statement is not meant to exclude disinflation, if by that we mean anti-inflationary measures, including such reduction in prices as can be absorbed without a general reduction in wages. This is possible because in periods of inflation it often happens that prices run ahead of wages. There is then scope for a certain amount of price deflation without a reduction in wages. But one ought not to expect too much from that.

Moreover, our statement that deflation and mass unemployment are excluded does not mean that literally full employment can or should be guaranteed all the time; or that literally all wage rates must be secure from any downward adjustment. What is meant is that a general reduction of all or most wages is virtually impossible under present day conditions and, happily, is not necessary for the maintenance of full employment, a healthy economy, and for the preservation of equilibrium in the balance of payments.[5]

For the reason stated above it would seem unwise to restore convertibility without providing flexibility of exchange rates, at least

[5] If I say that it is virtually impossible and with skillful policies unnecessary to carry out a general deflation of wages and prices, I mean *money* wages. But even the most skillful policy cannot always avoid a reduction in the level of *real* wages except at the price of creating a certain amount of unemployment. If a country lives beyond its means, covering the deficit by U.S. aid, running into debt or losing gold (if it has any to lose and is not a gold producer), restoration of equilibrium necessitates a fall of real income and hence in the real wage level irrespective of the method by which equilibrium is restored. This follows from the fact that equilibrium requires an increase in exports and/or fall in imports which leaves fewer goods available for domestic use.

Even trade unions can be bought to understand that fact. For example, labor unions in Holland voluntarily accepted in 1951 a cut of 5% in their real income in the form of higher prices uncompensated or insufficiently compensated by a rise in money wages.

until equilibrium of the rates under convertibility has been found. By flexibility I do not merely mean that some of the now inconvertible currencies should be devalued prior to or simultaneously with the introduction of convertibility and then provisionally stabilized at the new level until they are once more adjusted, if it appears that the first adjustment was either inadequate or too drastic.

This system of "the adjustable peg" under which there are occasional sharp adjustments in the exchange value of a currency while rates are rigidly pegged at a constant level during the intervening period, is the one envisaged by the Bretton Woods Agreement. It has worked in an unsatisfactory and, in fact, unstabilizing fashion. Nobody can calculate with precision beforehand how large a devaluation will be sufficient to maintain equilibrium under convertibility. In consequence each government in order to be on the safe side and to avoid the embarassment of having to repeat the operation, will tend to devalue too much rather than too little. Therefore the method of the "adjustable peg" does not provide the necessary flexibility.

What I mean by flexibility is a freely fluctuating or floating rate, the value of which is determined by demand and supply in freely accessible markets. Canada offers the best recent example of this freely fluctuating exchange rate. The Canadian dollar was set free several years ago and has been allowed to undergo fluctuations ever since. Such a system does not exclude the existence of an exchange stabilization fund operating to smooth out day-to-day oscillations, as the British Exchange Equalization Fund operated during several years after Sterling went off gold in 1931. This was another highly successful experiment in freely fluctuating exchange rates.

Two objections are often raised against floating exchange rates, (a) that they stimulate speculative and disturbing capital transfers, and (b) that they impede trade by introducing additional hazards. Experience has shown that the system of "adjustable pegs" is much more vulnerable on both counts than the system of freely floating exchange rates. This is well illustrated by British experience in 1947 and 1949. When currency is under pressure, as Sterling was in 1949, the country loses gold and dollar reserves and more and more people expect a depreciation. If the currency is pegged, the risk of speculating against it is almost entirely removed, because the speculator can be virtually certain that the value of the currency will not go up.

If Great Britain had possessed a floating exchange, the dollar price of Sterling would have drifted down earlier. There would also have been some speculation against Sterling. But soon a point would have been reached where some speculators would begin to expect recovery. The risk that a currency may go up is ever present under the floating exchange regime which tends, compared with the pegged system, to put a check on adverse speculation.

Under the old gold standard, so long as it was held sacrosanct, there was, of course, no motive for this kind of speculation. But there is no gold standard any more, and even if it were to be recreated, there would not be confidence that parity would be held in the case of crisis.

The adjustable peg system has another disadvantage which should not be taken lightly—it puts responsible people in a morally dubious position. Up to the last moment before they carry out their decision to depreciate they have to protest solemnly that they have no such intention. In 1949 the British Chancellor of the Exchequer was Sir Stafford Cripps, a man of the highest moral standards. He was compelled to deny emphatically and publicly that he would depreciate sterling, at a time when it must have been clear to him that depreciation was unavoidable, or when he had already made up his mind to take the plunge. A system which forces responsible statesmen deliberately to deceive the public cannot be a good one.

Persistent and massive speculation against a currency ("capital flight") is invariably the consequence of inflationary policies, political instability or the threat of war. In recent years there has been much capital flight out of France (into gold or dollars) but little out of Germany or Austria, although these countries are much more exposed to Russian aggressive acts than France. This suggests the overwhelming importance of monetary and financial policy. Experience has also shown that in peace time it is very difficult to prevent capital from leaving a country, if the causes which induce capital flight are powerful and persistent. Control measures designed to prevent it have proved in the end to impede rather than capital movements.

Stable exchanges are undoubtedly helpful to business. But mild fluctuations—and not more would be required except in rare emergencies—are much less inconvenient and disturbing to international trade than the alternative of rigid controls. Moreover, the inconvenience of fluctuating rates can be substantially reduced by permitting and organizing well functioning forward markets in foreign exchanges.

Freely fluctuating rates become definitely inconvenient to any government that persistently inflates its currency, thereby bringing on a steady downward drift in the rate of exchange. For precisely this reason the system of free rates is now unpopular with many governments. A freely fluctuating rate is a sensitive symptom of inflation. It makes concealment of the disease more difficult and hence enforces a certain measure of discipline on Governments and Central banks.

In the past the gold standard imposed even stricter discipline. But under present conditions, characterized by rigid wages and a horror of unemployment, the harsh discipline of the gold standard would nowhere be accepted. Therefore, the gold standard is not a realistic alternative to freely floating exchanges. The only alternative is the system of "adjustable pegs," with or without the straight jacket of exchange control, or outright inconvertibility. That floating exchange rates are preferable to exchange control and inconvertible currency goes without saying. And it has become evident that the system of adjustable pegs easily leads to undesirable results.

Of course the above is not to be taken as a recommendation for a floating dollar rate with respect to gold. Moreover, there will be quite a few currencies strong enough to remain on a stable rate with respect to the dollar and gold. Switzerland, Portugal and several dollar countries in Latin America belong to this group. The Canadian dollar has been floating for some time, but its variations have been small and will probably continue to be so that it can be said to belong to the dollar area.

THE U.S. TARIFF, AMERICAN PRODUCTIVITY AND CONVERTIBILITY

It is often claimed that convertibility cannot be restored without a drastic change in U.S. tariff policy. There can be no doubt that a further reduction of U.S. tariff rates, simplification of the extremely burdensome customs procedures, and elimination of existing uncertainty with respect to import policies, would go far to hasten and facilitate the introduction of convertibility and to ensure its lasting success. The higher the U.S. tariff, and the more burdensome the customs procedures, the greater is the effort required abroad to increase exports to the U.S. Thus a correspondingly larger fall in imports from the U.S. (i.e., U.S. exports) is necessary to restore the international trade and payments balance without artificial dollar aid.

It is, however, probably true that if U.S. tariffs were stabilized at their present level, and customs procedures simplified, an equilibrium between exports and imports could be worked out—of course, on a lower level of U.S. exports and imports than would otherwise be possible, and with less insurance against future upsets.

From a political and psychological standpoint a lowering of U.S. import duties would be a tremendous help in persuading foreign countries to restore convertibility, and to persevere in the policies essential to make convertibility a permanent success. It would put the responsibility of failure squarely on the shoulders of the foreign governments. These governments will certainly use the U.S. tariff, if it is not reduced, as a welcome excuse for not introducing convertibility or for abolishing it again in the event difficulties appear after convertibility has been introduced.

There are, however, some economists who take the pessimistic view that irrespective of what happens to the U.S. tariff, the "greater productivity" of the U.S. economy makes it virtually impossible for other countries to balance their accounts with the dollar area without discriminatory restrictions on the import of dollar goods. According to these writers the tariff is a matter of minor importance because the U.S. can out-compete and under-sell the rest of the world (or large parts of it) all along the line, unless the other countries protect themselves against this ruinous American competition by special discriminatory measures.

While this theory implies a great compliment to the efficiency of the free enterprise system of the U.S., it is bad economics nonetheless. The most elementary principles of international trade tell us that however poor or unproductive or inefficient a country, it need not be afraid of being undersold all along the line because trade and the profitability of trade to all concerned depend on *comparative*, not *absolute* cost, efficiency, and productivity. The fear abroad of superior U.S. general productivity is the fallacious counterpart of the equally unfounded American fear that the low general level of wages (compared with the U.S.) in many parts of the world will lead to a flooding of the American market unless it is protected by a tariff wall designed to equalize the difference in labor cost.[6]

The truth is, of course, that the high wage level in the U.S. is the consequence of the high productivity here and the low wage level abroad is the result of the low productivity there. The difference in the wage level no more prevents profitable international trade between any two countries than does the difference between the general level of their productivities. Given the lower level of productivity abroad, the foreign wage level must be lower than the U.S. wage level or else foreign exports to the U.S., and to other countries where they meet U.S. competition, would be even lower than they are and the balance of payments in even greater deficit. Similarly, given the relative wage levels as they are, productivity in the U.S. must be higher or else the U.S. balance of payments would be in hopeless deficit. In short, higher productivity in the U.S. and lower wages abroad are two sides of one and the same coin.

The dynamic version of the productivity theory, which stresses not the different *level* in productivity but the allegedly more *rapid advance* of productivity in the U.S., is only slightly less vulnerable than the static version. Countries that advance slowly *may* be hurt, but *need* not be hurt by the faster progress of their trade partners. If the rapid advance of country *A* takes place more or less evenly in most of its industries, its international trade position will not be changed much, because its position depends on comparative and not absolute productivity, and comparative productivity is not changed by a uniform advance in efficiency. In fact *A*'s trade partners will benefit in this case from *A*'s rapid progress, because *A*'s national income will rise, and hence *A*'s demand for foreign goods will go up.

If in country *A* export industries advance faster than import-competing industries, *A*'s trading partners (the more slowly advancing countries) will again benefit because they will get their imports on more favorable terms. Only if *A*'s advance is more rapid in import-competing industries—if natural rubber is replaced by synthetic rubber, or silk by rayon and nylon—will *A*'s trading partners be hurt. That does not mean that trade is no longer beneficial. It only means that it may be less beneficial than it was before and that a readjustment is necessary, which may be painful during the transition. There

[6] This would imply an unfavorable turn in the U.S. balance of payments and a glut and drop in value of the U.S. dollar in the exchange market—the opposite of the condition of dollar scarcity which has actually prevailed for a long time.

is, however, little that can be done about it except to soften the impact on the industries immediately concerned.

Gloomy forecasts to the effect that other countries are likely to advance so fast as to make trade impossible, or to impose painful readjustments, have been made many times over the last hundred years. This view was popular in Germany around the turn of the century and was used by nationalistic and socialistic economists and publicists as an argument for high protection and Government direction of trade.

Experience constantly shows, however, that countries with reasonable policies quickly recover from infinitely worse disasters than the loss of a few export markets. Two very striking examples are offered by recent history, namely the amazingly rapid economic recovery of Western Germany and the Netherlands. This recovery has occurred with respect to both internal production and international trade, despite unparalleled war destruction, despite trade dislocation, despite division of the country in the case of Germany and the loss of a rich colonial empire in the case of Holland. Poor countries like Finland were able to put their economic house in order while comparatively rich ones like France suffer from perpetual inflation and balance-of-payments troubles. Some war-ravaged countries staged a rapid recovery while others, which remained neutral and profited from the war, nevertheless find it difficult to balance international accounts.

Anyone who cares to learn from recent history should realize that currency convertibility depends primarily on proper monetary, financial and economic policy. If liberal economic and prudent financial policies are pursued, even the most serious material war damage can be repaired in a few years. However rich a country, its balance of payments can be ruined and the stability of its currency jeopardized almost over night by lax financial policies.

21. THE PROCESS OF INTERNATIONAL CAPITAL MOVEMENTS

Norman S. Buchanan

Excerpt from *International Investment and Domestic Welfare* (New York: Henry Holt and Co., Copyright 1945), pp. 232–236. Reprinted by permission of the author and the publisher. At the time of original publication the author was with the University of California, Berkeley.

Let us assume that a group of citizens of country D (the "debtor" country in what follows) offer for sale in the capital market of country C (the "creditor" country) a new issue of securities.[1] Let us assume further that these securities are bonds of a corporation in D and that the sale is successful. What has occurred so far? Certain persons in D *via* a corporation, have obtained buying power (bank deposits) in country C in exchange for which they have given a promise to pay the principal sum borrowed at maturity with interest in the interim at an agreed rate. A transaction has occurred in the capital market of country C which has international aspects and implications. Up to this point no "movement" has occurred other than a transfer of the ownership of certain bank deposits in C from nationals to foreigners. Yet in a sense a transfer is a movement; and it would be customary to describe what occurred as an international capital movement, or more correctly, as the first of several steps in an international capital movement.[2] A more precise statement, however, would be to the effect that the movement or transfer thus far

---

[1] One could rewrite what follows in terms of an increased desire on the part of investors in C to make investments abroad in D. Indeed, as a description of what has happened in times past in the development of backward areas it might be more appropriate to indicate that the lenders usually took the initiative. Yet in the postwar period the initiative will likely reside with borrowers in the sense that they will be pressing their needs in a vigorous fashion.

[2] One reason for speaking of the first step as a capital movement is that the full complement of steps may require a long time. Borrowers and lenders have occasionally overlooked the delayed consequences of international capital movements to their disaster.

was monetary in character, suggesting thereby that something more was involved.[3]

Let us return to our example. The borrowers in D now have bank deposits in C. At this juncture two extreme cases set the limits to the possibilities of what the D borrowers may desire to do with their newly acquired bank deposits. Assume for the present that C and D are the only two countries. In that instance the first possibility is that the D borrowers may wish to spend their bank deposits entirely on commodities or services available in country C.[4] If this be the fact, then the D borrowers acquire their merchandise, arrange for its delivery to their place of business in D, and, except for the interest and principal payments to be made in the future, the transaction is closed. The initial monetary transfer has been succeeded almost immediately by a transfer of goods. Exports from C to D are larger than they would have been had no international capital transaction occurred. Observe, however, that there is no requirement that the goods movement consist of machines or capital instruments. It may just as well consist of wheat or canned goods or services of some kind. There is no logical necessity that any particular *kind* of export effect the real transfer.

The alternative possibility at the other extreme of course is that the borrowers in D desire to spend the whole proceeds of their loan in their own country D. Clearly in this instance the possible sequences of development are more numerous than in the previous case, depending upon the assumptions that are made concerning the volume of employment in C and D, the foreign exchange relations between them, the composition of aggregate demand in the two countries between domestic and foreign goods, and others. Primary developments must also be distinguished from secondary or induced developments. Let us first consider the case of stable exchange rates,[5]

---

[3] Cf. the following, ". . . the *first* thing which happens when an international capital movement is to take place, is usually that part of the monetary buying power of one country is put at the disposal of people in the other (the monetary transfer). This first step is eliminated only where goods are sold abroad on long-term credit or in case imports of goods are financed by permanent loans after the shipment of the goods." Iversen, C., *Aspects of the Theory of International Capital Movements*, Copenhagen and London, 1935, p. 45.

[4] The reasons why they may desire to spend in C may be various. For instance, the goods required may not be available at home or not available at such attractive prices.

[5] The assumption of stable foreign exchange rates implies that there are banks, a central bank, or an exchange fund willing to increase or decrease their

with less than full employment in country D, and inquire as to the primary effects of a loan negotiated in C but which the borrowers desire to spend wholly in D.

The borrowers in D will sell their newly acquired bank balances in C to the banks in their own country, receiving in exchange bank balances in D currency. Since we may assume that, they then proceed with their project by hiring laborers and buying domestic materials. But the increase in employment generated in D means an increase in domestic incomes which, in turn, are spent on consumption or investment. The rise in incomes, however, is likely to cause two further consequences. First, some of the increased consumption will be a consumption of imported goods, and hence tend to raise imports from C (the only other country under present assumptions). Second, with a higher level of incomes possibly a larger fraction of the goods usually sent abroad (or of goods both consumed at home and sent abroad) will be purchased by domestic consumers.[6] Thus commodity exports from D may fall off somewhat. But the combination of these—a tendency in D for imports to rise and exports to fall —will serve to diminish the bank balances in C that the banks in D purchased from the original D borrowers. In other words, the expansion of investment and incomes in D, through their effect upon imports and exports, converts the monetary transfer from C to D into a real transfer, i.e., a movement of commodities. Yet here again no logic requires that the goods transferred be of any particular kind and type.[7]

If substantially full employment prevails in D, the sequence is slightly altered. The immediate expenditure in D of additional funds will serve to raise prices above the level that would have otherwise prevailed. The additional expenditure cannot increase aggregate output in the short run because we have assumed that unemployment is negligible. Increased expenditure can only raise prices. But a rise in prices in D relative to those in C will increase D's imports and diminish its exports, and thereby eliminate the balances abroad

(or its) foreign exchange holdings or gold holdings when others offer to sell or buy foreign exchange at given prices.

[6] The rise in incomes in D is assumed to be unaccompanied by a corresponding rise in incomes in C. If incomes also are rising in C no such shift need necessarily occur. As we shall note subsequently the loan would tend to have the reverse effect in C, i.e., to lower incomes and employment.

[7] The transfer theoretically could be effected, of course, entirely through a decline in exports from D to C. C lends to D and C simply reduced its imports. Its gross exports need not rise.

in C accepted by the D banks when they supplied deposits at home in D to the original borrowers.[8]

If we drop the simplifying assumption of only two countries the essence of the analysis is not substantially changed. Let us assume that the D borrowers wish to spend their C balances not in C nor at home in D but in a third country X. In this case an additional step is introduced. The banks in C must be willing to reduce their deposit liabilities through a (temporary) reduction in their holdings of balances in country X. The D borrowers then procure their merchandise and proceed homewards. But what of the real transfer? Clearly it has already occurred between X and D. But what of C, the lending country? Unless the banks in C are willing to see their balances in X permanently impaired (and there is nothing in the loan transaction *per se* to suggest this) then they will take steps to restore their balances in X to their previous level. (Under flexible exchange rates they will perhaps charge higher prices for X currency.) Imports from X will thereby be discouraged and exports to X from C will be stimulated. Both work in the direction of restoring the C banks' balances in X through raising exports from C to X relative to imports from X to C. One could also supplement the classical argument here by assuming that the purchases of the D borrowers in X stimulate employment and incomes in X and so tend to raise imports in X relative to exports. Similarly one could argue that the reduction in bank deposits in C [9] would react unfavorably on either employment and incomes and hence on imports, or upon prices, if there is little unemployment, with a similar result.[10] In any case the money transfer

[8] If we assume flexible, instead of stable, exchange rates the argument need be altered only slightly. The essential modification is that the adjustment need not occur entirely through changes in incomes or prices but the exchange rate itself, i.e., the price of one currency in terms of another, can also ease the process. The borrowing in C for expenditure in D will tend to raise the price of D currency in terms of C. That is to say, more units of C currency must be paid for a unit of D currency or, as it is expressed with almost equal frequency, less D currency is obtainable for a unit of C currency. Regardless of the mode of expression the effect of the loan transaction on the rate is to raise imports and diminish exports in D and vice versa in C. A single loan transaction unless of great size, however, would be unlikely to alter the exchange rate perceptibly. A stream of foreign borrowing with flexible exchange rates is another matter.

[9] Bank deposits are reduced because the banks in C have surrendered foreign assets against the reduction of domestic liabilities, the deposits.

[10] This assumes that the reserve position of the banks determines their lending policy. But this need not be the case. An "offsetting" policy, such as followed by the Federal Reserve authorities in the '20's would avoid the need for any deflation in C as a consequence of the lending transaction.

is followed by a real transfer, in this case three cornered, such that exports minus imports in C, the lending country, is a greater figure than before the loan was granted. The real transfer is from C to X to D, although the time sequence in the case discussed was actually from X to D as one step and from C to X as another.

We stated initially that the relationship between the money transfer and the real transfer could be elucidated by an examination of two extreme cases: first, where all the proceeds of the loan are to be spent in the lending country; second, where the proceeds are to be spent entirely in the borrowing country. It is self-evident, of course, that these are merely two "pure" cases at the extremes. What would be likely to occur in the real world would be some combination of these two extremes, with the complication of the borrowed funds being spent partly in third or fourth countries. Yet it should be clear from what we have suggested that the sequence would be a mixture of the pure cases already considered. The net result would be the same; a monetary transfer succeeded by a real transfer, unless one introduces the special assumption that for some reason the borrower wishes to hold idle balances in the lending country, at home, or in third countries.

22. Britain's Experience as a Creditor Country

Sir Arthur Salter

Excerpt from "Foreign Investment," *Essays in International Finance* (International Finance Section, Department of Economics and Sociology, Princeton University), February 1951; pages 2–10 excerpted and slightly shortened. Reprinted by permission of the author and the publisher.

I. INTRODUCTION

Britain's great creditor period was from about 1880 to 1913, which lasted, it is interesting to note, only a third of a century. It is well, at the outset, to note the more important differences between Britain's position and that of America.

1. During her great creditor period Britain, a small island with no important domestic raw materials and minerals except coal, had a population which expanded rapidly till it consumed twice as much food as has ever been produced on her own soil. She was the pioneer in industrial development, and when her overseas investments first began to develop on a great scale industrialization in other countries was only at an early stage.

2. Britain's trade with customer and borrowing countries was for the most part therefore essentially complementary. Typically she exported railway equipment to the Argentine, which did not manufacture it, and bought maize which she did not produce. She had also in her colonies primary producing areas with which trade was similarly complementary; and in these British rule gave the competent administration and the political security required to ensure that economic development would not be impeded or its rewards lost.

3. Even in underdeveloped areas outside the British Empire political conditions were much more favourable for foreign investment in the half century preceding the first world war than they have been since or are now.

4. Foreign investment during this period offered greater rewards than most investment by the British investor in enterprise at home, and the difference was more than enough to compensate for any

moderate extra risk. Domestic industrial expansion was mainly financed by ploughing back profits (then of course facilitated by the lower level of taxation) rather than by issues in the London market, and the general home investor was for the most part confined to Government bonds etc., of which the yield was substantially less than that promised by overseas investment. One consequence was that the machinery for promoting foreign investment was much more developed than any available for home investment.

5. In Britain's great period the world's currencies were anchored to a metallic basis, usually gold. Exchange rates were stable within the narrow limits of the gold points. There were, except in rare cases, no transfer difficulties or exchange controls.

6. Aided by these circumstances Britain's policy, and the practices of her traders and financiers, were ideally suited to a "creditor" country. She had no tariffs or quotas or other impediments to equal trade. She both imported and reinvested freely. Her foreign loans were not during this period "tied" to expenditure on British products. Her imports amounted at the peak to between a third and a quarter of her whole national income and throughout the whole period, 1880–1913, considerably exceeded her exports. In that period her annual earnings from foreign investments were, on the average, about £100 million of which about £60 million were used to finance imports in excess of current exports and £40 million were re-invested. In the last ten years of the period (in spite of a continuing import surplus) new foreign investment averaged over £150 million, and in the last year, 1913, it almost reached £200 million ($1 billion at the rate of exchange of the time), equivalent at present prices to about £600 million, an astonishing figure for a small island with a population of some 40 million.

There was, therefore, no "sterling" gap in the sense in which there has since the war been a "dollar" gap.

7. In all these respects America's problem as a creditor country is different and such as to make a "creditor policy" more difficult. It is true that, partly as a result of the depletion of certain resources during the second world war, she is likely to be more dependent upon imports for certain essential materials including iron ore, copper, and oil. Except, however, for these and a few articles of luxury (which together cannot be expected in themselves to maintain her balance of trade at anything like the present level) she produces and makes all she needs as well as or better than others, and in terms

of man-hours more economically. Any great expansion of imports from other countries must consist largely of goods which enter into direct competition with her own manufacturers and are only able to compete successfully because of the advantage of lower wage costs, with perhaps "devaluation" as well, which from the point of view of the domestic manufacturer seems "exchange dumping." This makes it much more difficult for her than it was for Great Britain to abolish tariffs. The differences in regard to foreign investment are no less important. The absence of stable currencies is one obstacle, the less favourable political conditions in most parts of the world a second, the opportunities for highly remunerative home investment a third.

8. These differences, however, while important, must not be exaggerated. For example, Britain's foreign trade in her creditor period was not wholly complementary, and its development to the point it reached was only made possible by a deliberate policy which subordinated to it the interests of the home producer and manufacturer.

British agriculture, for instance, denied either subsidy or protection during this period, became unprofitable in the 1880's; and the land under wheat was reduced by half, from 3.6 million to 1.8 million acres, between 1874 and 1900. Moreover a quarter of British imports were of manufactured goods which competed directly, without tariff handicap and often with the advantage to the foreign exporter of lower wage-costs, with domestic industry. For the British Empire, and other primary producing countries in which British capital had been invested, produced more raw materials than could be sold to Britain alone: they exported the remainder to Europe and the U.S.A., which in turn sent manufactured goods to Britain. Only in this way could the international accounts have been balanced at so high a level of foreign trade. Britain's creditor policy, therefore, though favoured by circumstances, was only pursued as far as it was with difficulty and against the protests, unsuccessful throughout the period which ended with the first war, of the interests which suffered from a free trade policy.

9. It is obvious that America cannot so far expand her imports that they would occupy a place in her economy comparable with that of Britain's imports in her creditor period. But nothing approaching that, of course, would be required to enable any probable dollar gap to be closed without a reduction of America's exports. The imports needed for that purpose would absorb only a small fraction of the

home market of the manufacturers affected; and any resulting loss or difficulty would be compensated by a fully equal gain in external markets to the same or other American industries. The problem of achieving an appropriate creditor policy, therefore, though in some respects more difficult, is in other respects proportionately a smaller one for America than it was for Great Britain.

When every allowance is made for differences there remains much that is interesting and relevant in the British experience.

II. BRITAIN'S RECORD 1880–1913 [1]

Britain's period as a great foreign investor reached its peak and its conclusion on the eve of the 1914 war. It may be said to have begun half a century, or its very large-scale development a third of a century, before then. In 1854 the total of British investment was only about £200 million. In 1880 the total of British investment was £1300, in 1905 £2000 million and in 1913 over £3700 million; with an allowance for investments not represented by negotiable securities, which are not included in the above figures, the 1913 total was about £4000 million, equivalent to about £12,000 million at current prices.

It is this period, from 1880 to 1913, that will now be examined.

During this expanding third of a century Britain's investments and the income from them increased at a much greater rate than the total wealth and income of the country. Between 1880 and 1913 the national income was not quite doubled (it rose from £1200 million to £2250 million). While at the earlier date, however, the income derived from overseas investment was about £50 million, in 1913 it reached £200 million, a fourfold increase. This income was 4% of the total national income in 1880, 7% in 1903 and 9% in 1913. As the British national income (with increased population and depreciated purchasing power of the pound) is now estimated at over £10,000 million, a maintenance of the 1913 proportion of foreign investment (without any continuation of the rate of increase) would have brought the total up to £16,000 million and the income up to £900 million. In fact Britain is now, on balance, a debtor and capital importing country.

[1] In this part of the Essay I have drawn freely on *The Problems of Foreign Investment* published by the Royal Institute of International Affairs in 1937. In order to avoid numerous footnotes I content myself with this general acknowledgment.

The actual yield on overseas investments shows the motive force behind this great expansion. In the decade 1870–1880 the average yield on all foreign bonds was 5.5% and on other foreign securities nearly 7%. The average yield on Consols during this period was 3.8%. In the first decade of the present century there was still a large margin in favour of foreign investments, which give an average yield of 5.2% as compared with about 3% on Consols and 3.5% on home securities generally. On the other hand there was little or no margin in the case of Colonial investments. Indian Government Loans were issued at a rate which yielded only 3.2%, Indian Railways 3.87% and Colonial and provincial loans 3.7%. Dominion and Colonial governments could indeed borrow more cheaply in London, just before the first war, than those home borrowers whose bonds were not trustee securities. This favourable rate of borrowing was helped by the fact that the Colonial Stock Acts gave trustee status to Empire Bonds—almost the only instance of government intervention favouring overseas investment. It also well illustrates, however, the confidence of the British investor in overseas areas under British administration and the special importance which the Empire thus had as a field of expansion for British overseas investment.

The geographical distribution of the investments is equally interesting. In the early 19th Century the main British investments had been in Europe, where they served to accelerate industrial development. In the period now under consideration, however, they had been switched to countries which were largely or mainly primary producers. By the end of our period (the outbreak of the first world war) the distribution was as follows:

Area	Percentage
U.S.A.	20
Canada	14
Australia and New Zealand	11
India	10
Argentine	9
Europe	6
Rest of the World	30
Total	100

Not less important is the distribution of the investments between different classes of borrowers and enterprises.

Mr. Herbert Feis [2] has given a detailed classification of British investments in December 1913 from which the general pattern can be clearly seen. The total value was about £4000 million divided as shown in the above table between the Empire and the foreign countries.

Railway securties take the first place, since in the period in which the investments were being made railway construction was the most important development taking place in the world. They account for 40% of the total. Loans to government authorities, central, state or municipal, come next with 30%. Four other main groups, raw materials, banks and finance, commerce and industry, and public utilities together account for the remaining 30%. The great bulk of the capital raised was in the form of securities yielding a fixed rate of return, though in South Africa in particular the general investor invested substantially in equity stock. In many cases, however, the bonds subscribed to by the general public in this way were issued by a British Company whose investment was "direct," in the sense that it controlled the actual enterprise—e.g. railways in the Argentine and in China.

Some four-fifths of the British investment in Governmental and railway securities was in countries dependent upon the profitability of agriculture as an export industry.

The other most notable features of the system of foreign investment were these:

A large, and increasing, proportion of the earnings and dividends was absorbed in the form of an excess of imports into the United Kingdom over exports. At the same time enough was re-invested to increase total investments at the rate already indicated. This re-investment was an essential part of the system from the point of view of the borrower, as well as the lender; for repayments, particularly of Government borrowing, were normally made out of the proceeds of new loans, and the prospect of further borrowing was the best incentive to a debtor to keep up service payments.

British loans during this period were not "tied." The borrowers could freely use them to buy from foreign countries as well as from Britain. The bulk of the business doubtless went in fact to British industrialists, but the fact that the borrower was free to go elsewhere was a protection against exploitation and a help to the development of multilateral trade.

[2] *Europe the World's Banker 1870–1914,* Yale University Press, 1930.

The machinery through which these investments were arranged was highly developed and efficient. In the early years of Britain's export of capital, for a quarter of a century after 1850, the machinery and methods were in several respects unsatisfactory. A select Committee [3] of the House of Commons in 1875 had revealed weaknesses and abuses in the system by which loans had been issued to several countries in South America, as the Senate's investigation did in the American system about half a century later. But by 1880 the British system had been reformed and throughout the period which is now being discussed, in which Britain was the greatest lending country, London was the best equipped centre for the purpose; and it retained its superiority after that period ended. The British issuing houses developed traditions and rules of practice which attracted and safeguarded the investor. In a well known passage the Macmillan Committee [4] described the position in 1931:

"When he (the investor) is investing abroad he has the assistance of long-established issuing houses, whose reputation is world-wide. When subscriptions to a foreign issue are invited by means of a public prospectus, it is almost certain that that issue will be vouched for by one of these issuing houses whose name will be evidence that it has been thoroughly examined and the interests of the investors protected as far as possible. For the issuing house's issuing credit, which can easily be affected, is involved, and it is very highly to its own interest to make sure that the issue is sound. If, as must from time to time happen, something goes wrong with the loan or the borrower, the issuing house regards it as its duty to do everything it can to put matters straight, and, indeed, to watch continuously the actions of the borrowers to see that the security remains unimpaired. These duties are sometimes very onerous and involve a great deal of labour and expense, as well as judgment, skill and experience."

In addition to arranging long-term investment of this kind by the public, London developed an elaborate and extensive system of short-term financing of international trade through the acceptance houses and the discount market, which is described at length in the Macmillan Report. Until the first war the claims in respect of acceptances were roughly matched by bills and deposits held in London on foreign account. These short-term operations yielded

[3] Select Committee on Loans to Foreign States *Report*, 29th July, 1875.
[4] Committee on Finance and Industry *Report*, Cmd. 3897, 1931 (henceforth referred to as *Macmillan*), paragraph 387.

profits which were a substantial addition to Britain's "invisible exports"; and since the acceptances were directly linked to the actual movement of goods, the system was safe as well as profitable, so long as there was an approximate balance between them and the obligations in respect of the foreign deposits and short-term credits. In the inter-war period this balance was no longer maintained, and short-term foreign deposits made London very vulnerable in a world financial crisis. When the Macmillan Committee wrote its report (in 1931) the absence of any institutions for financing domestic enterprise had become a serious defect in the British financial system. But up to the first war there was little need of capital from the general investor or of institutions in London to encourage and collect it. Overseas investment during this period profited from this fact.

Till at least late in the 19th Century the development of home industry was financed mainly out of profits, or by direct personal arrangements between individuals. Of total national savings (including profits ploughed back) of nearly £400 million a year, rather more than half went to home industry, a little less than half abroad; but of the former only a small fraction was obtained from the general investor through the mechanism of the London market. The great bulk of home investment came from those who had personal knowledge of the particular businesses. One consequence was that capital was in a form which made the return vary with changing fortunes. Either the business was individually owned, or its capital was mainly in the form of share-capital (equities), whether "ordinary" or "preference," of a joint stock company. There was no undue weight of fixed debt involving an annual charge independent of profits. The capital structure was thus such as to afford an elastic buffer against bankruptcy in a period of depression. A further result was that the savings of the general investor who had no personal knowledge of a promising home enterprise were not required for industrial development at home and were therefore available for foreign investment and were attracted to it by the specialized and responsible issuing houses.

America's situation and system in the same period presented a striking contrast. Her domestic industry was before the first war expanding rapidly enough to absorb all, and more, of the capital available for investment. She was a net importer, not exporter, of capital. Her financial system was as clearly better fitted than the British to attract the general investor's savings to home invesment as it was less well fitted to guide them towards foreign investment. All important industrial issues in the United States were sponsored by some responsible issuing institution, whose name appeared prominently on the prospectus. The banks or issuing houses engaged their credit in the eyes of the public for the soundness of the issues, and accordingly maintained a close and intimate association with the industries concerned. They gave the public real guidance of a kind not available to the British home investor.

The relation of Britain's foreign investments to her balance of payments is often misunderstood. Throughout the whole of the period now under consideration, 1880–1913, the increase in her foreign assets was not due to any investment of a surplus of current earnings from an excess of exports of goods and services over payments for imports; for there was no such surplus, but a deficit. It was wholly due to the investment of a part of the income derived from earlier investments. It was only in an earlier period, which terminated soon after 1870, that the resources for foreign investment came from an excess of current exports over imports. In the whole period from 1870–1913, when total foreign investments increased from about £1000 million to nearly £4000 million, the total new investments made were only about 40% of the income from past investments during the same period. The relevant statistics are given in Mr. C.K. Hobson's *Export of Capital* [5] of which Mr. Devons has analyzed the significance.[6] He summarizes the record in the following striking table:

Period	Average Annual Income from Overseas Investment [*]	Average Annual Capital Exports [*]
1870–1875	48	55
1876–1880	48	−1
1881–1893	75	48
1894–1904	100	24
1905–1913	155	143

[*] £ millions

He comments justly "This British experience merely illustrates the essential point, which is so often overlooked, that a capital-exporting country soon finds itself in the position of being able to maintain its investment by re-investing income."

[5] C.K. Hobson, *Export of Capital*, Constable, 1914.
[6] *Manchester Guardian*, January 18th and 19th, 1950.

("Re-investment" must of course be understood in the national, not the individual, sense. To the individual investor the annual return from his foreign investments was a part of his income, which he would spend or invest at home or abroad as he might decide on personal grounds. But his foreign earnings however spent contributed to a surplus in the national balance of payments available for new foreign investments.)

23. INTERNATIONAL INVESTMENT TO-DAY IN THE LIGHT OF NINETEENTH-CENTURY EXPERIENCE

Ragnar Nurkse

Columbia University

Reprinted from *The Economic Journal*, LXIV (December 1954), pp. 744–758, by permission of the author and The Royal Economic Society.

A paper prepared for discussion at the Conference of the Association of University Teachers of Economics at Sheffield on January 2, 1954. My thanks are due to Mr. David Butt and Sir Donald MacDougall for a number of valuable and helpful comments.

To many Americans to-day the problem of international investment is doubtless a source of perplexity and even of some irritation. Ever since the last world war great expectations have been placed on the export of private American capital as a means of bridging the dollar gap as well as financing world economic development. In reality, private foreign investment throughout the period since 1945 has fluctuated at a low level and without any sign at all of an upward trend.[1] This is most disappointing. We suspect that the export of capital from Great Britain was one reason why the international economy of the Victorian era did not know of a chronic sterling shortage. We recognise, above all, that foreign investment was associated during that era with a tremendous spurt in world production and trade. There is in America a feeling of nostalgia for the nineteenth-century environment that made this flow of capital possible. The question is: why can we not re-create that environment?

The answer, I submit, must start from the fact that the circumstances in which overseas investment, and more especially British investment, went on in the nineteenth century (which I take to have ended in 1914) were in some ways quite exceptional. To realise this is of more than historical interest. So long as the peculiar features of that experience are not fully appreciated memories of wonders worked by foreign investment in the past can only lead to false hopes and frustration.

[1] Cf. *Federal Reserve Bulletin*, October 1953, pp. 1039–42.

Recently researches have made it possible to estimate approximately the percentage share of her national income that Britain used to lend abroad. Occasionally one finds the same proportions being applied to the present American national income as an indication of what the United States could or should do. Over the fifty years that preceded the outbreak of the First World War, it seems that Great Britain invested overseas an amount equal to about 4% of her national income. In the later part of the period (1905–13) the ratio was as high as 7%. If the United States to-day were to devote similar percentage portions of her national income to the same purposes, she would be exporting funds to the tune of $12 billion or, if we apply the higher percentage, some $20 billion each year. These figures are almost absurdly large and tend to confirm the view that there was something unique about Britain's foreign investment.

It was unique in that the greater part of it—roughly two-thirds—went to the so-called "regions of recent settlement": the spacious, fertile and virtually empty plains of Canada, the United States, Argentina, Australia and other "new" countries in the world's temperate latitudes. It was unique in that it went to these places together with a great migration of about 60 million people,[2] including many trained and enterprising persons, from the British Isles as well as Continental Europe. The conditions that made this flow of private capital possible do not exist to any great extent to-day, and probably cannot be re-created.

It was in the newly settled regions, which received two-thirds of the capital exports and practically all the emigrants, that nineteenth-century international investment scored its greatest triumphs. The remaining third of British capital exported (or more accurately a quarter, since some went to Continental Europe) was employed in a different type of area, where its achievements were much more dubious: tropical or sub-tropical regions inhabited, often densely, by native populations endowed in some cases with ancient civilisations of their own. The areas that formed a minor field for overseas investment before 1914 are the major problem to-day: the truly backward economies, containing now about two-thirds of the world's population. The empty and newly settled regions, from which international investment derived its brilliant general record and reputation, are to-day, in *per capita* income, among the most prosperous countries in the world.

[2] This is a gross figure; some of the migrants returned.

Labour and capital are complementary factors of production, and exert a profound attraction on each other. The movement of labour to the new regions attracted capital to the same places at the same time. And the other way round: the flow of capital stimulated the migration of people to these places. To some extent, it is true, the parallel movements of capital and labour might plausibly be interpreted as two separate effects of a common cause; namely, of the opening-up of the vast reserves of land and other natural resources. But the complementary nature of the labour and capital movements, based on the complementarity of the two factors, is equally plain. Any barrier to the transfer of one would have reduced the flow of the other. Labour and capital moved along side by side, supporting each other.[3]

In the twentieth century the situation is totally different. The capital exports from the United States can be viewed rather as a *substitute* for the movement of people. Capital and labour are still complementary, and still basically attract one another. But as things now are, restricting the movement of labour in one direction increases the need, if not the incentive, for capital to move in the opposite direction. Cheap labour, instead of being allowed to come to the United States to work with American capital there, is to some extent supplied with American capital abroad (supplied by the American Government as in the years since 1945, if not by private profit-seeking investors, as in the 1920s). The underlying pressure—not necessarily the profit motive, but what we might call the global social pressure—is very strong for more capital to move out from the United States to work with the cheap labour in the world's backward economies. But notice that in this situation, in sharp contrast to the predominant nineteenth-century pattern, capital is being urged to go out to work with people that have not grown up in a capital-minded milieu, and may not be culturally prepared for the use of western equipment, methods and techniques.

With this situation in mind, we can perceive what I think is the basic rationale of the present American emphasis on direct business investment as a means of financing economic development. The advantages rightly attributed to it are, first, that it goes out with Amer-

---

[3] It is interesting to observe that the parallel nature of the two factor movements shows itself also, according to Professor A.K. Cairncross [*Home and Foreign Investment, 1870–1913* (Cambridge, 1953), p. 209], in the close agreement with which capital exports and emigration from Britain varied from decade to decade between 1870 and 1910.

ican enterprise, tied up with American "knowhow," and, secondly, that it is likely to be productively used, not swallowed up—directly or indirectly—by immediate consumption in the receiving country. Since, however, in the low-income areas the domestic market is small, this type of investment tends inevitably in such areas to concentrate on extractive industries—mines, plantations, oil wells—producing raw materials for export mainly to the advanced countries. This is, in effect, the so-called "colonial" pattern of foreign investment, of which American oil operations abroad are now an outstanding example. It has its drawbacks as well as its virtues. But, in any event, the stress laid—even in the original Point Four programme —on direct investments in economically backward countries should not, in my opinion, be dismissed as merely a product of conservative business ideology; it reflects in part an essential difference in the present-day environment of international investment as compared with the nineteenth century.

In the aggregate flow of capital in the nineteenth century, the "colonial" type of venture played a minor role. Looking at Britain's foreign investment portfolio in 1913, we find that, of an estimated total of about £3,700 million outstanding at that time in nominal value, 30% was in loans to governments, as much as 40% in railway securities and some 5% in other public utilities, so that no less than three-quarters of the total was in public or public-utility investments. The rest includes banking, insurance and manufacturing companies, as well as investments directly in raw-material extraction. The total should be increased by making some allowance (say, £300 million) for private holdings and participations not represented by securities listed on the London Stock Exchange; but that would make little difference to the proportions indicated. It is therefore far from correct to assume, as is sometimes done, that the "colonial" form of enterprise in the extraction of mineral and plantation products for the creditor country was the typical pattern of foreign investment. To call it the "traditional" pattern might be justified in view of its history in earlier centuries. But in the nineteenth century its total amount was comparatively small; and what little there was of it appears to have been concentrated, as one would expect, in colonial and predominantly tropical areas.

To the new countries, by contrast, capital moved chiefly through the medium of securities carrying a fixed return (*i.e.*, bonds and preference shares) issued by public authorities and public-utility undertakings. To these countries, it appears, capital could safely be sent in the form of relatively untied funds, with a good chance that it would remain capital there, because the people in these places, having come from Europe themselves, knew what to do with capital and how to handle it. Cultural adaptation was no problem.

These countries—the "regions of recent settlement" that absorbed the bulk of British overseas investment—were offshoots of European civilisation.[4] For Britain, or at any rate for Europe as a whole, investment in these areas was essentially a process of capital widening rather than deepening. Indeed, when Britain sent capital out to work with Swedes, Poles, Germans and Italians emigrating overseas, she may have done so at the expense of the deepening which her own economy is said to have needed in the period just before the First World War. But international investment in the nineteenth century was, of course, unplanned, and was determined by private rather than national advantages. French and German activities in Eastern Europe and the Near East were an exception in this respect. As Professor Viner has remarked, "the French loans to Russia . . . bore a close resemblance to the programme of military aid to Western Europe which we are now embarking on."[5]

Great Britain's national advantage, apart from the return flow of interest and dividends, seemed to be handsomely served through cheaper food and raw materials, though this benefit was shared by other importing countries that had made no corresponding investments and, besides, as we now realise, was derived in part from *Raubwirtschaft*, through soil depletion and erosion in some of the rich new plains (for example, in the virgin grasslands of the Mississippi valley).

Production of primary commodities for export to the industrial creditor countries is characteristic of the "colonial" pattern of direct

[4] The precise composition of this group may give rise to some debate, though essentially the line is clear. It takes in Canada, the United States, Australia, New Zealand and South Africa. In South America it certainly includes Argentina and Uruguay, rich farm and grazing lands in temperate latitudes settled predominantly by recent immigration from Europe. I would perhaps include also the southern tip of Brazil, to which the same description largely applies, and in which most of Brazil's productive capacity, including immigration as well as foreign capital, has been concentrated since the middle of the nineteenth century.

[5] "America's Aims and the Progress of Underdeveloped Countries," in *The Progress of Underdeveloped Areas*, edited by B.F. Hoselitz (Chicago, 1952), p. 184.

investment in economically backward areas. In the regions of recent settlement foreign investment can also be said to have been induced essentially by the raw-material needs of the industrial centres— especially by Great Britain's demand for the wheat, wool, meat and dairy products, which she decided not to try to produce for herself, and which these temperate regions were particularly well suited to produce. The capital that came into these regions did not, however, enter into primary production itself, but was employed above all in building up the costly framework of public services, including especially transport, which laid the basis for domestic industrial development, as well as for the production of raw commodities for export. These areas are now, and have been for some time, pre-dominantly industrial,[6] a fact entirely compatible with the large or even preponderant share of primary products in their export trade.

Nineteenth-century foreign investment centered on the railway— that "great instrument of improvement," in Lord Dalhousie's phrase. If account is taken not only of railway securities but also of the use to which many government loans were put, it seems that well over half of Britain's external investment before 1914 went into railway construction. The great bulk of this was in the newly settled countries. The Indian railways, though an important individual item, accounted for less than one-tenth of the total of overseas railway securities held by British investors in 1914. The United States and the Argentine alone accounted for more than half of that total. In the new countries the railway was important as a means of migration. The great pioneer lines—first in the United States, later in the Argentine and elsewhere—were deliberately planned and built *in advance* of current traffic needs; they themselves created the settlement and economic growth that eventually led to a full demand for their services.

Although individual promoters sometimes played the most conspicuous part, the railways in the new countries were built, as a rule, if not directly by governments, at any rate with extensive government assistance in the form of land grants, subsidies and guaranteed returns to the investors. In view of this fact, one can safely say that the bulk of international investment in the nineteenth century depended on government action in the borrowing countries. In French and German capital exports, some of which also went to the

---

[6] See F. Hilgerdt, *Industrialization and Foreign Trade* (League of Nations, 1945), pp. 26, 39 and *passim*.

new world, the proportion of government loans and other public investments was even higher than in the British case.

It is true that the transport revolution, to which the cheapening of British food imports (especially in the years 1880–1900) was largely due, was a matter of steamships as well as railways. While railway construction overseas was a major object of international financing, British shipbuilding counted almost entirely as part of British home investment. Since ship and railway building had much the same effects on international trade and the terms of trade, the distinction between home and foreign investment appears in this case somewhat arbitrary. In the internal economic expansion of the new countries, however, the railways had, of course, a very special part to play, rather different from that of the ships. And so we hear, for example, that "in the Argentine, the railway is like a magic talisman: for wherever it goes it entirely transforms the economic and productive conditions of the country." [7]

Overseas railway investment became predominant from about 1870 onwards. But this does not mean that the earlier part of the century can be ignored. While the total of foreign investment was much smaller then, so was everything else. We should note that by 1870 Britain's overseas assets had already grown to about the same order of magnitude as her annual national income. Capital imports were a prominent feature in the economic history of the United States for many years before the Civil War.

It is clear that the main flow of capital in the nineteenth century was not to the neediest countries with their "teeming millions," which were indeed neglected, but to sparsely peopled areas where conditions for rapid growth along familiar western lines were exceptionally favourable. If we were to look round for similar opportunities in the twentieth century, I do not know where we should find them if not in the further development of the same regions of recent settlement; or else perhaps in Siberia—a vast area reputedly

[7] A.B. Martinez and M. Lewandowski, *The Argentine in the Twentieth Century* (London, 1911), p. 108. A statement such as this applies to a type of region with the particular physical and human characteristics already noted. It would not apply in the same way to a country like India, where, for reasons that cannot be entered into, the railway "did not give rise to a flood of satellite innovations" and "destroyed more employment opportunities [e.g., in traditional village industries] that it opened up" (L.H. Jenks, "British Experience with Foreign Investments," *Journal of Economic History*, 1944, Supplement, p. 75).

rich in natural resources, which may be longing for an injection of skilled labour from Europe and capital from the United States.

Once the main facts about the nineteenth-century capital flow are set out in something like their true proportions,[8] it is curious to see how little they fit in with some pre-conceived notions that have been widely current. Bernard Shaw, for example, in Act I of *The Apple Cart*, made one of his characters talk about England sending her "capital abroad to places where poverty and hardship still exist: in other words, where labour is cheap. We live in comfort on the imported profits of that capital." Consider, more seriously, the summary which Mrs. Joan Robinson gives (in *The Rate of Interest and Other Essays*, 1952, pp. 157–8) of the views of Rosa Luxemburg:

"The capitalist nations are surrounded by primitive economies, each insulated from the others like a nut within its shell, waiting to be cracked. The capitalists break open a primitive economy and enter into trade with it, whether by enticing its inhabitants with commodities they have never seen before, by political cunning or by brute force. Now exports to the primitives provide an outlet for the product of the last batch of capital goods created at home. After a little while another nut is broken, a use for more capital is thereby found, and so on, as long as the supply of untouched primitive economies lasts. . . . When the stock of unbroken nuts is exhausted, the capitalist system collapses for want of markets."

This is one variant of neo-Marxist doctrine and, like others, it neglects some crucial facts. No pre-existing markets were conquered in the new countries. Markets were *created* there by labour, enterprise and capital all drawn from Europe. In the industrially primi-

---

[8] I have thought it superfluous to give detailed references to the well-known sources, such as the works of C.K. Hobson, L.H. Jenks, H. Feis and the Royal Institute of International Affairs. Among recent essays and articles that I have found useful, the following should be mentioned: N.S. Buchanan, "International Finance," *Survey of Contemporary Economics* (Vol. II, ed. by B.F. Haley, 1952); P. Hartland, "Private Enterprise and International Capital," *Canadian Journal of Economics and Political Science*, February 1953; Sir Arthur Salter, "Foreign Investment," *Essays in International Finance*, Princeton University, February 1951; Brinley Thomas, "Migration and the Rhythm of Economic Growth, 1830–1913," *The Manchester School*, September 1951; L.H. Jenks, "Railroads as an Economic Force in American Development," *Enterprise and Secular Change* (ed. by F.C. Lane and J.C. Riemersma, 1953); H.S. Ferns, "The Establishment of the British Investment in Argentina," *Inter-American Economic Affairs*, Autumn 1951; J.F. Rippy, "British Investments in Latin America, End of 1913," *ibid.*; A.H. Imlah, "British Balance of Payments and Export of Capital, 1816–1913," *Economic History Review*, 1952 (vol. V, No. 2).

tive countries markets were and have remained unattractive because of mass poverty. Why is it, for example, that in the 1920s Canada, Australia and New Zealand, with already quite highly developed industries of their own and with a combined population of only 17.4 millions, imported twice as much manufactured goods as India with her 340 million people? [9]

The American public also, perhaps because it lives in one of the new countries itself, does not always appreciate the peculiar nature of the nineteenth-century investment experience. Some of us are too apt to forget—or to take for granted—all that went with it and to assume, from that experience, a "simple equivalence of the pace of capital transfer and the pace of development." [10] Keynes in 1922 made a remark that is worth recalling: "The practice of foreign investment, as we know it now, is a very modern contrivance, a very unstable one, and only suited to peculiar circumstances." [11] He cautioned against extending it by simple analogy to a different set of circumstances. Private foreign lending in the 1920s can be viewed in part as a backwash of the great momentum which it had gathered before 1914. Was it because in Central Europe foreign investment was applied to a situation to which it was unsuited that it came to grief there? It might perhaps have worked; Hitler did not give it a chance. Yet the fact is that it did not work.

Will it work, and if so, how will it work, in the "under-developed" areas of which we hear so much to-day? The preceding remarks have all been leading up to this question. My purpose here is to present the question, against the background of past experience, rather than try to answer it. In the time that remains I will only hazard a few brief comments on three general topics: direct business investment, public-utility investment and governmental grants.

The assumption I am making here—that it is the low-income areas that constitute the main problem of international investment in the mid-twentieth century—may be challenged as arbitrary and not entirely justified. The most profitable opportunities may still be in the "regions of recent settlement." But having regard to their high income levels, these fortunate regions can, in the present discussion, be left to provide, by and large, for their own development needs.

[9] F. Hilgerdt, op. cit., p. 84.
[10] Honor Croome, "The Dilemma of Development," in New Commonwealth, November 9, 1953, p. 487.
[11] A Revision of the Treaty, p. 161.

For reasons mentioned earlier, direct investments by American business firms—usually financed from corporate reserves rather than security issues on the capital market—are thought to be particularly well suited to the economically backward countries. But they have their shortcomings also. In the life of an industrially primitive community they are apt to create not only a dual economy [12] but also a dual society, in which conditions for the diffusion of western technology may actually be the reverse of favourable. Foreign business investment is not always a happy form of encounter between different civilisations. Besides, if techniques are to be of wide and permanent use, they must be adapted to local conditions. The methods of giant corporations, whose foreign operations are sometimes only a side-show, are often too standardised to favour such adaptation. And so the local economy may not get much help from the example they give; the example is often inapplicable. Let us remember that the Japanese acquired industrial techniques very effectively before they began to receive any substantial foreign business investments. Also the technical assistance programmes now in operation remind us that there are other ways of spreading technical knowledge.

As a rule, when foreign business enterprise is attracted to economically backward areas, it is mainly for the production of raw materials for export markets, for the simple reason that the domestic market in such areas, even if protected by import restrictions, is generally too poor to afford any strong inducement to invest.[13] The natural result is a "colonial" investment pattern, open to the familiar

[12] Cf. H.W. Singer, "The Distribution of Gains between Investing and Borrowing Countries," *American Economic Review, Papers and Proceedings,* May 1950.

[13] From the latest comprehensive figures for American direct investments (*Survey of Current Business,* December 1952), it can be seen that of the total invested in Canada and Western Europe at the end of 1950, 23% was in extractive industries, as much as 60% in manufacturing and trade, 6% in public utilities and 11% in miscellaneous activities, including cinemas and other entertainments. Of the investments outstanding on the same date in all other countries, which with a few exceptions are economically backward, 60% was in extractive industries, mostly petroleum and mining, with 20%, 17% and 3% respectively in the other groups. This pattern is by no means new. We know that in 1929 only one-fifth of total American direct investment was in manufacturing, and 84% of this was in Western Europe, Canada, Australia and New Zealand. "Only to a very small extent, therefore, did American direct investments enter into manufacturing for the domestic market in under-developed countries." (United Nations, *International Capital Movements in the Inter-War Period,* 1949, p. 32.)

criticisms that it tends to promote lopsided rather than "balanced" growth, and that it makes for instability due to high dependence on foreign demand for one or two staple products. If this type of direct investment is to take place in any considerable volume, it presupposes a long-run prospect of rapidly expanding demand in the industrial centres for the raw materials which it seeks to provide. Despite the forecasts of the Paley Report, there is no firm assurance of such an expansion except for certain minerals. Governmental purchase agreements alone cannot give this assurance in the absence of favourable basic demand conditions. A temporary stimulus might be got from the removal of United States tariff protection on primary products (such as sugar, copper, wool), but little can be hoped for in this direction.

In the last few years one of the chief economic obstacles to a greater flow of business funds to low-income countries has been the high level of business profits obtainable at home, from developing American natural resources and catering to the American mass market. Conditions may change. It is not inconceivable that business investment abroad might greatly increase in the future, and that it might bring substantial benefits to the poorer countries. Yet, on the whole, it seems unlikely that direct investment alone can become anything like an adequate source of international finance for economic development. It played, as we saw, a minor part in the nineteenth century. Can we rely on it to play a major part to-day? I doubt it.

What is most urgently needed to-day is a revival of the public or public-utility type of international investment that used to dominate the scene. The International Bank has hardly begun to fill the gap left by the disappearance of this type of private foreign lending. If the past cannot be reproduced, it is all the more imperative to devise a new pattern suited to present needs and conditions. Critics have wondered how much of nineteenth-century foreign investment would have survived the tests and rules laid down by the International Bank. The Bank, being dependent on the private capital market for most of its loanable funds, inevitably reflects to some extent the attitudes of the private investor. And the private American investor is still waiting for a change in the weather, and remains unimpressed by statistics showing that only 15% of the dollar bonds (not counting direct investments) floated in the 1920s by under-developed countries—that is, aside from Central Europe—have proved a permanent loss.[14]

It is said that there are not enough productive projects in the low-income countries to absorb much more money than is now going out. It is pointed out that the Marshall Plan, which accustomed the world to the sight of a large dollar outflow, was not a plan of new development so much as one of reconstruction, in an area where a solid industrial foundation and the "know-how" of a skilled population already existed.[15]

No doubt this point has considerable force. But if there are not enough projects, can we not ask for international technical assistance to design them and to draw up the blueprints? Lack of basic services, such as transport, power and water supply, is a particularly serious bottleneck in the poor countries. Because of this the *physical* environment—quite apart from the obvious difficulties arising from the political or social climate—is unfavourable to private investment. A large foreign firm producing raw materials for export may find it profitable to set up incidental facilities such as roads or waterworks, of which the local economy, too, can make some use. But the general utility of such things often depends in haphazard fashion on the technical features of the firm's main activity. It may be fairly high in the case of a railway built by a mining company from the interior of Peru to the sea-coast. It is virtually zero in the case of the pipe-line in which Arabian oil is pumped to the Mediterranean.

In the United States a hundred years ago public authorities, as well as private promoters, played a leading role in the drive for "internal improvements," financed in part by foreign capital. There is no question that ample scope exists for international financing of public improvements in the poor countries to-day. Until these countries have acquired a skeleton framework of such facilities, conditions will not be particularly attractive for the more varied and smaller-scale business investments there. Even with such basic improvements, of course, the individual business investments, domestic as well as foreign, may fail to materialise, because of other obstacles. It is conceivable, therefore, that some of these public works would

[14] Cf. the Gray Report (1950), p. 62.

[15] It will be remembered, however, that some of the Marshall Aid was in effect passed on to "under-developed" countries (especially by way of the United Kingdom, whose overall balance was in equilibrium in 1948–49 and in surplus in 1950).

turn out to be white elephants. But the risk has to be taken; any form of capital investment is, in the last analysis, an act of faith. However hard it may be for the pioneering spirit that opened up the new countries to apply itself to the low-income areas to-day, not much can be achieved without that spirit, and no international organisation concerned with development can remain untouched by it.

Apart from the distribution of the promoter-function, there still remains the question of finance. If the profitability of American business at home has kept down direct investments abroad, a simple comparison of bond yields does not explain why "portfolio" lending cannot get started again. However, while the private investor has been standing on the side-lines, we may have witnessed the beginnings of a system of international grants-in-aid and low-interest loans from government funds. The reference to the principle of Equal Sacrifice with which Roosevelt defended the Lend-Lease programme may some day appear significant in retrospect. I need not point to other signs and landmarks. Let me just quote a few recent expressions of opinion. The man who gave his name to the Marshall Plan, in accepting the Nobel peace prize last December, said that it was "of basic importance to any successful effort towards an enduring peace that the more favoured nations should lend assistance in bettering the lot of the poorer." [16]

Dr. Herbert Feis, the historian of nineteenth-century foreign investment, has expressed himself as follows:

"A sense of obligation has won its way in the world to the effect that a wealthy country has a call of vague dimensions to provide means to assist poorer and suffering countries. To give free admission to [it] would bankrupt us and demoralise others; but to ignore the obligation wholly would be . . . out of accord with the effort in which we are engaged, to bring together the nations of the world in peaceful and co-operative understanding." [17]

Even if we hesitate to accept the assumption that world peace can be bought or that material progress makes for contentment, the fact of growing pressures for international income transfers must nevertheless be recognised. It may be precisely because the problem of international investment is now, unlike what it was in the Victorian

[16] *The Times,* December 12, 1953.
[17] "International Economic Outlook," *Proceedings of the Academy of Political Science,* New York, May 1953, p. 59.

era, concerned in the main with the backward economies that the need for such transfers is felt to arise.

The difficulties which American trade policy encounters in following the British nineteenth-century example might also be taken to point to unilateral income transfers as more in accord with the underlying situation. With commercial foreign investment an adjustment of the trade balance to the return flow of interest and dividends cannot normally be long postponed, while gifts permit an export surplus indefinitely.[18]

The idea of international grants-in-aid is essentially a consequence of the increased gaps in living standards and of the closeness of contact that is creating at the same time an increasingly acute awareness of these gaps—a situation without historical precedent. This awareness is perhaps the most fundamental obstacle to the resumption of private international lending. In contrast to the position of the backward economies to-day, income per head in the principal debtor countries of the nineteenth century—the newly settled regions—can never have been far below European levels. Interest payments from poor to rich are now, it seems, not only basically unwanted by the rich countries but indeed are felt to be somehow contrary to the spirit of the age. And although public grants (for "social overhead capital") and private foreign lending (for more specific investments) can ideally be looked upon as complementary rather than conflicting sources of finance, it is easy to see

[18] However, I cannot fully share the view that, just because of the growing return flow to which it normally gives rise, foreign investment of the orthodox sort can be no more than a short-period remedy for international imbalance. When in support of this view it is said that the increase in Great Britain's foreign assets from 1880 to 1913 "was due wholly to the reinvestment of a part of the income derived from earlier investments" (Salter, *op. cit.*, pp. 9, 53), it seems to me that a somewhat arbitrary causal attribution is made between two items on opposite sides of the balance of payments, a procedure always of doubtful validity, and particularly so when one of the items represents payments on capital account, while the other belongs to the income account. That the individual British investor, on the one hand, was under no obligation to reinvest the interest he got from abroad is obvious. From the national viewpoint, on the other hand, all one can say is that the British current account, including foreign interest earnings as well as earnings from merchandise exports and shipping, showed a surplus, which was balanced by the outflow of capital. Britain had an excess of merchandise imports over exports throughout the period 1880–1913. Yet it is conceivable that if British foreign lending had come to a complete stop in (say) 1890, a disequilibrium in the international balance of payments—a "sterling shortage"—might have been felt in the succeeding quarter of a century.

why in practice the two do not mix at all well. This applies not only to grants but also in some degree to international loans from government sources.

Persistent attempts in the United Nations organisation to set up a system of international grants under U.N. auspices—from the UNEDA proposal of 1948 to the SUNFED report of 1953—have foundered on the rocks of American opposition. Yet American practices and pronouncements alike have kept world expectations alive, and this has continued to some extent under the Republican administration. Two notable declarations by President Eisenhower last year attracted wide attention: one was the statement in April about "devoting a substantial percentage of the savings achieved by disarmament to a fund for world aid," the other being the so-called "Atom Bank" proposal for the international provision of atomic energy for peaceful purposes.

It must be recognised that international unilateral transfers have no necessary connection with the subject of foreign *investment*. They may be for current consumption or for military use. Even if they are intended for, or tied to, particular capital projects, a net increase in the overall rate of accumulation is not always assured. If they are to make an effective contribution to economic development, they call for domestic action in the receiving countries—fiscal, monetary and other policies designed to withhold resources from immediate consumption and to direct them into capital formation.

But once the receiving countries are capable of devising the necessary controls for the productive use of outside aid, they should be equally capable of using such policies for the mobilisation of potential *domestic* sources of capital (*e.g.*, skimming off resources now absorbed by luxury consumption, making use of labour set free from the land through better farm methods or recruiting any surplus labour already existing on the land). It is far from my intention to suggest that in these circumstances foreign aid becomes unnecessary. Yet this consideration does shift the emphasis upon the need for domestic policies to ensure that in the overall use of resources, domestic as well as external, investment is given top priority.[19] Here is the main criterion, and a body such as the World Bank has in this respect an even more vital role to play in the backward

[19] This theme is developed in my *Problems of Capital Formation in Underdeveloped Countries* (Oxford, 1953).

economies than that which the E.C.A. and the O.E.E.C. performed under the Marshall Plan.

These remarks on international grants and their possible uses may all be idle speculation, for which, perhaps, I should apologise. The practices alluded to may turn out to have been temporary devices related to particular emergency conditions. What I have said on these controversial matters should have been put in the form of questions—and extremely tentative questions at that. But they are, I think, questions which a survey of the present state of international finance inevitably draws to our attention.

V. Multilateralism and Capital Movements

COMMENTARY

A major theme of this book has been the nature and consequences of balance of payments disequilibrium and the means of adjustment. We have thus far confined our attention almost entirely to "free market" means of adjustment—alterations in price levels, in national incomes, and in exchange rates. But especially since the start of the Great Depression nations have, in fact, generally relied heavily on various direct controls and interventions by government to "protect" their balances of payments.

MULTILATERALISM AND DISCRIMINATION

Frisch (selection 18), it seems fair to interpret, believes that that for an indefinite time exchange control will be a prominent feature of international economics, and, furthermore, this need not be wholly regrettable. The world being what it is, he suggests that the appropriate choice is not between exchange control and no exchange control, but rather between "optimum" exchange control and unduly burdensome exchange control.[1]

[1] In another article, in which he proposes a plan of internationally coordinated, multilateral exchange control, Frisch thus sets the stage: "With the change in economic philosophy which had gained momentum in the depressions between World Wars I and II, and had continued to grow through the last war, and with the drift toward more direct control and stronger influence by the state on the course of economic affairs, it was only natural that the extremely difficult balance of payments situation in many countries should lead to very extensive application of import and export regulations. . . . The more difficult the balance of payments situation is, the more we must be prepared to see international trade take on the form of bilateral agreements. . . . One cannot expect that an individual country which faces the problem of 'export or die,' and which has by experience discovered the power that it has to

488

Table I gives Frisch's initial unbalanced situation. In his problem, there is the dual objective of eliminating all national *overall* deficits and surpluses with a minimum reduction in the volume of world trade; this objective is to be achieved within the constraint of not increasing any nation's exports. If the deficits of countries *A* and *B* and the surplus of *C* are to be eliminated by exchange controls, the controls may be either (a) non-discriminatory, or "proportional," or (b) discriminatory, or "non-proportional."

Table I

Exporting Country	Importing Country A	B	C	Total Exports	Surplus
A	–	5	1	6	
B	3	–	2	5	
C	8	1	–	9	6
Total Imports	11	6	3	20	
Deficit	5	1			

Table II

Exporting Country	Importing Country A	B	C	Total Exports	Surplus
A	–	3.23	1	4.23	
B	1.94	–	2	3.94	.05
C	5.18	.65	–	5.83	2.83
Total Imports	7.12	3.88	3	14	
Deficit	2.89				

---

influence its own economic affairs through direct controls, shall be willing to accept an abstract argument about the damage done to international trade as a whole through the bilateral agreement and therefore give up such agreements. . . . One must look for a system of trade agreements that can meet the bilateral agreement on its own ground, i.e., which can give the individual countries the same sort of obvious advantage as the bilateral trade agreement can, but which at the same time is as free as possible from the limitational effect of the bilateral agreement." "Outline of a System of Multicompensatory Trade," *Review of Economics and Statistics*, XXX (November 1948), p. 265.

Table III

Exporting Country	Importing Country A	B	C	Total Exports	Surplus
A	–	4.15	1	5.15	
B	1.64	–	2	3.64	
C	4.36	.85	0	5.21	2.21
Total Imports	6	5	3	14	
Deficit	.85	1.36			

Table IV

Exporting Country	Importing Country A	B	C	Total Exports	Surplus
A	–	3	1	4	
B	3	–	1	4	
C	1	1	–	2	
Total Imports	4	4	2	10	
Deficit					

If *A* and *B* are to restrict *all* of their imports proportionally (*C*, the surplus country, need not restrict imports), by what proportion or proportions? One possibility is for *A* and *B* to act as a unit in determining a common proportion by which to reduce their respective imports. *A* and *B* have total imports of 17 and exports of 11; therefore, they may reduce their total imports by 6/17, i.e., multiply their imports by 11/17. This would give Table II. But this obviously will not do: although the trade balances have been greatly reduced, they have not yet been eliminated.

A second "proportional" possibility would be for *A* and *B* each separately to curtail its imports by the apparently appropriate ratio to balance its own trade. *A* has imports of 11 and exports of 6; therefore, it may restrict imports by 5/11; and *B* restricts by 1/6. Table III gives the results. Again we fail to achieve all-round balanced trade immediately, i.e., directly with a single dose of restriction.

There is a solution, however, as Frisch illustrates. There is some coefficient by which we can multiply the imports of *A* and another to apply to the imports of *B* such that we obtain a balanced trade pattern (see Frisch's Table III). It is assumed that *C* maintains her imports although her exports—and consequently also her income, in the absence of domestic stabilization policies—are falling.

While the proportionality method has eliminated all balance of payments imbalances, it has done so at the cost of greatly reduced trade, the volume now being only 9.39. It may be possible to achieve the objective of balance at less cost through discriminatory restrictions by *A* and *B*. One rule of discrimination could call for each country to restrict its imports from all nations with which it has an import balance. Each country sees to it that it has no import balances, and thus each country's trade is balanced, as in Table IV. *A* restricts imports from *C*; *B* restricts imports from *A*; *C* restricts imports from *B*.

The volume of trade is slightly greater in this case than under the proportionality procedure (10 compared to 9.39). But we can do still better if *A* and *B* discriminate against imports from *C* (although *B* has an export balance with *C*), and if *C* does not curtail imports at all. That is, the *overall* deficit countries (*A* and *B*) discriminate against the *overall* surplus country (*C*), cutting their imports from *C* by the amounts of their respective total deficits. As seen in Frisch's Table IV, this discriminatory approach allows multilaterally balanced trade with a trade volume of 14.

Frisch goes on to show that if more than three countries are involved, initially the imports of deficit countries from surplus countries may be smaller than their total deficits. In such cases, deficit countries will have to restrict imports also from countries originally in balance (and the latter must then curtail their own imports in order to avoid deficits).

This approach to problems of balance of payments disequilibria has been widely criticized. Hinshaw, for example, denies that it provides a strong case for discrimination:

. . . any superiority which discriminatory import restrictions may have as a means of minimizing a contraction in international trade depends upon whether the appropriate (and continually changing) formula of discrimination, as derived from the trade matrix, is complied with by all countries. Even in situations involving as few as four countries, the correct formula is not likely to be stumbled upon by accident, particularly since it may require countries already in balance to reduce exports and imports. Under realistic conditions embracing many countries, only the highest degree of international cooperation would insure the superiority of discrimination as a method of minimizing contractions in the volume of international trade. The trade matrix would have to be continuously scrutinized; detailed balance-of payments data for all countries would have to be obtained at frequent intervals without appreciable lag; and all countries would have to be willing promptly to adjust their imports and exports to the changing requirements of the matrix formula. From the outset, cooperation would be required not only on the part of the deficit countries but also on the part of the surplus countries (which would have to agree not to retaliate) and on the part of the countries already in balance (to which a directive to contract imports and exports might seem unfair).[2]

MULTILATERALISM AND CONVERTIBILITY

In Figure I we diagram the data of some of the foregoing tables: Ia gives the initial, unbalanced situation; Ib, the solution of "proportional" restriction (Frisch's Table III); Ic, a severe discriminatory restriction (our Table IV); Id, Frisch's discriminatory restriction (his Table IV). Ib, Ic, and Id are alternative situations of multilateral balance, i.e., each nation is in overall balance vis-à-vis the rest of the world, and Ic is also a

---

[2] Randall Hinshaw, "Professor Frisch on Discrimination and Multilateral Trade," *Review of Economics and Statistics*, XXX (November 1948), pp. 273–274. See also the critiques of J.J. Polak, "Balancing International Trade: A Comment on Professor Frisch's Paper," *American Economic Review*, XXXVIII (March 1948), pp. 139–142; Gerald M. Meier, "The Trade Matrix: A Further Comment on Professor Frisch's Paper," *ibid.*, (September 1948), pp. 624–626; Anthony Y.C. Koo, "A Note on Professor Frisch's Trade Matrix and Discriminatory Restriction of Imports," *Review of Economics and Statistics*, XXXIV (February 1952), pp. 77–79.

case of bilateral balance. World trade volume in situation Ib is
9.39, 10 in Ic, and 14 in Id.

Since each country is bilaterally balanced with every other
country in case Ic, there are no problems of currency con-

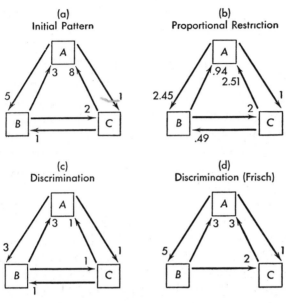

Figure I

vertibility (see Haberler, selection 20). Each nation earns
just as much of every other country's currency as it requires to
pay for its imports from each of the other countries. The situation is different in Id. While each country's *total* imports
and exports balance, no country is there bilaterally balanced
with any trading partner. Country A, e.g., has an export balance with B and an import balance with C: A has surplus
earnings of B-currency and equal deficiency of C-currency.
But there is no inherent difficulty, for A not only *wishes* to use
its surplus B-currency to cover its C-deficit, but C is *willing* to
accept B-currency, for C has a deficit of the same amount with
B. Similarly, both B and C can use their surplus currencies to

cover their deficits, for their respective creditors require such currencies to cover their own deficits.

This multilateral-balance situation of Id is quite different from the multilateral-imbalance situation of Ia. In Ia, A again has a surplus in trade with B; also A has an import balance from C, and C is a net importer from B, as in Id. But in Ia, A's deficit with C (of 7) is larger than its surplus with B (of 2); furthermore, C has no use for 2 units of B-currency, for its deficit with B is only 1. A has total exports of 6 and imports of 11, which is financial probem enough, but if only 4 of its exports to B can be used to cover current imports (i.e., 3 pay for imports from B, and 1 is accepted by C), her problem is intensified.

Thus we may state—as a first and unelaborated approximation—that the fundamental condition of convertibility is that *each* nation in the trading community be in *overall* (but not necessarily *bilateral*) balance.[3]

The Frisch approach to balance of payments problems—centering on direct trade controls rather than on fundamental adjustments of prices, incomes, and exchange rates—represents a point of view quite different from that of Hilgerdt (selection 19). The gains from unrestricted multilateral exchange lie at the very core of the traditional theory of international trade: freedom of traders to buy and sell where they please means inevitably a multilateral trade pattern. Frisch is, of course, not oblivious to the advantages of multilateralism. Indeed, his objective is to retain as much multilateralism as possible—within the limits of his overall approach. But, as Hinshaw remarks, Frisch's ingenious scheme is "the essentially restrictive goal of minimum-contraction-via-discrimination."[4]

The issue thus joined might be designated the choice between two alternatives: the search for the discrimination formula of least cost versus the search for the equilibrium ex-

---

[3] ". . . convertibility . . . requires that each country shall be able freely to use its accruing foreign exchange in order to acquire any good or currencies in the world; and this in turn implies a . . . highly important condition for convertibility of the currency of one country: *convertibility of all currencies of its partners in international trade*." C. Goedhart, "Conditions for Convertibility," *Economia Internazionale*, VIII (March 1955), p. 288.

[4] Hinshaw, *op. cit.*, p. 274. Meier (*op. cit.*, p. 625) holds that "the skewness of the matrix may be symptomatic of different kinds of disequilibria. The

change rate. It may be that the first alternative is our best hope: we may have to be content with minimizing losses rather than maximizing gains. But the costs, even if minimized, are great. Ellis holds that "it has become apparent how disastrously those payment arrangements which have grown up in the absence of convertibility—clearings and exchange controls—have abridged the efficacy of the market forces." [5] This abridgment involves more than the loss of "only" economic efficiency narrowly conceived, for the price system, or market mechanism, is a powerful method of community and inter-community *organization*.

International equilibrium and currency convertibility are not ends in themselves and like free markets in strategic raw materials and low taxes, it may be well to sacrifice them to important national and international objectives. It is the conclusion of this study, however, that trade discrimination and exchange restrictions on current transactions are not only economically harmful, but they are responsible for a misallocation of resources which the free world can ill afford if it is to defend itself against internal and external aggression. Paradoxically, however, the defense program is frequently cited as one of the reasons why nations cannot achieve equilibrium and currency convertibility.

. . . world trade is directed by a monstrously complex network of trade and payments arrangements which has minimized the role

---

disequilibrium may be of a cyclical or non-cyclical character and, under the latter, either a price disequilibrium or a structural disequilibrium. Even though the payment effect may be present in all these cases, it is apparent that discriminatory import restrictions would not be the best type of policy in each case. To contend that non-proportional import restrictions should be adopted whenever a skewness appears, is to deny the validity of arguments which stress internal recovery programs for cyclical disequilibrium, devaluation for price disequilibrium, and certain internal measures for structural disequilibrium." Polak (*op. cit.*, pp. 141, 142) adds that, under the Frisch proposal, "deficit countries would have to eliminate not the imports they could do without, but imports from a specific source of supply. Forced to concentrate their reduction in imports on one or a few countries which happened to follow from the matrix, they would have to accept a commodity structure of imports which might be quite incompatible with full national output. . . . If serious disequilibria in international trade and payments were dealt with, not by the necessary fundamental adjustments, but by successive doses of discrimination, the 'specialization' advantages of the remaining international trade would continually decline and the volume of international trade would lose all value as an indicator of international welfare."

[5] Howard S. Ellis, "Changing Concepts of Convertibility and the Future of Currencies," *Journal of Finance*, X (May 1955), p. 182.

of market forces in determining what nations will produce and what they will sell to one another. . . . The free world cannot compete with the Soviet sphere in this struggle for world power without some kind of an organizing principle. In the absence of political unification the principal coordinating force available to the free world economy is the operation of unfettered markets for goods and capital. In the broadest sense therefore the defense of the free world and its institutions depends upon the creation of a payments mechanism which will permit the unrestricted operations of these market forces.[6]

ECONOMIC GROWTH: CAPITAL SUPPLY, FOREIGN EXCHANGE REQUIREMENTS, AND SAVING

A conspicuous part of plans and proposals for the economic growth of "underdeveloped" areas—and the continued growth of "advanced" countries—is investment, or capital formation. This involves foregoing the immediate consumption of some of the current output, since investment consists of current output not currently consumed. The excess of current production over current consumption can be devoted to adding to the stock of tools and machines, factories and other production facilities, schools and roads, and inventories. The excess of production over consumption measures saving as well as investment, for incomes are earned in production, and saving is income received and not consumed.

A country may be poor largely because of a low level of capital formation; and capital formation may be low and increasing slowly, if at all, because the country is poor. This "vicious circle" is generally treated only in terms of inadequate supply of capital (and that is our emphasis here), but we may note in passing that there can be a problem on the demand side—paradoxical though it may seem for a capital-poor nation to have an inadequate demand (as opposed to desire) for capital. "The supply of capital is governed by the ability and willingness to save; the demand for capital is governed by the incentives to invest."

[6] Raymond F. Mikesell, *Foreign Exchange in the Postwar World* (New York: The Twentieth Century Fund, 1954), p. 523.

On the supply side, there is the small capacity to save, resulting from the low level of real income. The low real income is a reflection of low productivity, which in its turn is due largely to the lack of capital. The lack of capital is a result of the small capacity to save, and so the circle is complete.

On the demand side, the inducement to invest may be low because of the small buying power of the people, which is due to their small real income, which again is due to low productivity. The low level of productivity, however, is a result of the small amount of capital used in production, which in its turn may be caused at least partly by the small inducement to invest.

The low level of real income, reflecting low productivity, is a point that is common to both circles.[7]

With respect to the supply side, capital formation requires the use, or absorption, of real resources. These real productive inputs need not be entirely domestic if a nation can import from abroad: the goods and services actually available to a nation for consumption and investment (V) may be larger or smaller than domestic production (P). Omitting government from the model, we may say that $P = C + I + X$, and $V = P + M - X = C + I + M$. If imports are larger than exports, V will be larger than P. Furthermore, imports can be financed in various ways. In addition to paying for imports with the proceeds of exports, they may be purchased with loans from abroad or acquired as foreign gifts. As discussed in Part II, a nation which borrows and receives gifts can consume and invest beyond its currently earned means.

A nation's sources of foreign exchange may determine the feasible extent of its investment program. Suppose that Country Alpha's balance of payments is initially in equilibrium. Now, if there is an autonomous rise in the level of Alpha's investment, uncompensated by other changes, Alpha's income will rise; the increase in income will induce an increase in Alpha's imports, and a balance of payments deficit appears. Thus domestic investment can lead to a balance of payments problem even though the investment expenditures themselves are entirely on *domestic* resources.

[7] Ragnar Nurkse, *Problems of Capital Formation in Underdeveloped Countries* (Oxford: Basil Blackwell, 1953), pp. 4–5.

Perhaps Alpha can obtain a loan or a gift abroad to supply the additional foreign exchange. What is the relation between the increased supply of foreign exchange and the increase in investment? The question can be rephrased in either of two ways. (a) With a given increase in the rate of foreign exchange receipts, what is the maximum possible increase in the rate of investment? (b) In order to permit a given increase in the level of investment, what is the increase in the rate of imports which must be financed? We wish to determine the value of the "expansion ratio," $\Delta I/\Delta M$, the ratio of the increased rate of investment over the increased rate of imports (which equals the increased rate of foreign exchange inflow).

The autonomous change in investment (assumed to be repeated each time period) multiplied by the multiplier gives the change in the level of equilibrium income ($\Delta Y = k\Delta I$); the change in income multiplied by the marginal propensity to import gives the change in the equilibrium level of imports ($\Delta M = m\Delta Y$). Thus we can write:

$$\Delta M = mk\Delta I$$

$$= \frac{m\Delta I}{1 - c} = \frac{m\Delta I}{s + m}$$

$$\frac{\Delta M}{\Delta I} = \frac{m}{s + m} \quad \text{or} \quad \frac{\Delta I}{\Delta M} = \frac{s + m}{m}$$

As illustrated in Table V, with the marginal propensities to save and to import assumed there, we can say either that (a) with a given increase in the rate of foreign exchange receipts, Alpha can raise the level of investment by one-third more than the increase in imports which can be financed, or (b) with a given rise in the level of investment, Alpha must be prepared— in the absence of an effective income-stabilization policy—to finance an induced increase in imports equal to three-fourths of the increase in investment.

It is apparent from the equation for the expansion ratio that if $s = 0$, then $\Delta I/\Delta M = 1$. That is, if imports are the only leakage to offset the investment injection, the expansion ratio

TABLE V

$c = .6;\ s = .1;\ m = .3$

Ind ΔC	Ind ΔS	ΔM = Δ(M − X)	Aut ΔI	ΔY
			100	100
60	10	30	100	160
96	16	48	100	196
117.6	19.6	58.8	100	217.6
150	25	75	100	250

is unity. But if $s > 0$, the induced imports are less than the autonomous investment, and the ratio is greater than unity.[8]

Domestic investment spending is expansionary, and a rise in national income will tend to increase import expenditures and thereby create (or add to) a balance of payments strain. But suppose that the government of a developing nation acquires a loan from abroad, uses all the proceeds to import capital goods, e.g., tractors, and sells the tractors to domestic buyers. Will this expand money income and thus induce additional imports which cannot be financed out of the now-exhausted initial borrowing?

Money national income rises only if spending on current *domestic* production rises. In this illustration, such expenditure does not rise if the government "impounds" the receipts from selling the tractors (or collects sufficient additional taxes). Domestic residents have paid domestic currency to their government for imported goods; if the government does not respend the money it collects, national income does not rise. In fact, income will fall if the buyers of the tractors have curtailed other consumption or investment spending. Thus, whether the government's foreign borrowing-importing-selling is inflationary, deflationary, or neither, turns on (a) what domestic procedures the government follows and (b) whether the buying

[8] This discussion is based on a portion of J.J. Polak, "Balance of Payments Problems of Countries Reconstructing with the Help of Foreign Loans," *Quarterly Journal of Economics*, LVII (February 1943), pp. 208–240, reprinted in H.S. Ellis and L.A. Metzler, editors, *Readings in the Theory of International Trade* (Philadelphia: The Blakiston Co., 1949), pp. 459–493.

of the imported goods from the government is done with newly created or heretofore idle money or with funds made available by curtailed consumption and investment.

We have noted throughout the volume that effective handling of balance of payments problems may necessitate appropriate domestic policies, the exercise of monetary and fiscal responsibility. A related type of discipline is required if aid and loans from abroad are to be effective in promoting capital formation. For the hard fact of life is that would-be developing nations must, in a real sense, do their own saving.

Suppose that Alpha consumes all of its own output and thus saves nothing. Could it not still build up its capital equipment with resources received as gifts or loans? According to the usual definition of saving as income currently received (earned in current production) and not currently consumed, the answer is yes. But it will clarify matters to modify the saving definition. Let us define saving as the gap between consumption and the *whole* of resources over which the community has command— including resources received from foreigners. Thus, foreign aid, which increases the total resources at the disposal of the economy of Alpha, will not contribute to Alpha's capital accumulation if Alpha uses the additional resources simply for more net current consumption.[9]

While outside aid can supplement domestic saving by giving the economy additional resources, it cannot supplant saving. The receipt of foreign aid and investment *allows* greater capital accumulation. Also, as an alternative, it allows greater consumption. If Alpha wants to develop through capital accumulation, presumably it should spend its additional foreign exchange on something other than solid gold Cadillacs.

[9] "In an all-inclusive view, a country that is importing capital equipment is *ipso facto* saving, in that it is abstaining from the enjoyment of the consumer goods it could have imported in place of the capital goods brought in, or else abstaining from the consumption of the goods that it now exports in order to pay for the imported equipment." Nurkse, *ibid.*, p. 110. *Net* consumption (of domestic plus imported goods) must not rise by the amount of the additional imports. Capital accumulation can be promoted by importation of goods other than capital items if concurrently domestic output of consumption goods is curtailed and the domestic resources thus freed are shifted to producing capital goods.